THE HOPE TRAIN

I WAS NOT SUPPOSED TO BE HERE

Laura Rabb Morgan, EdD

ISBN 978-1-63903-685-1 (paperback)
ISBN 978-1-63903-686-8 (digital)

Christian Faith Publishing, Inc.
832 Park Avenue
Meadville, PA 16335
www.christianfaithpublishing.com

Printed in the United States of America

To the memory of my mother and father, dedicated servant leaders who continued the legacy of "The HopeTrain," and to all my brave ancestors who made it possible.

Preface

I have so many titles for my memoir, but why do I think "I Was Not Supposed to Be Here..." is the appropriate subtitle? It just seemed that so many times in my life I found myself where "I was not supposed to be." Really, when you look back on it, my birth was not supposed to be. It was not planned; my parents had to get married. I have wondered if they really loved each other or even knew what loved was. They got married because my mom was pregnant, and in those days, girls who found themselves pregnant and out of wedlock normally got married if the guy didn't run off. I am thankful my dad chose to do the right thing and marry my mom. I am also grateful that I entered this world with two parents who chose to stay together all of their married lives. Even if they didn't love each other when they got married, I know they cared for each other, due to the way they worked together to make sure all of their children were cared for and shown much love, maybe not in words but by deeds.

Looking back, I wonder if both sets of my grandparents, Dave and Carrie (paternal grandparents) and Rosie and JD (maternal grandparents) had to get married. I know Rosie and JD had what you would call a shotgun wedding because my great grandmother told me that she made my grandfather marry my grandmother because she was pregnant. She told me that later, after the birth of the child, she had to apologize to my grandfather because it was obvious the baby was not his because the baby was light skinned and both parents were dark skinned, and she knew my grandmother's previous boyfriend had been light skinned. Regardless, my grandfather did the right thing and had twelve more children by my grandmother. Both my paternal grandparents had passed on by the time I was born. I have a picture of my paternal grandfather, but I am still searching for a picture of my paternal grandmother. Fortunately, I have a picture of my paternal great-grandmother (Amy). But I am still missing that connection with my paternal grandmother (Carrie).

I can't help but wonder if she and my paternal grandfather had to get married as well. To be honest, it was my curiosity about her that drove me to write *The Hope Train*. I realized that women often lost much of their identity when they took on the name of their husbands, and it is hard to trace their history because of it, and I didn't want anyone to forget my paternal grandmother because she did indeed exist; otherwise, I wouldn't be here to document her story—*our story* in what became our *Hope Train* the Rabb-Herron, Hampton-Rabb *Hope Train* that is nowhere near the end of the line.

Indeed, I was not supposed to be here, but I am, and all I can say is that *God* provided when I boarded *the hope train* because He was evidently the conductor on the day I was born. He made it happen, and I am forever thankful. He has put me in so many positions that I was not supposed to be in over the years, and He brought me through. When I sashayed into this world as Laura Mae Rabb at six pounds and eight ounces at Charity Hospital, Shreveport, La. Caddo Parish, I am sure my parents had no idea that I was *at risk* of not achieving very much in life. I was born in rural America to poor black and uneducated parents, and according to some's definition, I was *at risk*, coming out of the womb. Well, somebody should have told the Master because He paved a way for me on evidently what was the *hope train*, and I took it.

What I regret is that the way was so rocky at times that I have the bruises to show for it. What I also regret is that the way did not have to be so rocky. My ancestors were taken from their home country years before I was even thought of and made slaves to make the lives of others better without compensation, thankfulness, or love. That is not to say that if my ancestors had stayed in Africa (where my DNA dictates) life would have been a bowl of cherries, but at least they would have felt at home, a place where they belonged and hopefully felt loved by their own people. But to be captured and enslaved for over three hundred years, some never know what freedom felt like or what it meant to be loved. Whenever I meet Africans today, I sometimes see *fear* in their eyes but never *hopelessness* that I see in some African Americans born and raised in America. Yes, indeed, I was not supposed to be here.

Growing up, I never heard much about slavery. There was very little about it in the history books we used in school or said about it in the classes we took—classes that were taught by black teachers (Hardy Kindergarten, Jerry A. Moore Elementary School, and Webster High School, Minden, Louisiana). All my teachers were black from kindergarten through twelfth grade, and the majority were black through undergraduate school at Southern University in Baton Rouge, Louisiana. I know I was three generations removed from slavery; some of my teachers had to be two generations removed from slavery. But at the time, African Americans were not writing history books. They were mostly written by whites, who did not feel the same way about slavery obviously. They obviously wanted to forget about it as if it did not happen; as if my race had not been tarred by slavery and later by segregation and racism, a tarring that even generations can't remove if ever; and as if we would not notice or feel the differences made between our races that one was heaped more affluent than the other and not wonder why.

By the age of fourteen or so, I started to notice particular differences that upset me and made me curious. For instance, my curiosity led me to wonder why my mom was called by her first name by her boss's children, yet my friends called her Ms. Dinkie. Why were white children allowed to disrespect my mother like that, and yet I had to call their parents Ms. Leona and Mr. Junior. It didn't make sense to me; I was angry and mad at that difference because, to me, my mother deserved just as much respect as their parents. She was after all a *mother* too. This love for my mother led me to be an avid proponent of the Civil Rights Movement when it came to Louisiana.

Another difference I noticed was that black people got out of the way of white people when they were passing by each other, even to the point of stepping off the sidewalk until the white people passed. Also, I was told early on by my mother not to look white people in the eyes. I had noticed other black people lowering their gaze when talking to white people. This became a habit of mine, not out of respect for white people but out of hatred for the degrading way black people were treated by them. This is something that I knew I had to squash because, as a Christian, I knew it was a sin, and I would go to hell for it. My eyes were opened when I learned not to judge people by the color of their skin but by their individual actions.

Another difference that stood out was the behavior of one of my mother's male coworkers at the Coffee Cup restaurant, especially when he was in the company of the white boss or any other white man. His name was Daniel Blue. He could make the best pies. I noticed that he would refer to white men as "cap'an" while smiling and laughing, even though no jokes had been made. I think it was short for *captain*. I figured it was a moniker that black men started to use after getting out of the service, but I don't think Daniel Blue was ever in the service.

I knew growing up that we were poor, but I didn't realize that this was by design, not of our own doing. I realized that at some point before I was born it was illegal to teach blacks how to read and that you could get killed or brutally beaten if you were found with a book. I later discovered that we were thought of as animals. Why would animals need to know how to read? I have to leave this train of thought because it is too depressing. I think whites who wonder why African Americans have a hard time trusting white people even today should read *The Hope Train*.

It is ironic that reading would become one of my favorite pastimes growing up. There was very little to do in our small hometown, so I took to reading. We didn't get a television until I was about fourteen years old or so. Then we weren't allowed to look at it for very long. So I had plenty of time to hone my reading skills. To this day, reading is one of my favorite pastimes. I didn't realize, growing up, that knowing how to read would make my life a lot less challenging. As an African American, it would be challenging enough. I didn't need illiteracy as a crutch as well to limit my abilities even more.

What were my dreams growing up? I know I wanted to get a college education and get married and work a full-time job. But it was never about becoming affluent. It was only after I got a college education, got married, worked on several full-time jobs, and then retired that I thought if I were more affluent, I could help my race and my son more. But this thinking was late in coming; it should have been at the forefront of my thinking from very early in life. Investing early on toward retirement was my idea, not to help an entire race. It would be impossible. Now, I know that every little bit helps. We were raised to give what we had, and I definitely did that as much as possible, not realizing that saving and investing early on would have helped me to be able to give back more later on and that the generation coming before needed to help the next generations achieve more. My dreams were of surviving as they had been for my parents and their parents before them and so on.

Remember, I was not supposed to be here, so how could I dare to dream when my life had been one of survival. It is obvious to me now that my son's life will be one of surviving as well, only different from mine. I can only hope that his children will have a different viewpoint as they ride *The Hope Train* as descendants of Dinkie and David Rabb. When will my race stop surviving and start to just live their lives and realize they are supposed to be here and the conductor is God?

Acknowledgments

I started writing my memoir almost twenty years ago because I couldn't get my relatives to write the history of the Rabb-Herron Family. All I wanted was six chapters, representing the six children in the family. I would write about my own family, so I ask my own siblings to send material for that chapter. No one sent me anything. I knew that if it is not written, then society would consider it had never happened. I didn't want my family to be forgotten. I was the family historian, so I knew the history of my mom's and dad's families somewhat. I decided against writing a family history and just to write about what I knew best and that was my own story. I started out writing for my son and his future family, but I think future Rabb-Herron-Hampton's descendants and others will find benefits in reading it as well.

I want to start out by acknowledging my parents for making me possible. Without their input, there would be nothing to write about. I also want to thank my siblings and my cousins who added flavor to my life each and every day as we grew up and even into adulthood.

I have met so many people throughout my life as neighbors, teachers, classmates, students, colleagues, or associates. They are too many to thank individually; however, I want to acknowledge them for the incidental learning that I acquired because it helped to make me who I am as well.

Last, but not least, I want to thank my dissertation chair, Dr. Amy Rose at Northern Illinois University, for informing me that when history is written, it is never forgotten, and while African Americans rejoice in their oral history, much of it cannot be authenticated. I wanted to authenticate the history of Laura Rabb Morgan by writing this memoir. I wrote it primarily for my son, James Jr. But I do believe it will benefit others to read about how I persevered through the storms of my life and how my husband and I, even though we were raised as different as night and day, are still married and getting to know and love one another still to this day in our senior years.

The Hope Train has been a rough ride, but it was well worth it. Hopefully, my son's travels alone on this railroad track will be less bumpy. I pray!

Chapter 1

THE EARLY YEARS

Infancy to Five Years Old

The Beginning

It's dark outside, and only the glow of the moon lights our way. My sister Bobbie and I held tightly to our mom's hands as we walked toward the outhouse late one night. If you grew up in a rural area in the south early on, you would know what an outhouse is. Let's just define it as an outdoor toilet. My sister and I waited outside as our mom used the outhouse with the door open. It was so eerily quiet. I was scared, and I was pretty sure my sister Bobbie was too. I can only imagine how big our eyes were as we waited for our mom to finish. From the very beginning, I was always scared of outhouses. To me they were big wooden boxes with a big hole that you sat on and did the number one or two. The problem for me was that you couldn't see the end of the hole. I imagined falling down into the hole and being swallowed up by it so many times. That is a nightmare I had for years as a child and even today. This walk to the outhouse was one of the earliest memories I have of my childhood. I was probably about three years old and my sister two.

outhouse

At the time, our mom (Dinkie), our dad (David, or Dave, as my mom and most adults called him), and Bobbie and I lived on the Rabb Family Farm. The farm was bought in the 1920s by my paternal grandfather, David Rabb, Sr. My dad, also David Rabb, and his siblings grew up on the farm. So when my dad married my mom, he brought her to the farm. At first they shared a house with my Aunt Velma and her husband Uncle Clyde, which was then the family home. By then they probably had their oldest daughter Alma Jean. Later, another house was built on the farm, and my mom and dad moved into it. I think before I was born.

Stories about how our parents met and married were told to me later on by my aunts. It seemed that our dad saw our mother playing basketball one day, and he liked her legs and spoke to her. Our aunts said that our mom had the biggest and prettiest legs. I think I take after her because I have received compliments about my legs all of my life. According to our aunts, our mom was a pretty good basketball player. This was hard for me to visualize because I just remember her after giving birth to nine babies, one of whom was stillborn (a boy), and having the laugh of my life one day when she couldn't get her legs across a girl's bike. However, her love of basketball would be pivotal in our lives later on. Our dad and our mom had gotten married about six months before I was born as my cousin Alma Jean [our Aunt Velma's (our dad's oldest sister's) oldest child] and about six months older than me so brazenly told me later on in life, to let me know that my mom was pregnant before she married my dad. Somehow she found out that our parents got married in October, and I was born in March. I know they got married in a church. It was Aunt Velma's and Uncle Clyde's (Aunt Velma's husband) church, and Mom and all of us would later join (Spring Lake Church of God in Christ). The Church of God in Christ in the day was very Orthodox with a strict doctrine especially for women, no makeup, no pants for women, no cutting your hair, no dancing, no basketball, etc. Because my mom had loved playing basketball when she was young, she felt it was harmless and allowed us to do things she felt were harmless even if they were against church policy. My sister Dorothy was the captain of her high school basketball team. We often went to school dances and loved them. We also cut our bangs. Our high school, Webster High School, didn't allow girls to wear pants, so that was not an issue. Growing up with those limitations early on helped me to set limits for myself as a teenager and as an adult that has served me well all of my life.

I think I was in high school when I found out that my mom and dad had to get married. I don't know if it was a shotgun wedding or not because my mom's parents always seemed fond of my dad and vice versa. I felt because they had to get married before they were ready, my parents often overprotected us. With seven girls, only one of us got pregnant before finishing high school. All of us graduated from high school on time, including our one and only brother, David Jr. I think this was a feat my parents were very proud of. After I graduated from high school, both of my parents started to go to night school to get their GEDs. Unfortunately, life got in the way, and they never got them

Besides my mom, being a teen pregnant mom, my grandmother (Rosie), her mother—as told to me by my maternal great grandmother (Lillie)—was pregnant before she got married to my grandfather. She told me that she made him marry my grandmother but later had to apologize to him after the baby was born because the baby evidently was not his. The baby was light-skinned, and both my grandparents had dark skin. This was my mom's oldest sister, my Aunt Elnora. I never discussed this revelation with my Aunt Elnora. Here it was my mom, her mom; both had to get married. The way they both talked about illegitimate babies, you never would have thought they had to get married as well, just like young girls in my day. I grew up thinking having sex out of wedlock was a sin. Girls in my day, I believe, were ostracized by older women and men in the community when they got pregnant out of wedlock. Now it seemed many of these same people did the same thing.

To this day, I wonder how my mom felt when she found out she was pregnant. I don't know why, but I often wonder if she enjoyed sex. Yes, I wonder if her first encounter was my dad taking advantage of her. I am not sure, but I think the Rabb boys were considered a catch since their family owned their farm. My mother's parents were sharecroppers. That meant that some white family owned the farm; they just worked and lived on the farm, like their family did when they were slaves. As a matter of fact, even after slavery ended, in Louisiana, black people were not always allowed to own land.

My dad and Aunt Velma tells the story of how their father came to own his property. They said that at one time in Louisiana that white people threatened to take the land away from all blacks who had bought property, so my grandfather sold our farm to a white man that kept it until it was safe to give it back to him. It seemed quite a few black farm owners did that; the difference, however was that the white man gave our farm back to my grandfather for $1.00. But in some cases, the white farmers didn't give the farms back to their black owners.

I found this out one day when we were visiting my mom's grave. It was just after attending my dad's funeral. One of my dad's first cousins, whom I really didn't know that well, was visiting his relatives' graves at the same time. He told us that their father's property had been stolen by white people, and he never understood why my grandfather didn't help his father keep his property. This seemed to have caused some disconnect between Rabb families, and that was probably why my father didn't visit them often even though they lived in the same small town. I had noticed that some kids in my school had the same last name as mine, but I had no idea they were relatives. My Aunt Velma said that some of our grandfather's property was stolen from him as well. I thought it was a white man, but it turned out to be a black man (I would find out later from my brother, who looked into who owned the property adjacent to our farm).

My father and his five siblings were all born and raised on the farm. I believe their family home had burned down before I was born or soon after. For some reason, I remember a house with two sides and a big hallway in the middle, where you could see through to the other side. There was also another family living on the road leading to the farm. This was my father's first cousin Stud Rabb and his family. At some point, they moved, and there are no remnants of their home now. Even the road leading by their house is gone and that entrance to the farm closed.

Even though my parents lived with Aunt Velma and Uncle Clyde when they first got married, a house was built next door for us and the rest of the siblings still living on the farm and their spouses. This house (rehabbed) is still on the farm. I was the first baby brought to this house, my parents' oldest child and only child for one year. I have no baby pictures or early childhood pictures. I always resented that fact. It would have been nice to see what I looked like as a child. That is why I have so many baby pictures of my son and other children in the family.

My Aunt Velma and Uncle Clyde lived with their children in the only other house on the farm. They eventually had seven children altogether and raised all of them on the farm. My mother looked upon Aunt Velma like an older sister. She loved Aunt Velma and had the deepest respect for her. Aunt Velma was the only Rabb daughter, so she would often say my mother was as close to her as a sister.

After their parents, David Rabb and Carrie Herron Rabb, died, Aunt Velma finished raising the Rabb children still left at home. I think Uncle Jasper (Jap) and Uncle Sedric (Sed) had left home by this time. So Aunt Velma, who had left for college and had been there two or three years by the time her mom died, had to come home to take care of the family. According to Aunt Velma (as told to me during an interview in 2006 for our Rabb-Herron family reunion souvenir booklet) their mother died giving birth to her last baby, a girl. Uncle Nate was about six years old when she died. I am not sure what happened to their father. I believe my father was fifteen when he died. Aunt Velma was the oldest Rabb sibling, then Uncle Jasper (Jap), Uncle Sedric (Sed), my father David (Dave), Uncle Colonial (Long), and then Uncle Nathaniel (Nate), the baby.

I spent the first five and a half years of my life living on the Rabb Family Farm in the new house that was built. I remember that my mom, dad, myself (I was their firstborn), my sister Bobbie, and later my brother David Jr., Carrie, and Juanita shared the first bedroom of the house. My dad's brother, my Uncle Nate (or Nathaniel Rabb), and his wife (Aunt Cille or Lucille) shared the second bedroom; and my dad's brother Uncle Long (Colonial Rabb) and his wife (Aunt Johnny Bell) and their children shared the last bedroom. I think there were only five rooms. The dining room and the kitchen were shared by all families.

By the time I was born or soon after, Uncle Jap and Uncle Sed had already left home, probably for the service and they never came back to live in Louisiana, just only for visits. Growing up on a farm in the '40s and '50s had to be hard on black kids, so when they had the opportunity to escape, they did. It was amazing that my father and his siblings had the opportunity to go to school. They all, except Uncle Nate, went to St. John Elementary School, which was connected to St. John Baptist Church, which as I understand it, was co-founded by our great-grandfather Tom Rabb in Claiborne Parish, or Homer, Louisiana. Uncle Nate, the baby, never learned how to read. Other than my Uncle Long and Aunt Velma, I knew very little about my father's siblings.

I do not remember the birth of my siblings Bobbie and David, but I think I remember the nights Carrie and Juanita were born, especially Juanita. I remember my Aunt Velma coming to our house in the middle of the night and getting us up to go to her house. We didn't know what was happening; we thought our mom was sick or something. As we were leaving one time, I remember my Aunt Hag (Aunt Harriet) coming through the door. She never came to our house. She lived across the fields from us. I wasn't sure if my dad had gone to get her or if she walked across the fields in the dark. I know that when we returned in the morning that there was a baby crying. My mom gave birth to I think Bobbie, David, Juanita, and Carrie in our house on the family farm. I would learn later that Aunt Hag was a midwife. She had delivered the babies in our home. I was my mom's first baby, so they took special precautions and took her to the hospital. I was born in what was then called Confederate Memorial Hospital. Louisiana was a former confederate state, I was later to learn, thus the hospital's name. The name has since changed. My siblings Dorothy, Linda, and Vickie (in that order) were born in Minden, Louisiana, in what was then called the Minden Sanitarium. Of course, that name has changed now too. I think I remember my dad taking us to see our mom in the basement or colored section of the hospital, probably to see her after Vickie was born (she was the last of the babies born.) I hated basements because they were so dark, and I always imagined the rest of the floors falling in on it. Going to the colored section of the hospital and being afraid of the basement was probably the beginning of me being paranoid.

coal oil lantern

Laura Rabb Morgan, EdD

wood burning stove

churn

iron

I don't remember much about our lives on the farm, but I do have very vivid memories of some of the happenings. If you look at how the Amish live even until this day, that was how we lived during the time I lived on the farm. We had coal oil lanterns for light and woodburning heaters and stoves to cook our food. Most of the food was fresh from the farm, from the milk we drank to the meat, vegetables, fruits, and nuts we ate. We lived off the land. I remember helping to churn butter from the milk we got from the cows using a milk churn. My Aunt Velma had a chicken coop; she would give us some of her eggs and chickens. I think my mom helped her with the chicken coop. It was smelly to me, and I remember being afraid of the chickens. All of our baked products were made with fresh unpasteurized milk and hand-churned butter. I remember the food tasting so good and definitely different from the food we cook today. Our clothes were pressed with an iron that was heated on the woodburning heater or the stove. You had to use a piece of cloth to hold the iron because the whole iron was hot, and it could burn your hand.

chamber pot

smoke house

storm pit

ice box

galvanized tub

At night, we used what was called a "slop jar" (chamber pot), I believe. You could do number one in it, and I believe as young kids we did the number two as well. Then the contents were tossed in the woods or just on the yard. During the day, we would do our business in the woods sometimes, just out of sight. We had a smokehouse to smoke, cure, and store the meats. We had a well for water. If a storm came up, especially one that had lightning and thunder, we would go to the storm pit. All of our food was cooked on a woodburning stove. We had an icebox. I remember a truck would deliver big chunks of ice to our houses. The ice was put in the icebox, and it would keep the food cold for a little while. I can't forget the bathtubs we used to take baths in. My friend since college called them number 3 galvanized tubs. All my life, I just called them tin tubs because they were made of tin. We would wash our face and hands in a washbowl or washbasin.

There were so many people that we always took group baths. I don't think the water was changed until the last person. The grown-ups and the children did not take baths in the same water. Hot water was boiled on the woodburning stove, and of course, it would be mixed with cold water, both from the well. We had to make several trips to the water well to get enough water for our baths. Most of the time, we just washed up in a waterbasin. All those items we used on the farm would be antiques now and worth some money, but nobody knows what happened to them; they just didn't disappear. Aunt Velma believed that while they were at church on Sundays, antique dealers would roam the property and get those priceless items. I remember years later as an adult paying $20 for a scrub board (as a memento), or rub board as I pronounced it as a child, when we'd had several of them on the farm.

wash basin

water well

scrub board

Whenever, there was a storm, evidently we went to the storm pit. I don't remember going to it while I lived on the farm. The storm pit, I guess, was leveled or my family just stopped using it because it no longer exist either. The storm pit was essentially a hole dug in the ground large enough to fit all of our families. There was a door to shield it off from the elements. Besides the outhouse, the storm pit was probably my second most dreaded place on the farm. It also caused me many nightmares. To me, it was like a grave or being buried alive. I kept imagining what if we couldn't get out. I hated being on the farm when a storm brewed. I was so happy when Uncle Clyde said that it was safe to be inside of the car in a storm. One time, I persevered through a storm beside him in a car. It was scary, but it was better for me than the storm pit.

Aunt Velma, even though she had some college education, chose to raise her kids and stay on the farm and not go out and work. However, listening to her children, it was chosen for her by Uncle Clyde. I don't know exactly why he didn't want her to work. Maybe he saw her life changing or getting ahead of him. I don't ever remember him having a full-time job, even though for some reason he always wore suits. He and Aunt Velma would start to receive welfare checks because they were both handicapped. Aunt Velma had one leg longer than the other, and Uncle Clyde would eventually become legally blind. Aunt Velma just said that after a bout with the measles, she woke up one morning limping. I remember Uncle Clyde could see initially, and after he had surgery on his eyes, his sight got worse. And then one day while I was visiting the farm, he was cutting wood, very carefully, and a piece shot up and hit him in his eye. After that, he was permanently blinded. They both lived the rest of their lives on the farm and on welfare. They eventually got electricity, gas stoves and heaters, refrigerator and freezer, hot and cold running water, and a bathroom. I do know they didn't have a car for a long time until my Uncle Nate gave them a car. This probably hampered them a lot as well, especially after we left the farm. I am sure my dad took them to town to shop prior to them getting a car. After they got the car, Aunt Velma probably had to learn how to drive because she was always the driver until her kids learned how to drive. They could always practice driving on the farm. Even after she got a car, Aunt Velma didn't try to find a job off the farm. I think this may have been a sore spot between her and Uncle Clyde, but she never said a word. She and Uncle Clyde seemed to agree on most things.

Before Uncle Clyde was permanently blinded, he would go with Aunt Velma into the pastures early in the morning to milk the cows. After he was blinded, she would go alone. She had to find the cows, and sometimes they would have wandered deep into the woods. One morning when I was a teenager and vacationing with them, I asked her if I could go along. We had such a long walk. She allowed me to milk one of the cow's udders. The cow's udders were so warm that I jumped back initially. The milk was warm itself. Aunt Velma didn't seem scared, so I wasn't scared. The woods were so quiet, except for the occasional sounds of crickets and birds.

Alma Jean was probably with us because we always did everything together. However, I am pretty sure she didn't go with Aunt Velma any other times. Uncle Clyde would churn the butter if you put the churn right in front of him. Also, before he was blinded, he helped Aunt Velma with the chicken coop. Now it was all her task. They had chickens of all types and turkeys. They would kill them for food sometimes and use their eggs for cooking. When they killed the chickens, it was a sight because they would run around headless until they died. This was scary to us as kids, but we got used to it. Aunt Velma was a woman I respected very much; she was a hardworking woman. It seemed from the time she got up in the morning, she never sat down.

Besides outhouses and storm pits on the farm, I was also scared of the water wells on our farm. Of course, at night you could hear the howls of animals at night, but that didn't scare me as much as the outhouses, water wells, and storm pits. They were holes in the ground that I would often imagine myself falling into and not being able to climb out of them or being shut in for life in the storm pits. Once or twice, I was brave enough to look inside of the hole of our outhouse, and I was always looking down the water well. Needless to say, the outhouse had a lot of what at the time we called *do-do*, and the water well looked so deep and never ending. Some water wells had pumps, and you couldn't see where it ended. As a kid, I loved pumping water from the water pump, as long as it had a pump. We had one at our church. But on the farm we used a bucket. We would lower the bucket down until it hit the water, let the bucket fill up, and then pull it back up. Most of the time, this was done by the grown-ups, and we would take the pail full of water back to the house.

water pump

Most of the real farming on the farm was left up to my father. He never seemed bitter that his brothers had left the farm or that his two siblings were handicapped. He just did what he could do with the energy he had left (which oftentimes seemed boundless). Plus, with the crops he had on the farm, he could feed his large family as well. My mom loved the fresh vegetables from the farm. You never heard her complaining about them. Otherwise, she hated farming. I don't think she ever helped with the planting.

At first, my father would use a horse and wagon to help him on the farm, and later he got a tractor. I don't think he ever could afford a new tractor, so he bought used tractors. After the fiasco with the cotton when I was in high school, he never tried again, even though he now had tractors. Before the tractors, I remember feeling so sorry for him when we were harvesting the cotton because he had to plow all of the rows behind a mule. That looked so hard. I felt so sorry for my daddy and proud of how he was taking care of us at the same time. I thought he had to be the strongest man alive. My father always worked a full-time job, and then farmed in the evenings and on Saturdays. He only rested on Sunday—he believed in that—even though he didn't always go to church on Sundays. I believed this hard work kept my father physically fit. Even when he passed away at the age of seventy-four, he still had firm chest and legs.

While we lived on the farm, I remember us all sleeping in one room with a big woodburning potbelly heater in the middle. I am not sure if it was called a heater, but that's what I am calling it because it is what we used to keep warm in the winter. I don't think there was another heater in the house, so I am not sure how Uncle Long and Uncle Nate's families kept warm at night. There was a stove in the kitchen, so the heat from the stove probably was used to heat the rest of the house.

There was an accident, and Bobbie was burned on the heater in our room. I don't know if I was rocking her or she was rocking herself; somehow she slipped and fell on the heater. I do remember her face being burned and that side of her face looking different from the other side for a long time. I also remember my mother not allowing rocking chairs in our house after that. I don't think my parents took Bobbie to the doctor; they probably used home remedies. Home remedies were big with black families when I was growing up. My father seemed more versed on them than my mother. Probably because he was six years older than my mom. She was only eighteen when he married her, and he was twenty-four. His family seemed to have believed in voodoo and superstitions because he often talked about it, whereas other than some superstitions about food, my mother very seldom spoke of such things. Like I said rocking chairs were taboo in our house. In his one and only visit home that I can remember, Uncle Jap left two small rocking chairs. He had bought for his two daughters but didn't have room to carry them back to California, so he left them at our house. My parents put them in the attic and left them there for years, almost until we were too old to rock in them. When they finally got them down and allowed us to rock in them, we had a ball and eventually tore them up. Uncle Jap's daughters never got them, and he never asked about them either. I don't think he ever came back for a visit after that visit when he left the chairs at our house. At the time, I didn't have any idea how far California was from Louisiana.

Another incident I remember was birds descending on our house on the farm. It was a swarm of black birds. It would have reminded you of the movie *The Birds*. I think that was why I was so fascinated by the movie every time I saw it; even today it scares me. I remember my father running around trying to shew the birds away. To this day, I have no idea why they just decided to descend on our house.

I also remember that Uncle Jasper or Uncle Jap at some point left his two sons for my dad and Aunt Velma to take care of and left for California. I think he and his wife, Aunt Mildred, were separating, and she was taking the girls to California. I am not sure how long the boys stayed with us on the farm. Brot or Ira (or Iva) stayed with us, and Junior or Jasper Jr. stayed with Aunt Velma and Uncle Clyde and their family in the other house on the farm. The boys were very helpful to my dad and Uncle Clyde on the farm. I think they were teenagers at the time. We got attached to the boys. I think Brot (short for brother) slept on a cot in the dining room in our house.

What I remember mostly is when his mother (Aunt Mildred) came from California to get him and his brother, she didn't come alone; evidently, she brought some of her siblings with her. There was a standoff. My father and Aunt Velma were arguing that Jasper had left the boys, and they were only giving them to him. Whereas, Aunt Mildred was saying they were her boys, and she was taking them to California. The boys were saying; they wanted to stay with us. Eventually, they got in the car with Aunt Mildred, and left and we would not see them again until they were grown and had children of their own.

Another time I remember a man called Joe Crawford coming to our house on the farm. He was Uncle Long's wife Johnny Bell's brother. He was tall and slender and had a very nice voice as I remember, and he was what you would call handsome. He was talking to my mom on the front porch, and I felt that he liked my mom. I was concerned because my dad was not home, and my mom was acting funny, laughing and smiling at this stranger. She seemed very girlie to me. Thinking about the incidence after I grew older, I couldn't help but think that my mom must have had a crush on him when she was younger. His family lived up the road from our house. After that, I would always stay close to my mom whenever he came around, which wasn't often. I don't think I said anything to my father about him, though. I am sure I would have told him if I had ever caught this man and my mom in an inappropriate situation, which I did not, and I never felt that way about another man I saw my mom talking to again.

There is one vivid memory that I don't think I will ever forget that occurred when I was on the farm because I was so impressed by it. That memory was of the day that black men and women from the community came to our house to help my dad slaughter some of our animals and the women helped to dress the meat from the animals. I remember the women making sausages patties and link sausages. They would grind the lean pork and fat up and add seasonings. The patties were fatty but they were tender and tasty. Plus add, sliced smoked ham with red-eye gravy, scrambled eggs, homemade biscuits with freshly churned butter, homemade syrup or canned jelly, and you never ate so well. When the meats were plentiful, my mom would cook two or three meats for us for breakfast.

We had a smokehouse on the farm near Aunt Velma's house, and some of the meat was put in there. Some of the meat was put in our icebox. The icebox had a big chunk of ice in it, and that's how the meat was stored for a few days. It was a bloody scene that day, but I remember it well. I was impressed with the camaraderie of people helping one another. I believe they helped one another build houses as well. I remember a lot of laughter among the men and women that day. I am sure my dad and maybe my mom did as well return the favor to these men and women.

Both my mother and my Aunt Velma grew to be very good cooks. When I was old enough and saw Aunt Velma cooking on the woodburning stove, I couldn't believe how she did it. After years of using it, she really got very good at cooking food on it and in its oven. It amazed me, so I probably would have learned how to cook with it, if they had not gotten a gas stove eventually. My mother chose to cook as a career. She became the head cook on most of her jobs. She was an excellent worker. She would get my sister Bobbie and I jobs alongside her when we grew old enough. I marveled at her energy level. Bobbie and I would be hired as dishwashers or short order cooks (hamburgers, hot dogs, etc.). Because we had little hands, we were too slow for my mom, so she would help us, if not do it herself. She would allow us to do our homework if things were slow and no bosses were around. What I admired about her mostly was that she let Bobbie and I keep our little money to do with whatever we wanted. We didn't even have to use it for our lunch money at school. This was amazing, considering how poor we were and how many kids our parents had.

The only other vivid memory I have while we lived on the farm is going to school with my cousin Alma Jean Lawhorne. She was Aunt Velma's, like I said, oldest child. She was born in 1946, and I was born in 1947, only six months a part. When she was six and I was five and it was time for her to go to school, she was too scared to go to school by herself, so Aunt Velma begged my mom to let me go to school with her. I think she was scared that Clarice and Bernice would do something to her—what, I do not know. Clarice and Bernice lived in a house across the street from our farm. They lived with someone called Collier Kidd and Ms. Theodosia (I believe they were their parents or grandparents). Alma Jean was going to have to walk to school with them every day through the woods, and she was scared. So my mom agreed to let me go, and I started to school at St. John's School when I was five years old. My mom helped me to learn my lessons, so I persevered. Everyone was bigger and taller than me. I think my mom and Aunt Velma would walk us to meet up with Bernice and Clarice, and then together we would all walk through a trail through the woods to get to school.

I went to school there from September to November 1952. At some point, the school was burned down. We were not in school at the time. I remember we saw black smoke bellowing in the air from our house. After that, we all went to school in the church that was next door. In the school, we had all been in two big rooms, if I remember correctly; now we were in one big room, the church's sanctuary. At lunchtime, we would all eat outside. I remember there was a water pump. In our classrooms, we were taught how to make paper cups and later pump the water into the cups to drink. I didn't know it then, but going to school early and being in that room with all those grades and listening to the teachers and students must have been good fertilizer for my brains because I excelled in school from that point on. I could probably be a poster girl for preschooling. Neither my mom nor my dad graduated from high school.

My dad had gone to St. John School. I believe St. John School was called a parochial school because it was a school connected to St. John Baptist Church. From what I understand, it was cofounded by my great-grandfather, Tom Rabb. My grandfather David Rabb was a deacon in the church. I have a picture of him posing with other of St. John's deacons, I believe. The church evidently was initially a white church, and then black people were allowed to attend and sit in the back probably. I am not sure if it was called St. John's then. It was where my great-aunt Harriet (Aunt Hag) met and married Archie Jones, a white boy or a very light-skinned black boy. Evidently, he took a liking to my aunt in church. According to relatives, Archie

Jones's white family disowned him after he married Aunt Hag. According to what I heard, he was an alcoholic, and my Aunt Hag shot his leg off after he attempted to beat her in a drunken rage. She killed one or two of her sons in the same way. When I met Archie Jones, he was what they called peg-legged with one wooden leg. I wasn't sure he was white or just talked like it. After a while, I was told the whites started going to a different church and the blacks continued on at St. John's. My great grandfather Tom Rabb and another man I was told helped to purchase the church from the whites. I think the area our farm is located in is probably what you would call the unincorporated section of Athens, Louisiana.

My mom went to school in Athens, Louisiana, and she often talked about her teachers. Even though I can't remember the name of the school now, it was initially a church as well. Aunt Natherine says the church was named St. Rest Baptist Church. The school only went to the eighth grade as well. They later built a school, and it was called Hillcrest. She and her siblings often talked about a 'fessor LoPo. I didn't understand what they were calling him at first; eventually I figured out the *'fessor* was short for "professor." Professor LoPolk was the principal of the school in Athens that blacks were allowed to attend. At first I thought LoPolk was a made-up name, until someone stood up in our church, Spring Lake, when I happened to be visiting and introduced herself as a LoPolk (I think she was Professor LoPolk's sister). I remember thinking, *It is a real name.* I even met Professor LoPolk at my grandmother's funeral and still didn't understand the pronunciation. He was a tall light-skinned handsome man even in the later stages of his life. My dad knew him as well. It seemed like the entire community loved and respected Professor LoPolk.

After I started to school with my cousin, I kind of liked it. I remember a lot of grades being in the same room. I wish I had pictures of my days at that school, but I don't. It was my introduction to education. I was five years old at the time and was put into the first grade. I don't think they had kindergarten. I remember vividly learning how to make paper cups so that we could drink water from the water pump. When my family and I visited my father's church during one of our reunion outings in 2010, I was surprised to see that the water pump was still at the new and improved St. John. The school, however, burned down soon after I started to go. I think my mom or dad walked over after we saw the smoke in the air and found out that it was the school burning.

Alma Jean and I must have followed because I have a vague memory of standing by the store near the burned down school with other people just looking at the rubble. After that, we had to go to school in the church. I only have vague memories of going to school in the church. They never did rebuild the school. Later, my cousins would take a bus to a new school that was built for blacks called Hillcrest. I think after segregation became illegal and racial integration occurred, Hillcrest became an elementary school and all the kids (black and white) went there. It became Athens Elementary School, and the high school students went to Athens High School. Like I said, Athens, Louisiana, is where our farm is located and our hometown.

Another vivid memory I have is that of my dad taking my mom and us to visit her family in Athens one time while we were living on the farm. I do know that we rode in a wagon; maybe it was before my father got a car. My mom's parents had always sharecropped. So I remember they were on this big farm, but they didn't own it, but I didn't know it at the time. I had no idea how significant it was for my father's family to own their own farm. Most of the farmers in the area sharecropped. I would later find out that meant that they were allowed to live on the farm as long as they worked the farm for the white family who really owned the farm. Even though they were supposed to get some payment for doing so, most of them received payment via the shared crops they harvested.

My mom and her siblings were big on storytelling, so they often told us stories about growing up as sharecroppers. It seemed that my mom and her sisters had to learn how to cook at very young ages. According to what we were told, the girls knew how to make biscuits by the time they were six years old. Evidently, my mom and my aunts would make breakfast for everyone before they went to the fields to pick cotton or whatever crop they were harvesting. My mom and her sisters would go with them to help and leave early to make lunch for everyone, then go back and continue working the fields. From what she said, her mother (Rosie or Monmon, as I would nickname her) and my grandmother was always pregnant and resting in the bed, so the girls cooked. My grandmother had fifteen pregnancies, I believe. My grandmother may have picked some cotton, but mostly she took in laundry from white people who lived nearby. She might have cleaned their homes as well. I think she preferred housework to fieldwork. She was a pretty good cook, though. I remember she would make the prettiest coconut cakes, but would never offer us a piece because she had too many mouths to feed herself. Ironically, she would be the one to introduce me to cotton picking and chopping.

Evidently, my mom did not like living on a farm, so in 1952 we moved to Minden, Louisiana, a town nearby and closer to the Shell Plant where my father worked. Many people in the community were upset, I am sure, that we moved because my father was their ride to the Shell Plant etc. I remember one of my great-uncles (Uncle John Thomas, my maternal grandmother's brother or half-brother) saying that one time my daddy was fired from the Shell Plant, his riders went to the boss and told him that they wouldn't be able to come to work the next day because my dad was their ride; they had to hire my dad back because they would be losing too many workers. My dad got his job back. I don't think he missed a day. Transporting people was my dad's third job until he got sick later in life. I don't think my father was ever without a car. As a matter of fact, my father's baby brother Uncle Nate told us, after my father got sick in his old age, that if we got our father a brand-new car he would be all fine again. Of course, we didn't take him up on that offer for fear my father would kill himself or others due to his mental state at the time. Nevertheless, we moved to Minden.

The things that probably caused my mom and dad to move from the family farm included the fact that my dad's job was closer to Minden (he worked at what was called the Shell plant—I didn't figure out this was ammunition until much later in life); my sister Bobbie having gotten burned on the woodburning heater while rocking her rocking chair that my parents had gotten for us, which scared my parents to death; and a flock of birds that had flown into our home one day. However, I think the main reason they moved was that Mildred, my aunt that was married to my father's oldest brother Jasper, came home to get her boys. They were a big help on the farm. Without them, my father had to take care of the biggest load because all the other adults on the farm had physical incapacities. Evidently, working full-time, traveling over fifty miles to and from his job daily, and working the farm on evenings and weekends got too much for him.

It must have been hard on my father to leave his handicapped brother and sister on the farm with their families. How were they going to take care of the farm now? I think he assured them that we were not moving far, and he would be there as often as possible, especially on the weekends. So when he should have been with us or resting, he was at the farm, helping out. Not only did he help out on the farm, he still had one of the only cars in the area, so he would take neighbors back and forth to town to shop. People were not doing as much farming as they used to because many of their kids had left and moved to other states and cities.

My father had four brothers, but three of them left the farm for greener pastures as soon as they could. They went to California, Texas, and Ohio. My father himself had gone to Washington and even Canada for a short while. My Uncle Long, if you remember, was handicapped. I think he had cerebral palsy, but not a severe case, or he had polio when he was young, as the story goes. It did not affect his speech that much, and he could still walk. He didn't need a cane until old age, like most people. He had seven kids, and my Aunt Velma (married to Uncle Clyde) had seven as well. My Uncle Clyde seemed not to be very helpful on the farm. He started having trouble with his eyes early on and went legally blind when I was in junior high school, I believe. Therefore, much of the helping out on the farm was left up to my Aunt Velma and Uncle Long. Uncle Clyde and Aunt Johnnie Bell (Uncle Long's wife) didn't do a whole lot. I think they would help with the planting and harvesting when they could. Aunt Velma would guide Uncle Clyde.

I remember the day Uncle Clyde went totally blind. He was cutting wood, and one piece flew up and hit him in the eye. I think he went to New Orleans for surgery, but when he came back, he wore patches on his eyes for a while. But he was now totally blind. We would all help him out if possible. Some of the times, we would tease him about who was helping him out and try to get him to guess. He seemed to always know us; he remembered our voices even after we grew up. Like I said earlier, Uncle Clyde and Aunt Velma had a big chicken coop, where they raised chickens and turkeys. When Uncle Clyde passed away, Aunt Velma got rid of that chicken coop immediately. Obviously, she was tired of taking care of the chickens mostly by herself.

I remember the morning we moved to Minden as if it were yesterday. I remember my cousins, the Lawhornes, looking so sad because we were moving. I knew they were going to miss us because there were so few kids on the farm or close by. We were going to miss them as well. My father had bought a car, and he was moving us in it. I think it was a black Ford; it seemed so big to me. I remember driving up to our new house out front and seeing it for the first time.

Chapter 2

THE MOVE (1952)
OUR NEW HOME

In 1952, our dad and mom moved us to a brand-new home in Minden, Louisiana. This is where I lived from the age of five until eighteen. Even though the farm life had it advantages, I was happy that we moved to Minden. Now we had indoor hot and cold running water and—thank You, Jesus!—an indoor toilet. No more trips to the well to get drinking or bath water. No more trips to the outhouse in the middle of the night with our mom or to the woods in the middle of the day. I couldn't believe it. Like I said, this was a new house. This is probably what you would call a subdivision because most of the houses looked alike. They were painted white and had a colorful trim. Our house was white with green trimming and located on 511 High Street. We now had neighbors within hearing distance. It seemed like we could whisper, and our neighbors would hear us. I remember always trying to keep my siblings quiet. No one lived in the house to the right of us when we moved. Mr. and Mrs. Harvey and Hattie Sims and their kids lived in the first house on the block and Ms. Lena and her husband lived next door to us. There were eight houses in the subdivision. Four of the houses were on High Street and four on North Fairview Street. The first house on North Fairview was vacant when we first moved (Mrs. Lettie Milner and her family moved in later). Ms. Della and Mr. Ralph lived in the next house, Ms. Angeline and her kids lived in the next, and my soon-to-be friend Pat Black, her mom, grandmom, and other siblings lived in the last house. Six of the houses were new and looked just alike.

The day we moved on high street, there was a white man mowing the grass in the field across the street; he was evidently clearing it for something. It turned out that he was building a cement company that would soon start up across from our house. We probably breathed in a lot of cement dust into our lungs over the years. Nobody questioned what it would do to the environment or our health being located right across the street from a populated area, probably because the people were black. My father had asthma before we moved there, but we all had a touch of asthma later in life, including myself. I have had my lungs x-rayed, and I was told they looked good. My mom would later go to work for that white man; she called him Mr. Junior. His wife was Ms. Leona. She ran the restaurant they owned and where my mom would later go to work and Bobbie and me as well.

Even though farm life had it advantages, I was happy that we moved to Minden. Forget the fact that our house only had two bedrooms for five kids and two adults at the time. We were all so little then that we could care less. My mom and dad put two big beds in the kids' room and one big bed in their room. Later they would add a cot to their room for the babies to sleep as they grew. Until then, they slept with my mom and dad. The only one I remember sleeping on the cot was my youngest sister Vickie. I don't remember her ever sleeping in the bed with us. I left home when Vickie was eight. I was ten when she was born. At some point in time, the babies would move into the kids' room, and one more space had to be made in the beds. The mattresses in our bed had cotton in them, probably actual cotton from the cotton fields (probably our own) because sometimes we could feel the wood stalks that somehow were left in the cotton.

Anyway, I think my mom made the mattresses, I don't think they were manufactured. For sure, I know that the quilts were hand-produced because I saw my mom and her sisters and my grandmother quilting them. The quilts were so heavy they would keep us warm at night because even though now we had a gas heater, my mom or dad always cut ours off at night because they feared a fire would start. They would only leave it on if it was really cold outside; even then my dad was skeptical about doing so. The heater in the bathroom was always left on. That was nice, so you didn't have to sit down on a cold toilet at night. My mom and dad kept their heater on all night. I think my dad thought as kids we might accidentally start a fire or sleepwalk into the heater (me, I think, as I was the only one to sleep-walk). One thing I do know, those quilts were heavy, and we would get up tired in the mornings. I am pretty sure it was from tussling with those quilts all night.

When we moved, Juanita was the baby by then, so my parents had five kids at the time. I assume all five of us and our parents shared that one bedroom at the family home on the farm. Dorothy, Linda, and Vickie were born in Minden. To us, we now lived in the city; we had next-door neighbors now. You could hollow from your porch to their house to get their attention; that was not true on the farm. You had to walk a distance to your nearest neighbor. There were several empty houses on our block initially, but they soon filled up. We quickly got to know the neighbors especially the kids. I will always consider the kids that lived on our block like extended family.

Eventually, we became to feel quite at home on high street. When we moved, my parents had five kids: Bobbie, David, Carrie, Juanita, and me. Like I said, Juanita was the baby at the time; she was about nine months old when we moved. There were some older kids in the neighborhood, but I was happy to see that Patricia Black (nicknamed Pat) and Melvyn Thomas (nicknamed Sister) were my age. Melvyn lived in a house that was up a slight hill and right next door to Pat. They were lighter-skinned girls. I noticed that early on because most of the people in my family had dark skin tones. I had no idea what the differences in skin tones meant at five.

Our new house had two bedrooms. This seemed sufficient for seven people at the time. My parents put two beds that resembled queen-size beds in the front bedroom (this was where the kids would sleep) and one full-size bed in their bedroom, the back bedroom. We had two bedrooms, a bathroom, a living room, and a porch. I have to mention the porch because it was the center of our entertainment all our lives from 1952 until 1977. When I got married and my parents had our house rehabbed and got rid of the porch to enlarge the living-room area. The front porch meant a lot in black Southern homes in Minden at the time and, I daresay, the South period. A lot took place on the front porch—fights, street watching, games, and weddings. Only one of us got married on our front porch, and that was my sister Linda in her first marriage. Three of my aunts got married on my grandparents' front porch. Melvyn Thomas's sister Jean got married on their front porch. If you didn't get married on your front porch, the front room was the next best place, especially if you were pregnant. When we were young, the beds seemed too big, and you could fit four kids in them comfortably. But as we aged and grew, they got to be too small. By the time I was eighteen, I was ready to have my own bed. When I got to college and had my own bed, it was like heaven to me. I missed my family, but not enough to give up my new bed.

When we moved to High Street in Minden, we didn't know that the property had been a lake before. My mom had tried over and over to get a garden to grow or to plant flowers, but whenever it rained as it often does in Louisiana, the seeds would be washed away, so nothing ever grew. She was finally successful with flowers, but never with a garden to her—or should I say, my father's—dismay.

Attached to both our homes, the one in Athens and now the one in Minden, was a front porch. This seemed to be a staple for Southern homes. Our porch was the center of our entertainment, especially in the summer. Everything either started or finished on our front porch. It was the first place we went in the morning and the last place we left in the evening before going to bed. The city had placed a light right in front of our house, so we had light, especially when there was no moon light. We would spend hours just sitting on the porch staring at the sky and the stars, trying to find the Big and Little Dipper or the man in the moon. Most summer nights were not cloudy, so our imaginations just ran wild. We loved being outside and was often encouraged or just sent outside by our parents, who wanted some quiet time after working all day, and we readily gave it to them.

In the spring and summer months, my dad divided his time between a full-time job, working on the farm, or serving as a jitney taxicab for people on nearby farms in Athens. He would get off work around 4:00 p.m., come home and change clothes, and go to the farm and work until around 9:00 p.m. If he had any energy left when he came home, he would help us with our homework if we had a problem. On Saturdays, he would go to the farm early. Sometime on Saturdays, he would stop farming and start driving people from nearby houses or farms back and forth to downtown Homer, Louisiana, or nearby Athens, Louisiana. He would get home around 8 p.m. in the evening on Saturdays. On Sunday, he stayed home all day and rested. He refused to work on Sundays, even around the house. My mom would ask him to fix this or that over and over again; but if he couldn't get to it before Sundays, which was most of the time, it didn't get done. Most of the time, he would have to get someone else to fix it, which if he couldn't use the bartering system, it would take a while to get done because he didn't have much money.

On the weekend, sometimes we would go to the farm to help Daddy. Most of the time, since farming work was hard and could be dangerous and most of the time in the sun, we just played with our cousins the Lawhornes. What the Lawhornes and us loved to do most of the time was just walk around the woods near the farm and hunt for wild berries, peaches, pears, and plums. We had pecan and black walnut trees on the farm as well. Sometimes we would go to the fields to check to see if we could find a ripe watermelon. Most of the watermelons were red, but we loved it when we opened one, and it was yellow. We would eat the watermelons right in the field. I don't think watermelons ever tasted so good as it did right there in the field. Unfortunately, we cleaned the trees of their fruits, so now hardly any fresh fruit grows on our farm, or as adult, we might be too scared to venture into the woods now, and definitely not our city-slicker children.

On one of our visits to the farm, Daddy asked Bobbie, David, and me if we wanted to ride one of his horses. I really wanted to ride the horse, but I said no because I was scared. Bobbie and David said yes, and he put them on the horse and rode them around. I was so jealous of them, so I wished I had said yes. Now, whenever, I get the chance to ride a horse, I do—and I love it. Sometimes on visits, he would take us for rides in his wagon; I loved that too.

As we got older, our dad put us to work, and the farm was not fun anymore. We had to help him plant, water, but what I regretted most of all was picking cotton. One summer, my parents decided they were going to put all their efforts into growing cotton. They even hired people to work to chop and pick the cotton. Daddy was supposed to pay us as well, but he did not, and it took us a long time to forgive him for that. He said he paid us by making sure we had a roof over our heads and food on the table. But we thought, *he promised*. Don't promise children and then come up with an excuse. I think he knew, since he was paying the Lawhornes, that if he didn't promise to pay us as well, we would have put in a halfhearted, effort and I am sure was right. We wanted to make money to go to the fair and actually enjoy ourselves for a change. We went to the carnival fair in our hometown every year, but we only had enough money for food; maybe we were given $2 a piece or less. We were heartbroken when he paid the Lawhornes and didn't pay us; they had more money at the fair than we did. I think Daddy felt bad about not being able to pay us money as well. I think they only made about $900 off the cotton, so they didn't have much left over after paying the hired help. They never tried to grow cotton again. I know he heard enough from us, especially my sister Bobbie because she wouldn't let him forget it. She even brings it up to this day—just a few weeks ago, as a matter of fact. Man, can she chew on a bone forever.

My dad was the only able bodied man working the farm. Like I said, Uncle Clyde and Uncle Long both lived on the farm, but both were handicapped. Uncle Long did as much as he could. I assume both his boys did as well. I know his oldest son left home early just like his uncles before him, probably because he feared farm work. None of my dad's other brothers ever came home to help out on the farm.

They did come home, though, especially Uncle Sed and Uncle Nate. They were both handsome dark-skinned men. My uncle Nate and his wife lived in the bedroom next to ours when we lived on the farm for a few years, and I know we heard them being affectionate often (now I know what was going on; I didn't then). We also used to visit them in Dallas, Texas, in their home, and I would often see them being affectionate. Their relationship gave me ideas of how I wanted my own relationships to be when I grew up. I wanted an open loving relationship in public and private. My parents were not affectionate in front of us. I knew they were; otherwise, they wouldn't have had eight kids, even though I knew my dad was just trying to get enough farm hands, and then my mom supported with household chores. I remember the first time I saw them kiss in front of us. My mom was washing dishes, and my dad came up behind her and gave her a kiss. I screamed, "Daddy kissed Mom!" so everybody could hear and come running. They both looked shy, but I was happy to see them being affectionate for once. I had often wondered if my mom enjoyed sex (I hope so because I truly enjoy sex and having a jaw-dropping climax is amazing). She never discussed sex with us girls, not even after we started having our periods. We learned mostly about sex from books and our girlfriends.

My uncle Sed had a light-skinned wife, and everybody seemed to think she was cute. I know Uncle Sed loved his wife, and my Uncle Nate loved his wife. To me, they treated their wives like queens. I never saw much spousal abuse on either side of my family, maternal or paternal. I did see my father and mother fight one time. I was very young and got scared when I saw my dad inches away from my mother's throat with an ice pick. I thought he was going to kill her, so I ran out the door, hollering that my dad was going to kill my mother. By the time I got to the front yard, both my parents were smiling at me, saying they were only playing. The neighbors had run to our yard, so my parents were really embarrassed. I think this embarrassed them so that they never had another physical fight. I am pretty sure they were not playing that time. I hate to think that my dad really would have killed my mother that day, though. I did see my mother standing at the door late one night with her coat on and looking intently at my father. I asked her where she was going (I was pretty sure she was leaving my father). She said "nowhere" and for me to go back to bed. I made sure she went back to bed as well. I am sure they'd had a fight. They did their best to keep any disagreements just between themselves, and that had to be hard in our small house. My parents did not like airing their dirty laundry; they never wanted anyone to know when they were hurting, financially or otherwise. I know my mom always took her problems to the Lord; I don't know where my dad took his.

I think Juanita, the baby when we moved, shared my parents' bed, and later my parents put a cot in their room, and this would be the second bed for the babies. We eventually got a foldaway bed for my brother to sleep in the hallway. As he grew, the living room couch opened up into a bed, and that's where he slept until he graduated from high school. We utilized every nook and cranny of that house at one point in time. I remember some of us sleeping in the kitchen on what we called a pallet (several quilts) when family members would visit. These were the crazy times. Because we had a toilet, my father's family members who visited always wanted to stay with us instead of with Aunt Velma or Uncle Long, who still lived on the farm and had an outdoor toilet.

We got to know all the families on our block, and I will always consider them like extended family members. We only had a few disagreements. Most of the disagreements were with the Thomas family for some reason. When we moved, my eventual friend Melvyn Thomas's parents were married and living together with their three girls and three boys. Ms. Lucille was Melvyn's mother, and Mr. Buck was her father. I remember them fighting a lot when I was growing up. I remember their kids (led by John Luther, the oldest boy) coming to our house when our parents were not home and jumping on the beds and messing up our house for some reason. I am not sure if my friend Melvyn caused any of the damage, but I do remember Jean Thomas (the oldest) stopping the destruction. I tried to stop them myself to no avail. When Momma and Daddy got home, they went marching up to the Thomases' home to confront Ms. Lucille and Mr. Buck about what their children had done. I do know my parents were angry, and the kids never did it again, even though we were home alone a lot. All of us eventually became very good friends. I used to go and talk to Melvyn or Jean on their back porch for hours on end. Melvyn and I went to kindergarten through college together. It was on the back porch where Jean told me she was pregnant by Tommie Washington. I didn't even know they were going together. I knew Tommie's siblings, but I did not know him or even that he and Jean were going together. Jean and Tommie got married soon after she graduated from Webster High School, the only black high school in Minden and where we would all go later. They got married, like I said, on their front porch. I remember she wore white even though she was pregnant at the time.

Shortly after we moved to Minden, Juanita was asleep in my parents' bedroom, and my mom made us not bother her so she could sleep. She was always shushing us when the baby was around so the baby wouldn't start to cry. I found out later that this was not always a good thing for a baby, that talking to the baby and talking while the baby was around even if the baby was sleeping helped develop their vocabulary. Even if they couldn't understand the words now, their brains were absorbing the words anyway. Go figure!

This time, though, my mom was spending time with one or two of the women in the neighborhood in our kitchen. For some reason, I went in to check on Juanita and noticed that something was different. Juanita was fast asleep on the bed in a diaper. It was hot, so she was sweating and had no cover. I noticed that her navel looked different. I had always been intrigued by the fact that her navel was so large, but something had changed. I felt her navel, and it was hard. Most of the times before when I would touch her navel, it would be soft. I knew this was different, so I told my mom about it. She immediately stopped talking to the ladies and checked on Juanita. She and the ladies agreed that Juanita should be taken to the hospital immediately. It turned out that she had to have surgery because she had a hernia. My mom was glad I had disobeyed her and checked on Juanita. I know that Juanita was taken to the hospital in Minden, and that was where the surgery took place. I don't think our parents took us to see her there, but we were glad when she came home.

My mom's babies were always small and red-looking with curly hair at first. However, when they started on table food—or should I say pot liquor (liquid from cooking beans or greens) and bread mashed together—they would start to gain weight fast. Dorothy, Linda, and Vickie were pretty big babies. I used to have to throw my hip to carry them because I was so small. After I grew up, this throwing of the hip affected how I walked, and I think it still does to this day. In the sixth grade, I think, a friend asked me why I always threw my hips when I walked. She wanted to know if I was trying to be sexy, something I knew nothing about, but I realized that I was throwing my hips at the time because I was used to carrying my mother's big babies and throwing my hip so they wouldn't fall.

Whenever my mom had a baby, the women in the neighborhood would come over to help out around the house until she healed. They would feed the baby, comb our hair, make sure we were bathed, and cook dinner for us. The women would insist that my mom just rested. I thought this was a nice thing to do, and my mom seemed to appreciate the attention and the chance to get to know her new neighbors. She was not one to visit with our neighbors in their homes, and neither were they normally. I think the attention pregnant women get is cherished by some women so much that some get pregnant just for the attention. I noticed this attention myself when I got pregnant and relished it sometimes.

I don't think in my mom's case that she had eight babies because she relished the attention she got when she was pregnant. I really think my father was trying for more boys so he could have more help with the farm. They had two boys; but one was stillborn, and the other, my brother, David, seemed to hate farm life just as much as my mom. The one attempt my dad tried to make him a farmer, David broke his leg. I think that upset my dad, so he never tried again. David later became a lawyer.

My father felt that farming was not for girls. He had solid traditional ideas about what boys and girls were supposed to do. I remember after my brother turned twelve, and my sister Carrie was about eleven, that he said that David would no longer help with dishes, that there were enough girls to do the dishes. To him, the girls were supposed to do the housework and boys the outside work or the farmwork. He also said that David was no longer to iron. However, Bobbie and I took care of that. We ironed David's blue jeans so poorly on purpose that David forbade us from ironing them, so he took back over the ironing of his clothes because only he could get them just the way he liked them. At the time, boys wore beautifully starched and ironed jeans with a crease. It was a tiresome chore to get them that way.

My mom never breastfed any of her babies. I asked her about this later in life when I decided to breastfeed my own baby; and she said nobody did it and that they were probably following the lead of white women at the time. She fed her babies evaporated milk that had been watered down. Evaporated milk could be kept in the cabinet a long time. However, once you hydrated it, it had to be kept in the refrigerator. I remember the bottles had to be sterilized and the milk warmed when the babies were small. As the babies got older, she didn't feed them baby cereal; she fed them pot liquor, mashed-up corn bread, or food from her mouth that she had chewed. She would feed them with her fingers. I would learn later that this pot liquor was probably healthier for the babies because the vegetables in the black household were often overcooked; and the nutrients, especially the water-soluble vitamins, would leech into the liquid. I think this trend of blacks overcooking their food probably started on the farm when they had no place to store the food safely, so they just left them on the stove to keep them warm and free from germs, and probably waiting for the men to come home from farming all day. This trend of blacks feeding their babies mush made from pot liquid or pot liquor, as most people called it, was good because most of the water-soluble vitamins would be in the pot liquor, like vitamin C and the B vitamins. Even though blacks ate a lot of raw fruit, they chose to cook most of their vegetables. The only vegetables I saw them eat raw were sweet potatoes, tomatoes, cabbage in slaw, lettuce, onions, cucumbers, and carrots in salads. My mom's babies would start to lose weight once they started to feed themselves and run around, and most of them didn't like vegetables by this time.

After moving to Minden, my mom tried to get me enrolled in the first grade at J. L. Jones Elementary, but she said I was not old enough, so they wouldn't accept me. She found out that the kids in the neighborhood were going to Mrs. Demp Hardy's Kindergarten, so she enrolled me in her kindergarten. At first, my mom would walk with me to school, and then when I got comfortable, Melvyn Thomas and I would walk together to Mrs. Demp's kindergarten. Mrs. Demp was Melvyn mother's sister. Sometimes, when we would arrive at school, Mrs. Demp would not be ready, so she would invite us into her home to sit until she opened the school. The school was right next to her house. I think her husband had built the one-room school for her. I think my neighbor Pat and her cousin Hazel must have been in kindergarten there with us, but I don't remember them.

Because I had already been going to school, I already knew my ABCs and my colors. I was happy about that because then I could keep up with the other kids in kindergarten. In the springtime, Mrs. Demp asked my mom if her kids could participate in the Easter Program at New Light Baptist Church. Mrs. Demp was in charge of the Easter Program. I was surprised when my mom said yes.

I don't remember graduating from kindergarten, but most of my siblings have pictures of themselves graduating from kindergarten. I guess Mrs. Demp started formal graduation services the year after I graduated, because Bobbie graduated the next year (1954), and she has a graduation picture. Even my baby sister Vickie has a graduation picture. I get jealous every time I see their pictures because more than likely, this is the youngest picture we have of them. None of us have baby pictures, so the kindergarten picture gives you a good idea of what you looked like at the age of five or six. I don't have that luxury. I have no idea what I looked like as a baby. I think the earliest picture I have of myself is sixth or seventh grade. My parents didn't buy many of our school pictures because they couldn't afford them. I guess they bought my sixth grade picture. I'm pretty sure it was sixth grade because I was not wearing glasses. I still wish I'd had a baby picture, but hardly any black folks around my age had baby pictures. If you did, you were probably middle class (for black folks) at the time.

Like I said, I couldn't believe my mom told Mrs. Demp that we could participate in the Easter Program at New Light Baptist Church. To my knowledge, New Light was the only church on Crichton Hill when we moved to Minden in 1952. Most of the Black residents on Crichton Hill belonged to New Light. All the kids in my neighborhood went to church there, except for a few who still went to their churches on the outskirts of Minden. My mom had grown up in the Methodist Church, and my dad was Baptist. After my mom married my dad, she became a member of Spring Lake Church of God in Christ or Sanctified church (kids in my neighborhood called us holly rollers because when we got "happy" [shouted], we rolled around on the floor; the name always embarrassed me), following in my dad's sister Aunt Velma's footsteps. I believed Aunt Velma joined after she married Uncle Clyde. She probably had been torn between her mother's (Carrie Herron Rabb) church, which was Union Grove Baptist near Homer, Louisiana, and the Rabb's family church, St. John Baptist Church. So she just joined her husband's (Uncle Clyde Lawhorne) church after she married him. You could say Crichton Hill was a church community; everything was centered round the church and its activities. Our social lives centered round the church. When we started to school, it was church and school, and in that order.

After participating in our first Easter Program at New Light, we were hooked. We loved practicing after school, which we did for a week or two before Easter Sunday. On Easter Sunday, we would all come back to church in the evening and present the program. It seemed as if the whole community attended the programs. The church was always packed, even with people who didn't generally attend New Light, like my mom and I think my dad. I just don't remember him inside the church. Maybe he stayed outside and talked to some of the men. Most of the kids in my family got the chance to participate in the Easter programs at New Light, I believe. There was a hierarchy in the Easter program: the older you were, the more lines you were given. The older kids always wore the sheets and did something like a praise dance to end the program every Easter to the song "On a Hill Far Away" or the "Old Rugged Cross" by George

Bennard. I think Bobbie was the last of my family to wear the sheets and perform the praise dance. David probably didn't do it because I think it was only girls who participated. The older boys might have had something else to do, but David didn't ask to participate because he was mad that Mrs. Demp had called him "Bucky Beaver" because when he was younger, his two front teeth were bigger than the other teeth. But other than David's problem with Mrs. Demp, we all enjoyed participating in the programs at New Light.

My mom started sending us to New Light Baptist Church for Sunday school, but for some reason, she didn't go. She was still a member of Aunt Velma's church, so whenever possible, she would go there to church or with her family to her family church, Barnes Chappel Methodist Church (I think). All of us kids loved going to New Light because they had a lot of programs kids could get involved in. Unfortunately, after one of the deacons saw Bobbie and me put nickels in the church offering, he made a comment about it, and Bobbie told Momma, and she didn't allow us to go to church there again. I can't remember what he said. I am not sure if I was paying attention to the sermon or not. But as I got older, I realized that all families paid tithes, and that plus the offering was used to pay the bills of the church. So we were taking advantage of the activities of the church, but we were not supporting the church. I didn't understand it because we were just kids; our parents didn't attend the church. My mom and dad went to other churches. They would only attend if we were on program. To be honest, I don't even remember my dad attending church that much even then. Maybe some of the men had been trying to get him to join New Light because my dad was Baptist, but he never did. St. John was his home church, even though he seldom attended it either.

After Bobbie told our parents about the negative comment, Mr. Hardy, the deacon (and Mrs. Demp's husband), had said, my mom started taking us to her church most Sundays, Spring Lake Church of God in Christ. It was kind of a culture shock to us because it was so different from New Light Baptist Church. There were more singing, shouting, and clapping of hands, and I found out later the members of the church were called *holy rollers* because, like I said, when people got "happy," they would roll around on the floor. We loved the church because it was active; you didn't get as bored as with the Baptist or Methodist churches. By now, we had gone to our mom's family's church and didn't understand the singing. They would do a lot of moaning, which we did not understand. To this day, to understand the church services and the songs are very important to me and my judgement of whether I like a church or not. I loved the services at Spring Lake because they were simple to me, and the songs were often the same words over and over again and quick to learn.

John Fountain, a journalist with the *Chicago Sun Times* in Chicago, also attended the Church of God in Christ in his youth, and he loved it as well. He wrote about how the church was when he was growing up and how it had changed, but not for the better. On Sunday, November 5, 2017, he wrote, "She was a mighty church, and he continued with the 'holiness' church. 'Saved.' 'Sanctified.' The church where so-called holy rollers rolled around the church's floors, overcome by the Holy Spirit." My family and I belonged to such a church, and members would indeed roll around on the floor in a jerking fashion and speaking in tongues. This type of event definitely occurred every night of our revival. Most churches in the south had revivals. It seemed like a social event, even in our church. Members who had stopped coming to church and others from the neighborhood who had never attended and weren't looking for a church somehow would find out about our revival and come to church. The churches probably collaborated in some way so they wouldn't hold their revivals on the same night. Revivals were big money-making events for churches as well. Looking back, I can say that from the age of five to eighteen years, my social life was centered 'round the church.

Whenever we had revival at Spring Lake, Brother Doc, Sister Leana Cope's husband, would come to church; that would be the only time during the year that we saw him. Even then, I don't think he came into the church. He would set up something like a canteen outside of the church. This was where he sold food and drinks. We loved going out there to get a soda pop from him. We would try to sneak out there before the church services were over and stay as long as possible. A lot of the older kids would be out there courting. I think some people came and just stood around the canteen area, making it more of a social event instead of a religious event. The area would be well lite, so whenever things got boring inside the church, we would peer out there with longing, wondering what the adults were doing.

During revival, our church was packed. I was always amazed at the number of people because in the daylight, there didn't seem to be that many people in the area. But they came out of the woods whenever we had revival at our church. People who didn't normally go to church would come out like it was a social event. I think it was the hope that they would get turned around, and maybe some of them did and start to go to church regularly even if it wasn't our church. But needless to say, there weren't that many social events in the area, so school events and revivals were high on the list, I assume. I wonder now if alcoholic beverages were consumed on the church grounds during the revival. I don't think so because back then even church buildings were respected. I think you could have left money in the church, and no one would have bothered it.

My mom didn't often go to church at night when we were little, but she always went to revival nightly, which was held about six nights: Monday, Tuesday, Wednesday, Thursday, Friday, and Sunday nights. They would have a barbeque on Saturday sometimes. I remember going to one of the barbeques, and my mom allowed Bobbie and me to wear blue-and-pink matching pedal pusher sets. This was unusual because we weren't allowed to wear pants to church. I think my mom figured it was okay because Bobbie and I were little, and we weren't saved yet. Bobbie does not remember this event. I remember it vividly because we never wore pants. The women would bring cakes and pies to sell, and Brother Doc would sell barbeque and soft drinks. The barbeque was a big hit, and the food would run out quickly. This was more like a fund-raiser for the church. I couldn't help but wonder if some of the money didn't go in Brother Doc's pocket. But then he probably bought the food and drinks to sell.

Revival ended on Sunday, and it was a big day, plus a very long day. All the families would bring food to church. I think they called it box lunches. All week, you could hear people asking one another, "Are you bringing a box on Sunday?" Nobody, to my knowledge, ever got sick, but for years we didn't have a refrigerator to put the food in or stove to heat it on. I remember us having some perishable foods, like potato salad, chicken and dressing, greens, etc. One of the members, Sister Carrie, didn't live too far from the church, so I believe some of the church members would go to her house and reheat the food, especially the food that went on the pastor's table. The pastor's table was always set with the best food and utensils. The minister and his wife didn't have to lift a figure. The sisters in the church would take care of everything, even after attending services every night, cooking all day on Saturday and attending Sunday school and church services during the day.

My mother would do all this and even after she had worked full-time all week. She would always demand Saturdays and Sundays off. She would often sleep through church services; she was so tired. We would tell her about it later in the car and laugh at her; she would laugh along with us. I have so many pictures of my mom sleeping at inappropriate times, but didn't think to take one of her in church, where I don't think she ever missed a time sleeping. I think with eight kids and an unaffectionate husband, my mom was tired to her core from the day she got married and until she died.

On most Saturdays (especially doing revival), she always washed and ironed (of course, we helped) and fried our hair. I say fried because that's just what it was. When you fry, you put food in hot grease. Well, my mom would grease our hair and then fry it. I think some black people consider a straightening comb (that's what we called it in our house; I think some people call it a hot comb) a blessing, but I would never call it that. I think God meant for black women to wear their hair naturally. With seven girls, my mom would often ask her sister Elnora to help out. Then and again, Elnora would probably offer her help because she had no children and enjoyed watching us get ready for special occasions like revival. She would sometimes go to church with us. This was seldom because we didn't have any room in our car.

On the last day of revival on Sundays, we would spend all day at church. After daytime service, we would eat and just wait at the church for nighttime service. Often after we (the kids) ate, we would go walking down the road or up the road, whichever we decided. We didn't walk in the woods because we had on our Sunday shoes and dresses, and to be honest, we were probably scared of woods we were not used to. Most of the time, it would be the Rabbs and the Lawhornes walking together. We had fun just talking, most of the time about the different church members, especially Sister Carrie, who couldn't sing if her life depended on it. But every Sunday Sister Carrie would lead a song, and nobody knew the words, so we couldn't follow along. One of the things I liked about Spring Lake or the Church of God in Christ was that anybody could lead a solo. We didn't have a choir at the time; we the congregation would sing all the songs together, except when Sister Carrie started a song in her own tune that no one had ever heard of. We'd have to be back to church before evening services, so we didn't walk too far. During evening services, we'd have communion and washing of the feet, like Jesus did. I forgot one thing: we also had baptisms on this Sunday of all the people who came to Christ during the week at the altar calls. The minister could tell if you were saved if you spoke in tongues and sometimes rolled around on the floor. As children, we would go to the altar for years before speaking in tongues or rolling around on the floor. Sometimes I wondered if we spoke in tongues and rolled just to end the ordeal. To this day, I am not sure. I am sure I spoke in tongues and rolled around the floor and was saved. I do know that afterward I never doubted that God was the Father, Son, the Holy Ghost, and my Savior. My cousin Alma Jean and I found God during the same revival. I think Queen and Bobbie found it the following year. It was like as we all got to a certain age, it was time to find Jesus and get baptized.

We begged our mom to allow us to participate in the programs at New Light, and she did until we were older. We no longer went to Sunday school or church services there, though. We missed so many of the programs at New Light. Even today I think the black Baptist Church places a high priority on education. New Light had an education building. One of the programs I enjoyed, I believe, was called Sunshine band. Women in the Sunshine band would invite young girls in our neighborhood to have tea with them and then do crafts. One of the crafts I remember was embroidering. I embroidered a piece that I thought was beautiful. My mom placed it on her dresser, and it was there for years. I was so proud of it.

Another program I just loved was the Vacation Bible School. It seemed the whole community participated in Vacation Bible School at New Light. I think Ms. Demp was in charge of this program as well. The school ran for one or two weeks. One activity most of us liked at the school was Bible bowl. The teacher would ask us to find a Bible verse to see who could find it first. It was a way of learning the Bible and the teachings of God because when you found the verse, you had to read it. For some reason, I was not afraid to read the Bible verse in front of people. Most of the competition was between me and Melvyn Thomas. I didn't know it at the time, but this was a way of horning our reading skills during the summer when school was out. To me, there is no book more difficult to understand than the Bible. However, I don't remember us looking up the words we didn't understand like we did at school. When we got out of Vacation Bible School, we would often continue the Bible bowl in our different homes and on our front or back porches because we enjoyed it so much.

Probably, the activity my siblings and I enjoyed the most about Vacation Bible School was the picnic at the end. We would take a bus to the picnic grounds (black side of Lake Bisteneau; whites used the other side, but I never saw it or them then because we weren't allowed on that side), where we enjoyed participating in fun games and especially riding on the paddleboats. These boats were manned by older kids from the neighborhood. I only went out on the boat one time. I remember my neighbor Noochie Gilbert was paddling the boat, and we got stuck. He had to rock the boat back and forth to get it loose. I was afraid we were going to drown. We weren't too far from shore, but I was scared and very glad when we got back to shore. The food was cooked in big black pots right there on the picnic grounds by men and women. Most of the time, we had fish, maybe hot dogs, potato salad, chips, soda pop, etc. I always loved the food. I remember they played music, and some of the kids would dance. We all had so much fun.

My mom knew we missed the programs at New Light, so she and the ladies at Spring Lake started to do some programs. I think the first program we had was a Mother's Day program. We loved it because we never had Mother's Day programs at New Light. My aunt Velma would give us our speeches and then later we would get them ourselves from Mother's Day cards from the store or poetry books from the library. Spring Lake had very few members and a small number of kids, so we all had speech parts on those occasions when we had programs. We even started having programs at Christmas too, along with Easter programs. One time, I remember us having a fashion show as a part of the Easter program. These occasions were always fun. My cousin Alma Jean and I were the oldest kids in the church for a long time. There were some older kids when we first started, but they either got married or left or, in the case of Deacon Morris or Big Boy, he and his wife divorced, I believe, and their kids started going to church with their mother.

Since Alma Jean and I were the oldest kids at Spring Lake, we were often given additional responsibilities. I was given the opportunity to teach the first little kids' class. I don't know what they did with the little kids before that. They started to purchase material for the little kids Sunday school class, which consisted primarily of little cards with Bible scripture and stories. I had fun teaching the little kids. I really should have chosen to become a primary school teacher as a result, but I didn't. I never would have been given the opportunities that I had at Spring Lake at New Light because there were so many older kids, so in the end, it was a blessing for me that my mom chose the smaller church because we were able to horn our reading skills and our leadership skills. Unfortunately, our social skills did take a hit because most of the kids at our church were our cousins. As a result, we got to know our cousins real well, and we enjoyed being together, but our conversations were limited.

My mom even started having Vacation Bible School at Spring Lake. By this time, I was in college, so I didn't participate. Before

I graduated, though, she did talk the holiness churches in Minden to have Vacation Bible School. We would end it with a picnic even. Even though I didn't attend, my mom would end Vacation Bible School at Spring Lake with a picnic also. My mom led all these activities because she knew what they meant to her kids. She didn't like her kids sitting around all summer with nothing to do. I wonder if she knew kids got in trouble that way. She didn't allow us to go to parties like other moms in our neighborhood because she didn't know the families. The only houses we were allowed to visit were our neighbors' and those of my mom's and dad's families. The only other place other than church or school we were allowed to spend time was the local library on Crichton Hill. My parents were extremely protective of us. My mom and dad were both leaders in their own right. I now know they were servant leaders because they became leaders when they felt there was a need and good for their own kids.

For as long as I can remember, I was always shy. Looking back the shyness was more than normal because it took me so long to come out of the shyness. At home and at Spring Lake church, I was not shy or quiet most of the time; but at school, with more people, I was deftly shy for some reason. I was even scared to raise my hand to answer questions even when I knew the answer. I grew out of my shyness somewhat by my senior year in high school, and to me, this was very late. I always equated it with a lack of confidence, but I am pretty sure now that it was more than that. What got me through was, I hated it. I hated being shy. So I worked on it. I worked on coming out of my shell and worked on trying to understand it. I think the shyness was innate, and I believe more encouragement from my parents and teachers would have helped. My parents probably didn't understand the magnitude of the situation, or they didn't know how shy I was because at home I was vibrant and in control. As I grew older, my shyness was compounded by my belief that I was very ugly, and who wanted the ugly girl to speak? It took me awhile to get over that feeling, then and again, I am not sure I ever really got over it. It is an everyday battle to fight the feeling that no one wants to hear from the ugly girl, now ugly woman. I think you can say unequivocally that I was more than a late bloomer, if I ever fully blossomed.

I think my perception was related to my skin color or other people's perceptions of me growing up because I spent so much time in the sun. My skin tone was very dark. After living in Chicago and being inside most of the time and with less sunlight in the winter months, I have a lighter skin tone. I noticed that most black Chicagoans who go on vacation to sun-drenched states come back darker, everybody mentions how tanned they are. Me, on the other hand, when I go south and come back darker, I think of myself as getting back my real color, not tanning.

I think I owe more of my personal development to my church and to my family more than my schools. At school, I was never chosen as the lead in anything until my senior year, whereas at church I was able to lead from, let's say, eighth grade on because I was one of two older kids. My cousin Alma Jean was the other one. I think Alma Jean was shy as well. I really think she majored in drama at college to help her get over her shyness. She didn't have the ugly-girl syndrome though because she started to attract boys when she was a teenager. At church, we would kind of take the lead from each other because we had no one else to compare ourselves to. That was kind of like that all my life. I had to take the lead because there was no one else available or willing to do it, so I had no one to pattern myself after.

At home, I developed more because I was the oldest and was called upon to stretch myself more. I was the first to do a lot of things. The first to cook, the first to pay the bills, the first to go to work, the first to plait hair, the first to make a bed, the first to clean the whole house. My sister Bobbie was next to me in age by one year, so we did a lot of things together, but normally I would do it first. It got to where I expected to be the first in everything. I remember when my daddy bought my sister Carrie candy for her birthday; this was the first time any consideration was given to anyone's birthday. We were lucky if someone said "happy birthday" to us. Birthdays were never special in our house; there were too many kids. I believe my dad bought the candy for Carrie on a whim, or maybe Carrie was his favorite because she was named after his mother, or maybe he bought it for her because her birthday was on Valentine's Day. Besides, he had never, to our knowledge, bought our mom candy on Valentine's Day. I don't really know why he bought it, but I only remember thinking, *I am the oldest. I should have gotten candy first.* My sister Bobbie and I gave daddy a mouth full for not buying us candy on our birthdays before, we should have been first. To me, my parents very seldom, if at all, made a difference in us as kids; my younger siblings may not feel the same. They tell me now that I was treated special sometimes. I didn't see that; I only saw my parents going out of their way to treat us equal. When daddy bought Carrie candy, this was out of order. Bobbie and I made sure he bought us candy on our birthdays. We would remind him often. The next years and all subsequent years, he never bought anybody anything else on their birthdays, not even our mother. To be honest, he never bought my mother anything on any day that I can remember that even remotely resembled something personal. I don't think he ever saw his dad do things like that for his mom. Then again, he was young when she died, and they were poor.

Our church was very small. Till this day, I consider the members of the church my church family. We knew everybody in the church, even though we never went to their homes. We felt a connection to them through the church. Even Sister Carrie, one of the mothers of the church, was near and dear to our hearts even though we had many laughs at her expense (we meant no harm). Out of church, we would often mimic her singing. I often wondered if her bad singing made me super conscious of my own voice. I can't carry a tune even though I was in the choir for three years in high school. I even led a few songs at church, but man, was I scared to sing in public normally. I was scared to speak and sing in public, but the fear was tripled with regards to solo singing. I really think I am tone-deaf. I believe that is why I have a hard time to this day with speaking proper English. I just don't hear myself. At times I still murder the English language. I just don't let it get me down or the fear of saying something stupid get me down now, whereas I used to worry whether I split that verb or not. Now my thinking is, *If God had wanted me to speak perfect English I would have been born in England.* As it was, I was born in America, the descendant of slaves, whose language was robbed of them through no fault of their own. My former slave relatives were field hands and had little contact with whites who spoke English. Plus, it was illegal for a long time to even teach blacks how to read or write. We were quicker to learn math because we didn't want to be cheated out of our money by anyone, even white folks.

Elder Kirkpatrick was the minister at Spring Lake when we started going there. He had so many talents. To me, he was a great preacher. He played the piano, and he could sing and speak English quite well. He had a nice quality to his voice. I don't know if it was because he was my first minister or not, but I had a lot of faith in him and what he said. When he quoted the Ten Commandments, I took them to heart. He would often give us lessons for life in the pulpit. He always started his sermons speaking softly, but before he finished, he would be screaming almost and dripping in sweat. This was the way pastors preached in the Church of God in Christ, and some still do. I am thankful that he started out softly because when he started screaming, I often couldn't understand what he was saying or couldn't follow him. To this day, he is my favorite preacher. I love the way he would be so cordial to some of the members with praises from the pulpit whenever they did something he admired. I will always be appreciative of him for making my mother the Sunday school superintendent.

Brother Will Morris, the old Sunday school superintendent was getting older, and he suggested to Elder Kirkpatrick that he name Sister Rabb, my mom, the superintendent, and he did. I am pretty sure my mom was named because we always got to church every Sunday before everyone, and my mom would sometimes start the Sunday school any way. I don't think they ever gave her a key to the church, but they should have. Brother Joe lived down the street from the church. He was one of the deacons in the church, so he would open the door. Often we would drive down to his house to wake him up. We would be deep into Sunday school by the time Elder Kirkpatrick and the rest of the members got to church.

Every Sunday, especially in the wintertime, we would fight with our mom about getting to church on time. We would argue that we were always the first ones there and had to sit in the cold car waiting for everyone. Sometimes no one would come because it was so cold;

then we would go back home. All of us kids would be shouting *thank you* inside whenever that happened. My mom was steadfast, and my dad was steadfast as well about us being on time for things, especially work, church, or Sunday school. We grew up with this ideal, and to this day, most of us get to things on time. Whenever I am late for something I get anxious. I always try to get to places on time or early. Those roots were set in me by my parents, and I am happy about it now. I was not when I was a child, but now I am. My on-time track record took a hit when I had my one and only baby. This caused me a lot of anxiety. I couldn't figure out how to get my baby and myself ready on time. How did my mom do it with eight children? Go figure.

Sister Kirkpatrick, our minister's wife, was very nice as well, even though she was old-fashioned. She always wanted things done a certain way. I remember one day she told us that she ironed Elder Kirkpatrick's underwear, his shorts, and T-shirts. I thought this was going too far; who would see his underwear? It seemed as if she treated him like a king at home. I couldn't help but to wonder how he treated her. Did he treat her like a queen? I doubt it. I am not sure when that trend of treating men like they were royalty in Southern black households started, but I know the women didn't get the same treatment. I think it started because the men had to work hard all day in the fields. But then and again, I am not sure because the women often worked right alongside them and still had to go home and cook breakfast, lunch, and dinner and clean the house and take care of the kids; whereas after dinner, the men could go to bed.

Royalty wasn't much, though. It simply meant sitting down at the table, and your wife or one of the children would put your filled plate before you; and if you wanted more food, someone would get it for you. Also, it meant, you did no housework. If something was broken around the house, the men would fix it if they knew how, and often they didn't (especially my father). Otherwise, they did nothing around the house. Often things would have to fall apart before they were repaired, if ever. I think the women helped with the homework most of the time, unless they had less schooling than their husbands, and then the husbands would assist. This is how it was in our home (my dad often helped with the homework, especially the math, because he liked it; my Aunt Velma said it was their mother's favorite subject), so I am guessing it was the same in most Southern black households.

One thing I noticed when I came north is that most Southern women who came north were married. I am pretty sure it was because the men loved the royal treatment when they were courting and cherished it and wanted it in their own homes, whereas Northern women may have demanded the royal treatment for themselves as well, definitely more than Southern women.

My father received the royal treatment until Bobbie, Carrie, and I went off to college. Then my sister Juanita was the oldest girl. She didn't like cooking, so she would let Daddy sit at the table for the longest time, waiting for his food. One day she asked him what was he sitting there for, and he said, "Aren't you going to fix my plate?" and she said she wasn't, and he'd better get his own food, and he did from then on, unless our mom was home or one of us older girls were home. I think all the younger girls took Juanita's lead.

I didn't mind fixing Daddy's plate because he worked very hard. He worked a full-time job and often went to the farm when he got off work. When he came home, all he could do was take a bath, eat, and go to bed. He would be in the bed before dark sometimes; he was so tired. After we started helping Daddy on the farm, I realized how hard the work was. Sometimes you would be in nothing but sun all day, and that was so hard on your body. It was while working on the farm that I realized how hard it had to be for slaves, working day by day in the hot sun. When I think of some slaves being born and dying as slaves, working from sunup to sundown in the hot sun, I cannot imagine the pain. I could just see some of them dying in the fields from sunstroke. I can imagine the evening shade was a welcomed joy. Sleeping and resting must have been their favorite pastime.

When I imagine three hundred years of slavery, it makes me want to drop to my knees and say, "God, *why!*" What did black people do to deserve such misery? Working in the fields made slavery imaginable for me. Until then, as a child, it was unimaginable because as a Christian, you could not imagine so-called Christians treating human beings so inhumane. But even today, Christians treat other humans inhumanely and justify it as God's wishes. That is sacrilegious because it is obviously man's wishes. Those slaves are still owed back wages; no one voluntarily does hard labor in the heat of the day for free, especially to make others richer. There is simply no justification. Their descendants are owed those wages with interest.

As I saw it, my dad was still doing hard labor and bringing us along with him. Farming to me was hard labor. When I saw how hard my dad worked plowing the fields behind those big mules with the *hot* sun beaming down on him with no shade in sight. I would look at how he was sweating and get scared for him. He would be dripping with sweat as he tried to put in eight hours or more because he didn't have much free time to farm, so he had to make the best of it. I started to develop my mom's hatred of farm life. She very seldom came to the farm with us as we helped our dad.

My dad never exercised like walking, running, etc.; farming was sufficient exercise for him. I was amazed that even when he died, he still had his musculature. I am sure it was because he did such physical labor on the farm with very little help. I am pretty sure that on his full-time job, he gave more than eight hours of work in eight hours. He and other Southern black men, I am sure, gave more of themselves because they were always fearful of losing their jobs. As I saw it then, the men, like my dad, really had it hard. Plus, outside of the house, they were mostly treated like children and not men, so when they came home, it was the place they could feel like men, and women and children were there to treat them as such.

I noticed at church that the men were still treated like royalty. The women always fixed their plates. At our church, the minister's wife was treated like royalty as well. I think Sister Kirkpatrick was a little embarrassed about this type of treatment because she was used to serving others, especially men.

I started to notice that women were not allowed in the pulpit (the place where the ministers sat in large chairs) in our church. It was weird because even though my dad was not a member of our church, he could go into the pulpit, and my mom could not, just because he was a man. I didn't understand that thinking. To this day, I do not understand why women were not allowed in the pulpit, and no one has sufficiently explained to me how that tradition started. Female missionaries would come to our church all the time and preach, but they had to do it from the floor and not the pulpit. I think this policy in the Church of God in Christ is still adhered to today. Women, I do believe, still cannot become ministers in the Church of God in Christ. I think there were a lot of off-shoot churches because of this policy, where women could become ministers.

There was definitely a difference in the way men and women were treated in the Church of God in Christ. I remember when one of the girls mentioned to Sister Kirkpatrick that she wanted to become a lawyer. Sister Kirkpatrick gave her a real dressing down about it, saying something like lawyers can't be Christians because they have to lie all the time. I think the girl changed her mind after that because she eventually got married and had a lot of children. She never became a lawyer. I am not sure she even got a college degree, but I do know that she went to college. Now, on the other hand, when my brother said he wanted to be a lawyer, everyone at church, including Sister Kirkpatrick, was all smiles. I thought, *What happened to lawyers can't be Christians?* I think they had passed away by the time my younger sister Dorothy said she was going to become a lawyer, so she didn't receive any backlash.

The church was a big part of our lives growing up. It seemed our lives centered on church and school, and that was it. We were poor, so we didn't go to the movies. Plus, it seemed everything was against the church's rules. We were not supposed to smoke, drink, play basketball, dance, wear makeup, wear fingernail polish, cut our hair, wear pants, go to parties, etc. I could go on and on with the don'ts. There seemed to be very few dos except serving God, and we got that. My mother's love of basketball when she was a kid saved us. She would allow us to do some things that were against church policy. Before we became saved and sanctified, she would say that she was the only one that was a member of the church, so we didn't have to follow the rules of the church. But even after we became members, she still would allow us to do some things that were forbidden.

Eventually, I came to love the people of Spring Lake; they were so warm and loving. They were always teasing us kids. One of the deacons would give me a big peppermint candy cane sometimes. I loved those candy canes. I always felt special when he gave it to me. I felt singled out for some reason, and that made me feel good. He may have given other kids candy as well, but I only remember him giving it to me, and that gave us a special connection. His name was Brother Will. Everyone called one another brother or sister at Spring Lake as well.

Spring Lake was a Church of God in Christ church. Bishop Charles Harrison Mason or C. H. Mason was the head of the church at the time. The headquarters was in Memphis, Tennessee, where they held convocation every year. A local convocation was held in Shreveport, Louisiana, every year, and we would always go. My mom would later in life go to the national conventions every year. To this day, I have not been to one of those national convocations, even though Bobbie, my sister closest to me, has lived in Memphis all her grown up life, where the conventions were held. I always said it was because crowds were not my thing. To be honest, that is true: I don't like crowds. I always look for the exit signs. Crowds make me anxious. They have always. I believe it started when I was in high school. I would get anxious every time I would have to go to the auditorium for an assembly of the whole school. Maybe it had something to do with being packed like sardines in our car every Sunday with the rest of my siblings. I am not sure; I just know I don't like crowds to this day.

After we stopped participating in New Lights' Vacation Bible School, my mom would take a week off from work to have Vacation Bible School. She held it at Lone Spring Church of God in Christ. I am not sure how, but she had gotten to know the women at that church. One of my classmates from school, Velma Washington, attended Long Spring. She and I got to know each other better at Long Spring while attending the Bible school there. Some of the moms would be the teachers. The Bible school was held only a week because my mom couldn't afford to take too much time off work.

As my mom made friends in Minden, she would invite them to our church, Spring Lake. Many of them accepted Christ as their Savior at our church, but could not go to church with us every Sunday because they didn't have cars, and our car was already full. Some of the women my mom helped to bring to Christ started going to the small holiness church on Crichton Hill where we lived. I don't think there was a pastor; the members would just carry on the service. Our neighbor Sister Grider joined the church. Sister Moore and Sister Gibson also helped to form the church. Sister Moore and her husband Deacon Moore were leaders in the church. These three ladies, along with my mom, would have prayer services during the summer months with us kids. We would go from house to house, and of course, we had to be properly dressed. This was one way us kids didn't lose our reading skills over the summer because we had to take part in prayer, testify individually to how God has been good to us, read Bible verses out loud often, and lead songs. When the prayer services came to our house, my mom would cook a snack and make Kool-Aid, and of course, the house had to be spick-and-span (clean). We never minded the prayer services because it was something to do. By now my mom worked at night and my dad during the day, so my mom was always available during the day for prayer services.

As we got older and our neighbors started having members of their families to pass away, my mom and dad and some of the other neighbors started a benevolent club. I think initially they would meet once a month and paid dues. The dues were used to purchase flowers for the loved ones of families who were grieving or provide them with cash. I think some people tried to turn it into a social club, but my mother was not having it; she refused to allow them to drink. I have no doubt that after she left the meetings that some people would stay and drink. Most of the meetings were held at Ms. Ocie's house; she was one of neighbors and Noochie's mother. We knew Ms. Ocie liked to drink because she was often slurring her speech, and her eyes would look funny.

I think you could call both of my parents' servant leaders for what they did in the community, church, and work. They often picked up the slack when they thought something was needed, especially when it came to their children. My mom set an excellent example for us as children. Observing her mother and grandmother, I could see they were strong women. Even though my mother was often soft-spoken, she knew when to speak up, and everybody knew she meant what she was saying, and she could be trusted. My dad was shy and often took my mom's lead, except when it came to farming.

However, when it came to the "Civil Rights Movement," my dad's shyness disappeared. I remember when we marched downtown as a group. He, all of a sudden, started walking in front of everyone as if he was the drum major. I was so proud of him. I remember smiling and thinking, *This is very serious if my dad is coming out of his shell*. My dad also hated to be taken advantage of on the job, so even though he couldn't read or write that well, he took on the position of grievance chair with his union at the Shell Plant or Louisiana Ammunition Plant. He would dictate the grievance for us, and we would write it for him. This scenario was hilarious sometimes, but he held on to the position. He would later become a deacon in St. John Baptist Church, his home church after he retired from the Shell plant. My mom and dad both led the Benevolent Club in our neighborhood, my mom as chair and my dad as treasurer of the club.

There were a lot of kids in my neighborhood and around my neighborhood. We walked all over these neighborhoods. We would play anywhere, but our favorite places were our backyard and across the street in an empty lot. After school, my sisters, brother, and I would often play ball in our backyard. I was the oldest, so until my brother got big enough, I was the pitcher. Our ball was a sock filled with something. We had to pinch hit for the younger kids. My husband laughs at me to this day when I tell him we used to play ball with a sock ball. But we always had fun; the neighbors would often join us. When we got older, the kids in the neighborhood would go across the street to vacant lot to play. The men in the neighborhood, including my father, made a clearing in the field across the street from our homes where we could go and play. I remember playing a lot of hopscotch over there with my friends. We didn't know who owned the land, but it was our playground growing up. We also played in the street behind our house. We couldn't play in the street in the front of our house because it was too busy most of the time. The street behind us was a dirt road. My friends Melvyn, Pat, and Ada Mae lived on this street, Fairview Street. Most of the people in the neighborhood didn't have cars, so the street was not that busy. We would roll tires up and down the street, race one another, and the boys played marbles. When the boys were older, they made some little wooden cars out of crates, and they would race one another. These were happy times for us.

I don't remember getting in too many fights at all or even yelling at one another the way kids do today. In the summer, we would play until dark. We had a streetlight in front of our house and a porch light, so many of the kids would come to play on our front lawn. We would sit on the porch for hours and hours. I think at that time you could call porch sitting a sport. We would sit and watch the cars and people pass by. As we got older, we would make up games for the kids to do, like race around the house for some dumb prize. Not only would my younger siblings run around our house, but the neighbors' kids would also. They all seem to enjoy it. One thing for sure, it was good exercise for them. I don't know about me and probably my sister Bobbie or one of my friends there, content to sit on the porch and watch the younger kids run like crazy. Kids in the day were definitely not sedentary. We either walked or ran wherever we were going.

When it was raining outside, which was often, my sisters, brother, and I would make up our own games. We would turn the chairs over and play house, or we would set the chairs in order and play school, or we'd play jacks or dolls. In our house, dolls were always paper dolls. We would play for hours with paper dolls. I can't remember if any of the paper dolls were black. I am pretty sure none of them were. I remember my friend Melvyn got a black doll for Christmas that was very big. It was the prettiest doll any of us had ever seen. She had straight black hair and lovely black skin. We loved that doll as if it was our own. I don't know what happened to that doll.

Whenever anyone got a gift for Christmas in our family, we all got a gift. The reality was that most of us only got one gift for Christmas, probably in a shoebox wrapped with paper from a paper bag. All the decorations on our Christmas trees were handmade made from ornaments our teachers taught us how to make at school. My dad would go into the woods near our home and cut down a pine tree, and we would decorate it the best we could and put lights on them every year. The teachers at the time had this habit of going around the room asking kids what they got for Christmas. I would always say what I got and what my siblings got as if I got them by myself. For instance, when Vickie got the doll, I got a doll. When David got the bike, I got the bike. My classmates never knew the difference. This was an embarrassing time for me for some reason. I knew I was lying, but I felt embarrassed that I only got one thing, and sometimes that was clothes. The only doll I remember getting was one without hair, a rubber doll, I called her, a white rubber doll. Bobbie and I both got them. I also remember getting a little cash register and a little typewriter. We had told our father that we were taking typing in high school, and we needed a typewriter. So for Christmas, he got us this little kid's typewriter. You could hear us complaining a mile away. My father eventually got us a Royal typewriter that we wore out the ribbon typing our assignments and practicing on. I will always be grateful for him for buying that royal typewriter; Bobbie and I both became excellent typists.

One thing I would always say was that I got fruits, nuts, and candy, and that was the truth. My father and mother would always give us a big brown paper bag filled with fruits, nuts, candy, etc. We cherished those bags all day; we would keep them as long as possible. We would take turns looking in one another's bags to see how much was left. Also, you protected your bag because you didn't want anybody stealing your goodies. We didn't steal that much in my family, though. But if someone got hungry, you might miss an apple or an orange.

My dad would buy a big wooden box of raisins and bags of what we called Christmas candy. He would save some of it for New Years, and he would give us some then. We loved those raisins. They were big raisins with seeds and not like the small raisins we get in the paper boxes now. The candy was all different colors, and they only sold it at Christmas for some reason.

My brother had friends that would often visit before we got up in the morning, especially on a Christmas morning. They would come in, yelling, "Get up, Rabbs!" when my parents weren't home. If it was Christmas, they would come after we had gotten up, opened our gifts, and had breakfast and went back to bed. They saw us girls at our worst, but who cared? No one liked these boys anyway, and they were too young. Picture this: we would have on regular clothes, panties on our heads over the pink curlers used to curl our hair, attempting to keep our pressed hair from napping up overnight. Early on, they would cover hair that was rolled up over paper rollers we had made. I doubt if any of those boys gave us any thoughts as well. I remember thinking that boys would never put those pink rollers in their hair. I was working, and I think it was the '70s when I first saw a boy with pink rollers in his pressed or permed hair. I couldn't believe it. We also wore plats or braids as children; I thought boys would never do that as well. Well, I stand corrected; some of them wear the braids now (since the '80s) better than I ever did. I am thankful my husband and my son are not in that bunch. Their hair is always done the old-fashioned way, and so are most of the males in my family, even the in-laws.

Christmas was my parents' favorite holiday, it seemed. My mom would cook up a lot of food. We always had chicken and dressing, not turkey and dressing. I don't know why. I think it was easier to handle chickens when it came to killing them. I remember my parents killing a rooster for Thanksgiving one year in our backyard. My dad just wrenched the neck off or chopped it off with an ax (I can't remember exactly how he did it). What I do remember very vividly is that rooster jumping headless around our backyard for what seemed like hours, but it had to have been only minutes. After it stopped jumping, my mom took it in the house and put it in a bathtub of hot water and took the feathers off him. Then she boiled him and used the broth to make dressing. At other times, she would just use a hen to make chicken and dressing. She said that the rooster was tougher to eat but that he made the best dressing. We agreed because my mom could make the best chicken and dressing. We were all grown when my mother started cooking turkey and dressing. To this day, however, I use the chicken broth to season my dressing, even though I cook a turkey as well.

Probably, the toys we enjoyed the most that we got for Christmas were the bicycle my brother got, the bicycle my baby sister Vickie got, and the swing and sliding board set we all got. My dad put the swing set up in the backyard, and the whole neighborhood would come over there to play with us. They even tried to swing in the set when we weren't home. Some of our neighbors had fences around their property, but we never did. It didn't dawn on us that the swing set wouldn't last that long if we allowed everyone to use it. My dad was afraid someone would get hurt, so he cemented the legs of the swing down. We used to swing so high on the swing or push the kids real high. Sometimes we would swing high and jump to see how far we could jump. My dad was right to be afraid. However, I don't think anyone ever got hurt on the swings.

The swings themselves didn't last, however, I know the poles probably were in the ground when we sold the house. Somebody stole the bikes over time. My brother's bike would probably have been an antique. I think it was a Schwinn bike. I remember the tires being extra big and sturdy. I think you would call it a *dirt bike*. The whole neighborhood rode that bike up and down the hill in the front of our house. My dad bought most of these toys at a discount from a company he worked for. Other than the years he worked for the company (and I can't remember the name of it), our Christmases were somewhat bleak.

One year, my brother got a tent for Christmas. The tent was so he could go camping with the Boy Scouts. My brother was a Boy Scout, and my sister Juanita was a Girl Scout. For some reasons, I don't think any of the rest of us joined. It probably cost something, and my mom and dad couldn't afford it. I know you had to buy a uniform, and that had to turn my parents off, not because they wanted to; it was they just had to have priorities on what they spent their money on.

My brother went camping with the Boy Scouts once that I can remember, and he took his tent. It was raining so hard they had to come home. I don't think anybody knew how to pitch a tent so it wouldn't drown them. My brother was afraid he would never go camping again, so one day, he pitched the tent in our backyard. He and our neighbor Willie Miller were going to spend the night in the tent. I think Willie's mom knew, but my mother didn't know. When she came home from her job late that night, she made Willie go home and my brother David come in the house. The tent was just an eyesore in our house after that. It took up space until somebody (probably me) threw it out. With ten people and two bedrooms, who had room for a useless tent.

After the bikes got old, we would leave them outside; that is how somebody stole Vickie and David's bikes. We didn't have a whole lot of stealing in our neighborhood, very little criminal activity. We would sleep with our doors and windows open often.

We slept like this until me and Bobbie caught Elmer Lee peeping in our window late one night. We decided that he was a Peeping Tom and didn't really trust him after that. Elmer Lee was a boy from the neighborhood, and we knew we could handle him if need be. We always slept with sleeping clothes on. Notice, I called them "sleeping clothes" because that's what they were: regular clothes (our old and worn clothes) that we often slept in at night. During the summer, we would often sleep in our slips because they were cooler. Sleeping in the cool summer breeze is probably one of my favorite experiences of growing up in Louisiana. Now, don't get me wrong, Louisiana was plenty hot.

The hot sun would bake the sand that we would have to walk on to go to the store or whatever. We would go to the store for our neighbors for a nickel or a dime. If we got a quarter or fifty cents (few and far in between), we were in heaven. Oh yes, this was another way I made money growing up. They didn't want to go themselves because of the heat. We would sometimes be barefooted and run to the store, but our feet would get parched. I learned to run between the shade from the trees, where it was not as hot; this saved my feet. It never dawned on me that we could have gotten sunstroke being out in the sun like that; all we thought about was getting that nickel or dime. Growing up, we didn't have air-conditioning, but somehow we kept the house somewhat cool. My mom and dad would buy a fan. Notice I said *a* fan—one fan, that's all we had. Wherever our parents were, that's where the fan was. So most of the time, us kids suffered with the heat. We used to bring (more likely steal, who was going to miss fans?) paper fans from church to fan ourselves with at home. If we didn't have a paper fan, we would use anything. We would often be ingenious with what we would fan ourselves with.

My mom had her sixth kid on my first day of regular school. She had been preparing me for school. She had even taught me the Lord's Prayer, which would prove very important to me later on as well. She had said that she would take me to school, so I was looking forward to it. I am sure she had bought me new clothes and shoes that I was looking forward to wearing for the first time. When I got up, my dad told me that my mom was not home and that my grandmother would take me to school. I was so disappointed; I am pretty sure I was mad and asked millions of questions. Back then, adults were not used to answering kids' questions, so I was confused as to why my mom was not at home. My dad took me over to my grandmothers, and she walked me and my Aunt Nat or Natherine to school at J. L. Jones. Nat was put in the second grade; I think this was her first day of school as well.

My mom's parents (JD and Rosie) and the rest of her siblings had moved to Minden. At first, they had left Athens and moved to Lake Providence, Louisiana. I only remember my parents taking us to visit them once in Lake Providence. Later, they moved to Minden and did not live too far from J. L. Jones or Webster High School, the black elementary school and high school. I called my maternal grandparents Monmon and Pawpaw; the story is, I couldn't pronounce *mama* and *papa*. They became Monmon and Pawpaw to all the grandkids.

My family was big and poor while we were growing up. But as kids, we didn't realize how poor because early on we didn't have television to see how affluent people lived. We knew we were not rich because we passed bigger and prettier homes on the main street of Minden where white people lived. We knew there were a lot of white people who lived in Minden, but we didn't go too far into their neighborhoods; we only saw the outskirts. My perception as a kid was that if we went into their neighborhoods, they would kill us or beat us up. I grew up being very scared of white people, all white people. We were taught to not to talk to them unless we were spoken to and not to look at them. So I grew up not seeing white people. The only place I saw them until I started working with my mom at the Coffee Cup was downtown Minden. We were taught not to look them in the eyes. I remember seeing black people looking down whenever they saw or even spoke to white people. I couldn't understand why, until I started reading and hearing about slavery and how blacks were treated and expected to act around white people. I realized that as a result of the way I was raised, I didn't see white people. The statement reminds me of the movie *Sixth Sense*, where the child says, "I see dead people." It really was as if white people were dead to me. They were not a part of my world. The only black people who went into white neighborhoods were maids, cooks, or gardeners. We would have to pass by white neighborhoods whenever we went to the store or downtown; we were always careful and scared at the same. I never remember passing their homes when I was not scared. White men especially scared me as I got older; I would probably start running whenever I saw one of them. I think this fear was passed on to girls in the neighborhood by the women even before we knew about slavery and how black women were often raped and would have their master's babies. The black women never said anything about it; it was just a feeling. I don't think any of them felt safe around white men either, and I would later learn rightfully so.

Our hometown, Minden, was dry, so people had to go across the line to buy the booze. Growing up, I didn't even know what "going across the line" meant. My father would often say that he was taking someone across the line when he would get dressed up and leave on Saturday evenings. By "dressed up," I mean a clean pair of khaki pants and a khaki shirt. My mom would look a little funny, but I never heard her object. She knew he was taking some guys and probably gals across the line to drink, but he would probably meet women himself, but she never went with him. Plus, he was going to earn some money for being the driver to support his family, so how could she complain?

My mother did not drink or smoke; I don't think she ever had a taste of either one in her life. She and my father got married when she was eighteen, and she joined the Church of God in Christ, where it was a sin to drink or smoke. My father never smoked, probably because of his asthma; but he did drink, I would discover later. I think I had seen him sneaking around drinking beer in our yard several times, but he hid it well. For the most part, my siblings and I were never around people who drank in our presence, so to this day, I get nervous when I am around drunken people. I soon make a quick exit if people are drunk and cursing, both things I did not grow up around.

My friend Pearlie was accustomed to liquor being around her house. I would see the liquor bottles whenever I visited her house. Now I can't remember, but I think there were empty liquor bottles, but maybe there was a combination. I never understood keeping empty liquor bottles around; people never used them for any other purpose. I think they thought some of the bottles were pretty; I can see the women thinking that. But I think the men kept them around as a badge of honor. I think the first real birthday gift I bought my husband was a fifth of Crown Royal liquor. I bought it for him because I knew he liked Crown Royal, and I thought the bottle was pretty. I tasted it and thought it was horrible, even after mixing it with ginger ale. My husband had always mixed it with ginger ale. There was not enough ginger ale in the world to make crown royal taste good to me. I didn't know when I bought the Crown Royal that alcohol was a problem with the men in his family. I had only known him a year by then, so I knew very little about his family.

The ten of us would live in that two-bedroom house together for over fifteen years. One by one, as we got older, we would leave the house. I was the first to go to college. After college, I never stayed in that house again for any length of time. When I left that night for college for the first time, I had no idea how my life was going to change from that moment on. I don't know when we started the tradition of always eating peanut and butter cracker sandwiches (we would take turns making them), bowls of cornflakes and milk, homemade chocolate chip cookies, or homemade chocolate cake on our front porch every Friday when my parents got paid. These items were a special treat for us. We loved it when it was our turn to bake the sweet treats because you could keep more for yourself. I remember my brother David putting his cookies under his pillow and slept on them over night to keep them from us. As if, we wanted the hard cookies he had baked. The boy couldn't cook. He called himself teaching us how to cook eggs once and his eggs turned out green. We laughed so hard we couldn't catch our breaths. I also remember my mom saying one time, "I'm tired of those black cakes." We loved everything black—chocolate cake, chocolate ice cream, chocolate candy, etc. We hated vanilla ice cream and most things white. Looking back now, I think we were taking a stance. My mom didn't mean what she said in a derogatory sense, but her culture or "whites" at the time had led her to believe black was a bad thing. My mom had no idea that by using the word as she had, she may have led "us" to believe that as black kids ourselves, we may not have been good enough and that the world could get tired of us because we were black as well.

Our lives definitely changed after we moved to Minden. Mrs. Demp's kindergarten and New Light played a big part in this. My life began in small towns. Both Minden and Athens were small segregated towns. So when I started to school, it was segregated. Black and poor people lived in certain sections of town. I really didn't know where the white people lived. I think blacks were hesitant to go outside of their neighborhood boundaries. I know I was taught to not go in the white section of town; I was almost afraid to look in their direction. At some point, I was told as a child not to look white people in their eyes. I really didn't know why I was taught this, but I thought of all white people as bad people, people, who would kill or hurt you. This was a big pill for a young girl to swallow, but it was my reality at the time. It would take years for me to trust white people or even see them.

Chapter 3

EARLY YEARS OF SCHOOLING

Six to Twelve Years of Age

After kindergarten, I started to school at J. L. Jones on the other side of town. When I say other side of town, my town was so small that you could walk from one side of town to the other. Plus, the other side of town was across the railroad tracks. When you look at it, I lived on the other side of the tracks. I didn't realize this was a negative term until I heard it on television later. It seemed when you were born and raised on the other side of the tracks, you were generally poor. At least, it seemed that way on television. But most of the time, these were white people. There were not a lot of black people on television when I was growing up. Plus, in my hometown, poor black people lived on both sides of the tracks. With that being said, I didn't realize that there was such a divide in my hometown with where you lived until I was grown.

My first day of school was September 4, 1953. I remember that day so well because I woke up thinking my mom was going to take me to my first day of school across town at J. L. Jones Elementary. But when I woke up, my father told me that my mom was in the hospital and that my maternal grandmother was going to take me to school. My grandparents and my mother's siblings had moved to Minden after we moved to Minden. My aunt Elnora already lived in Minden when we moved there. She was my mother's oldest sibling, therefore, my oldest maternal aunt. My dad took me to my grandmother's house that morning, and I walked to school with her and my aunt Natherine, who was only a year or two older than me; she was going to be in the second grade. I don't remember much of what happened that day because I was so upset that my mom was not taking me and if she was okay or not. I just couldn't believe she had deserted me like that. My sister Dorothy's birthday is September 4, 1953; she was born on my first day of school. I always remember her birthday. My mom had deserted me because in the night she had gone into labor and had to be rushed to the hospital. I remember being extremely upset about it. I think I experienced my first panic attack that day. Maybe I am exaggerating.

I remember those first few days of school. For some reason, we had no classroom, and we had school under a big tree near St Rest Baptist Church, which was in walking distance of the school. I guess they were rehabbing the school building. When I started to school, I was a scared shy little girl. It was ironic that my school life would start under a big tree. Remember, I was a country girl from the farm, and I was used to trees and loved them for the shade they provided on hot days in Louisiana, which was very often. I felt with the not so often cool breezes that my brain was wide awake and learning was easy. I loved being outside and learning. Ms. Wardlow was my teacher while we were under the big tree. I didn't like Ms. Wardlow because she had a hump on her back, and she never smiled. To me, she was mean, and the hump scared me. I believe she had scoliosis, of course; I just thought she was ill-deformed at the time. I often wandered if Ms. Wardlow had been a better teacher; I know she was more experienced.

Ms. Bridgeman was the other first grade teacher, and I thought she was pretty with her black curly hair. To me, she seemed very nice; I liked the way she treated her kids. I know that Ms. Bridgeman made a significant difference in my life, and I think I would have been too scared as an inexperienced child to open up to Ms. Wardlow. My parents should have explained to me what the hump was on her back, but maybe I never said anything about how it made me feel. Kids often don't share their feelings without being prodded. Kids need to know everything pretty may be misleading and not be what is right for them. That is why, after retiring, I became a strong proponent of social emotional learning for parents, teachers, and kids. Kids need to get in touch with their feelings early on in life, I daresay when they enter this world.

I am not sure how long we had class under the tree, but eventually, my first-grade class was held in a wooden building that was detached from the rest of J. L. Jones. J. L. Jones was close to Webster High School, so we would see the big kids going back and forth. However, a new building was being built for them, and I believe it was not ready when school started. The big kids went to school in a big white two-story building. There were some other red brick buildings, and that was a part of J. L. Jones as well.

When we moved to Minden, Louisiana, I had no idea that my family possibly had a strange connection to it. After reading the book *Roots* by Alex Haley and seeing the movie, I became extremely interested in my family history. I was envious of Alex being able to trace his roots back to the African village where his family hailed from. Afterward, I became our family's volunteer historian. African American families must record their family histories for future generations. Our past gives our future purpose. Every time I uncover an ancestor in my past, it is like rolling a stone away, opening up a treasure chest of our family's heritage. And when I find pictures, the meaning of the saying "a picture is worth a thousand words" goes from being surreal to being real.

I have been able to estimate that my great, great grandfather Sam Rabb was born around 1820. He was evidently born in South Carolina or that was where he disembarked the slave ship and later traveled to or was sold to someone from Alabama. In researching the Civil War records, I found a Samuel H. Rabb. He joined the Union Army and was part of the colored battalion that captured the city of Minden, Louisiana, for six months before the war ended. If Sam Rabb was part of that group, that would explain how the Rabbs ended up in Claiborne Parish (about thirty miles from Minden) and where my father and his siblings grew up. Ironically, my siblings and I would grow up in Minden, Louisiana.

When our classrooms in the wooden building were ready and our first-grade classes were divided again, I was placed in Ms. Bridgeman's class. I couldn't believe Ms. Bridgeman was going to be my teacher. I was so glad.

I think, for a while, my dad would take me to my grandma's house, and she would walk me and my aunt to school. But eventually, a bus was assigned to our route, and we had to take the bus to school. My mom (I had forgiven her by then) started walking me to the bus stop. I think Mr. Mims was our bus driver at first. I remember him because he would later become the principal of my high school after I graduated. From bus driver to school principal, it's possible—you just got to believe in yourself. I remember one of our bus drivers was also our school janitor. I think he drove us to school as well, then did his janitorial duties, and then drove us home. Later on, Melvyn Thomas, Pat Black, and Hazel Cosby, and I would start to walk together to the bus stop. We would walk together and talk. At the time, I didn't realize our talks would be part of my incidental learning early on and how important it was to my development and shaping my life. Who knew!

One day in first grade, soon after we moved to the school building, I was coloring a picture as instructed, and Ms. Bridgeman was walking around and noticed me coloring. She said for me to get up. She took my chair and placed it in another group. I was so young, but I knew that there had to be a difference in the ability levels of the three groups she had in her classroom. I was placed with the brightest kids. I had gotten used to coloring within the lines and cutting along the lines because I had done it in my other schools; plus, my mom had bought me coloring books at home to play with all the time. Now, they used standardized tests to separate kids with different ability levels back then; it was simply coloring or cutting along the lines to judge kids' ability and intellectual levels. Wow, how things have changed.

When I got to second grade, my teacher was Mrs. Mayfield. I remember the first day of school. She asked us to repeat the Lord's Prayer out loud by ourselves. If you could say all of it, she placed you in the brightest group. I remember Ada Green, and I knew the Lord's Prayer, and we were placed in the bright group. I was never tested again that I know of, but I was always in the bright group after that. The teachers would often give us some work to do, and then she would go off to teach the other groups. There were generally three groups. I think my group was made up of kids who generally got As and Bs, the next group Cs, and the last group Ds and Fs. The teachers seem to spend more time with the second and third group of students. It's funny how even in first grade, this grouping could stigmatize kids for the rest of their lives. You are considered one of the smart kids or one of the slower kids. These groups seem to remain the same all through school.

I think my sister Linda was born when I was in second grade. I don't remember my mom being pregnant, though. Linda was born November 1954. So by now, my mom and dad had seven children, and we still lived in the two-bedroom house on High Street.

In the third grade, Mrs. Mims (my bus driver's wife) was my teacher at J. L. Jones. She was often sick, and Mrs. Reeder would substitute in her class. In the middle of the school year, my siblings and I and the kids who lived on my side of town were transferred to Jerry A. Moore Elementary School. Jerry A. Moore was closer to my home, and it was a brand-new school. We could walk to school now. We had to take a bus to J. L. Jones. Jerry A. Moore Elementary School was about two or three miles from my home. Walking to and from school was excellent exercise for us. The surroundings of Jerry A. Moore were beautiful to me; we had nothing but open land. We could run and walk all over the school grounds. I loved that school. There were no big kids around, no mentally or physically disabled kids, no high school kids, and fewer kids in general. I was now in the third grade, and Mrs. Reeder was now my full-time teacher. She was also my neighbor. She lived not too far from my house. First, Mrs. Reeder and her family had a lived with her mother-in-law and father-in-law, and later they built a beautiful home right next door to them. I always thought they had a beautiful home, one of the nicest in the neighborhood. Her husband was a principal in a school not far from Minden. He had a speech impediment. I am not sure; he may have been hard of hearing. He spoke softly. They had one son and later had a daughter. I think they had the daughter after I graduated from high school because I don't remember her. I think she was a menopause baby for Mrs. Reeder and her husband. Their son Reginald was mildly retarded, and I think he died young. The daughter was born normal. Reginald was in the class with my sister Carrie. He never failed a grade, and he went to regular classes. I am sure Mrs. Reeder and her husband worked really hard with him at home. I don't believe Mrs. Mims ever did work full-time again; she was often sick but continued to work some at J.L. Jones.

There was a building on J. L. Jones's campus where special education students went. At first they would have lunch with everyone else, but they would run after us and scare us. Some of them looked different, and they couldn't speak English well even though some of them were older than us. One of these students was my neighbor; his name was Bill. Bill had cerebral palsy, I believe. He did not have perfect control over his extremities, and at the time, I thought he walked funny and carried his arms and hands weird. I was not afraid of Bill because I was used to him in the neighborhood. But some of the other special education kids did frighten me as a child. They didn't have mainstreaming at the time. I do remember that Mrs. Reeder's son, who obviously had some difficulty learning, was mainstreamed with my sister Carrie's classes, if I am remembering correctly. There were no special education classes at Jerry A. Moore. The kids who needed extra help were just mainstreamed into regular classes.

At Jerry A. Moore, Mrs. Reeder became my full-time third grade teacher. I loved Mrs. Reeder, I think to this day; she is still my favorite teacher of all times. She had such a calming personality, almost nun-like. Mrs. Graham was my fourth grade teacher, and I was supposed to have Mrs. White as my fifth grade teacher, but she missed so many days that Mr. Chapman, our principal, put some of us in Mrs. Duty or Mrs. Greenard's class. (At first, we called her Mrs. Duty, and then later she made us call her Mrs. Greenard; I don't know if she got married or divorced.) She was my sixth grade teacher as well. I remember she was very light-skinned and had light-colored eyes, like white people. Her speech pattern and body shape to me was similar to white people. She had shapely legs, and it was obvious that she knew her legs were an asset. She wore high heels most of the time. As a matter of fact, all the teachers wore high heels. Sometimes, in the classroom, they would take them off and put on comfortable shoes. But for the most part, the teachers wore nice dresses, suits, and high-heel shoes all day. I didn't particularly like Mrs. Greenard; I thought she was mean. I got the impression that she hated the principal. I saw her giving him what I thought were dirty looks several times. Most of the kids felt that he had scorned her for Mrs. Graham, and that's why she hated him (we never had any proof of that). Mr. Chapman eventually married Mrs. Graham.

Like I said, I loved Mrs. Reeder. She was a sweet teacher. She never raised her voice, and I don't believe she ever spanked any of us. We formed a band in her classroom. I can't recall any of the names of the instruments except the tambourines and banjos, but we all had some type of instrument to play. Every week, we had what was called assembly, and each week one of the classes would perform. Kids would give speeches; they would dance or sing a song. I figured out early on that I loved to dance. I was petrified of speaking before the whole school. As a matter of fact, I talked very little in class. I was a very quiet student. I was very adept at horning my listening skill in school. I talked at home because I was the oldest and had to keep everybody else in line. I don't remember ever hollering at my siblings, but I must have. Later on in life, my cousin Alma Jean told me that one of my siblings hated me. I never figured out which one, and nobody came forward after I told them what she said. So maybe I did holler at them and punish them too harshly. My parents had given me permission to spank them if they misbehaved. Plus, since we all went to the same school, I probably told my mom and dad if they misbehaved. Starting over at a new school was easy for me because I knew Mrs. Reeder already. She made learning so easy. Most of my neighbors my age were in her class as well.

It was funny; the friends I had in the neighborhood were never the friends I had at school. I was quiet and didn't like to participate in sports, so I sat on the sidelines with the other quiet kids, and we became friends. Most of them were not in the smart group (where I was), but we became friends anyway. Most of them did not even live in the city, so I could only talk with them at school. We eventually got a phone, but I still couldn't talk to them because most of them didn't have phones. The girls who lived in my neighborhood were more social than me. They were all lighter-skinned than me and raised in Minden and had more friends and more social skills. I was dark-skinned and, from an early age, thought I was not pretty. At some point in time, I started thinking I was the ugliest girl in school, if not in Minden. I am not sure when I came to that conclusion. Maybe it was when boys started to notice girls, and I noticed no one seemed interested in or talked to me, but I think it had to be earlier when I developed such a poor image of myself and probably from something a relative said. I know my younger aunts made me feel ugly all the time the way they treated me; it was if they didn't want to be seen with me. I think if I had not been so smart or believed in God with all my heart, it would have done more to my self-esteem. But as it was, I didn't let that revelation stop me from doing my best in school. I am sure, though, it did affect my self-esteem somewhat. I was a Christian, and I knew God loved me even if the boys didn't.

At Jerry A. Moore, I remember the principal (Mr. Chapman) would come in periodically and teach a lesson in arithmetic. You could tell he loved mathematics. His whole body seemed to come alive when he talked about it. He would often give us some words of wisdom as well, telling us what we were going to need to know when we got to high school and college. One day somebody asked me when I knew I was going to college. I told them always because it seemed like a normal progression because my teachers had talked about college so often and how they were preparing us for college. My elementary and junior high school teachers would talk about preparing us for high school, and my high school teachers would talk about preparing us for college. I even remember Mr. Chapman in elementary school talking about preparing us for college at Southern or Grambling, two black universities in Louisiana.

In the fourth grade, Mr. Chapman would come in to teach us a math lesson as well. Mrs. Graham always seemed to resent this interruption, but we could tell there were sparks flying between the two of them. Like I said earlier, later they would get married. Mrs. Graham already had a child. She never had any children by Mr. Chapman. I was kind of surprised that he married her because I thought she was mean. I liked Mr. Chapman; I call him one of my heroes. When I got to high school, he would let me work for him during the summer. He would pay me cash. Later, my sister Bobbie worked for him, and I think Juanita did also. We would be the only people in the building besides the janitor. It was weird being in the school when there were no kids, but I enjoyed being with Mr. Chapman. He had no children of his own, and I think he often thought of us as his children, so over the summer, he would give us some of his pearls of wisdom. I am sure they became a part of my cognitive development. Those were innocent times.

I think he taught us a couple of lessons in math in Mrs. Greenard's class in the fifth and sixth grades as well, but I always got the impression she resented it as well. I had the funny feeling that Mr. Chapman had dated her or that she wanted him too, but Mrs. Graham won the battle, and that was why Mrs. Greenard always gave him the evil eye whenever he came to her classroom to teach us a math lesson.

I never got the impression that these teachers were incompetent in math, but it was that Mr. Chapman just loved it, so and I think he wanted to teach so he wouldn't lose his touch with teaching. Plus, I think he wanted to get an idea of where we were as students. It probably also gave Mr. Chapman a way of evaluating his teachers. Of course, as students we had no idea of this. Besides, I don't think any of my teachers loved math the way Mr. Chapman did, and now I know how important for you (especially girls) to be taught math by someone who enjoys it.

My sister Vickie was born in the June 1955 during the summer, and I started fifth grade in the fall of 1955. Now, my mom and dad had eight kids. The last three were born in Minden. Like I said, they were big babies at first. I think Vickie was the first baby I realized my mom was pregnant. So I was not surprised when she came home from the hospital. I remember my mom wearing maternity clothes this time. She seemed happy while she was carrying Vickie. I was ten when Vickie was born, so I can always remember her age. I really don't have a problem remembering any of my siblings' ages because we were stair steps. It seemed almost every year my mom was pregnant, and so was my aunt Zack. Aunt Zack had nine kids by Uncle Chunk before he died. He died soon after the birth of their last baby. He was the first relative I knew to die in my family. Aunt Zack loved him to death. I would often see her sitting on his lap. Aunt Zack and Uncle Chunk lived next door to Aunt Elnora for a while, so I would see them being lovey-dovey whenever I visited Aunt Elnora. Vickie was my parents' last child. My mom was twenty-eight years old at the time. I don't know what they did for birth control after that, but she never got pregnant again. I was in the fifth grade now and beginning to feel kind of grown.

In the fifth grade, we had two grades in the same classroom; the fifth graders were on one side and the six graders on the other. What I liked about this arrangement was being so close you could not help but listen to what the sixth graders were learning, especially if you finished with your work earlier. It added to your confidence because if you learn it as well, you thought, *Well, sixth grade is not that bad.* Often we were given a chapter to read or busy work to do while Mrs. Greenard taught the sixth graders. We got to know the sixth graders real well because we were in the same class. I think sometimes she would blend our classes. Most of the sixth graders were my neighbors and I knew them from the activities at New Light Baptist Church. I looked up to many of the girls. Funny thing, I can't remember any of the boys. They probably didn't live in my neighborhood or weren't that smart. I was drawn to smart people. I wanted to model myself after them. I just remember Bobbie Nell, Gloria Bell, Mary Frances, and Ernestine. They were all very smart, and I looked up to them. Because I had no older sisters or brothers, I kind of always thought of them as my older siblings. As I grew up, there were times when they would stand up for me. As a matter of fact, all the older girls and boys who lived on my side of town, in my neighborhood, kind of looked out for the younger ones.

I remember one time, when I was walking home from school. I can't remember if it was Webster or Phillips (where I went to junior high school), the older kids stepped in and helped me out. I really didn't think I was in trouble, though. I remember, while I was walking home, some white girls were on a porch across the street from where I was walking. They called me over to their porch, and for some reason, I crossed the street and went over to see what they wanted. I think they asked me if I wanted some candy. Some older girls walking behind me saw what was happening and called me back over. It was then I started to wonder if I had indeed been in danger. In my hometown, blacks didn't talk to whites unless they were working for them. Whites didn't live in our neighborhoods; they lived on the outskirts of our neighborhood. Sometimes we would have to walk by their homes to get to ours. I never felt comfortable walking past their homes; I really can say I was petrified. We tried not to be alone whenever we had to walk past their homes until we were older and maybe not even then. We didn't drive through their neighborhoods. I think I can say blacks don't joyride through their neighborhoods, even today. Even though the schools are now integrated, the neighborhoods, for the most part, are still segregated. However, like in most towns and cities, some formerly white neighborhoods are now black neighborhoods.

It was in the sixth grade that I had many experiences that shaped my life. In the sixth grade, a gentleman by the name of Mr. Duty, a 4-H club representative, would come and teach us how to cook dishes. At some point, he talked about his career area and his major. His major had been dietetics in school. I thought food was probably a good major. I loved those food demonstrations. Plus, my mom was cooking for a living by now, and food seemed to be the center of our universe at times. In high school, when I was asked what I was going to major in college, for some reason, I said dietetics. Another student, Floristene, also said that she was going to major in it as well. My high school principal would never give me a home economics food class on my schedule in high school. I told him that I had planned on majoring in it in college, but he would never put it on my schedule. Mr. Hayes would always put me in choir. I hated choir; plus, I could not sing. Let's face it, I never tried. I didn't think I could carry a tune. However, I am not sure, but maybe it had something to do with my fear of public speaking, so that translated into not being able to sing in public, even in a group. I could sing at church. At times, I would even start a song, but that didn't help because we didn't have that many good singers in our church. I wished we'd had more oral reports in our elementary or high school classes; maybe I would have chosen a more financially lucrative career.

I think I was in the latter part of my sixth grade year when my period started. I had some idea of what that was not because my mom had told me but because kids at school had been talking about it. I remember one day Hazel Cosby came in late from recess because she was walking so slow. She had been walking slowly all day. We all (at least the girls) burst out laughing because we knew she got her period. Some of the girls had told the rest of us. All she did was walk slow and smile all day. I think she was the first to get her period in our class, and I think also the first to get pregnant. Of course, I didn't know she had gotten pregnant because her family moved, or she went to live with her mom in another state. Her mom and dad were separated at the time. Pat, Melvyn, and I used to stop by Hazel's house to pick her up on our way to the bus stop. She was Pat's cousin. Pat's mom and Hazel's dad were brother and sister. Her house was only about one-eighth of a mile from the bus stop. Hazel lived with her dad, stepmom, and her siblings. She got pregnant her freshman year in high school; she would tell us later at one of our reunions.

Because of her experience and the other girls clueing me in, I knew about periods. So I kind of knew what was happening when I noticed a dark excretion in my underwear after school one day. I called my mom and told her what was happening, and she told me to get one of the sanitary pads in the big blue box that she always kept in the bathroom and put it inside my panties. She showed me how to fasten it inside the panties later that night when she came home. Until then, I was walking slow, trying to keep it between my legs like

Hazel did that day. I now know this would have been the time my mom should have had the "sex" talk with me, but she never did. I don't think she did with any of her seven girls.

It was also in the sixth grade when I let temptation get to me. Mrs. Duty (or Mrs. Greenard, as she would eventually make us call her) had a Christmas tree made out of Styrofoam and red and green gumdrops. I wanted some of those gumdrops. I don't know how we did it or when, but Melvyn Thomas and I took some of those gumdrops off the Styrofoam tree and ate them. They were probably dusty because the tree was several weeks old. Mrs. Duty had it for decoration. We ate the candy on the last day; we didn't think she would mind. But Mrs. Duty did, and she gave us several taps with her board on our hands. Man, did that hurt. I was so mad at myself for stealing that candy. I never stole another thing. If I was tempted, I remembered that horrible feeling I got when the whole class saw me get a spanking for stealing gumdrops.

Seventh grade was pretty uneventful for me. I am not sure if this was the year I froze during a performance where I was supposed to play the flute or not. Melvyn Thomas and I were supposed to play the flute together, I believe. We had practiced. The night before my flute stopped on me, and I called Melvyn and told her she would be playing the flute by herself. However, in the morning it was okay, so I could play it. But when I got before the crowd, I froze. I also had to do the twist or the cha-cha on the program. I did the dance. Dancing before a group was never a problem for me, but speaking or playing an instrument was something else.

I don't think Mr. Chatman ever interrupted the seventh- and eighth-grade teacher Mrs. Dyer, and I am not sure why. She was short and pretty stocky and older than the rest of the teachers. Maybe he had more respect for her. She was a very good teacher. It was in her class that I discovered that I had a vision problem. I got my first pair of glasses when I was in the seventh grade.

One of my most embarrassing hidden moments happened in my seventh-grade class. We would often sit with our coats on because it was cold in the classrooms sometimes. This one day, I was taking my coat off, and I saw a small dead mouse inside of my coat. I was too embarrassed to scream. I don't remember how I got him out of my coat to put him in the garbage can. I probably used a sheet of paper. This was so embarrassing, but I don't think anybody noticed.

In elementary school, teachers often paddled your hands in front of the other kids if you talked when you weren't supposed to or did something else you weren't supposed to. For the most part, everyone was quiet and did as they were told. I don't remember any of the teachers going crazy on you with those boards. We didn't have any male teachers in elementary school. We only had two males on the campus, the principal and the janitor, most of the time. Jerry A. Moore was brand-new when we moved in, and it was always very, very clean. Even the bathrooms were clean. I remember at J. L. Jones, the toilets would often overflow, and we couldn't even use the bathrooms. Those were bad days. Most of the time, we were supervised, but it seems I remember some days the teachers would not be on the playground with us. However, otherwise, they were always around. They even sat with us at lunchtime. I wasn't very good at team sports, so I mostly played jacks with my classmates at lunchtime.

I don't remember having much playground equipment at Jerry A. Moore. What I remember is the spacious playground area surrounded by trees. There were no trees lining the street leading into the campus area, just bush. On arbor days, we would plant trees. I know we put time capsules under some of the trees, but since most of the school has been torn down after most of the building burned, I am not sure if anyone thought to look under the trees. Then again, the trees may still be there; I'll have to check it out.

I loved the playground as a kid. When I compare it to the playground my son's elementary school had in Chicago, it couldn't even compare. His school's playground was barely the size of the backyard we had at the house me and my siblings grew up in. Plus, it was fenced in. For me, coming from such a freeing experience, it seemed like prison. It seemed like we could run forever on our playground; my son's had only a few yards. Even with that, I think his playground had more playground equipment. We played football sometimes on our playground; I think the boys and the girls played it. I remember Etolia being very good at. I think it must have resembled something like rugby because I remember someone had to take the ball away from you. It was hard to get the ball away from Etolia. She was a strong girl, and the boys would give up on getting it from her. She would later play on the girls' basketball team in high school. Etolia was very nice, but I think most of the kids thought she was mean. I believe she was bullied because she was tough and didn't take any stuff. I say that because she seems to have, to this day, hard feelings about some of our classmates. I only saw her at one of our high school class reunions.

One thing I do not remember about Jerry A. Moore was not learning anything about African American history, just reading, writing, arithmetic, and just a little science and social science. We were constantly being reminded of what skills we would need in high school and later in college. I took the bait and worked hard to get good grades. I liked making the honor roll. Most of the girls in my neighborhood made the honor roll constantly. I loved learning. I don't think Black History Month had started yet in the '50s when I was in grammar school. It got to us late, like freedom did to some slaves in Texas. I doubt if my teachers even knew much about their own history; they were all black. I don't remember them ever mentioning slavery or why blacks and whites were in segregated everything, why we could go to the back of restaurants or use the outside window to order food period, or why there were colored and white fountains, bathrooms, etc. We knew that the colored areas were not kept as clean as the white areas. It was always very obvious. But these were taboo subjects in school. I have no doubt that learning about my history in school would have helped build my self-esteem. I think everybody thought it would make us angry—yes, angry enough not to be anyone else' slaves. I never thought of the slaves as being cowards; I thought of them (my ancestors) as being strong and brave. How else could I exist with what they went through; our race should be extinct. We were not supposed to be here.

I never worked to get on the honor roll; it just happened because I listened to the teachers and did what I was told. Like I said, most of the girls in my neighborhood made the honor roll. We were not competitive; we were just smart girls. What else was there to do beside study in elementary school? There was just nothing to do. We had very little to do after school that didn't involve the church (i.e., Christmas programs, Easter programs, Vacation Bible School were only a few weeks out of the year). The rest of the time, we (the kids) had to make our own fun. The adults didn't always supervise our fun. We had to be inventive; otherwise, we would be bored. Often what we did were games we did in school or church. But sometimes we made up games, like playing school. I had no idea that doing this was our being creative and would make us better students in high school and college and stronger as adults.

One thing I loved to do was play school or play games from Vacation Bible School. But during the school year, what we did most was study. There was no television until I was in high school in my house. I remember the Thomases were the first ones to get a television in my neighborhood. We would all go to their house to watch it, even if we had to stand outside and watch through their windows. So all we had to do was study. The teachers would make sure we knew how to do the homework before we left for the day. My parents had gone as far as seventh and eighth grades, so they could help us in elementary school, at least until the fourth grade. In the fourth grade, the mathematics problems got harder and my father couldn't help us. He liked mathematics, or arithmetic, which is what we called it then. I found out later that his mom was good in arithmetic, so she must have instilled that in her kids. I can't remember when we got a phone, but it must have been around the fourth grade because I remember calling my friends in the neighborhood to get help with math problems after the fourth grade. We would compare answers to homework questions. If we didn't have the same answer, then we would figure out how we differed and come up with the correct answer. We did this often; it was nice to have friends that could help you.

I don't think any of the parents in my neighborhood had graduated from high school. Only one of my aunts (Annie Laura) at the time (when I was in elementary school) had graduated from high school. I think she was in college when I was in elementary school. I know I very seldom saw her; she would come home on breaks. It seemed that when we lived in Athens, she had moved to Minden to live with Aunt Elnora so she could finish high school and then go to college.

Most of the kids in my neighborhood who went to Jerry A. Moore would walk home together, and that was the majority of the kids. The kids from Long Spring and Thompson Quarters would ride the bus. We had to walk about three miles—at least it seemed like it—to get to and from school. This was good exercise for us. No one at our school was ever teased about being overweight. No one in our neighborhood was that overweight, except for some of the adults (the women, I don't remember a single overweight man), but definitely not the kids. Sometimes it would take us a long time to get home from school because we would stop and gossip or hunt for fresh fruit or nuts on our way home.

I remember one day when we were walking home, my friend Ada Mae asked me why I was walking that way. I asked her, "What way?" She said that she thought I was trying to walk sexy or something and that I had changed my walk. It wasn't until later I realized what she was talking about. I had changed my walk because I was always carrying my mom's babies, who when they first came home were so little. After a while of eating pot liquor and corn bread that my mom fed them after they were old enough, they got big. I had to carry them on my hips, and I would swing the side of the body I carried them on because they were too heavy for me. This caused me to start to throw my hip even when I wasn't carrying a baby. I didn't notice this until she mentioned how I had changed how I walked. I think I still throw my hip when I walk; it stuck with me for life. Well, evidently, it made for a sexier walk. The first thing my husband ever said to me was, "I like the way you walk." He thought it was sexy. Later, I would develop a big butt and big legs. Add that to my sexy walk, I guess I became somewhat attractive to men. Maybe I had a chance of getting married. But it is amazing how what happens when you are young can shape your life forever.

I can see how some people in our neighborhood could envy us. Most of the time, because of the farm, we had enough food, and our utilities were never turned off unlike some people in our neighborhood. I think you could say we were comfortable. However, when we all got televisions, we realized just how poor we were, living in a two-bedroom house with ten people. I think we have to get rid of the term comfortable. But when you don't know any better, this is your reality, and it was comfortable for you. I bet people who grow up with pools in their yards all of their lives feel uncomfortable when they don't have one. I think our dreaming for better lives started with television; otherwise, we had no complaints, except for not having enough money.

We had one television, and it was in the living room. We could watch it for about an hour after we got home from school; then we had to turn it off and do our homework. We could turn it back on after we finished our homework. I always had a lot of home-work because I was taking honor classes. So I had to learn how to do homework with the television and seven other kids playing or doing something. We always turned the television off when my mom said so even though she was not home. We thought she would find out anyway. She would sometimes call home to check up on us. By now she was working at the Coffee Cup restaurant. She would call home, and she could tell us exactly where we were sitting in the living room watching television. She was only a couple of blocks from our house, so if we needed her, she could come home, walk if she had to. But most of the time, until I was old enough, my mom or my dad was home. After they thought I was old enough, they would leave us home for a short period of time by ourselves. If it was more than a few hours, my mom would get one of her brothers to baby sit us. Mostly, my uncles were a lot of fun. The only issue I had was with my uncle Jimmy. He took a liking to one of my winter caps, and he left our house wearing it one day, and I never saw it again. Because the next thing I knew, he had left for the service, and we didn't see him again for over twenty years. He and my uncle Little Johnny left home after they graduated from Webster High School and joined the service and didn't come home until years later. I don't think they even called or wrote for a long while. It was weird. I think they were trying to get settled in other states after they got out of the service and didn't want to come home until they had money. The first thing I said to Uncle Jimmy when I saw him was, "Where is my cap?" He had forgotten all about it. I told him how he left our house wearing my favorite cap, and that was the last time I saw him for the longest of time. It's funny how some of my memories are around clothing.

I remember I had a dress that I loved. For some reason, one of my neighbors, Miss Lena, started teasing my brother and decided since he lived with seven girls that she would put him in a dress. Unfortunately for me, she put him in my favorite dress. He fought her so hard that he tore that dress up; it had to be put in the garbage. I was mad at Miss Lena for years for that stupid incident. My brother was so young, so I am not sure he remembers the incident. My mom and dad kind of chugged it off, but I know at the time I didn't, and I know David didn't either. Grown-ups sometimes would play mean tricks on kids, thinking they were funny. Most of my life, even in high school, I wore clothes made of flour sacks, so to get a new dress from a dress store was priceless at the time. So this may have been funny to the adults, but sometimes it would scar kids for life. Miss Lena and her husband moved away while we were still in elementary school. Needless to say, I didn't miss them because of the incident with the dress.

Mrs. Francis moved into Miss Lena's house with her husband. At first they had no kids, but later they would adopt or raise Mrs. Frances brother's two children. I think he and his wife had separated, and she moved to California, and he didn't want to raise two children by himself. The kids were younger than me, so they became friends with my younger siblings. They were Wanda Jewel and Dwayne. Mrs. Frances wouldn't allow them off their property that often. My siblings would talk to them across the fence. Several of the houses on our block had fences. We didn't have a fence.

Mrs. Frances was our cafeteria supervisor at Jerry A. Moore. For some reason, it seemed she thought she was better than us, at least that is what my siblings and I thought. Two of my neighbors worked in the cafeteria, and she supervised them. This relationship seemed to have carried over in the neighborhood as well. To make extra money, she had a beauty shop built in her front yard. My mother would let her do our hair sometimes until she discovered that she wasn't very good at it. I don't think she ever made that much money in her shop.

She put a pop machine in her beauty shop, and I think she made more money from it.

Growing up, we never had enough money to buy much pop; but when we did, we would make a beeline to her beauty shop to get a pop or soda pop. Sometimes we would have to go into her house and get the key or wake her or her husband up to buy a pop. This was the start of our craving for pop. They were addictive. My addiction to pop would come much later because we couldn't afford it at the time. Our drink of choice or by default was Kool-Aid or water. We had tea on rare occasions. Very seldom did we have orange juice. The only time my mother bought orange juice was when she was giving us castor oil to keep us regular. Whenever we bought a pop, it was mostly Coca-Cola. We had a Coca-Cola plant in Minden. It was the best-tasting pop to us. For some reason—and I believe it had something to do with the water—Coca-Cola in Minden tasted different from not only the rest of the state but the United States. I loved it, and my siblings did as well. Later on, we would become addicted to Coke and Pepsi.

When we were young, I guess we would become irregular at times. My mom and all the other moms would give their kids castor oil, cod liver oil, or Castoria. Castor oil was given in orange juice. To this day, I can't drink orange juice without tasting castor oil. We thought castor oil was horrible. It was like drinking cooking grease. We could not understand the purpose. But most of us never complained of having stomachaches back then, and I don't remember a lot of colds. We very seldom missed school. If you did, you were home alone, and you were too scared. So even if you were sick, you would go to school if you didn't have a fever. Castoria didn't taste bad because it was sweet. I think my mom was scared we would drink too much of it, so I think she would hide it. They gave us turpentine on sugar for something as well. During those times, there was always some home remedy. Going to the doctor was out of the question unless you were half dead. I was half dead one time, and my mom took me to the doctor.

I was so weak. I had been vomiting and diarrheic for a while I could hardly lift my head up. When she finally took me to the doctor

I was so weak I couldn't stand up. My cousins happen to be visiting, and they thought I was going to die. I thought I was too. My mom gave me some soup that I was able to keep down, and I started to get better. I surmised after I grew up, I probably got dysentery from the sewage that flowed freely from under our house into a trench on our front lawn and into a ditch in front of our house. I guess when we first moved to Minden, the pipes for the sewage had not been laid down yet, or my parents couldn't afford the monthly payments. I am not sure, but I am pretty sure I got dysentery from it because that's where we played. I don't remember any of my other siblings getting sick from it.

We also had a cement company in front of our house. I remember when we moved in a man was over there mowing the grass and cutting down the trees. It turned out to be my mom's future boss, Mr. Junior, or at least he was called that. A lot of Southern men, black or white, were called junior if they were named after their father. He also owned the Coffee Cup restaurant where my mom got her first full-time job. They processed cement across the street from our house. My dad already had asthma. I am sure moving across the street from this cement factory didn't help any. I guess the black people who lived in our neighborhood had nothing to do with the zoning laws at the time. Several of my siblings and I have problems with breathing, but nothing serious yet. I still think some of that cement could be in our lungs.

In elementary school, we very seldom took off sick. I remember that one day I was actually sick and took off from school. I was so bored. There was nothing to do, no one to talk to; it was so eerily quiet. We didn't have a television or a radio, and the house was so quiet, and that was unheard of with eight kids. I was home by myself and scared to death. Nobody was in the streets, and hardly any cars went by. It seemed everybody was at work or school. When I went back to school the next day, my sister Bobbie had been chosen to be in the dance group for our school program instead of me because I was not at school. The one thing I knew I could do good was dance, so I was hurt.

I remember getting sick one other time, but this time, I was at school. I was sent home by myself. While I was walking home, I found myself surrounded by dogs. Someone had told me not to move if dogs approached me, or they would pounce on me. So I just stopped dead in my tracks when I realized what was happening. A man happened to be home, and he overheard the dogs barking widely and came to check it out. He somehow got the dogs to leave me alone. Afterward, I took off running home for fear I would run into some more dogs. My mom was home when I got there, and she calmed me down. Needless to say, I never walked home from school by myself again.

Like I said, I started my menstrual cycle at Jerry A. Moore. But until that day, my mom had not spoken to me about menstrual cycles that girls got monthly. She didn't mention to me that now I could get pregnant and have a baby. After taking care of so many sisters and my brother, I knew I was not ready for that. My parents did not have to worry; I was not getting pregnant until I was ready and until I could afford to take care of myself and a baby. I definitely did not want to be poor and having a baby. I wanted to be able to take care of my baby's needs.

When we left for the summer before my eighth grade year, we assumed we would be in Mrs. Dyer's classroom for two years, seventh and eighth grade. Over the summer, we heard that Minden would have a junior high school for blacks in the old J. L. Jones building. They had built a new J. L. Jones Elementary School close to the swimming pool in the black neighborhood across town. So after our seventh grade, we would be going back to that old building where the toilets always overflowed. Now most of us were on our periods, and things could get interesting.

So after our seventh-grade year with Mrs. Dyer, all of us eighth graders went to J. A. Phillips Junior High School. The school was named after Dr. Phillips, who was the only black medical doctor in town and who had passed away, I believe, that past summer or spring of 1960. I can't remember who my homeroom teacher was, maybe Ms. Jackson. She also was my science teacher. We now had to change classrooms; we never did that before. Mrs. Phillips (Dr. Phillips wife, now widow) was my civics, geography, and general business teacher. Mr. Carter was my mathematics teacher. Mrs. Jones was my English teacher, and Mrs. Harris was the choir director. We had a choice between choir and band, and I chose choir. I wish we had more than two choices because I didn't like choir or band. I didn't have a musical bone in my body I thought at the time even though I loved to dance. Mr. Turner was the principal at J. A. Phillips. Unlike Mr. Chapman; he very seldom came into the classrooms. We seldom saw him. He was nothing like Mr. Chapman. Mr. Turner had a secretary; I thought she was the sexiest woman I had ever seen. She had what I think boys would call a Coke-bottle shape.

I was kind of scared to be leaving Jerry A. Moore. Now we had to take the bus, and we would be surrounded by new kids from all over Webster Parish. I was still shy and seldom spoke in class, but I was definitely learning how to study. I had made good grades for the most part at Jerry A. Moore and was beginning to gain some confidence in myself. But I was still afraid of what Junior High School would mean for this still shy and now not-so-timid girl.

Chapter 4

MIDDLE SCHOOL YEARS 1960–1961

J. A. Phillips Junior High School

By the time I got to eighth grade, J. A. Phillips Junior High School had started. It was a new school, but it was in the old buildings of J. L. Jones Elementary. A brand-new school had been built for J. L. Jones, so the seventh and eighth grade classes in Webster Parish were now being held in the old J. L. Jones buildings, now being called J. A. Phillips, named after the late Dr. J. A. Phillips, the only black physician in town. I went to Phillips for my eighth grade year along with the rest of the kids in my neighborhood, and Bobbie went there as well for her seventh and eighth grade years. We again had to take the bus to school. We had always walked to Jerry A. Moore; now we had a shorter distance to walk. Even though we hated walking to school and got my dad or mom to drive us as much as possible, this walking kept us physically fit, and we didn't have a lot of colds or other illnesses growing up. We had to walk two or three miles a day;

now we only had to walk a couple of blocks to the bus stop in front of New Light Baptist Church.

My days at J. A. Phillips Junior High School, for the most part, were uneventful. What I noticed the most was that classroom structure changed somewhat. I don't think we were in groups any more or from what I could see. We now had to change class every hour. Plus, now the teachers lectured, and we had to take notes, and the books were harder. We had classes in subjects we never had before, like science, general business, and social studies. We had science, but no science laboratory equipment. Our science teacher was good, but she was not inventive. She could have gotten the parents together and raised money for some equipment. Plus, she could have taken us on field trips to farms to introduce us to animals or even just took us outside to introduce us to the environment. Instead, she just lectured us.

I did quite well in the classes, but I never raised my hand to answer questions even if I knew the answer. I was mortified that the teachers would ask me a question that I didn't know the answer to, and I would be humiliated. Sometimes kids would laugh when you didn't know the answer to questions. Now add that to my innate shyness, and the humiliation would be multiplied. Whenever I felt inadequate in something, I would think about it all night and sometimes still be thinking about it weeks later. Oh, let's be real. Some of the things I think about to this day, and I am in my seventies (that's how long humiliation can last). That is why I am so against bullying, especially among young kids; you never know when they can't just brush it off. So many people think kids just brush it off and never think about it again. Well, that doesn't happen all the time, especially with timid and shy kids like myself. I am glad I never thought about suicide because nowadays kids are committing suicide at younger ages, and this has shocked a lot of people.

At Phillips, a lot of the kids were new to me. I had remembered some of them from my days at J. L. Jones when I was in elementary school there, but some of them had come from other schools. Some of my classmates from Jerry A. Moore didn't follow us to J. A. Phillips. They either dropped out or went to other schools. Now we were all spread out all over the school in different homerooms and classes. Whereas, at Jerry A. Moore, we were all in one classroom, and that's where we stayed all day, so changing classrooms was totally different for me. We had so many teachers to get to know. Even with that, I still did well in school because at Jerry A. Moore, I had learned how to read and read well. At Phillips, though, I had to horn my notetaking skills, as well as reading.

This was a new experience for me because now we had to change classes and get used to more than one teacher. We even had a choir and band period. I chose the choir. We had to do one or the other. I couldn't sing or play an instrument. I don't know why I chose choir; it probably had something to do with the flute fiasco or the fact that my parents probably couldn't afford to buy me an instrument. Ms. Harris was our choir teacher, and Mr. Joe Miller was our band teacher. Ms. Harris was okay, but I didn't particularly like her. I thought she was to into herself and thought she was cute. Mr. Miller was an excellent band director. I thought the Phillips band sounded as good as the Grambling College band that came to our parades on Fair days often. I believe Mr. Miller had graduated from Grambling.

On the first day of choir, Ms. Harris had us come up and sing for her; then she would put us into a group. She put me in second soprano. After that, whenever, someone would ask me what I sang, I said second soprano. The time I sang for her was probably the one and only time I sang solo, except in church or at our summer prayer service we had in our homes. I was more petrified to sing than I was to talk in front of people, if you can imagine that. I don't know if we went to choir every day or not. I just can't remember. I do know that I started to hate choir then. Now, years later, I wished I had paid more attention. Back then, I thought my voice sounded too timid and didn't understand that choir could help develop your voice. Much, much, later, someone told me I had a good radio voice. I was floored. That was only a few months before I retired, and I probably didn't believe them anyway.

At Phillips, our school colors were black and gold, just like Grambling College. We were the Phillips' Panthers. Since this was the first year of J. A. Phillips Junior High, the students got the chance to pick the colors and the mascot. The band performed in the parade we had every year when the fair came to town. We got the day off from school, and we all went to the parade, and we would walk to the fairgrounds. Grambling College's band would come as well. It was fun times. Bands from all the black high schools in Webster Parish came. We had parishes in Louisiana because it was a Catholic state. Other states have counties. I will never understand why Louisiana doesn't change to counties; I guess it likes the distinction, being a confederate state and all. Shreveport had a fair the next week after our fair that was bigger. It was the Louisiana State Fair, so it was too expensive for us to go. Sometimes we would pass by in the car, and I would see how big it was and definitely wanted to go. Their fair was segregated as well back then.

We always looked forward to going to the fair but didn't have that much fun because we didn't have enough money. Blacks had one day, and whites had one day. I think the whites had a parade also, but we never went to their parade or attended the fair on their day and vice versa. When I did get the chance to go to their parade, I was surprised at how different their band uniforms were. Where the black schools always had rich colors; the whites had softer colors, like gray, pale blue, red, etc. We had black, gold, green, purple, etc. The white high school in our town had red and white as their school colors. To this day, every time I see red and white, I think of that segregated school in my hometown and how different they were treated than our black school. They were the Minden Tides, and we were the Webster Wolves. I never wear red and white, and it is the reason I did not want to be in the Delta Sigma Theta sorority in college because their colors were red and white. Something as simple as that can guide your life. I don't think I knew what their colors were at Phillips, though, because I didn't get the chance to go to their parade downtown until after I was out of high school.

The Phillips Junior High Band and the Webster High School band would perform together sometimes at concerts. Our junior high choir would sing, but I don't think we ever sang with Webster's choir. Mr. Miller and Mr. Shaw (the Webster High School band director) got along well. Phillips' band had majorettes, who also played instruments. They would later become majorettes at Webster High School.

The majorettes hung together, and they became some of the popular kids at Phillips and at Webster later. They were probably, besides the athletes, the closest we got to celebrities in our schools. Plus, most of us didn't have television. Also, going to the movies was a treat. Then again, in my religion, movies were a sin. Yes, going to the movies was a sin. My mom and dad never went to the movies. My dad never went, but to my mom, they were sin and forbidden in her religion. At the time, we had one black movie theater in Minden; and it was called the Cozy, I think, and one white theater, and it was called the Rex. When they closed the Cozy, blacks were allowed to buy tickets for the upstairs portion of the Rex. Sometimes people would drop pop over the railing onto the white people, and you could hear them cursing.

It's amazing my parents let us go to the fair. I had never given a thought of being a majorette. I wonder why because I loved to dance, but back then it seemed all they did was march in parades or up and down the football field and twirl the baton. It probably had something to do with the baton; I was not very good at twirling. I could turn a flip and probably could have gotten good at it if I had become a cheerleader.

Now in Chicago, we have a parade called the Bud Billiken parade. This parade is an annual event and started long before I came to Chicago. My husband makes it an annual event for himself; I don't always go with him. One time I did, and I heard this band that sounded so much like Mr. Miller's band from Phillips. Later, I found out that Mr. Miller had taught band at Chicago Vocational High School, and I am pretty sure it was his band. I don't remember seeing him with that band, but he probably had changed a lot by then. I'd had a crush on him when I was in junior high. He was probably my first teacher crush.

One of the new courses that we had was general business. I loved the class, and I excelled in it. Mrs. Phillips, Dr. Phillips' widow was, our teacher. I think the class was too easy for most of the girls, so they kept asking Mrs. Phillips to teach us shorthand. I think they all thought they might get the opportunity to be secretaries one day. I think they had seen women (white) as secretaries on television because women were always secretaries to the men on television. It seemed sometimes, if you saw a black person, they were either maids or butlers; and if you saw a white woman, she was either a housewife or a secretary. In real life, we never saw maids, butlers, or secretaries. What we saw were teachers and principals, and that's probably why most of the girls especially became teachers and principals. I don't think a single girl in that class ever became a secretary. Other than school secretaries, we never knew a secretary, and there were only two of those. J. A. Phillips and Webster had secretaries. The elementary school principals didn't have secretaries; at least Mr. Chatman didn't. At the time, I was the closest thing he had to a secretary. Mrs. Phillips gave in and borrowed some secretarial books from the high school, I believe, and started teaching us shorthand. I was the only one to pass her quizzes. I still use some of the shorthand techniques when I take notes to this day. Everybody was doing so poorly that I am sure these grades brought down their averages for the class.

One day Mrs. Phillips went on a tirade, scolding the girls on how they begged her for shorthand, and now they weren't studying it the way they should. She even went as far as to say that Laura Rabb was the only one that didn't beg me for shorthand and she is the only one doing well on the tests. You could tell she was mad. You could also tell the girls had no idea that shorthand would be so hard. Shorthand was like drawing, and we seldom had to draw, not even in elementary school. For the most part, we were either tracing or coloring between already prepared lines. Our creative skills were not developed in the artistic realm at all. We were never asked to go beyond stick people. It took me a long time to realize that these skills could be developed; I thought you had to be born with the ability to draw. I still think so, but with practice, you could do more than stick people. We grew up in a beautiful area of Louisiana; it would have been nice to be able to paint it. Needless to say, she stopped teaching us shorthand, and she had never tried to teach it to the boys. I can't remember what they were doing while we were practicing shorthand. I think the girls stopped thinking about being secretaries in the future.

Mrs. Phillips also taught us civics or social studies. This was the year President Kennedy was elected president and had to select his cabinet. One of our current events had all the cabinet members and their responsibilities in their particular office with the federal government. Mrs. Phillips had us memorize them, and she tested us on it. I can say this was excellent for my memorization skills. I got an A or a B on the test, and Mrs. Phillips praised me.

I can still remember one of the exams she gave us in her social studies class. I think it was the final exam because, to this day, it is the hardest test that I have ever taken in my life. She had a list of sentences written down, and we had to place the sentences in the order they appeared in our textbook. She had taken several sentences from each chapter, and we had to arrange them in the order of their appearance. I can't remember what grade I got. She had said that test would be on the whole book, but who reads every chapter in their textbook, unless the teacher gives you an assignment? Mrs. Phillip's had not gone over the whole book, so this test was unfair to me. Except for the current-events test, we just answered the questions at the back of each chapter, and she had not assigned all the chapters. Of course, even then, I did not read the whole chapter. I did what I now know as fast reading and then go to the end of the chapter to get the questions and fast-read to find where the subject was being discussed in the book and then answer the questions. Some sections were never read. I never sweated so much on a test since. I cannot remember what grade I made, but I think I got an A out of the class.

The only class I enjoyed in eighth grade was math. My math teacher was Mr. Carter. He was short and had the biggest head. The rumor was that he married one of his former students. Let's say you could not call him handsome, so everybody was surprised that she married him. Of course, the rumor was that she married him for his money. I know they had a son, and he was the apple of Mr. Carter's life. He may not have been cute, but he was an excellent math teacher; he knew his math. He would spend most of the hour chastising one person or the other. He would often make us laugh. When he spanked someone, he would take them in the closet. We never thought anything was weird about this, but he was the only teacher I had to do it. He took me into that closet one time, and I don't remember what I did wrong. Maybe I couldn't answer a homework question or something. I remember when we got in the closet he just laughed and said I better not smile when we got out of the closet. He never even touched me. Man, I had no idea he wasn't spanking those other kids when he took them in the closet. We all thought he did. No one ever said anything for fear the next time he would spank them for real.

As far as math goes, he said he was preparing us for high school. I think he could have spent more time on the subject, but he did get us ready for high school algebra. He taught us how to do equations, and this was a good lead in to high school math. Mr. Chatman in elementary school had wanted to make sure we had good sound math basics, and we did. We did so much drill and practice in those days, so I was prepared for Mr. Carter's class; and after junior high, I was prepared for high school mathematics, I would later find out as well.

Ms. Jewel Jackson was my eighth grade science teacher. I did quite well in her class. I think this was the first time I had science that I can remember. I don't remember us even having a science book in elementary school. Then and again, maybe that is because no teacher showed a passion for it, so it would leave a lasting impression on me. We may have had a little bit in elementary school, but I don't remember it. We still didn't have any equipment. Ms. Jackson seemed surprised that I always got As on my tests because I was so quiet in the class. I was too scared to ask questions and never raised my hand to answer questions even though I knew the answer. I remember her saying that she wanted to recommend me for the honor's science class in high school, but she wasn't sure because I was so quiet. Mr. Carter, my math teacher, told me he was recommending me for honor's math in high school. I really didn't know what that meant, but I knew math would be harder. Mr. Carter often said he was preparing us for high school math. When Ms. Jackson said that she wouldn't recommend me, all I remember thinking was, *What did the fact that I didn't talk have to do with the price of tea in China?* That is just what I thought; I remember that as clear as day. I guess in my naiveté, I thought you could go through life not talking. What I didn't know was that not talking early on curtailed my growth and development in so many ways, and I probably missed out on some of my blessings in life because of it. No one else questioned me about it until I got in graduate school, and the teacher said no one would get an A if they didn't talk in her class, so I started talking then and kept on talking after that. Someone should have said that to me early on in elementary school. What I did get were all As in conduct because I was quiet and didn't talk in class. I think I thought that was what the teachers wanted. I was always very good at following teachers' instructions. I should have gotten a grade in communication skills or social interaction from the beginning of my education. Besides being innately shy, the paddling scared me to death and affected my social and emotional growth. Now I know social and emotional skills development is just as important for you as academic skills development, and it should start in infancy. I am a proponent of social and emotional learning to this day.

We had a social event to culminate our eighth grade year. My mom bought me a pretty hot-pink dress. It was so pretty and for the first time I thought I looked hot (at least I hoped I did). Boys were supposed to ask us to go to the dance; no one asked me. So Mrs. Jones—I think she taught me English—paired me with Billy Joe Cosby. At the social, we were supposed to dance together. We didn't even sit together. I don't know why, but he sat clear across the room from me. At some point during the evening, they announced that we had to dance with our dates, and I saw Billy coming toward me, and I was scared stiff. It was the first time I had danced with a boy. I was so scared I don't even remember the dance; all I remember is him coming toward me. Needless to say, I felt funny every time I saw him after that. We hardly ever spoke to each other throughout high school. We both went to different colleges, and I don't remember seeing him again until our fortieth high school reunion, I believe. He looked the same as I remembered. He was still skinny; I can't say the same for me. Back in junior high school, we were just two shy skinny, socially inept teenagers trying to get through the night without stepping on each other's feet. I guess you can say he was my first date, even though we didn't sit together and only danced together once or twice.

The summer between junior high school and high school was interesting. I think it was the time that many of my friends experienced sex for the first time. I know they would invite me over to Helen Phillip's home during the day to meet with boys from high school. They said that Helen's mother was not at home. I said I couldn't go because I had to baby sit my brother and sisters and that was the truth, but I was really happy to have the excuse because I felt the high school boys were only using the junior high girls for sex. I was pretty sure they all had girlfriends in the high school. I noticed when they passed by Phillips, and we were on recess the boys would flirt with the girls. Webster High School was always on the same campus as J.L. Jones, now J. A. Phillips. They had built another elementary school, and Jones students transferred over there after we transferred to Jerry A. Moore.

Then they built a new low-level high school and eventually tore down the two-level white building that had been the elementary and high school at one time. They kept the old gym, and that was considered the auditorium, where plays, concerts, graduations, etc. were held. In order to get to the auditorium, the high school kids had to walk pass J.A. Phillips. They had a ramp, so they could even walk when it was raining. Plus, we shared a cafeteria. I don't think we had more than five hundred students on that plot of land, but we had over one hundred acres of land probably. Now, in Chicago, often you will have that many students in a building on one acre of land. I loved the campus; it gave you a feeling of freedom, something we still didn't have in the South, even though slavery had been abolished over one hundred years earlier. Like I said, whenever the high school boys passed the junior high school girls, they would flirt shamelessly. The girls loved it. I think they thought they were one-upping the high school girls and that the boys thought they were sexier or something. It never dawned on them that the boys were just using them to make the high school girls jealous or just to get their own kicks. No one ever thought about the fact that having sex with a minor was statutory rape. This was not even discussed in my neighborhood. Girls never thought about the fact that they could get the boys in trouble by having sex with them and vice versa.

I couldn't help but wonder what would happen when we got to Webster High School. After starting Webster, I noticed that the boys that had noticed my friends when they were in junior high seemed to distance themselves from them now, probably because their real girl friends were around. Some of my friends did get caught up in their relationships and dropped out of school and married some of the boys. One, I would later learn, got pregnant and left school. My best friend Pat eventually got pregnant and married her friend, only to get a divorced once the baby came and the boy graduated and left for the service and didn't even tell the service about the baby or Pat, as her mom informed me later.

Things changed for all of us in high school. I think we were all scared our freshmen year but excited at the same time. I am sure we all started to take on more responsibility in our homes as well and started to grow up. One of my friends, Bobbie Mae, for some reason over the summer decided to not continue with school and eventually married even though she was not pregnant by the older guy she had been interested in and always talked about. I had no idea it was that serious. I would see her sometimes, and she would never seem to regret her decision. I figured she would forget me, the quiet one who never spoke in class, as if she didn't have a voice. I was grateful to be starting high school.

Chapter 5

HIGH SCHOOL YEARS
1961–1965

Webster High School

My starting high school was a big deal in our home because neither my mom nor my dad had graduated from high school. I think they were as nervous and happy as I was, if not more so. It was the time I would find out just how much my mom and dad respected teachers. I had an idea by the way they bragged about someone called 'Fessor LoPolk," but I didn't know they would take their side over mine. Unless, my parents observed things firsthand, whatever adults said was god. They always respected the chain of command. But back then, I don't think kids were known as being as manipulative as they are now. In high school, my mom bought me more clothes as opposed to making them. I think my sisters were still wearing my hand-me-downs. To be honest, I didn't notice; I was too busy trying to fit in with my own attire.

The summer before I started to Webster High School, I tried out for their cheerleading team at Webster. I don't remember practicing a cheer. I just remember going to a meeting with the current cheerleaders. My aunt Natherine was a current cheerleader because she was already in high school. I think I called her for some advice, but she probably already knew with my nerdy and ugly self that I wasn't going to be selected. I don't even know how I got up the nerve to even try out. I think it had something to do with the fact that I loved to dance. I was scared of speaking in front of crowds, but I didn't mind dancing or cheering in front of them. As a matter of fact, I would show out a little bit if I could—in other words, try to outdo the other girls. I think I was trying to use the cheerleading team as my speech class in high school. I was starting to develop my own curriculum to get me out of my shell, and I shouldn't have had to do it. My school curriculum from elementary school through high school needed to be more developmental and personalized.

I don't think any of the girls from my side of town (Crichton Hill) were selected for the cheerleading team, but I didn't notice this discrimination at the time. Of course, I thought I wasn't selected because of my looks, which probably was true because they didn't check out my abilities. I wasn't given a cheer to do, and neither were the other girls. They told the rest of us that we could become pompoms if we wanted to, and I said yes. The girl was branching out, no matter how small.

Going to high school was exciting and scary to me. Webster was not completely new to us because we had used the cafeteria as the junior high cafeteria and the old gym or chapel as our auditorium. I loved Webster's campus. Webster sat on what I thought was a huge plot of land. It had a huge front lawn that the kids would sit on at lunchtime. There were benches and I believe tables for kids who brought their own lunches. The main building sat on a hill. On the side of the building was what we called the new gym and the stadium. The new gym was where we held dances, and the stadium was where we had football games as well as commencement graduation exercises outdoors. The property was always well kept. There was a ramp connecting us to the gym and almost to the old gym where Webster also had assemblies for all the students. This ramp went past Phillips Junior High. Now, as a freshman, I was one of the big kids walking past the junior high students on my way to assembly. I felt like I was growing up, and this kind of scared me. But I was ready for it.

I can't remember who my first homeroom teacher was, and that's weird. It seems I would remember that. For some reason, I think it was Mrs. Winchester. She was new to Webster, so she was probably only a few years older than us. She taught English and French. To me, she was one of the best-dressed teachers at Webster. I took her for freshmen English and two semesters of French. I remember thinking that I learned more English in her French class than I did in her English class. I will always believe that African Americans born in the rural South would have learned more English if they had taught it like they taught foreign languages because English is our second language; black English is our first language. I learned to write English quite well, I think, but speaking it was another thing. I am still not confident in my use of the English language; I gave up trying to be perfect and started doing the best I could. I am just grateful that this deficiency never stopped me from talking to giving speeches when I had to.

I remember in one of my French classes that Mrs. Winchester taped recorded us and played it back so we could hear ourselves. I didn't recognize my voice, and on top of that, I didn't like it. I sounded so nasally to me. It didn't dawn on me that this was probably due to a stuffy nose from allergies. I just decided that I didn't have a pleasant voice. This probably made me do even less talking in my classes.

We would sit close to the cheerleaders in the stands at football games and cheer. Now, pom-pom teams do much more. I would cheer my head off at the football games for my team; it was one of the ways I found my voice. I don't think we had uniforms; we just had to wear blue and white (our school colors), and we would have pom poms to wave around. Pom-pom girls traveled with the team if they had their own money, and because I was working at the Coffee Cup restaurant alongside my mom by this time, I traveled with the team often. I didn't understand that much about football, but I think it was being outside that made me feel free and unafraid to just let loose and scream, hollow, and cheer my team on to victory, even though half the time I didn't know what the score was. For some reason, being a pom-pom helped me with my self-confidence. I am really not sure why. I think having the money to go to the games without family and friends in tow and being okay with people I didn't know that well, even with the boys, I was okay. It gave me a feeling of independence and freedom. It was as if I could breathe. It was as if being out in the fresh air, I could finally breathe and be myself. I think I needed the oxygen. I felt the same way when we had school under the big tree in front of the church when I was in first grade. I was happy that my mom went against church policy and allowed me to go to the games as long as I had the money.

I can't remember who was my sophomore year homeroom teacher either. I do know that Mrs. Musgrow was my junior-year homeroom teacher, and Ms. Lillian Mitchell was my senior-year homeroom teacher. I remember that because some pivotal things happened during those years.

When Bobbie and I got old enough, thirteen or fourteen, we started to work in the evenings and on the weekend at restaurants where my mom was head cook and could talk her bosses into hiring us. The first restaurant was the Coffee Cup. It was owned by a man my mom called Mr. Junior Davis (I think) and his wife, Ms. Leona—the same people who at the time owned the Cement Company that was in the front of our house. I always felt that having a cement company across from our house couldn't have been healthy for our lungs. My dad had asthma, but he had it before we moved to Minden. I doubt if zoning laws would have allowed this company in a white neighborhood. Ms. Leona really ran the restaurant. They had two children, a boy and a girl. They eventually got a divorce and sold the restaurant to a man my mom called Mr. Henry. Mr. Henry was married and had children, but his girlfriend worked in the restaurant as a waitress. Later on, Mr. Henry sold the restaurant back to Mrs. Leona. Then she ran the Coffee Cup with her new and younger husband. We made $2.50 or a day or .32 cents an hour for working at the Coffee Cup talking about child labor. We were dishwashers and short-order cooks. The short-order cooks made the sandwiches, such as hamburgers, cheeseburgers, barbeque beef, etc. Mostly we were dishwashers. The best thing about working at the Coffee Cup was being able to eat the food. Bobbie and I both gained weight and developed hips working at the Coffee Cup.

We loved having a little money. We were in high school and could buy a few things for ourselves. My mom even allowed us to go to a school dance or two. She was really branching out. Her church was orthodox and forbade so many things, including football, dancing, cutting your hair, etc. But my mom told us that she wanted us to have fun. I think she remembered how much fun she'd had when she was young playing basketball. My aunt Elnora had told us that my mom was a really good basketball player growing up and that she wowed the boys with her big legs and pigtails. Of course, my sisters and I couldn't believe our mom ever played any sport. My mom, after having eight kids and nine pregnancies, couldn't even get her legs across a girl's bike and looked pregnant even though she wasn't. We tried to get her to ride Vickie's girl bike one day, and she couldn't even get her legs high enough to get on the bike. Of course, we all broke out laughing. My mom took it in stride. Having a little money to do things made high school more fun. I started to loosen up and not take things so serious.

I think I would say that I enjoyed high school. I know I never studied so hard. I was in honors science and honors mathematics all through high school—in spite of not being recommended by my science teacher Ms. Jackson for honor's science. Mr. Carter (bless his heart), my eighth grade mathematics teacher, did recommend me for the honor's mathematics classes at Webster. I think it came down to my high school principal, Mr. Hayes. He probably noticed my tendency to be on the honor roll most semesters and decided to give me a chance. I owe him a lot for that. I had the upmost respect for him. Taking those honor's classes set the tone for my life: hard work. It is because of those classes that hard work is normal for me. I am a stickler for details, following instructions, and researching ideas.

Mr. Hayes, to me, was an excellent principal. He could keep us quiet just by looking at us. If he had a hard time keeping us quiet, he would talk to us about respect etc. He had this very base voice and was long-winded, so most of the time, you would keep quiet just to keep him from talking. Mr. Hayes was a principal with principles, and he followed them. He had come from Texas to be the principal of Webster High School. He was married and had a daughter and a young son. The son was named Wilbur Hayes Jr. The son died early in life, and you felt the life slip out of Mr. Hayes as well. I really don't think he ever got over his son's death. People didn't go to psychiatrists in those days, and of course, Minden didn't have one, definitely not a black one. I think Mr. Hayes could have used one to help heal his pain. I think his daughter, Yvette, and his wife, Mrs. Hayes (kindergarten teacher) tried to help him get over the pain. I think you could call Mr. Hayes and his family the "first family" among the blacks in Minden. Everyone knew Mr. Hayes and respected him, and whatever he said was the word (I didn't know who the white mayor was, but everyone knew the name of the white sheriff—can't remember it now) because he was feared. Otherwise, Mr. Hayes and his family were royalty in my hometown.

I had no idea how important Mr. Hayes was to education for blacks in Louisiana and not just in Minden until I spoke with a photographer who started his business in Louisiana and had moved to Chicago, Illinois, and ended up down the street from where I lived in Chicago as an adult. I had remembered that Potter Studios had taken our graduation pictures when I graduated from Webster (the name was on the back of all the pictures). Then after I moved to Chicago, I noticed that a sign on a storefront that said "Potter Studios." I decided to use their services when my son graduated from kindergarten. Remember, I always wanted my own kindergarten graduation picture, so even though my son's school was not taking kindergarten graduation pictures, I decided to have one done for my son, James Jr. anyway.

One day while I was at Potter Studio, I asked the photographer if he remembered taking pictures at Webster, and he did. He went on to tell me the story of how Mr. Hayes saved his photography business. He said that Mr. Hayes stood up to the white establishment and hired him and other black photographers to take school pictures at Webster. Because of the stance Mr. Hayes took, other black principals followed his lead, and the black photographers were able to make a living and keep their businesses going. He said he owed Mr. Hayes a lot. I felt even more proud of Mr. Hayes.

Mr. Gibson taught honor's Algebra 1 and 2 and finite math. He said that he was preparing us for college freshmen algebra. I must say he did because I almost made two As in Algebra 1 and 2 in college. I got a B in Algebra 2 my freshman year because I missed an assignment. I arrived in class about five minutes late for some reason, and the teacher had given us an assignment to do over the holidays. I didn't know it, so that lowered my grade. I had asked my friend Pearlie, who was in the class as well, if he'd given any homework, and she said no. Then most semesters ended after the holidays. Now they end before the holidays. I loved finishing the semester after the holidays because I spent the whole holiday organizing my work so I could study for the end of the semester exams. When we arrived back from the holidays and Mr. Knox (I knew Mr. Knox because he had taught higher-level mathematics at Webster but left before my senior year) asked for our assignments, I was puzzled and asked Pearlie, "I thought you said we didn't have an assignment." She said that she wanted me to fail because I always got As. She was supposed to be one of my best friends, so I could not understand her logic. This was my first opportunity to realize that the definition of being someone's best friend is not the same for everyone. To me, you never wish failure on your best friend.

I want to mention that after Mr. Knox left Webster, there was a rumor that he was gay. It seemed the adults knew he was gay but respected him for his knowledge of mathematics, so being gay didn't seem to matter. Also, Mr. Knox was not flamboyantly gay; he dressed like the other teachers and carried himself similarly as well. I think as long as gays assimilated into the black society, they were not discriminated against. I think that tone carried over into white society as well—and does even to this day generally. However, today gays are encouraged to come out of the closet and be themselves.

High school was not a piece of cake for me. I was always studying. Our semester exams were comprehensive; meaning, everything we had from the beginning of the school year to the final exam in most of my classes. In May, especially in our math classes, our finals covered what we had learned the whole year. We had to review every-thing to be prepared for these exams. This was extremely difficult. You hardly had time to play when you got home. When I went to work at the Coffee Cup in the evenings, if my mom knew I had homework, she would wash the dishes or cook the short order items and let me study. If her bosses came around, I would jump up and stand by the sink as if I was washing the dishes. Sometimes my mom would let me go into the storage room and close the door and study. I felt a little guilty about this because then my mom was doing two jobs. This had to be hard on her, but she understood that studying came first.

On Sundays, we never went back to church in the evenings because my mom knew we had homework or were studying for exams. Most of us made good grades, but we were never rewarded for them. I don't even remember my mom and dad gushing over our report cards. I never thought about making good grades to make them happy; however, I innately knew that if I had made a bad grade, it would not have gone over well. I enjoyed studying; I enjoyed learn-ing. I would often work or read ahead in the books. I thought this was smart, until I met a guy who was taking graduate classes, and he made sure he got the books weeks before the classes started so he could read the whole book beforehand. He wanted to be prepared on the very first day of class. I thought this was going a little overboard, but I bet he graduated magna or summa cum laude, and I didn't graduate either in undergrad.

There weren't a whole lot of eventful things that happened in high school. I grew to love my school. To me, it was like the little engine that could. Even though we were small, about five hundred children, we would go up against some of the larger schools and win. Our teams (athletic and academic) played schools like Carroll High in Monroe, Louisiana; Booker T. Washington in Shreveport; Peabody in Alexandria, Louisiana; or the powerhouse St. Augustine in New Orleans. I went with the football team to these away games, I think beginning in my freshman year. I loved the atmosphere at these games. I think I liked the competition and winning. You could feel the hostility among the crowd the minute you got off the bus.

I remember one time we must have beaten Booker T. Washington, and they threw rocks at us on the bus. I think they shook the bus a little too. Needless to say, I was scared, and my opinion of Booker T. sank to an all new low. Most of the schools we played were bigger than us, but we would often win. Throwing rocks at the bus that one time at Booker T. was the most dangerous situation we faced when I was growing up. Nowadays kids fight and even shoot at one another. Kids have been killed at games here in Chicago and other cities while attending school athletic events.

Louisiana even had academic competitions against these same schools. We had what was called the LIALO rally (Louisiana Interscholastic Athletic and Literary Organization) among the black schools. I don't think the white high schools had the same competition, and after integration, it was demolished, which was a shame because it meant so much to black students who were not athletes. This was our academic Olympics, and it should have been enhanced instead of demolished. In the LIALO rallies, black high schools competed against one another in academic subjects (science, math, typing, civics, etc.), as well as choir, drama, etc. Most of us didn't know what the acronym stood for at the time, but these competitions were big things in our school. Whenever our football team came back from the state championship in football, they would be treated royally at an assembly of the whole school. Well, the academic teams were treated the same way in our high school. We got an award if we came in first or second.

I was chosen to represent my school in current events in my senior year in high school. I was taking Coach Flentroy's civic class, and he chose me and Larry Houston to represent our school in current events. I had been good at current events ever since our teacher Mrs. Phillips had given us a test on it in eighth grade. She told us she was going to give us a test on one of the current events about the United States government. I think it was the year Kennedy became president (1961). I started studying early, and when we took the test, I almost made a perfect paper. Mrs. Phillips really bragged on me; I felt proud of my memorization abilities. Practicing for all those Easter programs and Mother's Day programs really paid off too. I know Larry and I came in first and second in the regional competition, and I believe sixth and seventh in the state competition. He ranked higher than me at the state level and maybe the regional level as well; I think he was happy to best a female. Even though he was tall, he didn't play football or basketball; academics was his thing. He was pretty smart. We got along quite well—and still do to this day.

Larry had lived with his aunt and uncle on my side of town for a while. His aunt, I think, tried to do some match making, but I couldn't see Larry as nothing but a friend. Then at the time, I didn't really have a high opinion of myself. I probably didn't get her hints or thought he didn't care since she was doing the talking. Besides, he was always too skinny for me. Now, I didn't weigh much myself in elementary, high school, or college, so that was the pot calling the kettle black. Larry and I were the best of friends, though. He was and still is a nice guy, someone I have the utmost respect for. He is still skinny to this day. I can't say that about myself.

Ms. Gunn, my typing teacher, asked me to go to the LIALO Rally in typing that same year. Coach Flentroy had asked me first, so I felt obligated to be true to him, even though I figured my chances were better in typing. I took typing my senior year at Webster. Ms. Gunn said on the first day that if we followed her instructions and practiced, typing would take us far. I did everything she said. My dad even bought us a typewriter so Bobbie and I could practice. Bobbie was taking typing the same year I was; this was her junior year. At first, my dad had gotten us some type of toy typewriter. We told him this was not helpful at all, so soon afterward he brought us an old Royal typewriter home. We used it, and it definitely helped us to increase our speed while typing. In class, I followed Ms. Gunn's advice to the tee and did not look at the keyboard while I was learning. I learned the home-row keys. So to this day, I can type without looking at the keyboard. I could type fifty-five words a minute when I graduated from high school, and I think that was faster than the average person needed to get a secretarial job.

For some reason, I never considered a job as a secretary; I thought it would be too boring. I could not see myself typing all day and getting the boss coffee. Later on, much later, I saw where a secretary became the CEO of a Fortune 500 company after her boss retired, resigned, or was terminated. I was floored. I understood why, however. The secretary probably knew more about the company than any other person. She probably knew as much or more than her boss, especially a good secretary. I think after she got the job, she stayed in the position until she retired. I daresay the company is still afloat, and I believe it was a Fortune 500 company.

I made good grades in high school. I carried a B average or above all the way through. I aimed for Bs and As. I didn't realize that because of my grade point average I had to run for Ms. Webster. I tried to get out of it, but those were the rules: all girls with B averages had to run. I begged Mr. Hayes, our principal, to not make me run. I had only made one other trip to his office, and that was to beg him to take me out of choir because I couldn't sing. Plus, every year, I would choose home economics for my schedule; but every year, Mr. Hayes would put me in choir instead. He knew that home economics was not the right career stream for me. He probably thought with my grades in math and science that I should think about a health career, like medicine or nursing instead, but he never said it. It would be much later when I would realize that either medicine or law were probably the right paths for me.

Finally, my senior year, he acquiesced and put me in home economics. Some girls had been in those classes for four years now and were really good at cooking and sewing, whereas I was a neophyte. The funny thing was, I didn't like either cooking or sewing. This should have been a hint to me, but it wasn't. I guess I had no idea what else to major in, so I went with my first choice: dietetics.

I could not sway Mr. Hayes away from making me run for Ms. Webster. He said those were the rules, and all girls with B averages had to run for Ms. Webster. I kept thinking if I had known that, I would have made a couple of Cs over the years. It didn't dawn on me that was a warped way of thinking. Looking back, I wished they had made more of a learning experience for those of us running for Ms. Webster. The only thing they required was that we give a speech in assembly for one minute, I think. We should have had to answer questions extemporaneously like contestants do now in beauty contests and compete in a fashion show.

I think I was afraid of running for Ms. Webster because I didn't think I would get any votes, and it would be embarrassing. My friend Pearlie and I both had to run, and neither of us were the princess types, but she didn't have the issue that I had. She was a thespian and spoke in public all the time. There were a few other girls that I felt were not the princess types either, and they didn't seem to have the problem that I had. Like I said, all candidates had to give an election speech before the whole school. Pearlie loved giving speeches, so she was okay with that. I was scared to death to give that speech because of my fear of public speaking. My friend Etolia Rowe became my campaign manager. I think I got two votes: hers and mine. To be honest, I am not even sure I voted for myself, so I am not sure who the second person was that voted for me.

I couldn't believe that you didn't have to be pretty to run for Ms. Webster. I always thought those types of contest were beauty contests. My friend Pearlie became Ms. Drama, but under her name in the yearbook, they put "Ms. Home Economics," and under our friend Athelene Evans, they put "Ms. Drama." In reality, Athelene was Ms. Home Economics, and Pearlie was Ms. Drama. Pearlie is still fuming about that mix-up to this day. She doesn't cook or sew, and I think she thought it was beneath her. She would go on to become a lawyer. Plus, she had been so good in drama she won the LIALO rally in dramatic speech for most of the years we were in high school. I think that experience helped her to do well in law school after she graduated from college.

Pearlie couldn't understand how it had not been caught doing the editing of the yearbook. She didn't win Ms. Webster either but never complained about it. I was so glad when the contest was over that I didn't know what to do. I think my mother was kind of proud that I was running because she bought me a pretty dress to give my speech in, but she never said anything. I thought she didn't say anything because she knew I was ugly also. If she had said something, it probably would have made a difference in the way I felt about running for Ms. Webster. She was a good mother, but she didn't know how to build your self-esteem, and neither did my dad. I think all of us suffered as a result, girls especially. I daresay their parents didn't know how to build them up, and unfortunately, they followed suit with us. Our self-esteems were wrapped around the love that they showed us in what they did for us. This, along with our belief in, God helped to keep us afloat mentally.

In the twelfth grade, Pearlie nominated me for president of our homeroom, and I nominated her for secretary. I think we came up with this idea over the phone. We were both branching out. We won our elections. Our homeroom did more things that year; I made sure of it. We participated in the intramural basketball game. I think the score was 4 to 1. I am not sure if my team won. I know Coach Flentroy teased me for the rest of my high school days about playing basketball with my hands on my hips. At the time, the girls played half-court basketball, so I was a guard; and if they were playing on the other side, all I had to do was stand and wait for them to come back on my side of the court. So I would stand with my hands on my hips. Remember, I developed a problem with my walk when I carried my mom's heavy babies. Well, it affected my stance as well. My mom probably should have put me in ballet class, but I don't even think the white girls had ballet classes in my small hometown. We also played tag football. That was where I discovered I couldn't run. In practice, we had to run the length of the football field; I came in last. Man, was I in horrible shape. By high school, I had stopped playing and started to study after school, but remember, I never really played the athletic games in school anyway. I did take physical education for two semesters at Webster. I only liked it when we would dance. I even liked it when we did square dancing. But being last running the football field told me I had to do more.

I discovered in high school that taking physical education classes were good for me. When I first saw that I had physical education classes in the middle of the day, I thought I would be too tired for my other classes, and it was just the opposite; I felt more alive in my other classes. I think it was being physical got the oxygen circulating in my body, and I felt great and could think better. So when I went to college and graduate schools, I made sure to do something physical to get my juices flowing, and it worked for me. I think physical exercise was my upper, and that's a pretty good alternative to doing drugs.

At the time, some kids were taking something called no-dose to keep them up all night so they could study. I never tried it. I knew how to organize my studying so that I could be in the bed by midnight; I was no good after midnight. It was as if after midnight, nothing was going into my brain, so I would give up and go to sleep. I had to have my sleep; it was mandatory for me. At the time, I had no idea how important sleep was for you. I just knew what my body needed: to do well in school. I think a lot of those no-dose users probably graduated to harder drugs or cigarettes later in life. To this day, in my seventies, I use exercise as my drug of choice.

I am pretty sure I learned how to use *Robert's Rules of Order* somewhat during the year I was president of my class. However, we didn't have that many class meetings, so I never mastered it. Mrs. Lillian Mitchell was my homeroom teacher. Most of the time, she just let Pearlie and I take over the class. She very seldom gave us any advice. She must have told us about *Robert's Rules of Order*, or maybe I learned about them in my civics class with Coach Flentroy. I know I did not understand how important they were to organizing meetings.

The one thing I do remember is that our homeroom class had to do some type of event for assembly, so Pearlie wrote a play with me as the lead. Funny, she doesn't remember a thing about it. But I remember just one line in the play, and it was, "I didn't asked to be born, did I?" She wrote it, but she can't remember. I remember it because the audience laughed, right on time, when I said it. I wish she had kept the script. Her drama teacher helped her with the script. Acting in that play really helped me come out my shell. I should have chosen drama as my extracurricular activity.

Because I was in the choir at Phillips, it was chosen as my extra-curricular activity by Mr. Hayes my first year of high school. So for three years, I took choir every day for an hour, and all I did was study for my other classes whenever my teacher Ms. Shackleford turned her head. I never sang a note; I just mouthed the words. I am glad I did learn some of the words to the songs. So often when I see choirs sing on television, they are singing the songs Mrs. Shackleford taught us. I guess she taught us the classics. I was glad of the other experiences I got singing in the choir also. Every Christmas we would load onto a bus and go to various homes of dignitaries in Minden and sing carols. I loved doing that and even tried to sing some of Christmas songs. We also sang at the choir and band concerts, graduations, etc. I think we sounded pretty good. Often we had to stay after school to practice. Some of the kids became quite popular around school because of their singing.

At Webster, when we took pictures for the yearbook, clubs would take group pictures. I was in a lot of clubs according to the yearbook, but I don't remember us ever having meetings. This was an excellent opportunity lost because it would have given us an opportunity to hone our leadership skills and to become familiar with *Robert's Rules of Order.* I remember hearing about these rules somewhat in high school but not practicing them to any serious extinct. I think this was a serious neglect at all of my schools. More attention should have been paid to extracurricular activities that would prepare us for life and leadership.

The junior and senior proms were two events I'd like to forget happened in high school. I was so disappointed that I didn't have a date for either one. I had hoped Billy would take pity on me again and ask me, but he didn't. My father drove me to the prom my junior year and picked me up later. Then in my senior year, my father drove my sister Bobbie and I to the prom and picked us up later. She didn't have a date either.

I didn't take a picture at ether prom. I think it was too humiliating to take a picture by myself. There were a lot of girls without dates. We should have taken group pictures so we could have those memories, but I think we were all suffering. When I went to my senior prom, I walked in with a lot of boys hanging around the entrance. I realized that most of them didn't have cars and was embarrassed, so that was why they didn't ask any of us girls to the prom. My friend Druzella and I were supposed to be going with her neighbor Ronnie Sweeney. Ronnie lived next door, to Druzella and I think his mom, Mrs. Sweeney, was making him take Druzella. They never showed up. I called Druzella, and she said they weren't going. I can't remember why, and now she can't even remember that she was supposed to go with Ronnie. I don't think she ever showed up to the prom. Ronnie Sweeney could drive, but he also had epileptic seizures. I was prepared to go in the car with a guy who could possibly have a seizure behind the wheel; that was how desperate I was—I didn't want to walk into the prom by myself or have my father drive me to the prom again.

The one good thing about my prom was being able to wear an off the shoulder dress for the first time. I remember I had a can-can under it. Can-cans were pretty popular back then. Why? I don't know. They were cumbersome when you sat down, and where did you store them? My mom was still making our clothes sometimes, but she had graduated to regular off-the-rack clothes for me and Bobbie by now. We sometimes wore the can-cans under our skirts or dresses at school. We didn't do that often because the can-cans made it hard to fit into the seats in the classrooms. I wish I had a picture of myself in the off-the-shoulder gown with the can-can underneath. Looking back, I think probably getting a new dress was one of the reasons I went to the prom. Plus the fact that if you were a junior or senior, you had to pay for the prom, whether you went or not, and my family was too poor for me to pay for something and not take advantage of it, no matter how embarrassing.

Bobbie and I were no longer wore the flower sack clothing by the time we went to high school. At some point in time, I think flour companies stopped putting the designs on the sacks, and black mothers stopped using the flour sacks to make clothes. I am pretty sure a lot of black mothers were disappointed. After Bobbie and I took home economics and learned how to sew, my mom started buying fabric for us to use. She had even bought herself a Brother sewing machine, but she never mastered it. Bobbie and I started using it. I made quite a few pieces of clothing for my college wardrobe the summer before my freshman year, and I am sure Bobbie did the same.

One of the biggest arguments my mom and I had occurred over fabric. I was taking sewing the first semester of my senior year (no more choir), and we had to make a dress. Our teacher told us not to select fabric that had stripes because it would be difficult to match the stipes up. My mom and I were supposed to go shopping for fabric together; instead, she went shopping after she got off work and picked out the fabric herself. She came home with stripped fabric, and I cried. I took it to school and showed it to my home economics teacher Ms. Duty, and she said she would help me. I did have a time trying to match up the stripes, but I did the best I could, and the dress came out okay.

The next semester we had food preparation, and this was the part of home economics I was going to major in, so I was happy to be taking food. I thought I should have been in food the whole year, but that was not the way it worked. Mrs. Duty taught sewing, and Mrs. Lewis taught food preparation. I don't remember learning much in the food preparation class because the time was so short; we only had an hour. I do remember that we made an omelet, and I had never had omelets. Maybe we made some other foods, but I do not remember any of them. We had a fashion show at the end of the year, but I do not think I was in it. Most of the kids who had taken home economics all four years were in the fashion show. I wasn't disappointed because I didn't particularly like sewing. I liked the idea of making some of my own clothes, however.

Most girls started wearing some makeup in high school. Makeup was one of those forbidden things in our church as well. We could wear powder, but no lipstick. I remember putting on lipstick at my girlfriend Melvyn's house one day and had this weird reaction. It was later when I realized that I probably had an orgasm. We couldn't even wear fingernail polish. Girls in our church started wearing blush and clear nail polish later to compensate, but this was long after my time. I think I carried this only-wearing-powder into college. I really didn't start wearing makeup until I started to work, and then it was not that much. I never bought a lot of makeup. I really never learned how to use it. I did think that it made me look better. I felt that if I had known how to wear makeup or had been allowed to wear it in high school, maybe I could have landed a boyfriend sooner. I know I could have landed one if short skirts or hot pants had come into vogue by then, but sadly, they didn't until I was in graduate school.

I remember one night we had an event at Webster, and I wore powder. I remember our band director Mr. Shaw saying, "You girls sure look different at night." I thought he meant we looked cute with makeup (or in my case, just powder). I think I was floating on cloud nine for the rest of the night after this comment. I probably wore too much powder like most of the women in my church. Sometimes they would have on so much face powder that it would cake up on their faces after they started sweating, especially Sister Carrie's face. I think they were overcompensating for the fact they couldn't wear lipstick or rouge or eye makeup. I don't think they could wear jewelry either, and that may be the reason I have never worn ornate jewelry and felt out of place when I wore even the semblance of something ornate. We would play house when I was growing up, but we never played dress up and put on makeup because we didn't have anything but powder. Women wore something called rouge at the time. I think it was reddish in color. I never wore rouge; I thought it would make me look like a clown. Makeup is still my nemesis.

Recently, I asked my sisters-in-law if they wanted to play makeup. Now let me remind you we are all in our senior years, and they hollered together very loudly, "Noooooo." So I married into a family of nonfeminine women. I am pretty sure they never played dress-up either. I was serious, though. Even in my old age, I want to know how to apply makeup correctly and appropriately. I do think makeup enhances a person's looks. The first time I wore eyelashes, my husband gave me a compliment and said I looked different for some reason. I didn't tell him until much later that I had worn false eyelashes.

Courting for me in high school was nonexistent. Even though I had several crushes in high school, I was too shy to approach a boy myself. I remember one guy my senior year, I believe, coming to my house to court me. He lived in my neighborhood and had graduated from high school. When he came to my house, my mom and dad were sitting in the living room. It was as if they had been caught off guard. I think the guy and I had been talking on the phone a few times. I am not even sure I expected him. My mom and dad just stared at the floor. I don't think they knew what to do. The one other time I went out with fellow, they were waiting up for me when I got home. When the guy and I got back home, we sat on the porch for a while and just talked until my mom came to door and told me it was time for me to come inside. I don't remember how old I was, but I think I was over eighteen. But my mom told me that they couldn't go to sleep until I was home. It wasn't until I got married that I understood what they meant, and definitely after I had a child.

I decided early on that I was not going to have sex until I could afford to take care of a baby myself. I almost kept this promise to myself. I lost my virginity my first year out of college, but I didn't have a full-time job yet. I was still a dietetic intern, but I thought it was close enough (at least I was qualified for a job). The guy was so nice. I loved being with him. He was from Guyana. I think he was doing an internship in x-ray technology at the University of Wisconsin Hospitals at the same time I was doing my dietetic internship there. We ended our friendship before it got too serious because he had every intention of going back home to Guyana, and I didn't have any intentions of leaving the United States. I don't think I had a climax, but I found out that I enjoyed the intimacy we shared. I felt safe with this guy. Plus, he knew very few people, and I figured what we shared was just between the two of us, and maybe his other friend from Guyana that was in his same program. He was probably the guy who was meant to be my husband. I think he would have made a terrific husband and father. I knew that the person I would have sex with had to be someone that I would marry and be a good father to our children.

I don't remember anyone in high school trying to go too far with me. My mom wouldn't allow us to go to parties where there was dancing. We could only go to dances at school. I didn't get too many invitations to go to parties. I didn't even get an invitation to go to a party after the prom. I probably wouldn't have been allowed to go anyway. So I didn't even get the opportunity to go too far with a guy. I wouldn't have done it anyway because I knew the whole town would have known about it the next day.

My best friend and neighbor Pat Black got pregnant either our freshmen or sophomore year in high school. She told me while we were walking to the school bus. I remember her asking me if a friend of mine got pregnant, would I stay their friend? And I said of course, not realizing she was talking about herself. In her next breath, she told me that she was pregnant. We had talked about what to do if you ever got pregnant, so I thought she knew what to do to not get pregnant or how to abort the baby; but it didn't work, and she was pregnant by an older guy. The guy did marry her, and she dropped out of school soon. She moved across town into a trailer house. I would go to visit her as often as possible, but she looked lonesome. I never did see her husband in the trailer. I know he went into the service soon. After the baby was born, Pat moved back home with her mom. She eventually went back to school. We didn't take any classes together because she was a grade below me after missing so many days out of school. It was a time when pregnant girls were not allowed to go to regular school.

I know my Aunt Natherine got pregnant her sophomore and senior years in high school, and both times she had to drop out. The first time, Mr. Hayes allowed her to come back to regular school; but the second time, she had to go to night school (I think her class had graduated anyway). Both times, she laughed her way through her pregnancies; she never seemed to let it get her down. My grandmother was really disappointed in her both times because she wanted her to go to college because she was so smart; she was in honors classes as well. The second time, my grandmother was more devastated. I remember her asking me if a girl had gotten pregnant once out of wedlock and her parents helped her out, did I think she would do it again? I don't remember what I said, but later on I found out she was talking about Natherine. I couldn't believe she had gotten pregnant again too. I think she told me herself, just before Mr. Hayes made her drop out of school. It seemed those closest to me were getting pregnant. Pat and Nat, were both very close to me, and here I was, still a virgin.

One of my classmates told me at our forty-fifth reunion that he didn't notice me in high school. He went on to say that he didn't notice that I was so sexy, intimating that I was now sexy. Well, by now I was wearing tight jeans and tight dresses or skirts that showed off my assets. I think in high school I only had one tight outfit: it was a straight dress, and I didn't get it until my senior year. I started to notice that I did have a figure my senior year. I would have worn this dress every day if I could. I have it on in almost all of my yearbook pictures. You can't see me that well in all the pictures because my favorite colors were black and olive green; and since I was black as well, you could hardly distinguish me in all the pictures except for the ones taken outside.

I now know that Mr. Hayes probably put me in choir to help with my shyness and my speaking voice and language skills. I am not sure about the language skills because most of the songs we sang were Negro spirituals, and they were not always in standard English. If someone had explained to me that being in choir would help improve my speaking abilities and job potential after I grew up, then maybe I would have tried even in junior high school to really learn how to sing.

Mr. Hayes finally relented in my senior year after I got my mom to talk with him as well and took me out of choir and put me in one year of home economics. Like I said earlier, I took one semester of sewing and one semester of cooking; and to be honest, I didn't like either class, but I was still determined to major in dietetics. I would later discover that I probably should have looked to this area as a hobby and not a career. I liked gourmet cooking and still do. However, talking food all day bored me to death. Plus, working in a hospital was too medicinal for me. By that I mean it was too depressing; people were dying all around you. I didn't have the heart for it. Of course, plenty of people left the hospital looking healthy and happy, but the ones that stayed on my mind were those who came in looking healthy and happy but left looking sad and forlorn. I would have learned this if we had even toured a hospital when I was in high school or college.

We did tour a hospital when I was in college at Southern University in Baton Rouge, Louisiana, but we didn't get the chance to see the dietetics department, and I had thought that was the whole purpose in the field trip. I think we only saw one floor of the hospital. I am pretty sure the hospital was still segregated at the time, being in the South, so they didn't allow blacks on some of the floors. I got the chance to meet one dietitian. She was probably the only black dietitian in the hospital, but she looked white herself. Her husband turned out to be my swimming teacher at Southern. My girlfriends and I had often gossiped about how well-endowed he was in his swimming trunks. I think most of the girls didn't learn how to swim because most of the time they were gazing at him. When I saw his prim and proper wife, I really couldn't place them together. So here I was, choosing a career area that I still didn't know much about even after I graduated from college.

I think proper counseling and training would have made me choose a more appropriate career path. Until my senior year in college, I had never even met a dietitian. Mr. Duty—whom I had met in the sixth grade and had majored in food and nutrition at Grambling College, I believed—had worked for the 4-H program. We had a career day in high school for all four years, but there were very few careers other than teaching. They couldn't find that many blacks in our area that were in any other career. In my senior year, we did have a counselor. They made one of our best English teachers the counselor. I doubt if she had any training for counseling. She helped us fill out our college entrance applications and apply for scholarships and financial aid. She didn't really quiz us about our majors. I think she went from being one of the best English teachers to one of the worst counselors. I remember thinking we needed her more in English than in counseling. We could have done without a counselor (at least a poor counselor); we definitely needed a good English teacher.

Your senior year was when you did a research paper, I believe. Ms. Lillian Mitchell ended up being my senior-year English teacher, and she was horrible. She was also my homeroom teacher. It seemed she was always fussing at us about something. I don't remember learning anything in her classroom that could help us with a research paper other than how to do note cards and the different types of paragraphs. When I got to college, I got Cs in almost all of my English composition classes. I think I had two years of English, two literature, and two composition classes. I think I made poor grades in English for several reasons, but Ms. Lillian Mitchell was the main culprit. Mrs. June Turner would have done much better.

The other reason was the fact that most of my college English teachers were white. I could never understand what they were saying; plus, they always talked so fast. I think they were Northerners. Later, when I had other classes from whites in the North, I had the same problem. Much later, when I learned that I spoke ebonics (or black English), then I understood even more. But I still feel that my high school did not put as much attention on English classes as they did math and science, which I did quite well in at college. Plus, when you major in a scientific major, like nutrition, you don't get a lot of chances to write. Most of it is memorization, and I had an excellent memory. Because early on I didn't talk a lot, I learned how to listen, so I could memorize tons of information and regurgitate back to the teacher on exams. I found out later this doesn't necessarily make you smart, and it doesn't mean that you understand everything. I needed to learn how to think—more specifically, how to critically think for myself. My high school and college failed me in this area. I can say, though that my high school prepared me for the basics, and with that, you can go as far as you want. It just means you still have a lot of growing and learning to do on your own.

I think if I had had proper counseling and experiences when I was in high school, I would have chosen a more appropriate career for my personality and my interest. All my nutrition classes bored me. Then and again, it could have been my boring teachers. It's just my gut feeling that business would have been a better fit for me. I used to sell everything I could: berries, plums, worms, pecans, peaches, pears to make extra money. I was always trying to figure out how to make extra money. We were poor, so if we got a nickel to spend at school, we were doing well and better than most kids at that time. My parents very seldom had spending money to give us. We would have to scrimp and save the best way we could. Women in the neighborhood were always happy to get a pail of berries, plums, peaches, etc. so they could make pies, jams, jellies, etc. Plus, people did a lot of fishing, so when we got older and were no longer afraid of the worms, we would dig them up with our hands and sell them too.

My high school typing teacher had tried to stir me in the direction of becoming a secretary. I was an excellent typist and still am—even now, fifty plus years since I graduated from high school. I thought it was too boring. Plus, I thought, Why not be the boss who wanted to type all day? Later, I would discover that some secretaries would become the boss, even of Fortune 500 companies, because they sometimes knew as much as their bosses or at least where the information was recorded or stored. Some companies probably would have been lost without their secretaries, more so than their bosses. Of course, at seventeen, I could not see this happening.

My friend Pat and her husband divorced after he went into the service. She was probably a junior by then, and so we were still in high school. I don't think she ever heard from him again. I think when he got out of the service, he didn't even come home. She started to see other guys. Being on the sidelines watching to see what happened to her in her relationships made me promise myself that I would wait for sex. To me, it was important to know that a guy cared about me and only me before I gave into sex. Pat seemed to be a woman before she was ready and definitely before she could tell the difference between love and passion. Even though she was more ready than me, her mom and dad had separated when we were very young, and her mom was always ill or feigning illness, so Pat had to be the grown up in the house often because she was the oldest child. She learned how to cook and clean a house at an early age. I think that was the reason her biscuits in the 4-H contest were better than mine; she was already making biscuits for her family in elementary school. My mom hadn't taught me how to cook biscuits yet. I was too busy having fun being a kid. Pat didn't get that opportunity.

Going to the football games made me understand what it meant to hate somebody, but not really, really hate them. We hated Carroll High School, but when the game was over, we didn't think about them again until the next game. So we didn't really hate them as in *hate*. Carroll High was our nemesis because they often beat us. Booker T and Peabody High Schools would beat us too. Coach Flentroy was our football coach. He married my kindergarten teacher. He was Catholic, and the talk was that he and Ms. Bridgeman, my kindergarten teacher, got married in the only Catholic church in town, a white church. We wondered if he went there to church on Sundays. I couldn't see Coach Flentroy together with Ms. Bridgeman because he was a he man, and she was a princess to me. But the marriage worked out for them.

My favorite classes in high school were math and biology. I kind of enjoyed chemistry as well, but the teacher Mrs. Johnson spoiled it for me with our last assignment. She gave us to me the stupidest assignment. She made us outline the entire chemistry book. My sister Bobbie was taking chemistry under her as well at the same time. After I turned in my assignment to Mrs. Johnson, I saw her come marching into the cafeteria straight to my table fuming, telling me why I let my sister help me with my assignment. She said she could tell my sister had helped me because of the handwriting. I told her I did all the outlines myself, but she didn't believe me and lowered my final grade to a B. Bobbie and I were sisters, so our handwriting looks alike. I don't know if that is a genetic thing or not, but most of my siblings' handwritings look similar to mine and similar to our parents.

Math in high school was one of my favorite subjects. I really enjoyed taking math from my teacher Mr. Gibson; he was an excellent teacher. He was very thorough and just as passionate about math as my elementary school principal, Mr. Chapman. Mr. Gibson always gave us tons of homework. The math books always had the answers in the back. Most of the time, I would work the problem and then go to the back of the book to see what the answer was; sometimes it was just the opposite. Mr. Gibson always made us do all of our work to see how we got our answers. He also made a point of grading us down if we had the wrong sign. Some of the kids thought if I got the right number, why not give me credit? They didn't quite understand how important the sign was to the whole problem. The sign made a ton of difference, and he wanted you to understand that, so he would grade you down for not including the right sign in your answer.

In math, I would often work ahead with the problems just because I enjoyed doing math. I think the hardest math for me to learn was geometry with finite math a close second. I think that was because geometry required that you draw the angles, and drawing is not my forte. Most of the time, I did well in my math class. I made mostly As and Bs, I think. I remember taking algebra 1 and algebra 2 and geometry. When we were supposed to take trigonometry, the trig teacher Mr. Knox left and went to teach at Southern University. This was my senior year. They added a course in finite math, and Mr. Gibson taught it. To this day, I still wonder what trigonometry would have been about.

I loved taking math because it made me think. I figured this out early on, and that was why I was trying to take calculus in college, and my home economics advisor wouldn't let me. I probably wouldn't have done well anyway since I didn't have trigonometry. My friend Jacquelyn Bradford was taking it because she was majoring in mathematics. I looked at her calculus book and thought, *Man, this is hard*. I think Jacquelyn and I would have had fun figuring out the answers though. I loved math so much that if I went to sleep before figuring out the answer to a problem, I would figure it out in my sleep and get up the next day with the correct answer.

I had known Jacquelyn since third grade. In the third grade, I thought she had the biggest head for a kid. Her head seemed to shrink as she got older. She and I sat next to each other in Mrs. Mim's third grade class, but Mrs. Mims was out sickly most of the time, so the teacher I remember is Mrs. Reader (the substitute). Jacquelyn and I were both in group 1, the smart group. Jacquelyn always made As on the assignments. I missed her when we moved to Jerry A. Moore in the middle of the year. We lived on different sides of town, and we didn't have a telephone until much later.

We became friends again in high school because we took many of our classes together. In high school, I was placed in the honors science (despite my junior high school teachers' threats; the final decision was left up to Mr. Hayes and not her, and am I grateful for that) and honors mathematics classes, and so was Jacquelyn. I think I am spelling her name wrong; she may have spelled it *Jacqueline*. I became friends with another Jacquelyn in college, and she spells her name *Jacquelyn*, so that is where the confusion comes from. The Jacquelyn I met in college and I remain friends to this day, whereas my friendship with Jacqueline long ago fizzled, so much so that she didn't even tell me when her mother (Ms. Rosetta) passed. I was very fond of her mother; she was an adult you could talk to. Even after Jacqueline had moved out of her mom's home, I would go over whenever I was home just to talk to her mother.

In elementary school, I remember whenever the teacher would leave us by ourselves in the class, which was seldom, they would asked one of us to take names of students who were talking or disturbing the class. When they came back, they would paddle the kids whose names were on the list or lower their conduct grade. I don't remember the kids giving that kid a hard time. I remember that most of the time, the kid who took the names took it seriously, as if they were the pseudo-teacher. Teachers often called on the smartest kid in the class to take the names. I got called on to do it several times. I didn't enjoy it. Fast-forward to fifty plus years later, and teachers can't even leave the room without another teacher monitoring their classes. I can imagine the problems a name taker would have now. I can't remember if we carried on that name-taking ritual in high school or not. It seems that sometimes the teachers would leave a kid in charge or something, but my memory fails me after more than fifty years.

Mr. Tobin was my biology teacher. All the kids loved him because he was good at reciting poetry and had a fantastic vocabulary. He taught us biology with one microscope; at the most, two. The second microscope was used only by Mr. Tobin. His laboratory was very scarce in equipment. I don't remember us dissecting a frog, but maybe Mr. Tobin did; I just don't remember. He had some animals in formaldehyde in his room (I can't believe I spelled that word correctly on the first try; at least my Word didn't show that it was misspelled—I better look it up anyway). I got a sound science foundation from Mr. Tobin, so much so that I made excellent grades in most of my science classes, and a lot of sciences classes were required for nutrition majors. Basically, all science classes required of you was an excellent memory, and I had developed that through my programs at church and in my junior high social studies class.

If we'd had laboratory equipment in my science classes in high school, maybe I would have adapted to it and would have entertained being a doctor. As it was, laboratory classes in college frightened me. We had to dissect animals. At Webster, Mr. Tobin had done it, so we didn't get the chance to touch any animals. In college in one of my laboratory classes, we had to grow bacteria. I think the class was microbiology. My friend Jackie Byrd and I were lab partners. Neither of us knew what we were doing. We had to get a cow chip or cow manure and dissolve it and put some of its droppings in a petri dish. When Jackie was pipetting some of the manure solution up with her mouth to put it in the petri dish, she accidently got some of it in her mouth. She made the funniest face, which makes me laugh to this day whenever I think about it. I never laughed so hard. Plus, you should have seen us going into the pasture near our campus trying to get the manure. I daresay that one scene along made me decide I didn't want to be a doctor.

I remember taking French 1 and French 2 in high school under Miss Winchester. She had been my freshman English teacher. I think it was her first year at Webster. I thought she was pretty. She had the biggest butt and skinniest legs. By the time I took French, she might have been Mrs. Malone by then. She was best friends with my junior high choir teacher Mrs. Harris. They lived next door to each other on Talton Street. I remember wishing that if my English class had been taught like my French class, I would have learned more English. You had to practice French. I needed to have practiced English too because what I learned in class was not the same English I spoke at home, and it made it difficult to master in speaking and in writing. As a result, I learned to write English better than I speak it still (you be the judge as you read my memoir). Of course, after seventy years, I am better at it now, but I used to doubt my usage of English so that, I believe, it held me back. I was so afraid that I was going to massacre the English language if I spoke extemporaneously.

It wasn't until I became what I called a "black" activist that I became comfortable with my speaking voice. I was out of college and working at the time when someone came up with the term *ebonics*, meaning "black English." Man, did that make sense to me. What I was speaking was ebonics and not the "king's English" and if God had intended for me to speak English perfectly, I would have been born in England, and my ancestors would not have been slaves. How could I be expected to speak English as well as white folks when it was their native language and not mine? My native language should have been a tribal language, and it should never have been taken from me. I probably would have spoken it perfectly and not have been made fun of when I misspoke. As it was, I was always self-conscious about the way I spoke; it hampered my growth and development somewhat. Man, did I have issues, issues with the way I looked and the way I spoke. Other than being a pretty smart student, I am not sure what positives I had. But having a brain kept me on track to having a career and not dwelling on my negatives. I was always able to reason. I think growing up in an orthodox Christian family and church nurtured me to believe in God as my Savior who loves and protects me no matter what. So even though I had negative feelings about my appearance and speaking abilities, I didn't give into dwelling on those negatives. I persevered because God loved me, whether I found a man or a job.

I have to talk about my teacher Mrs. Smith. She was a very tall woman, and she was married to Mr. Smith. He was a teacher also, but I can't remember what he taught. I know he wasn't a high school teacher. They lived across the street from Webster. After I graduated from high school, they started a little restaurant, community center, or something on the lot next to their property. I remember going there one Christmas and dancing. It was something we needed in Minden, a place where kids could go and hang out and get to know one another outside of school and church. Mrs. Smith taught us general business. I don't think she touched upon shorthand at all. It was in her class that we opened kids' savings account I believe at our local bank. We also learned how to write checks and how to balance a checkbook. She could have taught us much, much more she was just so busy fussing at us or spanking some of the kids in class. She was death on chewing gum. If she caught someone chewing gum in class, she would hold up the lesson while she berated them. She would go ballistic if she caught you chewing gum, especially if you were stupid enough to pop it. To this day, if I see someone chewing gum at an inappropriate time, it gets my attention, and I immediately think of Mrs. Smith.

Another teacher I had was Mrs. Sims. I think she was my junior English teacher. She would sleep through much of our classes. She did assign a book for us to read. I chose *David Copperfield* by Mark Twain. I really enjoyed reading the book. I think it was the biggest book I had read at the time. She only assigned one book. We were in her class a whole year. What else did we do? I can't remember a thing.

Mrs. Frankie Mitchell taught me English my sophomore year. What I remember doing in her class more than anything is diagramming sentences. She poured that into us. I hated diagramming sentences, but you did learn the parts of a sentence. She even had us do bulletin boards of diagrammed sentences. Man, was she into diagramming—so much so that most of the time, I do not have a problem with grammar in a sentence or a paragraph; they just might always fit.

It's funny how foreigners come to America, and they are taught English the way I was taught French, and they end up speaking English better than me. See, I tell you that I should have been taught English the way I was taught French. In other words, I should have learned how to use it in conversation. What I was taught mostly was grammar and how to use it in a sentence. We used to diagram sentences. When I was taking English under Mrs. Frankie Mitchell, like I said, we even diagramed sentences for a bulletin board. I think that was going overboard. But it is the reason I can write English better than I can speak it to this day. I can generally tell when I have written a sentence wrong because you can go back and correct it. Whereas, what comes out your mouth can't be taken back, and what comes out of mind is generally what I have heard all my life, mixed with mispronunciations and poor grammar.

People who speak English well do not like being around people who speak it poorly, even black people. To me, it is funny how some people born in the same circumstances as I was speak English so well. I finally boiled it down to one thing: that I had a problem with tone. I am tone-deaf. That is why I sing so badly. I think if you know how to sing or can catch on quickly, even if you grow up hearing ebonics, you will learn how to say proper English and it becomes a part of you. English has never become a part of me because I am tone-deaf and just can't learn quickly, so much so that speaking it becomes second nature. But then again, to me, Oprah Winfrey can't sing a lick, and she speaks English perfectly. Oh well, so much for that theory. But then, maybe if she practiced singing the way she does talking, maybe she would get better at it.

I have gotten better at English over the years, but it took me so long. I even made myself take an English class after I had a graduate degree and had worked for over twenty years after college. This time, I made an A, and I came away understanding the power of communication. If you want to get your point across, it is important that you speak their language, so it was important for me to learn how to write and speak so that majority of the people could understand me, if I wanted to be understood as a person and a professional. I don't think it is important for you to learn two languages, ebonics and English. I think it is important for you to work on improving the language that most people speak, and that is English.

So even though I spoke ebonics, I continue to try to speak English better and to write it better. It will always be a work in progress. It took me a while to get over my fear of speaking in public due to my ebonics, but I knew I would never get better until I did. One thing that held me back was how to formulate extemporaneous questions. I learned how to write questions after I started teaching. I had to give many, many exams that I had to write, so I developed the skill of writing questions. Now formulating them on the run and asking a question of a speaker extemporaneously was another thing for me for a long time. I had to conquer my fear of public speaking and learn to not be afraid of hearing my own voice. To think if I had been made to talk more in school in kindergarten on, I would have been better a lot sooner. I just happen to go to school when the teachers loved listening to their own voices. I think they went through the same thing as I did where the teachers did most of the talking. I think they were evolving in this world of English speakers as well. Until college, all of my teachers were African American, so they had to learn English as well. For so many years, it was illegal to teach blacks how to read or write, so all we heard was poor English in our homes, especially if you were a field Negro. If you were a house Negro, you overheard proper English being spoken by the whites. Even some of the Negro children did as well if they helped out in the homes.

I learned how to write fast though in high school because we had to take notes, and most of the tests were essay tests. I don't know if my paragraphs were succinct, though. I learned that later on while teaching my own students and as director of Academic Support Services at Kennedy-King College later in life. I had to learn paragraph development. What I had learned in English class about the different type of paragraphs was important as well as topic sentences, detailed information, and concluding sentences and paragraphs.

We didn't have many comprehensive tests in high school or multiple-choice exams. I don't think the teachers had learned how to develop these exams. When I became a teacher, I took an assessment seminar that helped me to develop this skill. Now teachers get already-made comprehensive exams for their classes. There is nothing like developing your own exams because then you know whether your students had learned the information in a cognitive sense or not. I am not sure giving exams developed by someone else helps the teacher or the student understand the learning that had actually taken place in the class.

Another thing I remember about exams in high school, they were always given back to us, except maybe the final exam. We could take them home and figure out where or how we went wrong in our studying. Plus, we'd use them to study for our final semester exams. At that time, the final exam was based on everything we had learned for the semester or, in the case of math, the year. We used the exams as our study guides. Now in college, at least for some courses, teachers give students study guides for each unit of lesson. They do not give the students their exams back so they can use the same exam with students in another class. Plus, exams are only based on one or two, at the most, chapters. I think this has an impact on cognitive learning of the material. Supposedly students only retain 10 percent of what they learn anyway. Well, the new way of teaching and testing on only one chapter—I doubt if this statistic is even true.

Another thing I remember in high school was the tremendous amount of homework we had each night, each week, each holiday. Yes, the teachers would load us up for the holidays. Now parents actually want to take kids on trips during the holidays, so teachers don't give holiday homework. Now is the time more homework should be given over the holidays to prevent kids from getting into drugs and other mischief. What happened to taking vacation during the summer? Even though now I think summer school is not such a bad idea for some kids. I am sure in most cities the arrest records of juveniles spike in the summer. Kids need to be kept busy, and with most parents working and sometimes two jobs, who has time or energy to keep the kids busy doing creative things? Now even Vacation Bible School is no more than a week or a few days. What happened to two weeks? There should be more things to keep the kids busy and reading during the summer. Now most kids go back to school, and the teachers have to reteach reading skills for the first month to catch the students up.

I remember that during the summer, my sister Bobbie and some of the other girls in the neighborhood would do things to keep our reading levels up. We weren't trying. It was just that we were curious and in the habit of doing tons of homework that required reading, so we were bored to death otherwise. You really couldn't play in the heat during the day, but you could always read. My sister Bobbie and I would buy romance magazines and later novels with our little money and trade them with each other and other girls in the neighborhood. There were two other girls in the neighborhood, Addie and Alma—whom I would call slow learners—but they could read romance books. We always traded books with them. Bobbie and I would also go to the little library in our neighborhood and read also. When my mom got home from work, she would let us go to the library.

Bobbie and I read every book in that library and started in on the encyclopedias. Eventually, we would walk over to the library on the other side of town in another black neighborhood. They got a library after we had a library, or I am not sure where their library was until they opened the one close to my grandmother's house. I know that we always had a library on Crichton Hill as long as I can remember. It was a little one room white building. Its collection was extremely small. The librarian would often engage us in discussion (really neighborhood gossip). Jewelean was the librarian that I remember. I doubt if she had much training as a librarian. The library across town was a little bigger and had more books, but it was still lacking. Later, I would wonder how much more I would have learned if I'd grown up with a huge library with a librarian who actually led you in intelligent, stimulating discussion of topics—if I had actually had book discussions and met authors. I can only imagine that right now. My son has grown up with access to these types of things, and I doubt he has ever been in any one of those libraries when I didn't drag him to it. So growing up with it does not mean you will partake of it. What I do know is that all the activities I participated in over the summer helped me to be a better student in the fall when I returned to school.

I made a lot of friends in high school. I started to come out of my shell somewhat. Plus, by now we had a telephone, and I could call people. Most of the people I called were in my neighborhood just a house away at all times. Mostly, I called Melvyn Thomas or Ada Mae Morris because we were in classes together in high school and, of course, in elementary school too. Melvyn and I had even gone to kindergarten together. We went through all of our schooling together through college. I guess she is the only one I can say that about; I didn't realize it until now. She and I were very close. We would give each other birthday gifts. She would give me my favorite candy bar on my birthday, and I would give her favorite candy bar to her on her birthday. Her birthday was March 5, and mine was March 6. Most of the time, those were the only gifts we ever got for our birthdays. No one ever sang happy birthday to us on our birthdays; forget about a cake. Birthdays just came and went. I think someone would acknowledge that you were now one year older, and that was about it. Otherwise, you probably wouldn't even recognize your own birthday.

I didn't realize, until I was in my doctoral classes at Northern Illinois, how much Melvyn and my other friends from my neighborhood had meant to my education. All the girls in my neighborhood were conscientious about their education, and so was I. What if I had been in a neighborhood with girls who didn't' take their education seriously or was not smart. Melvyn, Ada Mae, and Pat were smart girls, and the neighborhood girls in the class ahead of me were smart as well. When it came to doing homework, we would help each other if we had a problem. We all did our homework. We didn't copy from each other. We only called each other to double-check our answers. My Aunt Natherine would help me sometimes as well, and so would my Aunt Katherine. They were my mother's sisters who were closest to me in age. My Aunt "Nat," as I call her, would help me most of the time. She was really smart and funny. She would always make me laugh. We are still friends to this day.

Nat got pregnant when she was in high school twice. Once during her sophomore year and again in her senior year, I believe. She didn't finish school with her class. She had to go to school at night. I think she got her GED or maybe even her high school diploma. As a matter of fact, she was in night school with my father. She used to tell me tales about how he used to sit in the back of the class. She said that he was kind of like their security guard because it would be mostly women in the class at night. My dad would walk them to their cars. I bet he was a riot when the teacher would ask him to go to the board. I think my dad was the first to attempt to get his GED; my mom would later join him. My father was always more helpful with our homework than my mother at first. She had trouble reading and doing mathematics. But after she started teaching Sunday school at church, she got much better at reading. She would read her Sunday school lessons and her Bible religiously. It was wonderful to see her confidence level grow the better she read. I guess my dad's did as well, but he always had us do his homework. He would have learned more if he had done it himself. Neither my mom nor my dad took the GED exam, and that is too bad. To me, when I graduated with my doctorate, they earned their GED because I was never ever supposed to get out of high school being black, poor, and growing up in rural America. It is a testament to my parents that I did.

Typing was one of the most beneficial classes that I took in high school. The skills I learned in Ms. Gunn's typing class are helping me right now as I write this. I am so glad that I had the attitude that I wanted to learn how to type and how to do it the right way. I took typing my senior year, I believe. My sister Bobbie was taking it at the same time. We both wanted to learn it correctly. I got very good at it, so much so that Ms. Gunn wanted me to go the LIALO rally in typing. I bet I would have come in first place too. But I told her no because I had already promised Coach Flentroy I would go for him in Current Events. I think Ms. Gunn tried to talk him into letting me go in typing, but he didn't flinch. I went to the LIALO rally in Current Events with Larry Houston. We became very close after studying for the competition. We won the regionals and came in fifth and sixth or something at state. We were still recognized at a special assembly by Mr. Hayes for our efforts.

Going to the state in Current Events was the first time I had been away from home, other than spending a week at my Aunt Velma's in the summer on our farm. I was scared to death. I think Webster had arranged for us to room with girls from Webster who were now attending Southern University. The LIALO Rally was always held at Southern University. Grambling College was the other black college and closest to us. The high schools in my area would go there for drama competitions. They also held drama competitions at Webster in our auditorium; maybe these were the regionals competition. We would be allowed to go during the day, and I super enjoyed the plays.

Grambling would present a play as well, and they were always the best even though they weren't in the competition. My friend Pearlie was never in the plays that I remember, but she always did the orations. She would win these competitions. I loved listening to her do her orations, I was always so proud of her. She did what I could never do. This talent would later help her in law school at UCLA. She was also a prolific writer. I have never read anything that she wrote because she wrote so small. Her lettering was so small that it was impossible for me to maintain my interest in what she was writing. She would sit next to me while we were taking an essay exam, and she would be writing forever. I would finish, and she would be still writing.

It's hard for me to remember my freshman year in high school. I do know that I took English under Ms. Winchester, Algebra I under

Mr. Gibson, and biology I under Mr. Tobin. I am not sure what else was on my plate, probably physical education because it seems we had it almost every year. I remember those horrible shorts we had to wear; they ballooned at the bottom, as if black women didn't have enough derriere. I wish I could find a picture of those shorts. It seemed they came back in style later in my life; they were similar to some hot pants that were worn. What did PE teach me? It taught me that you could enjoy any type of dance. We had to do a square dance, something we equated to white people's dancing, and we loved it. I've only square-danced a few times since then, and I always enjoy it. I think dancing or doing something physical is just my cup of tea; it never scares me. Even if I am horrible at it, I will try it. Whereas, getting up in front of people and talking still at seventy plus scares me, but thank heavens not quite as much anymore.

I remember when Pearlie and I were in some class—I believe it was civics, but I am not sure—and I think it was a class under Coach Flentroy. I know we had to argue Nixon vs. Kennedy. I think I was Nixon, and she was Kennedy. I know that was the beginning of our arguments against each other. We had some terrific arguments over the years, but they were always within reason. We never became mad at each other. We just were not afraid to express our opinions. I like to think that our arguing helped her in law school as well. We became very good friends. She was tall, and I was short. She was somewhat overweight, and I was petite. She had huge breasts, and I was a size 32B in high school. She had beautiful, well-shaped painted nails all the time, and my nails were misshapen and never painted. She was a prolific writer and reader, and I was and am a prolific reader. We both liked to talk, well, to each other. We kept each other on our toes. She never knew what I was going to say, and I never knew what she was going to say. Most of the time, it was just the opposite of each other. I think she enjoyed it; I was just frustrated.

My sophomore year is a blur. I am pretty sure I took French I under Ms. Winchester, English under Mrs. Frankie Mitchell, Algebra II under Mr. Gibson, biology II under Mr. Tobin, and choir (freshman, sophomore, and junior years) under Ms. Shackleford (who would later become Mrs. Holiday). I don't remember anything spectacular happening my sophomore year. I continued to travel with the football team to away games as a member of the pom-pom squad. Most of the time, I was by myself (no one from my neighborhood or my siblings was with me). I didn't know any of the girls or boys that traveled on the bus with us very well. Most of them were upperclassmen. I knew some of the band members, but they traveled on another bus. I would sit next to the bus driver, who most of the time was Mr. Buster Walker, my daily bus driver, so I was comfortable. I loved being away from home and seeing new faces. It was scary and exhilarating at the same time. We never spent the night away from home. I was glad about that I was not ready to spend the night away from home yet. I was a little slow with this unless it was a family member. My dad would always be there to pick me up no matter how late it got.

My dad taught me to count on a man. So if I had a boyfriend that I could not count on, he was not going to be my boyfriend for long. Men never kept me waiting—well, maybe one time—but they very seldom got a chance to do it again. My dad was very protective of his girls. I remember him saying that he wanted us to get a college education so we could take care of ourselves because a man wasn't promised to us and most of them weren't any good anyway. I also remember that after I moved from 7251 South Shore Drive to 7363 South Shore Drive just down the street, Daddy took a bus all the way from our hometown, Minden, LA, by himself to visit me in Chicago. He really surprised me, so I asked him why did he do it, and he said, "Because I had to see where you lived and to know you were safe." His statement let me know that I was indeed loved. It was this and other small things that my parents did for me and my siblings that let us know that we were very much loved even though we never heard early on or ever the words "I love you" from them. After I became an adult, I would say it to them and they would repeat it to me, but I don't ever remember them taking the lead. It would have been nice to hear those words coming from my parents, then maybe I wouldn't have doubted them coming from other people, even my own husband.

My junior year is a blur as well. I must have taken geometry under Mr. Gibson, chemistry under Mrs. Johnson, world history under Ms. Walker, English literature under Mrs. Sims (who was married to the only black dentist in Minden; he pulled most of our teeth), and French II under Mrs. Malone (Ms. Winchester was now Mrs. Malone), and of course, choir under Mrs. Holiday (I think she was married by now).

I liked chemistry and did good in it, and I was on my way to getting an A in it until Mrs. Johnson decided that my sister Bobbie and I had cheated. Bobbie was taking some science class under her, and I was taking chemistry. Since she didn't get to all the chapters in the book that year, at the end of the year, she assigned us to do an outline of the rest of the chapters. It was ludicrous assignment, but at least it made you read some of the material in the chapters and maybe retain a small fraction to prepare you for college. It took me forever to outline those chapters. I remember being up late at night past my bedtime. My mom had to buy me additional paper that was not in our budget.

I was eating lunch one day in the cafeteria after handing in my assignment to Mrs. Johnson, and I saw her walking hurriedly toward me, saying, "Laura Rabb, I know you got your sister to help you write these outlines." I told her *no*, that I had done it all by myself and that my handwriting probably changed because I was up so late and tired. Bobbie told her she didn't do it, but she said the handwriting was too similar. Well, we were sisters, genetically linked. As a science teacher, she should have realized that we might have similar handwriting. We all have similar handwriting in my family. When I look at some of the letters my mom used to write to me, I can see mine and my siblings' handwritings as well. I don't have any of my dad's handwritings to compare it with. He very seldom wrote anything. I wish I did; I must have his signature somewhere, if only on my marriage license. Mrs. Johnson did not believe Bobbie nor me. I probably should have gotten my mom involved in it, but I didn't. Mrs. Johnson gave both of us Bs that year. If the grade had been lower, I probably would have gotten my mom and dad involved in it because I was not used to making Cs. I don't think I made a C in high school and only a few in the colleges I attended.

In my senior year, I remember taking finite mathematics (it should have been trigonometry under Mr. Knox, but he had left Webster and gone to teach at Southern University by this time; I'll always wonder what I was supposed to learn in trigonometry); civics under Coach Haynes; English under Mrs. Lillian Mitchell (by then, the best senior English teacher had become our school counselor; I remember crying over this fact and knew that it would haunt me for a long time—I knew I was not going to get what I needed under Mrs. Mitchell and Physics under Mrs. Musgrow). Now I don't know how I knew it (maybe from the other girls and boys in my neighborhood who took English under her, I don't know); I just didn't like the way she looked. She looked mean to me, just by the way she walked, and she could make you stop talking just with a look. She had a horrible shape, and she walked gapped legged. I don't think I ever saw a smile cross her face. I hate to say it, but she was a lousy English teacher. She was probably the worst teacher I had at Webster. She did more fussing than teaching. I took typing (under Ms. Gunn), and home economics (under Mrs. Duty and Mrs. Lewis) as well my senior year.

The typing class was taught to me by Ms. Gunn. Ms. Gunn was a very stern teacher; she did not play. I remember her saying that if we learned typing right it would be an asset for us forever or something like that, and she was not wrong. Of all the courses I took in high school, the typing class was the one that has come in handy all of my life. It saved me so much money over the years. It was advantageous because not only could I type, but because I followed Ms. Gunn advice and learned how to type correctly, I could type fast and accurate. I owe this to Ms. Gunn and what she said. I decided I was going to follow her lead every step of the way. I learned the home row keys, I practiced without looking at the keys, I practiced typing faster and faster. When I graduated from high school, I could type fifty-five words per minute. Ms. Gunn would time us at the end of every class period. I remember having to type a research paper with footnotes and bibliography. I learned the different styles of writing, APA and MPA style. I can't remember if we wrote a research paper in Ms. Mitchell's English class, but I do remember typing one in Ms. Gunn's class, and this would help me later. I think we did note cards in Ms. Mitchell's class, but we didn't even do that well.

One of my favorite teachers in high school was Coach Haynes. For some reason, we got along well. Unfortunately, he didn't get along well with my friend Jacqueline Bradford. He gave her—or, according to him, she earned—a C in his class. I remember meeting her in the hallway one day and her saying to me that she just couldn't get civics under Coach Haynes. I couldn't understand because the book was so simple to me. She could get finite math but couldn't get civics; it was perplexing to me. That C would haunt her for the rest of her life. She was the salutatorian for our class instead of the valedictorian because of that C. She hates Coach Haynes to this day because of that C.

From freshman year on, I think we all thought Robert Walker was going to be the valedictorian of our class. He always got As. Then he had a health issue or girl issue, and his grades started to slip. So it was a toss-up as to who would be the valedictorian. When it turned out to be my friend Ada Mae Morris. I think we were all shocked. She was smart in all of the classes. What she could do better than most of us was speak extemporaneously. Plus, she spoke English well. I hated to see Jacqueline hurt, but I was glad my neighbor Ada Mae was the valedictorian. I think if Jacqueline had come in second to Robert, it would not have been a big deal for her because that was always expected.

At my school, Webster High School, boys came in at the top most of the time in the classes, until my class. For some reason, in my year, it all of a sudden got to be sissified to be smart for boys. I remember talking to a friend Albert Moore one day and asking him why he was only making Cs now and why he had left the honors biology class. He told me that only sissies made As and Bs. I could not believe that had come out of his mouth. I had never heard that before. It would be the first and not the last time I would hear that ridiculous statement. *Sissy* at the time was a term used for homosexual people or gay people. Another term was *funny*.

At the time, I had only heard this term used with regard to one of our teachers, Mr. Knox, one of the math teachers. Mr. Knox was a very well-respected teacher at our school. If he was "gay," no one seemed to care; he was a good teacher. I know he was serious teacher. He never ever smiled. I would later take a math class under him at Southern University, and I found him to be an excellent teacher. If he was "gay," no one ostracized him in our community. That's how I remember gays being treated when I was growing up. But I guess you could say Mr. Knox was in the closet, if you want to call it that. I just think Mr. Knox was being Mr. Knox. Later, gay guys would start to dress differently, and then I think people started to treat them differently in my hometown. But to this day, I have not seen a man dressed in women's clothing or makeup in my hometown. I think some gay guys want to be women and dress as such, and others just want to be guys who have sex with guys and still dress like a guy because that is who they are.

In Chicago, I have seen it all, men dressed as women and women dressed as men. In my twenties, I wore an afro and dressed in pants and masculine shirt-like blouses, and I am sure I was mistaken as a man sometimes. Who cares? I was comfortable.

I remember my freshman year going to the baccalaureate exercises and Mr. Hayes (our principal) asking the top four students in the class to stand up and it was all boys. The audience clapped and cheered. I didn't know that this was unique. In all of my classes, there had always been smart boys and smart girls. However, after we entered high school, I did notice that some boys who had been smart in elementary school all of a sudden were not. I remember that my friend Albert had been in my honor's science class one day, and I think it was after our first quiz he was no longer in the class. When I finally got the chance to ask him what happened, why he had dropped out of the science class, he said that he didn't want to be smart, that smart boys were sissies. I thought that was stupid. He also started dressing differently. He always wore suits to school; now he was wearing jeans and T-shirts. So now why some smart boys were being led to be dumb boys just so they would not be called a sissy. That did not make sense to me. Why dumb down yourself for others? To me, at all times you should be you; and if that meant being smarter than others, so be it. I had one brother. I remember him making Cs in high school most of the time. I don't know if he heard this lunacy statement or not and was trying to live up to it. I do know that he grew out of it and later became a lawyer.

I remember the day we were all hanging around waiting to see how we would rank in the class. For some reason, I ranked fourth or fifth initially, and then it swapped for some reason. I just remember Ida Faye Allums coming up to me saying that she now ranked ahead of me. I didn't question it because I didn't see what the fuss was all about. I didn't know at the time that how you ranked was that important. I was in the top ten. I would later learn that put you on some type of pedestal to be able to say that. That was never my aim; I was just living up to my potential. I would later hear the sayings the "top 10 percent" or "cream of the crop." Now I know that means: you are probably pretty smart. Later, I would learn that book smarts do not always translate into common-sense smarts.

Mrs. Lillian Mitchell was my homeroom teacher as well. For some reason, I was brave enough to run for homeroom class president at the urging of my friend Pearlie. I think she ran for class secretary. I wanted to run because I thought I could make the year more fun. Our classes in the past never did anything fun during intramural time. During my presidency, I remember playing in an intramural basketball game and a nighttime touch football game. We even put on a play that Pearlie Jean wrote, even though she doesn't remember it. I only remember one of my lines, and it was, "I didn't ask to be born, did I?" How can she forget that line? I doubt if she hadn't written the play, I would have played the lead. We had to perform the play before an audience, and I spoke. I figured out that I spoke because I had practiced. That gave me a clue to how I could speak publicly in the future. It is important that you be able to speak before a large crowd extemporaneously too; I avoided this type of speaking for years. I even avoided asking questions in class for the longest time because of the problem. At first, it was just being plain scared to hear my own voice, and later it was being afraid of my poor English and how I would sound. This wasn't the problem initially because I sounded like everyone else in high school. We all were from the south and poor, so standard English was not expected because we had our own version I would later come to learn as ebonics or black English. When everyone else sound like you (even the teachers) and never correct you because they are accustomed to poor English, you don't realize how poorly you communicate.

Like I said earlier, Mrs. June Turner was now our high school counselor. As a senior, she helped me with my college and financial aid applications. She was my schools first counselor, so I don't know who helped the kids prior to that, probably Mr. Hayes or different teachers. My financial aid application came back. It was sent back to me by my neighbor Mr. Musgrow. He was now the financial aid director at Southern University. I applied to Southern because it was near my home and in the state, but not too near, like Grambling College. I wanted to get as far away as I possibly could from my family. I loved my family, but with ten people in a two-bedroom house, it had become claustrophobic. At the time, it seemed Grambling and Southern were my only options. African Americans were not yet going to Louisiana State University, the major white university in my state, or any other white university in my state or in the South. Integration was just getting started in 1965.

My senior year was probably my most fun year in high school and the worst. I had to run for Ms. Webster because I had a B average. I hated it with a passion. Good I did not know that until it was too late because I probably would have made a few Cs on purpose. Mr. Hayes did not want being Ms. Webster to be just a beauty contest. He wanted Ms. Webster to be intelligent as well. I can understand that, but you should still have a choice. If you want to run, I begged him to let me out of it. He said no. So I ran, even though I thought I was the ugliest contestant of them all. I had to give a speech before the whole school. This was probably the reason I didn't want to run (my fear of public speaking). My mom bought me a cute dress that I loved to wear the day I gave the speech.

When I gave my speech, the bell rang. I just kept going. When the bell finished, I was finished. I looked at the faces of my audience, and I couldn't help but think they were all saying, "Saved by the bell." That poor kid. I got two votes, I think, I doubt if I voted for myself. Etolia Rowe, a friend, decided she would be my campaign manager.

I think she made posters for me. I was so horrified I don't remember them. I love her to this day for her efforts though. To me, she would have made a better Ms. Webster. She was pretty and didn't even know it. I remember her coming back to one of our reunions, and she was beautiful. I think at some point in time she must have realized that, but I lost track of her after high school, so I don't know if she ever really did.

In high school, she played basketball, so I think everyone thought she was a tomboy and she was. In junior high school, I remember she brought her lunch in syrup buckets, and she smelled like her clothes had been washed in the black washing pot. I knew the smell because our clothes smelled like that as well. We lived in the city, so we had more access to water and could rinse our clothes until they smelled good. Etolia evidently had well or springwater and couldn't or didn't wash her clothes to rinse over and over. Plus, her family evidently could not afford lunch money, and she had to bring her lunch. I think some kids used to tease her, and she never got over it.

My junior year was probably my worst year to this point because it was the first year that I crossed a teacher. Unfortunately, it happened with the teacher I most respected and patterned myself after over the years: my mathematics teacher, Mr. Gibson. Mr. Gibson had given us an assignment of rewriting all of our work for the year in ink and putting it in a notebook. I did as he said. My friend Ada Mae called me the night before we were to hand in the assignment and asked me what we were supposed to do. She hadn't gotten started. The next day, she turned in her assignment with some of it not in ink and didn't have all of the assignments. She got an A, and I got a B. I didn't understand it, so I told Mr. Gibson that he was a dirty man. He asked me, "What did you say?" and I was so mad that I repeated it. He stopped the class and went and got my homeroom teacher, Mrs. Musgrow. She asked me what I said, and I told her without remorse. I was still mad.

Now Mr. Gibson and Mrs. Musgrow were upset, but I was not backing down because I knew I had followed his instructions, and Ada didn't. I thought he was giving her an A because he liked her. All the teachers liked Ada, it seemed. She would later become our valedictorian. I sometimes thought they decided to give it to her because she spoke so well. When I got home, Mrs. Musgrow or Mr. Gibson called my mom and told her what had happened. My mom made me apologize to Mr. Gibson. At the time, I couldn't understand what all the fuss was about because when I said he was a dirty man, I was only thinking he was wrong in giving Ada an A and me a B. I wouldn't have complained if he had given me the A that I deserved. Now I know that "dirty old man" is synonymous to "lecherous old coot" or someone who flirted with young girls for sex.

I didn't use bad or curse words throughout my high school days. They were not spoken in my house, church, neighborhood, etc., and I seldom heard curse words anywhere. I didn't even know how to spell the word *shit* when I went to college. I learned how to curse in college when playing cards. The girls would often curse while playing cards. I picked up the habit—so much so that early on, the only time I would curse was when I was playing cards. I stopped that habit when I was in graduate school playing cards with some guys and cursed after winning a game. I must have said something like, "Take that, motherfuckers" or something. One of the guys—I believe his name was Leonard—stopped the game and took me aside. He told me that it was not ladylike to curse like that, especially when playing cards with men; they could get the wrong impression. Needless to say, to this day, I don't curse while playing cards, especially when playing with men. After that day, I tried to limit my cursing; it had not become a habit anyway except when playing cards. When I listen to young ladies cursing on the streets now, I can understand exactly what Leonard meant.

I get upset when I hear men cursing and get as far away as possible because I always think they are going to fight or something. My father never cursed around the house or raised his voice often. My mother never cursed or raised her voice often either. The houses in our neighborhood had thin walls, so if you talked loudly, someone could hear you. My mom and dad were always concerned about not disturbing the neighbors. When I was in college, I came across two tall, big guys cursing at one another; they looked like football players. I thought they were going to fight. I walked passed them hurriedly and looked back, and I realized that they were talking normally to one another. Talking loud and cursing was normal for them. I couldn't believe it. I started to realize that some men talked to one another that way when they were not in the presence of ladies. This was not the norm in my dorm; I seldom heard cursing unless it was at the card table.

My friends and I did pick up another bad habit after the "Civil Rights Movement." We started to call each other *mon nigero* or *mon nigger*. We knew by now that it was taboo to use the word *nigger*, that it had negative connotations and a word that white people had created and used to demean us as black people. I guess we thought we were giving the word some class. There is no way to class up the word *nigger*. Sometimes we also called one another "whore" and "prostitute." We would pass one another on the campus and say, "Hey, ho" and respond with, "Hey, ho," whereas nine times out of ten both, persons saying it were virgins. I know in my case, I *was*. I am so glad we did not popularize the word *bitch* like they do now. I cringe every time I hear it.

I was not accustomed to the word *nigger* being used in my presence either. The only time I remember my mom using it was when I was grown (or at least thought I was; I had turned twenty-one) and was arguing my point against her. As a matter of fact, I think I told her that I was not going to church, and she was saying that I was. I remember her reaching for me and I ran (for the first time), and she said, "I'll kill you nigger." I think she was shocked because I never ran from her before. I think she got out of breath and stopped running after me. She proceeded to get the other kids ready and left for church without me. I wanted to go to a James Brown concert in Shreveport, Louisiana, about thirty miles from our house, and I knew if we went to church (fifty miles from our house) that we probably would not make it back. There was a guy that had promised to take me to the concert. I didn't know him that well, but I wanted to go to that concert for one reason, to hear James Brown sing "Say It Loud, I'm Black & I'm Proud," my favorite song of all time. That song changed my life—well, that song and the "Black Power Movement" or the "Civil Rights Movement." Until then, I had felt like being a dark-skinned black woman was disadvantageous. I felt that I would never get a man and that I was ugly. After that song came out, I started to wear my black skin like a badge of honor. I was indeed black and proud. I had nothing to be ashamed of being dark-skinned. If I didn't know that, no one else would. It was as if a weight had been lifted off my shoulders, and now I could let my light shine. We started saying things like "blacker the berry, sweeter the juice." Prior to that time, I only heard black being used in a derogatory manner, like, "You so black you shining," or "You so black I could only see your eyes coming." I had never heard the words *beautiful* or *cute* used to describe an extremely dark skinned person. My husband even told me that his mother had told him not to bring a black girl to her house. Well, after we got married, she started to love my black draws (okay, I reverted to ebonics, not sure how to spell the word that we used when referring to panties), but somehow black panties doesn't sound as derogatory. I always treated her with respect and dignity, and she appreciated it. Before I forget, let me add that the guy I had the date with that my mom and I got in the fight over stood me up. I decided I deserved that—you should never ever fight with your mom.

After reading the book *Cane River* by Lalita Tademy, I came to understand why being black became equated with being at the bottom of everything. In the book, if you were white or almost white, you got what was good in life. And if you were black, you got the crumbs. Black women who had babies by white men, and if they were-light skinned or even could pass as white, used them to do things that their dark-skinned kids couldn't do, like buy a house or go places (passing as white) to get goods for the family. Having a white-black (mulatto child) improved your status in the neighborhood somewhat. That is ironic because most of the women who had black children were raped, and that is how they got pregnant. The white men used the women for their own needs. There was no love. No love most of the time, I believe, now that some of the black women and white men did love each other, an unforbidden love in the South at the time. From what I understand, some of the white men even sent their black-white children to college or even endowed money to black colleges for the purpose of educating their black-white children.

When I was in high school, so was my aunt Natherine. She was one grade ahead of me. My freshman year, I was a little scared, so I was happy she was there. I knew most of the kids, so I wasn't that scared. Like I said earlier, I think it was my sophomore and her junior year that she told me that she was pregnant and would be dropping out of school to have the baby. She came back after she had the baby, but then she got pregnant again. This time, she didn't come back to school; she had to go to night school. I believe Mr. Hayes refused to allow her back. I can't remember the policy, but I do know there were never any big-belly pregnant teens in our classes the way there is nowadays.

I remember at one school here in Chicago, the homecoming queen was pregnant. I think the kids elected her queen as a joke, but it wasn't funny. This young lady was having a baby that she had no way of taking care of while she was in high school, and she was placing an extra burden upon her family and placing her baby in a precarious position before it is even born. My aunt Natherine's life turned out okay, but she had problems that might have been avoided if she had waited, like getting a divorce and her son going to jail. There's nothing saying these things would not have happened anyway if she had continued her education and gone to college, but the chances are less. She was smart and popular in high school and ran with the popular kids. She was a cheerleader. I believe that is why I wanted to be one. She was lighter-skinned than me, and for some reason, I always thought that was why she was accepted more than me. And besides she, lived on the right side of the railroad tracks. At the time, though, I didn't know there was a right or wrong side of the tracks or that people made a difference in which side you lived.

I have to mention the baseball games that the black men used to have in my hometown on the weekend. I really don't know how organized they were, but I do remember how serious they were. My uncles used to play. My uncle Little Johnny was very good at it; he played baseball on our high school team. He had graduated when I got to high school, but every once in a while, they would allow us at J. A. Phillips to go to a game, and I caught one or two of his games. You had to walk a long ways from school to get to the baseball field.

We all would crowd the roads headed to games; we would have so much fun that we didn't mind the walk.

Recently, I found out that not only did the black men play baseball in my hometown; some of them were a part of a minor Negro League professional team. I had heard about the Negro Baseball League, but I never knew that they had a minor league farm system like the white teams. I definitely didn't know that there was a minor league team in my hometown. I found this out the summer of 2015, the year my class celebrated its fifty-year reunion. My aunt (by marriage) and my uncle just mentioned it while my sisters and I were visiting them after my reunion. I noticed a picture of black men in baseball uniforms, and my aunt said that it was her dad's team, that he was part owner of minor league Negro League team that was located in Minden. Whenever, I talk about this, people of my generation are surprised to hear that we had a minor league Negro baseball team in our hometown. Why hadn't we heard of this? This is another mystery. I think not talking about things we should be proud of and can serve as a role model for other African Americans is a learned behavior of African Americans. I am not sure if it's from our believing that what takes place in our community is and always will be second or beneath the status of what takes place in the white neighborhood, so why brag on it? Or is it something deeper, our being taught in church that it is a sin to "brag," that "humility" is a virtue. My uncle Sam played on his "wife's" father's team, which was how they met. Neither of them finished high school. My aunt said she got pregnant, or like she put it, it was because of "him." I just took that to mean that he got her pregnant, and they had to get married.

I remember when they got married. My grandmother refused to go to the wedding. I remember going to the house where they got married. I am not sure if I walked down there with my grandmother or not. I know she did not want him to marry Christine. I could not figure out why. She probably knew Christine was pregnant. However, she didn't ever seem to want her sons to get married. At the time, I thought she figured no girl was good enough for her boys; now I am not sure why. I know Uncle JD told me that Christine had always thought her family was better than ours and that marrying Uncle

Sam was marrying down to her. In other words, she was out of our league. I know she never did seem comfortable in our family; she was never very sociable. Of late, she seems to be more sociable, more talkative, and shares more. That is how I came to know her husband (my uncle) was a part of her father's Negro League, minor team. She didn't think it was a big deal, and evidently, my uncle didn't either; at least that was the way it seemed. Whereas inside, I am going, *What? We had a minor league Negro League team in our hometown at some point?* I was screaming inside; this was a huge deal to me. Young black boys, and girls for that matter, need to know this. They need to know of the potential, even though you come from a small town, that life exists outside of the walls of this town, which may be more lucrative for them and their families. We missed out on this when we were not fed this information.

Little Johnny was my favorite among my mother's brothers. I was surprised when he left for the army and didn't return home. My uncle Jimmy had left early on and didn't return home for years, and so did Little Johnny. Uncle Jimmy settled in California, and Uncle Little Johnny settled in Texas. They both had children, but we are not close to any of them because they lived so far away and seldom visited. To be honest, we didn't know they existed. My Uncle Jimmy was a rolling stone like the "Temptation" song. He had so many children, and none of them looked like him, so he just had to take the word of the young ladies. He had a child in my hometown, I guess, before he went into the service. The child didn't look like him, so I think my family for the longest didn't think he was his child. The child is still estranged from our family. We have invited him to family events, but he never comes. I think my mom and my aunt Elnora were the only ones that acknowledged the child. We would visit his family when he was little, and he would visit us. They didn't live to far from our home. He lived with his mother, grandmother, and aunt surrounded by love, so he grew to be, I believe, an excellent father himself and has a very nice life.

Walking was something that we did a lot in my hometown. When we were in high school, often my friends and I would walk wherever we wanted to go (i.e., to school, downtown, visiting friends, running errands). This was just the mode of transportation for us. Now I realize how healthy that was for us at the time. However, other than being afraid of white people, we weren't afraid to walk on the fringes of their neighborhoods normally. We would sometimes get heckled or called a derogatory name by white people passing us in their cars, but other than that, we enjoyed walking. On Sundays, my friends Melvyn, Pat, Hazel, and later Ada Mae would walk to the Dairy Queen to get ice cream and walk back home. We would walk slowly enjoying each other's company. We had to pass some homes of white people to get to the Dairy Queen. I am sure we would walk a little faster passing their homes. We never walked for exercise, which we were getting; we did it to socialize.

Picking berries and plums was another form of exercise we got that we didn't consider as exercise. During the late spring and summer months, we would pick berries and plums and sell them to our neighbors. What we couldn't sell, we would eat. The berry patches and plum orchards would be quite a distance from our homes, so we would have to walk. It seemed at times that every kid in the neighborhood would go with us to pick berries and plums. Somehow we coordinated our times. We would keep track of the plums and berries until they were ripened. Sometimes the kids would pick them before they were ripened, and we wouldn't have nothing to pick. Now developments have taken over the areas where we used to pick berries and plums, but you can still find some.

My first novel that wasn't a harlequin romance novel that I read through and through was *David Copperfield*. I think I was a junior year in school, and it was in Mrs. Sims's English class. I can't remember what we did other than read the book. I really enjoyed the book. I think I would have enjoyed it more if Mrs. Sims had actively engaged us in discussing our books, but most of the time, she slept in class. She was quite old by now and would sleep through class. Of course, we were not going to disturb her. I think we read a little Shakespeare in her class, but again, limited amount of discussion. I don't remember having to memorize or write a poem. Like I said earlier, there were no honors English classes at Webster High School, unless I didn't qualify. That and economics were subjects that I could have used more depth as evident by my grades in college. The one thing in English that I learned how to do was to diagram a sentence. Diagraming sentences was a very useful tool. I am very good at sentence structure and paragraph writing; it is composition and literature that I was sorely lacking in. I am better at composition, which I hope you can see, but I am still sorely lacking in literature.

It didn't help that most of my English teachers in college were white. I didn't understand most of what they said. I thought they were speaking a foreign language most of the time. They spoke so fast to me. When I came North, people said I spoke fast. Now I know I spoke a foreign language to them: Southern ebonics. I had been taught not to look at white people; now I am supposed to see them standing in front of the classroom. Coming from a segregated background, seeing white folks was new to me. Other than television, I had seldom heard them speak in person. Plus, now we are in the Civil Rights Movement heydays, and white people were not to be trusted. I am just lucky we only had two English courses that were required for my major, and I got Cs in both classes. I think I earned the Cs because I did try.

I don't remember getting teased that much in school. I know if I did get teased that I would have had a smart come back or simply ignored the stupid person. People would often make fun of my religion in front of me; I don't think they all knew what religion I was. Most of the kids were either Baptist or Methodist. Most probably thought I was Baptist since I went to New Light Baptist Church in my neighborhood most of my early years. But after we left New Light, I became a member of Spring Lake Church of God in Christ, what everyone called a sanctified church or holy-roller church. They called us holy rollers because we would roll around the floor when we would be in the spirit. We also clapped our hands, and the congregation sang a lot at our church. This didn't happen at other churches as often. I just ignored what people said and learned to love my church and its members.

Spring Lake was located back in the woods. For some reason, I loved that about it. It spelled freedom to me. At night, we would be in the church, and the only lights you would see would be ours. It was magical. I loved it during the summers, when we would have a barbeque at the church. We would drink soft drinks and eat barbeque. Brother Doc was always behind the stands selling candy, chips, barbeque, etc. He seldom came into the church. It seems the only time I saw him at church was during the revival or when we had barbeques. He was married to Sister Leana. She was a mainstay at the church. They lived in Homer, Louisiana. Our church address is Homer, but it was closer to Athens, Louisiana, the town I spent my first five and a half years.

My sister Bobbie doesn't remember, but I remember that it was to one of the barbeques at the church that my mom allowed us to wear pedal pushers. I think Bobbie had a pink outfit, and I had a blue or vice versa. Pedal pushers were pants, and us girls weren't allowed to wear pants in our church.

As a matter of fact, girls couldn't wear pants to Webster High School. If it was cold, we wore leotards to cover our legs or just froze and had ashy legs. At the time, Louisiana was not that cold, so we just bore the ashy legs and the wet (it rained all the time) weather with long socks if we had them. I think we didn't even wear pants when we picked cotton. That had to be rough on our little legs with the sharp-edged cotton stalks.

Mr. Musgrow, my neighbor, helped all the Webster graduates complete their application properly so they could get financial aid for college. At the time, we all got what was called National Defense loans that we would have to pay back. We did not have federal grants (that you did not have to pay back) at the time. (At least we didn't know about them, I found out later they did have them, but Southern gave them out like scholarships, I believe). Having to pay the money back later gave me extra impetus not to fail. Plus, it was said that if you made below a C, you could lose the loan. I had no other way to college, so I couldn't make below a C. I studied very hard in college.

My senior year ended with the prom, senior night, the commencement exercises, and the baccalaureate exercises. The whole town enjoyed the festivities. I should say the entire black community enjoyed the festivities at Webster. Your family didn't just come to the graduation exercises; it was the whole town. You knew almost everyone in the town. Football games, basketball games, and baseball games were treated in a similar way. Friday night, football games were enjoyed by everyone, even if you didn't have a child in school or on the field. Our social lives, at least I thought at the time, were built around church, home, and school.

The prom was a tumultuous event for me. I had gone to the junior senior prom without a date, and here I was again without a date again for the prom for my senior year. I had hoped some guy would take pity on me and invite me. My sister Bobbie was a junior at the time, so she was going as well. My mom bought us similar gowns. I remember mine was either purple, and hers was pink or vice versa. I know we had can cans under them. I never thought of not going to the prom, but I felt humiliated not to have a date. I don't know why it was such a big deal, but it was for me. I thought about the devastation of not having a date and not dancing one dance at the prom for years. So much so that when the class above mine, the 1964 class, decided to have as their theme, "Revisiting Our Prom," for their twentieth year reunion and invited my class, I decided to go and this time be the belle of the ball.

I knew I would have a date this time, my husband. I rented a limousine to take me and my "date" to all the events. We even went to the picnic in the limo since we had it for four hours; I had to think of something to do with it. We used it to take my nieces and nephews for a ride around the neighborhood. When I told someone about my renting the limo and going to the picnic, she said, "They must have thought you were country." That made me think about just what my friends thought when my husband and I drove up in a limo; I really doubt if they thought I was country, I think they thought I was showing off. Yes, I was showing off, and what's wrong with that, if that is what makes you happy. I bought a new dress for the prom that night, and I felt like the belle of the ball. One of my girlfriends called me early the next day at my mom's house and told me that everybody was talking about the dress that I wore and how pretty it was. I felt like I had erased the picture of that girl who felt awful those many, many years ago of going to her senior prom dateless after having been dropped off by her dad.

My dad had driven me to my junior prom, and then my sister Bobbie and I to our prom (my senior year). To tell how desperate I was to have someone to drive me to the prom besides my dad, I was willing to share a date. My friend Druzella was supposed to go with our classmate Ronnie Sweeney, her next-door neighbor. I think his mom, Mrs. Sweeney (a music teacher), was making him take her. Somehow it was decided that I could go with them. Ronnie was an epileptic and subject to seizures. We had witnessed him having several seizures at school. He was a very big guy, kind of the life-of-the-party type of guy. I had nightmares about him having seizures while driving us to the prom. But in order to not go by myself. I was willing to risk it. The night of the prom, even though Ronnie lived right next door to Druzella, he disappeared. We had no ride to the prom. My dad, as I said, eventually took Bobbie and me, but I don't think Druzella even came to the prom at all.

I remember when my sister Bobbie and I got to the prom, there were a lot of guys hanging around the door. I walked in with several guys. I remember asking one of them (I think it was John Wesley Thomas) why they didn't ask a girl to the dance, and he said, "*We* didn't have transportation." It had never dawned on me that most of the guys would not have transportation, not even a family car (many families didn't have cars at the time; just couldn't afford them). My family had always had a car, and sometimes two cars, so did most of the families in my neighborhood. Our town didn't have a bus system, but it did have a few cabs. Mostly everyone walked everywhere they wanted to go in my hometown or bum a ride with a friend, relative, or neighbor. I can imagine how desperate those young men must have felt with their families not having a car, or maybe they didn't have a driving license yet. I wonder if they spent years feeling unloved and uncared for because they didn't have a date for the prom or thought they were too poor to ask a girl to the prom. Rental cars weren't in vogue back then. Whatever the case, it made me feel a little better entering the gym all decorated with a bunch of guys and not just by myself, for everyone to stare at that poor, lonesome, ugly girl no one cared to ask to the prom. I still didn't get the chance to dance or take a picture with anyone. I don't have a prom picture like a lot of people do. My sister Bobbie has a picture from her senior year. My mom told her (senior now) and my brother (a junior) to make sure they took a picture together.

When I received an invitation to the twentieth reunion for the Webster High School class of 1964, I was surprised to see that they were inviting our class, the class of 1965. I noticed in their program they were going to have a "prom theme" type of dance for their big event. I decided I had to go. I was married by then and had a ready-made date. I had noticed in Chicago that even kids who lived in the federal projects took limos to their proms, so I decided to rent a limo for the weekend of activities. I also bought a dress that I spent more on than any other dress I'd ever bought. It was probably my first designer dress, and it cost me $800. The dress was couture, and the salesperson said that I would not ever see anyone in that dress, and I never have. The dress is hanging up in my closet now. If I ever wore it again, I would have to lose about fifty pounds and have it restored. There is a little discoloration, but not much. I still love the deep purple color. Purple has always been my favorite color. I always gravitate to that color in the department stores, that and black. I gave black up because my husband complained that I wore it too much. When he complained, I took a look in my closet and realized that I hardly had any clothing that didn't have black coloring in it.

I think I was undergoing to mild form of depression and didn't know it. I heard or read somewhere that black people report that they suffer less depression. I think it covers us like a mask, and we really don't recognize it. When depression is so familiar, it becomes your norm, and you wear it like a dress or a pair of pants. As a matter of fact, to be without it feels naked, so you hustle to put it on again to feel normal. As I look back, my depression was not a deep depression, but I remember crying myself to sleep at night for one reason or another. I also remember finding ways to get over my depression and to bring light into my life by throwing parties, going to the movies, out to dinner or plays. I loved to dance, and I did that almost every opportunity I had. When I was in college, I went to every dance, with or without a date.

College was next for me after graduating high school. I chose Southern University because it was the farthest away from home. I had only considered two colleges, Southern or Grambling, like most of the kids in my graduating class. Segregation was still very much in operation then, so most African Americans in Louisiana would go to either Southern or Grambling. Some in 1965 ventured out to apply to a few other colleges and did get accepted, but it was rare. Grambling and Southern, I don't believe, had to recruit much in state back then; now they do. The black kids graduating in my hometown now have more options due to integration.

Going to college had always been on my radar, even from elementary school. I had two aunts who went to college, one who graduated. My Aunt Velma had gone to Grambling but had to drop out her sophomore year because her dad died. Her mom had died I believe in child birth. So when her dad died, being the oldest and only female, she had to come home and take over the running of the house. She never did go back to college. My teachers always talked about college as well. Most of them had gone to college at Southern or Grambling.

Most of our commencement and baccalaureate program speakers were either from Southern or Grambling. Like I said, these were community events, so I went to them even if I didn't know anyone in the graduating class. So I heard lots of speakers. At my own graduation, Dr. Felton G. Clark, the president of Southern University, was our commencement speaker (at least I thought so, until my fiftieth reunion, when Floristene told me that our speaker did not show up). Dr. Clark may have spoken the previous year, and all I know is that I thought he was a great speaker. I believe he was known around the state as a "great orator," and rightfully so. I attended most of the commencement exercises; it was a part of the social life of our community. All of the commencement exercises were on the football field, and I loved it because I felt I could breathe; my anxiety did not surface like it normally did in crowds. I was very impressed by Dr. Clark as I was by most of the speakers from Southern and Grambling. For some reason, I held on to every encouraging word, and there were many. Some of the speeches were too long, but I didn't care. Growing up poor and afraid of life, I needed the encouragement. I had never spent much time away from home and my parents, except for one week a year at my Aunt Velma's with my cousins. I was scared to death of going away to college, but excited nevertheless. I knew the alternative was to continue sleeping in the bed with two other people in a room with seven people. That was not an attractive option for me. Going away to college to escape the crowded conditions of my home was a more attractive option at the time.

I remember the day I decided I was definitely going to college. I was in my father's cotton fields, and the sun was beating down over my head with no shade in sight. I started thinking about the slaves and how they must have felt. I could see them getting up early in the morning and toiling all day in the hot sun, picking or chopping cotton with no relief in sight. I could see someone bringing them a drink of water like my younger sisters had done for us. If we got overheated, we could find shade and sit down for a while. I was pretty sure the slaves didn't have this option. I envisioned them having someone on a horse with a whip, ready to pounce if they didn't give a 110 percent for no wages and very little food. I thought I would die in that hot sun; it was unbearable. I decided that I would go to college because of the slaves and my legacy. They had endured so much so that I could have a better life. I didn't want to let them down. I wanted to make something of myself so their toils in the hot sun would not be in vain. I felt so weak in that sunlight, but I felt what strength it must have taken for the slaves to endure in order for me to be here. How dare I let them down—they sacrificed so much.

We celebrated our fiftieth year Webster High School Class Reunion in 2015. Fifty years seem to have passed so fast. I did a lot of living, learning, growing, and regressing in those fifty years. When you are in high school, you can't even imagine fifty years from then. Sometimes I wish I could do it all over again, but differently. But in life, there are no do-overs, except in the movies. Now, it is fifty-five years, and some who were with us at our fiftieth have passed on, even my closest friend Melvyn. When I heard of her passing, I struggled, but it is imperative that you keep the hope train moving because you are not in charge of the schedule—God is!

Chapter 6

COLLEGE YEARS

Southern University (1965–1969)

Freshman Year

Going to college was one of the major turning points in my life. The summer before I left for college was hectic and exciting. I had taken sewing my senior year of high school, to the chagrin of my high school principal. I think he envisioned more for me than cooking and sewing, and at the time, I didn't. Because of the sewing classes, I had the confidence to make most of my outfits for college. I was so proud of myself. Most of the clothes were made from cheap fabric, so they didn't last long, but they got me through my freshman year of college. I was able to buy a few pieces of clothing because I worked at the Coffee Cup restaurant where my mom was still working. I probably sold berries, plums, worms, whatever—I was a hustler. I didn't know it, but I was.

The night I left for college, so did Melvyn and Ada (my neighbors), and so did many of my classmates from Webster. Melvyn had been a classmate since kindergarten and Ada since elementary school. I felt right at home with them by my side. Also leaving that night from across town were Pearlie Jean and Jacqueline Bradford (my best friends), Larry Houston, Vincent Wilson, Ida Faye Allums, Moses

Brown, Joyce Ivory, and Lee Venice Bell—all fellow graduates from Webster. We were all taking the train to Southern University in Baton Rouge, Louisiana—a historical black univeristy.

I remember, when we got ready to load the car, that I had expected my siblings to go with us. I think the only ones that could go were Bobbie and my brother, David, because the car was filled with our neighbors Mrs. Lettie and Sister Grider. Evidently, my mom had told them they could accompany us to the train station. I was puzzled as to why, but for some reason after I got over the shock of my siblings not being able to go, I felt loved. I felt they cared about me and were wishing me well. Later, they would send their kids to Southern as well and make that same trip to the train station. That is, if the train was still running because it did stop, and kids then had to take the bus or their parents had to drive them down. I didn't know one kid who drove their own car at that time.

Other than the surprise of my neighbors going to the train station with me, the one thing I remember from that night was something my brother said. He was looking at my friend Pearlie Jean mom's car, and he said, "Miss Pearl got may-pop tires." I asked him what he meant, and he said, "May pop any minute." I laughed so hard at his comment that it soothed the evening for me, and I wasn't as scared any more. The area we had to wait for the train was dark and dingy; everyone sat in their cars. I guess some had their headlights on to brighten the area. There must have been some type of light, but I don't remember it. I knew I was going to miss my family terribly. What I didn't know was that life as it had been would never be the same again for me. Life in Minden would not be the same for me ever again.

My life was about to change. I had never been away from home for more than a week, so this was a big change for me. It was a change I was ready for, though. After being in a two bedroom house with ten people for almost thirteen years, you need a change. I had already chosen my roommate during the summer orientation for freshmen. Euredell Williams and I ended up rooming together in Thomas Hall. Thomas Hall was one of three dorms in what was called the Triangle at the time. It was three dorms that were fairly new, and all three dorms housed freshmen. I loved the design of the Triangle, especially the individual suites. When you entered the suites, you entered the hallway. There were four dorm rooms to a suite. The bathrooms were straight ahead and two bedrooms on the two sides. Each side had a shower and a sink with a mirror on it. We could use either side if one side was busy. Seldom was there anyone in the shower when I needed to use one.

We had a live-in adult supervisor and a resident hall manager for each of the three dorms. I remember my friend from Webster Etolia Rowe's sister was the hall manager for Thomas Hall. Her name was Rosie Rowe. It gave me a sense of security knowing the hall manager. We also had a maid or housekeeper. She would sweep the suites every day, even take the trash out of our rooms. She would even make the beds if we had gone to get the linen. Once or twice a week, we could get fresh linen. All this help made me feel extraspecial. It was a very good introduction to college for a freshmen student who never had her own bed before.

I had stayed on the campus once before when I attended the LIALO rally my senior year. Larry Houston and I were participating in the Current Events category. We had studied all year. We were chosen by Coach Flintroy to represent the school. We had placed first and second in the regionals; that's why we got the opportunity to go to state. The state contest was always held at Southern University. This was an excellent idea because it gave kids the opportunity to be on a college campus and to get a taste of dorm life before actually going to college. I can't remember how well or how poor we placed in the state, but I do know that we didn't come in first or second. Mr. Hayes still recognized us at the next auditorium program, and I felt so honored.

Larry had been a friend of mine for a long time. At some point in time, he came to live with his aunt and uncle who lived on Crichton Hill. He had always lived with his grandfather on Peach Street across town. He lived on the same street as my grandparents. His aunt had made some innuendo about Larry and I being girl-friend and boyfriend once, and I told her that we were just friends. Larry was someone I could always talk to. He was too skinny to be my boyfriend at the time; at least that's what I thought. Not that I had a boyfriend. I just never saw him in that light. He also went to Southern University. We would eat almost every meal together, along with my friends Pearlie Jean and Ada Green.

I remember one day after he had crossed over the Omega Psi Phi line, he came to the cafeteria at Southern to eat with us, and he started using profane language. I couldn't believe it. He had never talked that way, and he had always been respectful. He had been raised by a minister. Larry's grandfather was a minister. I went off and asked him what had gotten into him and that I was going to tell his grandfather, like I even knew his grandfather. I just didn't appreciate being in the company of men who cursed. It always scared me to death when men cursed for some reason. Neither my father nor any of my uncles had ever used curse words in front of us. I didn't even know how to spell *shit* when I went to college. The girls in the dorms cursed some, especially while playing cards. I had even learned how to say a few curse words. But I still had problems when I heard men cursing, and I am not sure why.

I came across two huge football players cursing at each other one day while I was crossing campus. I thought they were angry with each other, and I could imagine two huge dinosaurs fighting each other. However, as I walked past them, I realized they were just talking to each other. I thought that was a strange way to talk to each other. It had scared me to death. I had hurried past them. This feeling I had about men cursing still exists with me today.

Minnie B. Anderson from my hometown was the resident hall manager for Baranco Hall, which was a part of the triangle. She had graduated from Webster High School the year before I did. Plus, she stayed only a few blocks from me on Crichton Hill. She was one of five girls that I considered older and wiser in my neighborhood. Bobbie Nell Musgrow, Gloria Bell, Mary Frances McClendon, and Ernestine Edwards were all in the class ahead of me. They also went to New Light Baptist Church, so I had gotten to know them while I was participating in the Easter programs and Vacation Bible School at the church. It seemed I was always following in their footsteps. Minnie B's room was just around the corner from mine, even though

I was in Thomas Hall. You could easily go from one hall to the other in the Triangle because all three were connected. Most of the freshman stayed in the Triangle, so all of my friends from Webster were never far away from me. Along with Minnie B, my homegirls Bobbie Nell and Gloria Bell also went to Southern. Having them all near me made me feel comfortable from day one at Southern.

The freshmen got to campus a week before the upperclassmen, so we were able to register without as much human traffic on campus. I couldn't believe how busy it got when the upperclassmen returned to campus. Even though the upperclassmen were not on campus yet, there were still so many lines. I already had a roommate and had been assigned a room, so that was one line I did not have to stand in. I just had to get the keys to my room.

I lived in Thomas Hall my freshmen year. Euredell Williams and I were assigned as roommates. I think we were assigned together because she was also majoring in a home economics program, which was clothing and textiles, and I was majoring in food and nutrition. She was from New Orleans. Initially, we did not hit it off. She seemed very into herself even though she had come from a family larger than mine, if I'm remembering correctly. Every night she had a bedtime ritual. She would take her shower, then lotion, and powder up. She even had moisturizer (I guess for her face). I would just take a shower and go to bed. I didn't understand why she did this every night. I saw her about thirty-four years after our graduation, and I was so surprised that she looked almost the same as she did from the day I had met her on Southern's campus. Her skin was radiant. Plus, the girl had the same hairstyle. I couldn't believe it. She really still looked like a teenager. My son was about thirteen at the time, and her kids were both out of high school. Yet Euredell had not gained an ounce as a result of her pregnancies; if anything, she had lost weight. To top that, she did not have a big stomach like I and a lot of women did after having babies. You would think after seeing her I would have developed a nighttime routine as well, but it would take me about thirty more years to do so and to figure out the importance. I was the type to go to bed after a night out with makeup on, which could be devastating to a person's face, I would learn later.

I loved living in Thomas Hall. I finally had a bed to myself. Thomas Hall was a part of three dorms that was called the Triangle. The other two dorms were Lang Hall and Baranco Hall. Our rooms were larger than the average-size college dorm room. We had beds that were larger than twin beds. I don't think they were full size, but definitely not twin size. We lived in a four room suite. There were eight girls in the suite, but only two to a room. Two of the rooms shared bathroom facilities, but you could use any of the facilities if yours was in use. I don't ever remember waiting to use the toilet or the shower. It was a nice arrangement. We also had a housekeeper. Our rooms were inspected by the resident hall manager I think twice a week. I know on Thursdays we got new linen. If we got the linen and put it on our bed, the housekeeper would make our beds for us. I believe she mopped and swept the floors as well. They kept the bathrooms cleaned. We had no television and no phones in our rooms. But I believe girls could bring radios and clocks. I didn't have either, but I believe Euredell did. She would wake me for class sometimes. My roommates, like my mom and dad before them, were my alarm clocks all throughout college.

One day, when I arrived back to my dorm room, I overheard Euredell say to her friends from New Orleans that I was from some little small country town up north. I thought she was being very nasty and discourteous. She and her friends were from the big city of New Orleans. She and I were majoring in home economics. I was in nutrition, and she was in clothing and textiles, so we had to take some classes together. By the middle of the school year, we were all friends. I would often go to dinner with her and her friends from New Orleans. By that time, Euredell had figured out that I might be country, but I was a smart country girl. She couldn't figure out how I could study so little and still make good grades. She was surprised when I made the freshman honor roll and participated in the honors program. My mom had come down to go to the program. Euredell did not make honors. One day she cornered me and asked me why I made such good grades. I told her that I'd had most of what we were studying in high school. She had a hard time with biology and chemistry and algebra courses. I did quite well in those courses because I liked them, and I'd had teachers in high school who had prepared me well.

One of my teachers Mr. Gibson had gone out of his way to purchase books for our Algebra II and finite math classes that he thought we were going to use in college. Over the summer months, he said that he was attending the University of Illinois at Urbana-Champaign. I didn't know he was taking courses for his doctorate that he eventually got. He was so smart. His wife was my sister Carrie's third grade teacher at Jerry A. Moore, I believe. Mr. Gibson was smart and nerdy, and his wife was outgoing and beautiful. I thought she was too much for him, but they made it. Mr. Gibson was my math teacher for all of my math classes.

Mr. Tobin was my biology teacher. I had two biology classes. All the kids loved Mr. Tobin because he seemed to have a large vocabulary and were often heard quoting poems. Mr. Tobin's science lab consisted of a couple of microscopes, plants, and few animals in formaldehyde. We didn't get the chance to dissect anything. I think Mr. Tobin dissected a frog while we watched. Mr. Tobin gave us a pretty sound foundation even with those limitations. Plus, I had chemistry and physics in high school. Again, with very limited laboratory experiences. So when I took labs at Southern, I always felt lacking. I was afraid of the animals we had to work with in all of my classes. I was majoring in nutrition, so I had a lot of science lab classes. I only did poorly in one laboratory, and that was because I couldn't understand the teacher because he had such a heavy accent. He was from Africa. I made a C in his class even though it was not that hard. I tried to stay away from instructors from foreign countries after that.

Southern was located in the southern part of Louisiana, a very Catholic section of Louisiana. During our freshman year, we had a lot of rules to follow. We had to attend vespers services (more of the Catholic tradition) on Sunday evening. We had to wear gloves. The year before freshmen, we had to wear hats and gloves; they were progressing. Before I graduated, I don't think vespers services were required of freshman anymore. We also had to go to all the social events: freshman ball, convocations, concerts, etc. In some kind of way—at least I thought—they kept track of when you didn't go to those types of things. I think they inspected our dorm rooms. I went to everything, even all the football games. In some of the physical education classes, they required that you go to the football games and write about what happened. They didn't have to require me to go; I loved football.

I came to love Southern's marching band. I had a crush on the band director. He was so handsome to me. My friends Jacqueline Bradford and Pearlie Jean Winzer initially didn't go to the football games and didn't want to. Almost everyone on the campus went to the games. It had to be lonely in the dorms. However, their PE teachers gave them an assignment to go to the games, so they started going and started enjoying it; they never missed a game after that. I don't know what it was about football that intrigued me because I didn't know much about it. I think it was being outdoors that I loved and, of course, the band. Southern's band was nicknamed the human jukebox, and I loved it. I thought it was much better than Grambling College's band.

I had my first real date at Southern University my freshman year. This boy from out of nowhere asked me to go to one of Southern's football games. I accepted, and he called for me at my dorm. I was so nervous, and he seemed to be shy. I didn't know what to say to him. I found out two things about him that disappointed me that night. First, his breath was not that pleasant. I didn't know how to tastefully tell him so. Secondly, I found out that he was majoring in agriculture. To me, agriculture meant farming, and that was what I was trying to get away from. This couldn't have been further away from the truth, but my naive self was in the dark about the potential of majoring in agriculture. I didn't encourage a relationship with him. I don't know what I said, but he got the message. He later met a girl, and I believe she was a freshman, and he was a senior. They eventually got married, I believe. She had more sense than I did. When I was a senior, I met the dean of Agriculture, and he talked about how he consulted with foreign countries and how much traveling he had done. It was then that I realized that I should not have let that guy get away so easily. Here I was, a country bumpkin dating another country bumpkin and thought I could do better than a future farmer. Boy, did I have a lot to learn.

I loved my freshmen year at Southern; there were so many boys. There seemed to be boys everywhere you looked. It seemed to be enough to go around. I said all those girls who can't get a boyfriend in high school should definitely go to college. I had several dates after my first. I even got invited to the ROTC ball. The guy that took me couldn't dance, but at least I could dance with the other guys. I remember a guy I had met in one of my classes asked me to dance at one of the balls. While we were dancing, I told him he was breaking my back. He said, "What do you think you're doing to my back?" (I was five foot three, and he was obviously over six feet.) I decided then that tall guys were out of my league. I never fantasized about being with a tall guy like most girls.

I forgot to mention that my first night on Southern's campus was dramatic. I'd had a long day registering for classes, came home, and got in the bed and slept like a baby. When I woke up the next morning, it looked as if all hell had broken loose. I had slept through Betsy, a hurricane. The lights were out, and trees were thrown all over the campus. We could not leave our dorm until they cleaned up. I had been so tired that I slept through the whole thing. I couldn't believe I had slept through my first hurricane. Living in Louisiana, you were always afraid of hurricanes. There was a house near my house in Minden that everyone said used to be a two-story house until a hurricane came though Minden, years before I moved to Minden. Later (2005), Hurricane Katrina would come through Louisiana and make Betsy look like a rainstorm.

We had not started classes yet, so the only thing that was disrupted was registration. Most of the upperclassmen were not on campus yet. I believe we were able to start classes on time. Most of my friends from Webster lived in the Triangle as well. Ada Green and Pearlie were suite mates. So I visited them often. They also lived in Thomas Hall. Ada Mae and Ida Faye Allums were roommates. Ada Mae became best friends with another of her suite mates, and Ida Faye became best friends with another of the suite mates. I think they eventually changed roommates. I didn't want to be in the same room with someone from my hometown because if we became upset with each other, then we wouldn't be friends again and become strange around each other when we went home, and I didn't want that. Some friends from Webster who became roommates even stopped talking to one another. I saw this over and over again.

Jacqueline Bradford and I did become roommates accidently during our sophomore year. She had arrived late for registration, and all the dorm rooms were taken up. She couldn't find a place to stay, so she bunked with me and my roommate and never left. I didn't like this at all. It was so crowded now. I still wanted the solace of Thomas Hall. They had to start putting three people together in some of the rooms because Southern's enrollment was growing. Jacqueline and I were both in Progress Hall, the honors dorm, because she and I had made the dean's list our freshmen year. Jacqueline had made a lot of friends, and now they became my friends as well. They loved to play cards. I had started playing cards my freshman year, but I really honed my skills my sophomore year. We would play all night sometimes, especially on the weekends. We played bid whist and pluck. The girls would sometimes curse one another and call each other *nigger* or *bitches* and use the words *motherfucker* while playing, so I started that bad habit as well. Progress Hall had upperclassmen as well because it was the honors dorm. So girls from my hometown like Gloria Bell and Bobbie Nell and some others that I didn't know well lived in that dorm as well.

I loved college life. Sometimes the fraternities would come over to the dorms and serenade us. Some of the candidates for class offices would come over to give campaign speeches. We would look out over our banisters. I loved it. Then on other days, all the girls would be going to social events all dressed up alone with me and my roommates or my date. I loved it. It was like a parade of fashion. I often would look at them to see if I was in fashion, which I was not most of the time. However, a lot of the other girls were not as well because many of them came from a poor family or a small town like I did. I didn't know some of those towns existed in Louisiana. There was an off-campus social life, but I didn't get involved in it my freshmen year because I wanted to do my best in my classes. Most of my weekends were spent studying. The only foray off-campus I did was to go to a movie with friends every once in a while.

After my freshman year, I would venture out to parties. However, I found out that most of the time, the guys were trying to get you to have sex with them in one of the back rooms. One time, I went back to one of those rooms with a guy that was trying to talk to me. When I saw how dingy the sheets were, I didn't even want to sit on them, much less have sex on them. I began to think less of the guy because of that. I doubt if we had another date. Even though I had always thought I was uglier than most girls, I still thought of myself higher than that. I was worth more than some dirty sheets in some random apartment, woods, car, or fleabag motel. Incidentally, the guys that took me to those places never did get sex from me. What they did get was my big mouth that I am sure they never wanted to hear again after that night. From the beginning, I decided that I would only have sex with a guy that I loved and I was sure (or thought) loved me back. I thought guys who tried to have sex with you in some frumpy room didn't really care about you, and I was right. The girl had values and a strong-willed character. I knew that having sex with someone you hardly knew meant trouble—real trouble if you accidentally got pregnant.

I had to fight myself out of several bedrooms at Southern. But the one I remember mostly is the date I had with a so-called gay guy. My roommate my sophomore year had asked me to go out with this guy. To this day, I am not sure why. She said we were going to the movies and that I didn't have to worry about the guy because he was gay. I went, and some kind of way we ended up in his room off campus. He said he had to get his wallet from his room, so he stopped by his apartment building on our way to the movie. He said for me to come up because it was dangerous for me to be alone in that area. So I went with him. When we got inside of his room, he pushed me down on the bed. I couldn't believe it when he jumped on top of me on the bed. I fought that idiot like a man and told him to take me home. I didn't even get a movie out of the deal. I was back home, and needless to say, I had some sharp words for my roommate. All she did was laugh. I didn't see anything to laugh about.

That would not be the last time that I had to fight my way out of situations when men thought they would get some without loving me or me loving them. I could never understand why they would want to have sex with some strange girl they hardly knew. I decided later that for most men, the hole (vagina) was the most important part; they could care less who it belonged to. Some men even decided that another man's asshole was sufficient. It was just another warm hole to sink their dicks into and come; that was all that mattered to some of them. My worst experience with almost date rape would come later while I was doing an apprenticeship in Chicago, while in graduate school. I'll say more about that later.

I have to say something about eating in Parker Hall my freshman year. Southern had several lunchrooms, and the freshmen ate in Parker Hall. Parker Hall was an old building. Most of the food was okay, but some of it was for the dogs. One thing they served was red beans and rice. I loved the red beans, but I didn't like eating beans and rice. So every time I went through the line, I would tell the ladies to hold the rice. They would look at me strange because rice was a Southern Louisiana staple. It was not a Northern Louisiana staple. We ate just as many potatoes, if not more, as we did rice. But in Southern Louisiana, they would even have rice for breakfast. Whoever heard of rice and scrambled eggs? Well, I did when I got to Southern. Like I said, rice was a staple. You would have thought you were in China or Japan, but no we were in southern Louisiana. They did serve grits for breakfast, which I was used to.

I remember one day during my sophomore year, they decided to switch up and serve us cream of wheat. Everybody started saying under their breaths, "What is this?" They and I had figured out that it was not grits. Cream of wheat had a different taste, and the kernels were smaller. All of a sudden people started throwing the cream of wheat all over the cafeteria. I believe that was the first food fight I had observed. Needless to say, they did not serve black kids cream of wheat again and try to fool them like it was grits.

I ate breakfast, lunch, and dinner in the cafeteria because I would always find myself hungry and broke late at night. Most girls would send out for food most of the time; I didn't have money to do that. Some of the food they served, we were very curious about. For instance, we thought the eggs were imitation and the hamburger meat was from horses. After, I did apprenticeships as a part of my requirement for my major in nutrition. I told everyone that the eggs were real because I'd had to crack them and that the hamburger meat was not horse meat. We didn't have the variety as kids do nowadays (they even have a McDonald's in some of their cafeterias—who would have thought?), but we had balanced meals. I loved it when I got to work with the baker and help him make those cakes all the students (plus me) loved; then I could eat as much cake as I wanted. For the most part, I didn't like working in the food service operations on campus. That was a hint of what was to come, but it was too late. I was a senior by then.

I would always get to the cafeteria early, especially for dinner, before all the food had been picked over. The men (mostly football players who had to get to practice) would crowd around the door to the cafeteria, and I would be bomb rushed by them when the lady opened the door to the cafeteria. I hated that, but I was determined to get the fresh food, and I was always hungry from going from class to class. Southern's campus was huge. You only had ten minutes to get between classes, and the instructors would close the doors after five minutes. Sometimes you had to run. So by lunch and dinner, I was hungry. Even with all that walking, I still gained some weight. When I went to college, I was only 93 pounds. By December, I was 118 pounds. I couldn't wear some of my clothes. I had to have new clothes for my sophomore year. I remember by the end of the semester, boys were checking out my butt. My clothes were fitting tighter because I had gained weight. I didn't realize that if I had continued to wear tight clothes, I probably would have gotten a boyfriend at Southern, but I wasn't giving out to anyone who tried to get me in bed because I was not ready for a baby.

By the end of my sophomore year, two of my friends had babies. Pat had gotten pregnant, our freshmen or sophomore year in high school and Melvyn had gotten pregnant by the end of our freshmen year in college. Both by men they stopped talking to after they had their baby. I could not understand how the love stopped after they had the babies. In both cases, it seemed like just a few weeks after the birth of the baby. I am pretty sure they thought the guys would be more caring after the baby and found out just the opposite. This was eye opening to me. I decided the ring should come before the baby then he would not be able to escape so easily.

One incident that occurred during my freshman year still haunts me. It was Valentine's Day 1966. I was walking across the ravine coming from Parker Hall with some of my friends when we were approached by some boys handing out roses. One of them was my homeboy Vincent Wilson. I asked Vincent why they were giving strange girls roses. He said that they were giving the ugly girls flowers because they knew they would not get any. He said that he wouldn't give me one because I was his homegirl. I couldn't believe they could be so cruel. I lost all respect for Vincent. I never said how I felt that day to him then or ever.

Over the years since college, he and I have worked pretty close to plan reunions; however, I could never get really close to him because of that day. Another event that floored me that he was intricately involved in was when he called another friend of mine, a classmate of ours, "an ugly girl," and I knew this friend had a crush on him. To be honest, to me, none of the boys handing out flowers to so-called ugly girls that day were handsome themselves. As a matter of fact, the girls would probably have called them ugly. So why would "ugly" boys humiliate "ugly" girls? I think because no matter how ugly, there are more girls than boys, so ugly boys can get a girlfriend, and that makes them feel more handsome than they really are. Just saying, call a spade a spade, will you?

While at Southern, I became enamored of sororities and fraternities. I loved to see them do their routines. You had to have a B average to get into them. I wanted to try to get into them, and I did my sophomore year. My friend Melvyn Thomas and I applied to be Alpha Kappa Alphas, and both got turned down. My friend Pearlie Jean got accepted by the Deltas. I am not sure how or when I met JoAnn Robinson, but she and I became fast friends, and she was accepted on the Alpha Kappa Alpha line. JoAnn was my suitemate. She didn't like her clothes, so she wore some of my new clothes. We were the same size. She even wore my coat because she wanted to impress the big sisters. I wore some of her clothes, but I didn't like them and thought they were old-fashioned. I didn't make it on the AKA line, but my clothes did. I cried when I didn't make it; it hurt me deeply. It was the debutante ball all over again when I didn't get chosen to be a debutante in high school. My friends Melvyn and Pearlie got chosen. What hurt more than not getting chosen was that Melvyn and Pearlie had been going to debutante meetings all summer but did not tell me. I am sure they felt sorry for me and didn't know what to say. But they really hurt me by not saying anything. These two incidents would haunt me forever. I eventually stopped crying every time I thought of them, but every time I was denied something, my thoughts would go back to these two incidents, and I would figure that I was too ugly and that's why I didn't get it, whatever it was. I think my family, church, and belief in myself kept me from dwelling on this negative stigma.

My sophomore year, my sister Bobbie started to Southern. I was a sophomore, and she was a freshmen. By my junior year, my brother David started to Southern. My mother and father had three kids in college at the same time. It was definitely a financial burden. My brother David had learned how to cut hair, so he started making money at Southern by cutting his dormmates' hair. I would go over sometimes to borrow some money from him. My roommates teased me that I was borrowing from my little brother. So what? He had it, and I didn't. He would make me grovel for some change, but he would always give it to me.

With eight stairstep kids, my mom and dad had children in all the classes at Southern for eight years almost. All of my siblings followed me to Southern, and all of us graduated except for one, my sister Carrie. At the time, I thought it was because she chose the wrong major, but it was probably because she didn't like college or studying. As a matter of fact, she may have had a learning disability that we were not aware of. I think teachers just thought you were slow or didn't like to study. Carrie was the one sibling that had the most trouble in school. I remember my father trying to teach her the multiplication table. He would say, "Nine times nine is eighty-one.

What is nine times nine, Carrie?" and she would forget or pretend to. To this day, I am not sure if she was edging him on, or she actually would forget. It didn't make sense. My father would get so mad. I remember him whipping Carrie while he kept repeating "nine times nine eighty-one." This was one time I thought my father was definitely abusive. I wonder to this day, if I asked Carrie what was nine times nine if she'd remember it was eighty-one. I don't think anyone else in the household would ever forget. We had to live through that scenario.

My father loved math. I would find out later that his mother loved math as well, so she would always worked with her kids with math. He was only able to help us with math through fourth grade, though. He and my mom had only gotten as far as the seventh and eighth grades. I think that was as far as the school went in those days for blacks and in the rural country area where they lived.

After I graduated from high school and started to college, my father and later my mom went back to school to get their GEDs. Neither one of them got it, but they did try. Once we all got into college, they had to work more than one job. I think they both had three jobs at one time. My father, you could say, always worked three jobs. He worked a regular job; then he farmed, and he also played Jitney cab for most of the people that lived in the St. John area on Saturdays after he finished on the farm. Sometimes, especially in the winter months, he didn't farm; he just chauffeured people to and from town. I didn't realize that was how he made additional change until late in life. Until my Aunt Velma and Uncle Long learned how to drive and got cars, he would chauffer them around too. Remember, they were both handicapped and were the only Rabb siblings who remained on the Rabb farm and raised their families there.

Sophomore Year

My sophomore year was tumultuous because I almost failed a course. I was taking sociology and I could not understand the teacher's teaching methodology. Plus, the exams were departmental exams. When I got a F for mid-term my mother almost had a fit. I was scared to death that I was going to flunk. I had never flunked a course in my life. I don't think I had made a C grade, now here I was flunking. I had to make some changes in my life. First thing I did was stop playing cards all night. My roommates still played cards, but I studied. Evidently, they had majors that didn't require as much concentration because they were still making As and Bs, whereas with me and sociology, that was not my case.

I met with the teacher to see if she could help me. I told her that my problem was the tests. I studied her notes and the text, but what I studied was not on the tests. The tests were departmental exams, not individual teacher exams. She said that she would see how well I studied in class. What she started doing was asking me questions in class; she would not go to the next student until she asked me something I couldn't answer. She never had to go to another person. I think she was astounded as to how well I did, so much so that she gave me a B grade at the end of the semester. I was still flunking the exams. After she gave me that B, I made the Social Science Department's honor society. I couldn't believe it. I didn't think I earned that honor. I was the girl who couldn't pass their departmentalized exams.

Sophomore year was tumultuous for another reason for me. It was the year that I applied to pledge the Alpha Kappa Alpha sorority. I did it for one reason: I liked their colors, pink and green. I didn't like the colors of Delta Sigma Theta, red and white. Red and white to me were the symbols of racism because they were the colors of the white high school in my hometown. I still have trouble with red and white together. You won't ever see me wear red and white, maybe red and maybe white, but never them together. Plus, you very seldom see me wear all white, and I think the reason for that is obvious, being that I am black. I was turned down for the Alpha Kappa Alpha sorority. My friend Melvyn was turned down as well. I think we had gone to the interviews together.

I remember I wore a burgundy dress that was a little too tight because I had gained some weight. I wore the dress because it was the nicest dress I had at the time. When I was turned down, I kept wondering if the ladies that interviewed me thought I looked like a whore in that dress. I also kept wondering if they thought I was too ugly. I also thought maybe one of the ladies who was the girlfriend of a football player who was flirting with me had convinced them to not let me in. When I say "I kept wondering," I mean that for years I thought about and cried about it.

I didn't handle disappointment very well. I remember how disappointed I was not to win the 4-H Club baking contest. This was more of a catastrophic failure to me. I don't know when I stopped thinking about it, if I ever did; it haunted me for years. I found out years later that the reason I didn't get selected was because a girl from my hometown that didn't really know me that well had convinced her sisters that I wasn't the type of girl they wanted. She lived across town from me, and I lived on Crichton Hill, which was literally across the tracks. I didn't know what the connotation meant at the time, but I am sure she did, and that was why she convinced them to vote against me.

Recently on a television reality show, one of the judges asked a young lady if she was down because she hadn't won the previous contest, and she responded, "No, I don't let things fester. That's over, time to move on." Boy, I wish I'd had her attitude; it would have saved me a lot of time and energy. But to my defense, I often used disappointments to grow from, at least I thought. I think to a point I did, but I am sure I didn't pursue things over the years because I thought I was too ugly or someone would judge me for it.

Junior Year

Later (my junior year), I decided to pledge a service sorority Gamma Sigma Sigma. I made this line and was able to go across. But it was the reason I didn't graduate with a 3.0 or better. I graduated with a 2.92, I believe. I was living in the Villa at the time. Juniors and seniors at Southern were allowed to live in the Villa. The Villa was an apartment building. It was built my freshmen year for families at first. It had a swimming pool in the middle of it, and the apartments had patios. I think it was connected to Southern University, and you had to be connected to the university to live in the dorm. However, at first it was coed and opened to married couples only. Most of them were adults, so they started having parties, and I think things got out of hand. Of course, underclassmen were invited to the parties. There were rumors of gang rapes etc. By my junior year, it had been turned into a female dormitory.

I was dreading my junior year because the junior and senior girls' dorms were on the old part of the campus, and the dorms were outdated, and you had to shower and use the bathroom down the hall, not in your suite like I was used to. I had gotten spoiled. I was lucky when I was chosen to live in the Villa. I was hoping we would be able to use the pool. To my dismay, they had drained the pool, and we were not even allowed to have parties around the dried-up pool. What I loved was that the building was fairly new and had a bathroom in the suites and not down the hall. There were one- or two-bedroom suites, and most of the time five or six girls to a suite. In addition, we had a kitchen and a patio. I loved it. I was able to stay there my junior and senior years.

During my junior year, I got a work-study job at the Villa. I had not done that before because I wanted to concentrate on my studies. Plus, I am not even sure I knew anything about it. What I liked about work-study jobs was that you were supposed to be able to study while on the jobs. I got a job in the Villa, so all I had to do was go downstairs for a few hours a day and call for a girl whenever a boy came to see her. Boys could not visit you in your apartment. It got so hectic, so many boys came looking for girls; I could hardly study. Plus, I was pledging Gamma Sigma Sigma, and my big sisters would make me do what I called "stupid" stuff. One night a big sister had me write "I will obey my big sister" a thousand times I think because I didn't do something in a timely fashion. I had a test in anatomy the next day, and I needed that time to study. I remember I ended up making a C on the test, where I normally made an A or B. I got a C out of the course, I believe, and I knew I would have made an A or B if my big sister had not interrupted my studying. I was so upset about that. When I crossed the line and had little sisters, I never required them to do anything stupid.

I think I had one other bad grade at Southern, a D or C, in economics. Remember, I got a C in a biology laboratory class too, but that was only a one-credit hour course. Both of these classes had something in common, though. They were taught by foreigners. I had a hard time understanding what they were saying. I was also shy about asking teachers questions. I would go home and read up on it myself or ask my friends who were also in the class what the teacher had said. Evidently, it didn't work because I made Cs. Most of my teachers spoke English but with sometimes complicated (to me at least) accents. I had a hard time understanding my white teachers as well. I thought they always talked too fast. I was thankful that most of my teachers were black and articulate. I had several science classes with over three hundred students and the teachers spoke well. To me, they knew how to lecture by repeating their statements sometimes. I never would have asked a question in those classes; I was too shy. I made Bs or As in those classes. I don't know how other students mastered those classes with foreign teachers. They must have stayed in their offices. I couldn't understand anything they said; plus, they spoke too fast. I needed a tape recorder, but they weren't in vogue back then. I am not even sure if they would have been allowed. I am pretty sure they are now in all colleges and classes. If they aren't, teachers wouldn't know anyway because some tape recorders are so small. Plus, with the proliferation and modernization of cell phone now, not only can you be tape-recorded, but you can be videoed. However, you never hear about college teachers getting busted. You often hear or see high school teachers doing stupid stuff. College kids are probably so intent on getting a grade from a teacher they wouldn't dare place something on Facebook about their teachers.

One of the things I loved most about being on Southern's campus was the social life. I'd had a very limited social life at home. It was mainly school and church, and that was it. Now there was so much that we could do: some we were required to do, others we could just do. Plus, living in the dorm with so many girls, every room was a social event. There were girls from all over Louisiana, and it was like they lived not only in a different part of the state but also a different part of the country. Their lives had been different from mine; plus, the language was different. Some spoke what they called broken French or broken English or Creole. Some of their parents didn't even speak English. They were black, for the most part, but many of them looked white. I learned that not all black people were alike, that there were regional differences. Not only was the language different, the foods were different as well.

I loved Southern Louisiana cuisine. It was so highly seasoned. I didn't like hot sauce; that was always on the side. The food in the cafeteria was not that highly seasoned because they had a lot of people with different tastes eating it, but my Southern Louisiana roommates cooked with a lot of seasoning. In my junior year, like I said, I lived in the Villa and had Southern Louisiana roommates. I still ate most of my meals in the university cafeteria, but my roommates did not. They cooked their food, and often it smelled so good. I would taste some of it, if they had enough. One thing that they cooked that got me hooked was liver. I hated liver until I walked in one day, and one of my Southern Louisiana–born and bred roommates was cooking liver. She had the house smelling so good. I was shocked when I found out it was liver. I had learned to hate liver because when I saw my mother cooking it, it looked so bloody and slimy. Most meat I could eat without thinking of the animal that was sacrificed so that we could eat, but not liver; you could see the blood dripping. I had tried to taste it when my mother cooked it, but I just couldn't. Now my roommates had it smelling so good I had to taste it. I couldn't believe how good the liver tasted. They had smothered it in gravy and served it with rice. I ate every bit. I wanted to know how they cooked it. They taught me, and I have been cooking like that ever since. The trick was in the seasoning. My mom had only used salt and pepper on her liver. Now these ladies not only used that, they also used fresh garlic, fresh onions, seasoned salt, onion powder, garlic powder, celery powder, etc.—you name it, they used it. They cooked like this all the time. My mom's food was good, but these ladies took their cooking to a new level with the seasonings. I started cooking that way as well, and I am pretty sure that is why my son developed acid reflux at an early age. Plus, I am pretty sure I didn't because my mom didn't use a whole lot of seasonings when I was growing up, and my digestive system was immature as well. I didn't think about what the seasonings would do to my own son's insides at such a young age.

Now, I must admit, I can eat liver any way you cook it now. Before my mom died, she still had not learned how to cook with all those seasonings I supplied her cabinet with, and her food still tasted great.

My junior year was interesting. I tried going to parties off campus a couple of time, but both times I was put off. I remember going to a party with a guy. He led me to a back room and sat me on a bed. I think he wanted to get busy on that bed. When I looked at the bed, the sheet was gray, not white. It was supposed to be white. The sheet was dirty, probably from not being washed at all or not washed enough. Two things: I didn't know this guy that well, and I was not sitting or having sex on a dirty bed. I thought he was crazy to even think I would do it. When I look back on it, some girls probably didn't mind having sex on that bed. Yes, I had developed high standards for myself. First of all, I am not having sex with someone I hardly know, and my environment had to be appropriate. Every time men tried to take me to sleazy hotels or transient hotels, I looked at them like they were crazy and refused to get out of the cars. I think they thought because I was a naive country girl from a small town, I was getting what I deserved. I know you do not have to be from a rich family from the city to have respect for yourself and your body.

I knew that sex meant the potential of pregnancy and having a baby. Why would I put myself in the position to have a baby by someone I did not love or knew that well? To me, that was setting you up for failure, and my family did not sacrifice for me to fail. I was not going to put myself in that position; it was ridiculous. I had goals for myself, and getting pregnant was not on the list just yet and wouldn't be until I could afford to take care of baby, with or without a man.

As you can imagine, I didn't go to many parties while I was in college. This was 1965 or '66, and I hadn't even heard of marijuana. I had heard of heroin because my health teacher had shown us a film in high school of some heroin addicts. Plus, I had seen a television show of teenage heroin addicts. After seeing these films, I knew I never wanted to do heroin or any drugs at all. I never changed my mind about that. My junior year, one of my roommates said that her boyfriend sold marijuana. I had never even smelled it, but when I did smell it, I knew what it was for some reason.

The only time I was even interested in going to a party on a weekend was when I didn't have a quiz or a test in one of my classes. It seemed that we were always being tested, so I seldom went out on the weekend, even to shop or go to the movies. I always used weekends to get organized to study or to study for tests. I would rewrite or type my notes and type practice exams. I never had a typewriter, but a roommate or friend from Webster High School did and always allowed me to use it. Southern also had typewriters in the library that you could use for ten cents; I can't remember how long.

Southern had so many social events on campus that I didn't really want to go to parties off campus that were not supervised. I loved going to events on campus and spotting that bald head of the dean of students. It was like having your parents watching out for you. Every class had a ball; it was like going to the prom every year. I loved it. I went to everything. The classical events at Southern taught me how to love classical music and operas. I couldn't sing myself, but I loved listening to beautiful singers of classical music.

My junior year at Southern (1967) was a year that was met with strikes and demonstrations on campus. I had taken part in demonstrations back home in Minden. Black people all over the country were demonstrating to fight discrimination, taxation without representation, the right to vote, or just the right to live life like other Americans. I remember one day we had been peacefully demonstrating, and we were sitting on the lawn of the men's gym, quietly commiserating, when the announcer on the radio said that there was an angry demonstration by students on Southern's campus. We all started laughing because we were following Dr. King's philosophy of peacefully demonstrating. That was when I realized that the press often sensationalized things for the viewers for monetary greed. Plus, another way of looking at it, since these DJs were black, they might have been trying to help our cause. One of the things we were demonstrating for was an overpass bridge so that off-campus students could get to their classes on time. There were train tracks blocking the entrance to the, campus and if trains were present, the gates would come down, and often you would be late for class. And if more than five minutes late, the door would be closed, and you couldn't get into class. Missing one class could have an impact on your grade for the class. The trains didn't seem to have a schedule.

Ironically, when I started teaching college classes, when I tried that tactic, I got called on the carpet by the president of the college. He said that student couldn't learn if they weren't in class, so no matter how late, it was the college's policy to let them come into the class. To me, I was following the policy that I was used to at Southern with underclassmen. I figured if they were late for class, they would not learn to be on time for a job and could get fired or given a poor evaluation. I thought of underclassmen as to still being in the training mode. However, I was teaching at a community college, and most of the students were adults. I was used to the first two years of college, which this was supposed to be, to have mostly eighteen- and nineteen-years-olds, but this was far from the case and definitely different from what I was used to. In one of my first classes, I had a student who was in her eighties. Her name was Mrs. Burnley. She was one of the sweetest women. When she graduated, she already had a job. I whispered that fact to the president at her graduation, and he announced it to the crowd, and they stood up and gave Mrs. Burnley a standing ovation.

Having a baby changed my life totally. After having a baby, I found myself having a hard time getting to work on time. Plus, sometimes I would get stopped by a train or two. So now I understood why some of my students were late all the time. They would have to get their babies ready for school or baby sitter or day care and take a train or/and a bus to school themselves. So I stopped locking my doors and allowed them to enter any time.

My homeboy Sam Mims was leading the demonstrations at Southern. He was president of the student body. I was so proud of him. He had been smart and popular at Webster also. The Student Government Association had invited Julian Bond and Muhammad Ali to our campus. After Julian Bond spoke, we were so hyped up about our rights as black people. After Muhammad Ali spoke, we were all hyped up about not eating pork. It was ironic that same day, we had pork in the cafeteria. I don't think anybody turned it down (after walking all the way from the men's gym to Parker Hall to eat, you were hungry). I would remember Muhammad Ali's speech in a big way later on in college.

We got the overpass, but not while we were at Southern. Future generations benefitted from our struggles, and that was a good thing. Every time I go back to Southern and go over the overpass, I think of how we came together as students for a cause. Unfortunately, I think because of our demonstrations that our president, Dr. Felton G. Clark, lost his job. He was nearing retirement anyway. I loved Dr. Clark. I should say I loved to hear him speak. He was a great orator, and you could tell that every time he got up to speak. Dr. Netterville, a vice president under Dr. Clark, became our president, and he was not as good of a speaker. He could have been just as good of a president, but to me and other students, he had a tall order to fill when it came to speech giving, and he was sorely lacking. Dr. Clark taught me that the delivery of a speech is just as good as the speech itself, if not more important. Mastering the art of giving a speech that keeps the attention of teenagers has got to be an art. Dr. Clark had often been the speaker at graduations at Webster. He was one of the reasons I chose to go to Southern.

I loved my apartment-style dorm room my junior and senior years at college. We had two bedrooms, a living room, kitchenette, and patios. We had a swimming pool in the center of the apartment complex, but they didn't fill it with water, to my disappointment. I loved the atmosphere. You couldn't have boys in your rooms. Like always, a boy would call for you, and you would go to the lobby to talk with him. I very seldom, if ever, had a boy call for me that I had to entertain in the lobby. If I had a date, I would be picked up, and we'd walk to the dance or movie. I never got the chance to sit in the lobby with a boy while courting. I would often see the girls and guys sitting together trying to talk to one another. Most of the time, they seemed like they were in pain. I think the girls just wanted us to see them with their men and to salivate about what we were missing. Well, they succeeded. Everybody wanted a boyfriend to sit in the lobby with. I really don't think most of us knew what a courtship should entail, and that is why so many of us end up in marriages miserable and mismatched with our spouses.

I remember having a boyfriend my junior year, but he was not on campus; he was in the service. I met him through my roommate Lorraine; she always had boyfriends. She was heavier than most of the girls, but she was talented and pretty and was often in beauty contests. She always had the best talent because she could sing. She was always hooking me up with boys that she knew. She introduced me to one boy who tried to rape me. He was the supposedly gay guy I told you about earlier.

She made up for it somewhat by introducing me to a boy she knew from Mississippi. She was from Oklahoma but had relatives I believe in Mississippi. He evidently liked me, so we started to write to each other while he was away in the service. I think during that time, all men wanted someone to write to them while they were away in Vietnam or wherever. I can't remember where he was for some reason. I do know that after we met for only one time and wrote to each other several times, he gave me a ring. My roommates and I squealed when we saw the ring. They and I thought it was an engagement ring. I wrote him back asking him what was the ring about, and he said it was a friendship ring. So I kept the ring. I was the envy of my friends. Ms. Never Having a Date had a ring. I couldn't believe it. I wore the ring every day until I gained so much weight I could no longer wear it. I still have it to this day. It had three very small diamonds. One of the diamonds is missing, but the ring still looks cute to me and brings back so many memories.

I can't remember how the guy and I broke up, but we did. I think he found someone else, and I was glad because I didn't really know him that well. We did go out one time during my junior year after my twenty-first birthday. We went to a lounge with some people, and I had a drink. I think it was a Tom Collins. I decided it was my birthday, and I was going to taste everybody's drink at the table. At six o'clock in the morning, I regretted doing that because I was vomiting my gut out over the toilet. I learned a lesson that night. I knew I did not like drinking. Plus, my mom was coming because my sister Bobbie was in the honor's program that day. If she had stopped at my dorm first, she would have seen me sick as a dog and probably would have taken me home.

It was either right before my junior year or my senior year at Southern that the Civil Rights Movement picked up in Minden when some white people from the north and James Farmer of CORE (Congress of Racial Equality) came to Minden. I attended meetings all summer and participated in several of the sit-ins. Our main head-quarters was the Fourteen District Building in Minden. We would show up there and find out what place we were going to integrate that day. I was very surprised when I was selected to go to Ed's Café, the place where my mother was working as the head cook. When we got to the restaurant and sat at the counter and attempted to order food, I noticed that my mom was peeping through the window the cooks would place the food generally. I was scared I was going to be arrested, but we left without an incident. I really can't remember if they served us or not. I do remember my mother being on the phone that night, talking to her friends and family members about us and how we had integrated her restaurant that day. Normally, black folks would have to come to the back door to order food. My mother seemed proud of us as she relayed the story. I was so surprised because she seemed so reluctant to participate in any of the civil rights pro-tests, whereas my dad did not. We had one protest march downtown Minden and I remember my dad leading the march as if he was the drum major. I was never more proud of him. It was obvious both my parents had morals, courage, and pride that nobody could take from them.

I remember asking them why they never told us any stories of bad things that happened to black people in Minden. They told us the story of how the white sheriff had attached a black man to a wagon by his balls (male genitalia) and drove him through the town. I realized then why they never told us such things as children they didn't want to scare us.

I told you earlier, how Muhammad Ali's speech about pork would come back to haunt me later. Well, one of my friends, Marilyn McElroy, was graduating from Southern; and I stayed on campus to go to her graduation. I was poor, so I bought a family package of pork chops (about twelve chops) so I could have them for lunch and dinner every day leading up to graduation. On the day of Marilyn's graduation, she came to get me and I couldn't lift my head off the pillow, I was so dizzy. I remembered Muhammad Ali's speech about pigs being hard to kill. After that experience and for years afterward, I would get a little dizzy any time I ate pork. I would learn later that it was probably the fat that was increasing my blood pressure and making me dizzy. I also learned that pork is the best source of thiamin (vitamin B1) and you needed it. So I still eat pork, but in moderation. I still get dizzy if I eat it more than two days in a row.

Senior Year

I continued to go to football games and a few basketball games my junior and senior years in college. I even got a chance to go to a few off-campus games. I remember, going to Florida &M University for a football game my senior year. I begged my mom for money to go to this game because I loved their band. I think or I know I went to the games, primarily to see the bands perform. Southern had a great band. I had a crush on Mr. Freeman, our band director; I often fantasized about him. He was so cute and cool, I thought.

Going to Florida A&M took a lot of courage on my part, but it was only the beginning. We stayed in their dorms. Their campus was hilly. All the men and women were taller to me. The trees were even taller. With their campus being so hilly, I could tell why their men seemed to be so skinny. I loved the competition between their band and ours. They were the rattlers, and we were the jaguars. The crowd went wild for both bands. Of course, we tried to cheer the loudest for Southern's band, but we were outnumbered.

By my sophomore, junior, and senior years at Southern, we were no longer required to go to activities, so I slacked off. You needed to slack off because after your freshman year, the courses got harder and harder—because now you were in your major courses and learning material you never knew. Now it would tell if you had good study habits or not. I knew I had to focus. My goal was to get my degree in four years. My mom tried to talk me into going to summer school so that I could get out sooner. I resisted because I needed a break from schooling during the summers. By the end of spring, I would be so tired of studying I thought I would go crazy, so I needed the summers to rejuvenate myself. I did go to summer school once or twice while I was at Southern. I went primarily to get ahead with my credit hours so that I didn't have to take more than fifteen hours a semester in order to graduate in four years. It was hot, but I enjoyed the summers. I loved going to the track meets. Plus, the atmosphere on campus was more laid back during the summers. Most of the students and the teachers were gone, and you would often find yourself walking alone. During the school year, there was a lot of hustle and bustle on the campus, sometimes too much, especially when there was a football game.

When I look back on good times at Southern, what comes to mind are the homecoming games and the Grambling and Southern football games. Everybody wanted something blue and gold and new to wear to the games. This was always a challenge for me because I was poor, and my parents could only afford so much. Often I would work during the summers at the same café my mom worked in to save a little money for school. This little money only went so far though. I made $2.50 a day and only worked on the weekend and sometimes during the week. I remember my mom made $25 a week, a $100 a month. My dad made $100 a week, about $500 a month. I found this out when I went to college had to apply for the National Defense Loan. We were poor. Multiply this by the fact that I was the oldest of eight kids, and we were beyond poor.

I think growing up with so little and not being able to do things impaired me for raising my own son while making more money because I didn't want him to suffer as I did. We used to get one gift for Christmas. In contrast, my son had so many gifts for Christmas one year that the whole living room was filled with just his toys. The very next year, he wanted the same thing. I realized then we had made a mistake. One time, I tried to get him everything—and I mean everything—on his Christmas list. Why did I do such a stupid thing? I say I because if it was left up to my husband, he never would have gotten him all of those toys. My only answer to that is,

I didn't want him to be like me, disappointed that you didn't get what you had wished for at Christmas. Oh, if I could do it again, I would make him earn every gift he got—with good grades, doing his chores, keeping his room clean, volunteering, etc. I didn't know we were raising a spoiled brat at the time. I say *we* because my husband is not totally innocent in this picture. There were so many other things he could have done differently as a dad, but his role model (his belligerent father) was worse than mine.

My senior year at Southern was when I started to grow up or come into my own, so to speak. I started to realize that pretty soon I would be on my own and responsible for myself. It was scary. I had to apply for my dietetic internship. Again you could only apply if you had a 3.0 or above average in your major classes, and I did. My friend Jackie did not and did not get the chance to apply for a dietetic internship. She started to work long before I did, so I thought this made up for her disappointment somewhat. My senior year was fun yet challenging/ I guess it was supposed to prepare you for the real world of work.

I was excited when I got an internship at the University of Wisconsin. Initially, I had just gotten an alternate position; then someone dropped out, and I got the internship. I was really happy at the time. I had no idea where the University of Wisconsin was located or what I was getting myself into, but I was ready for my real-life experiences. I was disappointed that my friend Jackie didn't get an internship. I know she was disappointed also. Southern used to post GPAs, so I know her GPA was not as high as mine. She did better in the nutrition classes than I did. She made As where I made B. I found the teachers and the subject matter boring at times. All of our business classes, except for personnel management, were taught by dietitians who knew absolutely nothing about business. Now they take the business classes, which is the way it should have been. Now at Southern, they call the School of Home Economics, the Family and Consumer Science Department, and they have a Family Financial Planning Program. That is a cooperative online program with eight other historical black colleges and universities (HBCUs). I found this out when I attended my fiftieth-anniversary reunion at Southern in

2019. I'd like to think that I would have been interested in this type of program if it had been offered when I was at Southern.

It was during graduation exercises that my friends and I noticed that there were a lot of short men graduating. We all had been overlooking the short men when it came to the dating scene. It turned out that evidently these were the smart guys. The guys who were going to make the money one day and could provide opportunity for you as their wives. I noticed that the guy I had stopped dating my freshmen year was leading his agricultural college graduates. The person who led the line was the person with the highest average in the major. This was one of the smart guys, and I had dropped him. I was the stupid one. We never met again, but years later, he did look me up in Southern's alumni directory and emailed me for a while. I think he married the freshmen I had seen him walking on the campus with—smart girl. He said that he was retired and that he had done a lot of traveling for his job and served on several boards now. I believe he said that he had four kids who were all grown up. He and his wife did not live far from Chicago. I couldn't help but wonder how different my life would have been if we had stayed a couple and married. My friends and I realized too late how stupid we were to overlook some of the guys on the campus as potential mates. These guys were probably looking at the pretty chicks anyway and would never have considered us. I wonder why people always want the people out of their league. I have noticed that about my son; he seems to always want the girls out of his league.

One of my son's girlfriends even told him that she wanted a man with some swagger. She eventually got pregnant and married a guy that had been a former gangbanger, even though now he was making a career of the military. I think her candor hurt my son, but he realized that she was probably making a mistake in her choice. But then this was a black man with a job and potential, so hopefully things worked out. I know one thing: my son has no swagger, and neither did his father. They are both just decent guys. My son does want to be rich one day, even though now, years after graduation, he is still looking for a full-time job. My husband just wanted a good job. I wish I'd had known this before I married him because my dreams were bigger. When you marry someone who doesn't share your dreams, they can definitely pull you down. Every time I wanted to step out of the box and do something different, my husband would say *no*. He was always scared to venture out. But then I am blessed by God. You get what you ask for, and I think I did because I didn't know any better. When I was at Southern, I had one goal, and that was to graduate. I think white girls (and possibly others as well) used to go to college with two goals, to graduate and get a man, and not necessarily in that order.

University of Wisconsin—Dietetic Internship (1969–1970)

During my senior year at Southern, all dietetic majors had to apply for dietetic internships. They said we couldn't get jobs as dietitians until we completed the internship. They had not informed us of this little tidbit early on. It was like this was a five-year major instead of four years, and I would not be able to work for another year. I was tired of being poor. My family was poor, and I needed a job. That was when I realized that I should have majored in business because I would be job ready or received my training on the job while making a salary. I applied for the internship and got on the wait list at the University of Wisconsin. My friend Jackie didn't get accepted into an internship, and I know she was extremely disappointed. She was able to find a job, though. I secretly envied her making money already. In fact, by the time I started to work, which eventually was two years later, we were probably making the same salary. The dean of the Home Economics School, Mrs. Thrift, called me into her office one afternoon and told me that I did get into the internship at the University of Wisconsin in Madison, Wisconsin, because somebody had dropped out. I was so ecstatic and scared to death. I don't think I had ever heard of Madison, Wisconsin.

I had to report for my internship July 1, so after I graduated, I just had a month to get ready. I needed a white work uniform and white work shoes. I hated wearing white as a uniform. At Southern, we had to wear the same thing. I tried to get something that fit me, but I still hated white. I think it had something to do with white people, slavery, and segregation.

This time when I left for Madison, Wisconsin, I was taking a bus instead of the train, and none of my neighbors came with my parents when they took me to the bus station. I am not sure if any of my siblings came either. This time, I knew that when I got on the bus, our lives would never be the same again. I cried after I got on the bus. When we got to the next bus stop, I got off to buy some snacks, and there was my father running toward the bus. I was scared because I thought something had happened. But he had my coat in his hand and said that I'd left it in the car. It was July, so I didn't need a coat, but I was going to be gone a year, so I was going to need it eventually. Plus, we knew Wisconsin was up north, and it was going to be colder in the winter. I couldn't believe my father had followed the bus. I knew then that without a doubt how much he loved me. I felt so loved. After I got back on the bus, I really cried. I was going to miss everybody, but I was ready for the challenges ahead, and they and Southern had prepared me. I was the first kid out of the nest, so to speak. I knew my parents were scared, but not as scared as I was. I had been one of those kids, except for my grandparents' home or my Aunt Velma's: I was afraid to stay with other people. I was always afraid of being away from the security of my parents. I was afraid I was going to do something wrong in someone else's home or get harmed by them in some way. Our church always wanted me to go to Sunday school conventions. My mom had begged me to go, but I was too scared. I don't think my cousin Alma went either, but her sister Queen took up the challenge and loved going. She would often talk about the people that she met, and I was a little jealous, but not jealous enough to go without my mama.

My bus trip was uneventful, but I was so happy my father had brought my coat instead of mailing it to me because it was cold on the bus at night. I had to change bus companies in Chicago. The Continental Bus stopped in Chicago, and I had to change to Greyhound. It stopped downtown Chicago. This was my first glimpse of Chicago, the town that would eventually become where I would spend most of my years. I had to walk about two blocks from one bus station to the next, so I got a chance to experience the heavy downtown traffic in Chicago. I saw the Civic Center, the place that would later become the main office for my first job. I noticed how tall the buildings were and a poor tree trying to grow on a small plot of land surrounded by concrete. This was a strange setting for me because most of the buildings I was used to didn't go above two stories, and there were plenty of land for the trees to grow on.

After I got to Madison, Wisconsin, I took a taxi to my dorm. I knew the dorm was a high-rise, so I had to prepare myself. I had never lived in a high-rise before. I think I had never been in any building over three stories, and I probably had never even been to the third floor. For the summer, I was going to be on the seventeenth floor, and I would not have a roommate. I got to the campus a day early so I could find my way around. I walked around the campus and found the University of Wisconsin Hospitals; this was where I was doing my internship. I timed how long it was going to take me to get to the hospital that next morning. I think I had to be there at 7:00 a.m., and I didn't want to be late. I had my mom call me at 6:00 a.m. to wake me, and I also set the alarm clock she had bought me. The alarm clock went off, and I got up. My mom called, and I told her that the alarm clock had awakened me. I was so surprised because I had slept in the room with roommates for years, and their alarm clocks would go off, and I would never hear them. My roommates would wake me if I had an early morning class. I couldn't understand why I never heard the alarm clocks, so I was scared I wouldn't hear it that first morning of my internship.

I got dressed in my whites that I hated and headed to the hospital. I found my way to the basement. As soon as I got off the elevator, a little white lady met me and said, "Good morning, Laura." At first I wondered how she knew my name, and then I remembered we had sent pictures. Later I would decipher not only had we sent pictures, I was the only black intern. There was one other intern from Louisiana, and she was white. She was obviously Southern but treated me nice all year long. I was never really comfortable around the white interns but got to know most of them pretty well. There were two Asians, a Californian, one from Milwaukee, one was a nun, several from the East Coast, and on and on. I think there were twelve of us all together.

Several of the dietetic interns were overweight. I couldn't help but remember how one of the dietetic students at Southern was overweight, and at the end of her program, she was told that she was too overweight to apply for an internship. We couldn't believe it—you wait until she is almost ready to walk the stage to graduate to tell her that. But here were two overweight white dietetic interns.

I found all of the dietetic interns pleasant enough. For the most part, they seemed like pretty smart girls. I got along quite well with the two Asian interns. Even the intern from the South was nice to me. As a matter of fact, other that the nun (who got a position in Chicago later), she is the only one that I had contact with after completing the internship. The nun was supposed to get a position working in a retirement center for nuns. We even had a field trip to the center that she was supposed to work in. She was full of energy, so I really couldn't see her working in the retirement home. So when I met her accidentally in a store on the south side of Chicago, I couldn't believe it. She said that the job in the retirement center didn't work out, that it was too isolating. It seemed she was only working a short distance from the store and only blocks from my home, but we never saw each other again.

The University of Wisconsin's campus was very busy, much more so than Southern's campus. I was there almost a week without seeing a single black person, and believe it or not, the first one I saw was someone I knew from Southern. I think it was during the first week I was there. I was walking on the campus and noticed this young black man walking toward me. It turned out to be Sylvester Love, a guy I had met in Southern's cafeteria. He never had a meal card, so he would go from table to table begging for food. This evidently worked for him, but I felt sorry for him. I asked him why he was there, and he said that he'd gotten a scholarship. I was so happy for him. We took each other's phone numbers, but we never really talked again. I think he was too busy, and I know I was busy.

The next black person I saw on campus was African. I couldn't believe it, and I thought, Don't any African Americans go to school here? He and I went on a date. He took me to a place that was right next door to my dorm, so I felt that I was safe. He seemed interesting enough, but we never dated again, and I seldom saw him on campus.

The campus was huge and not that far from town. I ventured to go shopping downtown because it was not too far from campus. The downtown area at the time was not that big. Plus, I was poor and had very few dollars to spend. We got a stipend of only $200 a month, so my funds were limited.

Later, I would visit the African American Student Center and found out there were quite a few African Americans attending the University of Wisconsin at Madison, Wisconsin. I was surprised when I met a South African student at the center who was white or mixed race, and that surprised me. I did not know there were white Africans. I believe this guy might have been of mixed race, but he looked white.

I went to several social events held by the African American Center. I met the director of the center. He was overweight but extremely friendly. He would later call me at home. It was doing his calls that I experienced my first phone-sex experience. The only problem was it caused me to have nightmares of us having sex and him falling on me and smothering me because he was so overweight. I discouraged his calls after that and didn't frequent the center anymore.

My internship was pretty uneventful except for my deciding that I didn't particularly like dietetics. First of all, I found out that most of the offices were in the basements of hospitals where the kitchens were located. Secondly, you had to wear white (I never wore white) uniforms, and lastly, you had to counsel sick patients on their diets, and some of them didn't live through the night. During the internship, we had to observe most of the departments within the hospital. We had to observe at least two autopsies. While I was in one autopsy, I sat next to one of the dietitians, and she said she had just counseled that patient on a diet the day before. Now here she was, watching the medical examiner take the organs out of his body, place them in cellophane bags, and stuff him with straw. I couldn't take it.

I hated to think of my patients dying and being stuffed with straw even though they were really total strangers to me.

As an intern, I was assigned to work with professional dietitians. We had rotations with the dietitians on the different floors of the hospital. You had to go on rounds with the professional dietitians, along with doctors and nurses. Sometimes the doctors would ask the dietitian a question or too about diets and the nurse about how the patient was eating. I would also go with the dietitian when she would visit new or old patients. Patients could request to see the dietitian. I believe the dietitians were supposed to make rounds often, but most of them were stuck in the basement office trying to write the diet orders placed by the doctors. As interns, we were taught to write diet orders. I found it easy to catch on to the routine of the dietitians I worked with—so much so that I was wondering why my degree had been so hard to get.

The dietetic office also had a few dietetic clerks. The clerks would assist with the diet orders. They would label them for the dietitians. I can't remember what else they did. The hospital also had servers (I can't remember there official title) who distributed the food to the patients. Each floor had a small kitchenette where the food was delivered to from the hospital kitchen; they would plate the food if necessary and take it to the patients. These needed to know what diets the patients were on. The only other black employee in dietetics other than me was one of the persons who distributed the food to the patients. I believe she was on 4 East, the first floor I served on after pediatrics. We got along well. I eventually would visit her home and spend time with her children and sometimes her husband. I don't have a picture of her, but for a long time I had pictures of her children. I remember she had two children, Michael and his sister.

I think I remember Michael's name because I was with Elsie and her children one day when we were in a store, and he took some candy, I believe, when Elsie discovered the candy when we got home. She walked Michael all the way back to the store to take it back to teach him a lesson. I can't remember exactly, but I believe she whipped him and lectured him all the way back to the store. I was embarrassed for Michael. I doubt that kid ever stole another piece of candy from a store.

After I left Wisconsin, I only saw Elsie one time. She came to Chicago to visit her relatives and came over to visit me. I took her across the street to visit James (my boyfriend at the time and later my husband). James lived across the street from me. I think we surprised him because he didn't have a shirt on. I guess he thought it was just me. To me, James had a beautiful body at the time, so it did not disturb me. Elsie kept smiling all the while we were there. When we left, she told me she thought James was cute or handsome or something like that. To me, she seemed a little surprised that I had gotten such a hunk. I thought James was okay, but hunk? No way, I thought. Now, don't get me wrong, I love my husband's body even to this day.

The University of Wisconsin Hospital was a research hospital, so patients came here when they were really sick, and many of them were using it as their last hope before dying. Some of my patients were terminal. I had to read their charts before I went in to see them, and sometimes it would say terminally ill. It was hard to talk to patients when you knew they were dying. Some doctors would place the patients they doubted would get well on very strict diets, hoping it would help them. Most of the time, they were looking for miracles, so they tried whatever they thought might help.

I had to go on rounds every morning with doctors and nurses. I had to pay close attention whenever they were discussing one of my patients. I had one patient that was on tube feeding; meaning she received all of her nourishments through a tube. She was unconscious. The doctors discussed taking her off tube feeding. They wanted her husband to sign for it. I was against it because I thought she would die. I am not sure what happened after I left the floor. As an intern, we had to rotate. I do know that before I left the hospital the next summer, I saw the patient sitting up by herself eating on another floor. So evidently, she didn't die like the doctors had thought. Her husband was sitting in the room with her, happy as a lark.

I started my internship on the pediatric floor. Soon after I started on the floor, John Glenn had circled the earth. Everybody was ecstatic that he had gotten back to earth safely, including me.

Every television in the ward was watching his heroics. The kids in the pediatric wing were so sick it grabbed your heart. I felt so sorry for them and their parents.

At the end of the summer, we had to move out of the dorms or pay the dorm fee. We were getting a stipend of $200 a month. This was not enough to pay for rent. I was surprised, but happily so, when two of the white interns asked if I wanted to share an apartment with them. After I agreed, we still needed a fourth. All the other interns had places to stay, so we put up a sign in the hospital to advertise for a fourth roommate. One of the nurses answered the ad. We found an apartment not too far from the campus, and we moved in. The nurse was my roommate. She and I only slept in the same room for about a month, and then she moved out. I will never know why she moved out, but she paid her rent anyway because we all signed the lease. I suspected that she moved out because she didn't want to live with a black roommate, or it could have been because our other two roommates were so filthy. There is no other word to describe how they kept their room and the bathroom. The nurse put a sign up in the bathroom asking us to please clean up behind ourselves. There would be long brown hairs all over the place. My hair was short and black, and so were the nurse's, so it was not ours. I couldn't believe anyone could be as nasty as my other two roommates. They would sleep with their boyfriends in their filthy room. I think I talked to them about it, but to no avail. I said "I think" because it has been so long ago.

I didn't know I was going to have to take graduate classes while I was doing my internship, but we had to take a class every semester. I was there for two semesters. The first semester, we took biochemistry. My professor I believe was a Nobel laureate. He was the worst lecturer I had ever had, even worse than the African guy I had in one of my laboratory classes at Southern. The biochemistry professor at the University of Wisconsin didn't have an accent; he just spoke fast with his head down. I thought I was the only one in his class that didn't understand him, but on the second day, his desk was filled with tape recorders. This was before small recorders. I wished I'd had a tape recorder. All the interns were having trouble with the class; one of them dropped the class. I wish I had dropped it.

One of my roommates had gotten permission to take another class because she said she had taken the class and gotten an A. She was very smart; I think she got an A in the higher-level class she took. After failing most of my exams, I decided to go and speak to the instructor. I was so nervous; I seldom had to see teachers, especially white teachers, about anything. I don't even recall the discussion. I know he didn't fail me. I think I got a D. I had to take another class; I believe it was advanced nutrition, and I got a B in it. The University of Wisconsin had 30,000 students at the time (on the Madison campus alone I believe) and I was able to register for my classes quicker than at Southern with 10,000 students. I didn't have to stand in long lines like at Southern. I dreaded registration at Southern, I hated long lines with a passion. At the University of Wisconsin they used computers for registration. I thought Southern probably didn't have them yet because it was a black institution. Then, also, I figured Louisiana is a southern state and they seem to be behind the northern states in some things.

I also noticed that the University of Wisconsin had a library for most of their colleges (i.e., Science and Medicine, Humanities, English, Social Science, etc.). I couldn't believe it. Here, the students had extra help, and it was centralized. I figured that was one of the reasons Dr. King pushed so hard for integration. He knew it would be years if ever black colleges caught up with white colleges with regard to resources. I now understood the need for Affirmative Action as well. In order for African Americans coming from black institutions to gain access to certain careers, they had to be given a chance. There was no way their education was going to be equal to those of their white counterparts. But if we were given a chance and if we worked hard with access to excellent resources, we could master their career programs at their institutions just as well as they did.

Southern University only had one library for all the colleges. It was always crowded and noisier than most libraries. Southern's library did have typewriters that you could use for ten cents. Whenever I couldn't borrow a roommates or suitemates typewriter, I had to resort to using the library's overused typewriters. Some professors would require that you type your assignments. This was in the late '60s, so personal computers probably had not been thought of yet. I couldn't help but think how far ahead blacks would have been at black universities if they had the same resources as whites at white universities. At the time, I thought all white universities had similar resources.

I lost my virginity with a guy from Guyana that I met at the University of Wisconsin Hospital. He was an x-ray technician there. He was so nice, and I really liked him. I loved his accent. We went to his room one night, and he was so sweet about it, so I had protected sex with him. This was my first time. I didn't get a climax, but I enjoyed the cuddling and our talk afterward. I think we only had sex once because I asked him if he was going back to Guyana, and he said yes, so I told him that I was not leaving the United States and that we should end it before it got too serious. So I stopped seeing him. I would see him at the hospital and wish that things had been different.

I did meet another guy while I was in Wisconsin before I met the guy from Guyana. He was a Vietnam vet and on disability. His mother lived in the same apartment building as a girl (Elsie) I had met in the hospital. She lived above his mother. Because of the campus, Madison had a lot of girls, more girls than guys with the war going on, so even guys who were just blue-collar workers had college girlfriends, married or not. Elsie told me that she would take pills that her husband brought home because she wanted to be treated also if he had venereal disease. I told her she was crazy for doing it. She did not trust her husband. I can't remember if she had gotten an STD before.

Elsie introduced me to Calvin; his mother's apartment was in the same building as Elsie's. Calvin took me out, and we started dating. Most of our dates ended up in his apartment. He had a roommate, so both of them would have women in their rooms. His roommate's girlfriend was American Indian. I thought she looked white. She didn't know how to cook, so sometimes I would cook for everyone, but this wasn't often because I didn't particularly like cooking. At home, my mom did most of the cooking. She was an excellent cook; she cooked for a living. Calvin was always trying to get me to have intercourse with him, but I wouldn't. I agreed to oral sex on me, but nothing else. I didn't want to have sex with someone unless we were getting married and I loved him.

When I went home for Christmas that first winter in Wisconsin, Calvin drove me to the O'Hare Airport in Chicago, which was about two hours away. I was very impressed and thankful. Over the holidays. I missed Calvin, and before I left, he was talking like maybe we would get married. I kind of felt like maybe I did care about him enough to love him, but I wasn't sure. While I was home, one of my younger neighbors got married. I was now almost twenty-three years old and felt like time was slipping away from me.

After I got back to Wisconsin, Calvin and I went out. We were sitting in front of my apartment building, and he started to ask me a lot of questions. He asked me how much money I planned to make when I finished my internship, and I told him not less than $10,000. I remember that he looked kind of funny. Later, I would think maybe he realized with his disability that he would never make that in his lifetime. I knew I didn't want to marry someone with just disability pay. So I started asking him if he planned on getting some training. If we were going to get married, he needed to make some progress toward getting this training, but I noticed he didn't show much interest. I know his disability was due to injury to his head while in Vietnam. He had a large sunken hole on one side of his head. It was very noticeable. I wonder if he developed some memory issues as a result of his disability; he never did elaborate on it. He might have had Agent Orange as well.

After I came back from my Christmas vacation, I was in for a surprise for two reasons. I had about decided to have sex with Calvin because I knew I was almost finished with my internship, and even if I got pregnant and we didn't get married, I would be able to financially support myself and a baby. I think I decided to have sex with him on Valentine's Day. The night before Valentine's, he called me and said he had to take his sister out of town and wouldn't be back before our date. However, I never heard from him again, even though according to Elsie, he was back in town. She had seen him visit his mother. I went to a Valentine's Day dance with Elsie, and there he was with a white girl. It hurt like hell that I had lost him to a white girl. I think this was my first heartbreak. But eventually, I got over it and said that I probably escaped a bullet with him and his family. His family had been a welfare family. The sister he took out of town, it was rumored, worked at the University of Wisconsin Hospitals and was also on welfare, which was illegal. I think he took her out of town to escape the law.

Most people in my family worked. There was only a few on welfare, and that was because they were disabled. My Aunt Velma and Uncle Clyde and Uncle Long and his wife were on welfare because they were all disabled. However, it was not generational; all of their kids either went to college or trade schools or got decent jobs later on. It still hurt like hell to lose a boyfriend to someone, especially a white someone. This was 1969, and it was not that prevalent to see whites and blacks dating. Later, it would almost become commonplace, but some blacks and whites do not accept interracial dating even today. Personally, I've come a long way with accepting that people should be with whomever they love. When I got on the plane to go home after my internship, I looked back on Madison, Wisconsin, and said goodbye and good riddance.

The second surprise I had when I got back in town after Christmas was the amount of snow that had fallen. I had on boots, but after I got out of the taxi, the snow came over my boots. I could hardly get in the door of my apartment building. The snow was pretty and dangerous. In Louisiana, we hardly ever had snow and definitely not as thick as in Wisconsin. Before the Cuban Missile Crisis, my mom would make snow ice cream. We loved it. But supposedly, we couldn't trust the snow after the crisis. Now I think nobody trust the environment to make snow ice cream. I think this is too bad because it was a fun thing to do with your parents. However, snow in Wisconsin was dangerous, especially if you were driving.

I was glad to be getting out of Wisconsin when my internship ended. I had a lot of experiences, some of which I'd rather forget. I had my first sexual escapade, I met some gay people, I got drunk for the first (no, second time, but this time it was due to haven taken medication and drinking afterward), I saw interracial dating for the first time, met an American Indian. I traveled throughout Wisconsin, and after I left Madison, Wisconsin, I didn't see another black person until I got to Milwaukee, Wisconsin. I saw my first red barn on a farm. All the barns I had seen in books had been red, but I never saw a red barn in Louisiana. But the farms in Wisconsin were like storybook farms with red barns and silos. This is probably where the book illustrators got the idea that barns were red. As I traveled throughout the state of Wisconsin, I couldn't help but wonder why the white people who hated black people just didn't move to Wisconsin. There are so many towns without black people.

By the end of my internship, I had discovered that I cared too much to work in hospitals. I oversympathized with the patients. When I went home every night, I couldn't get them out of my head. Working with sick patients was not for me; I needed to work with people before they got sick. I decided I needed to work in preventive medicine or preventive nutrition. On one of my rotations, the public health rotation, I decided this was the area I needed to concentrate on because you could prevent illness. I worked with the public health nutritionist, and she sent us out to various sections of town to work with other public health nutritionist or nurse in the area. We would also visit people in their homes. In one home, while the nurse bath the patient, I spoke with his wife. She was very chatty. She said that she and her husband had lived modestly all their lives and had saved to take a trip around the world when he retired. Either just before or just after he retired, he had a stroke, and now she was unsure if they would ever be able to take a trip together. I felt sorry for her and decided I would not wait to take trips, that I would enjoy myself while I had the energy and the health to do so. That is one promise I kept to myself. After I retired, I did not necessarily need to travel a lot because I had traveled and enjoyed myself.

The nutritionist in the public health rotation suggested that I apply for an apprenticeship in public health nutrition with Case Western Reserve University. At the end of the apprenticeship, which was for a year, I would have a master's degree. The degree would be paid for, and I would still get a monthly stipend. Plus, I had free room and board. I was really tired of school by then, but I decided to give it a try. I received the apprenticeship and had to report to Case Western Reserve University in Cleveland, Ohio in late August 1970.

At the end of the internship, we had to take the American Dietetic Association's Registration Examination. Afterward, we would be registered dietitians, similar to registered nurses. I had attended Southern for four years, and none of the teachers had ever mentioned that we would have to take a registration exam as a requirement for our jobs as dietitians. I found out by accident while I was walking with one of the administrative dietitians and one of my roommates. My roommate just happened to mention that at her white university, she had taken a sample registration dietitian exam. I asked them what that was, and they said that starting in 1970, all dietetic interns would be required to take a registration examination to become registered dietitians. If you were already a dietitian, you didn't have to take the exam.

Nobody had said a word to me, and now in a few months, I was going to have to take an exam that would help decide my career. I had no books because I had sold them when I graduated. I had no sample tests. For the first time in my life, I was on my own. There were no other black students that I could study with, and I didn't dare ask my white roommates. I felt, surely, they thought I was from an inferior university.

Then on the day of the registration exam, I started my period, and I always had cramps with my period, which made it hard for me to concentrate on tests. This had happened to me several times in my life time, and it had always affected the grade or score I made on an exam. I think the first time I'd had this problem was on the ACT or SAT exam at Webster because I just knew all of us had to take a test. Both times I hurriedly finished the exams so I could go lie down. I couldn't concentrate because my stomach was hurting so bad. I didn't even finish the tests at Webster. I felt that I had not done well on the registration exam as well because I could not concentrate.

I found out just before I left for Case Western Reserve in Cleveland that I had indeed failed the registration exam. I was sleeping on my parents' bed, and someone brought the letter to me and, after I read it, found out that I did not pass. I cried but didn't tell anyone. I don't even know if I told them I was taking an exam for my career. It hurt, but I felt more mad than hurt because I knew I would have passed the exam if I had known when I first started college that I had to take it to be a registered dietitian. I would have paid more attention in my nutrition classes and the books I used in them. Plus, I would have kept my books and my notes or bought more books.

I was extremely mad that the teachers at Southern, a historically black college or university (HBCU), didn't tell us about the test. I think they figured we would drop the major if they had told us. I think I definitely would have because I was on the cuff anyway. But that is still no excuse. They should have also signed up to be a test site for the exam, and they didn't. When I asked Ms. Johnson, one of my nutrition instructors at Southern, why they didn't inform us when I got the chance to visit the campus later, she said that they figured we would pass the exam if we were serious enough with our coursework. Looking back, I wish I had polled the nutrition students who got internships from Southern how many of them passed their registration exam the first time. I know the young lady from Tuskegee (an HBCU as well), who was doing the apprenticeship with me at the Chicago Board of Health, didn't pass her exam the first time. I felt vindicated somewhat. I understood the importance of integration now because some black teachers had a weird way of thinking, and discrimination probably limited their opportunities in the white dietetic world. Plus, it didn't help that segregation had probably limited their social skills, especially in a white environment.

I think it all goes back to slavery and segregation. The black teachers didn't feel comfortable with white teachers and probably felt inadequate at times; therefore, they didn't volunteer to take part in the sampling. As a matter of fact, they probably weren't even in the room when it was discussed and volunteers were recruited. Then and again, did they even attend the national convention of the American Dietetic Association? I know when I started to work at my college they didn't provide funds for traveling to and attending conferences for years. Whenever I went to a conference, I had to pay my way. This was hard on a college teacher's salary at the time. People often talk about how much teachers get paid most of the time; teacher salaries are low on the totem pole. Well, add to the equation keeping up in your field. To do this, you have to go to conferences, read expensive books (that aren't in the library), speak at conferences, etc. How do you do this on a teacher's salary? I went to some of those conferences anyway and found myself broke in retirement. That being said, the ADA should have recruited at least one HBCU's nutrition program with dietetic students to participate in the sample testing before making it mandatory for all interns. For all I know, maybe they did.

I went on with my life without being a registered dietitian. What I did not understand at the time was being a part of some organization, working with other people, would have helped me build my social skills and my understanding of how to work with people as a follower and a leader. I didn't get involved with the American Dietetic Association because I felt dietetics was not the career path for me. So what was my career path? I had no idea, but I chose to later become a home economics teacher.

The administrative dietitian that had unwittingly informed me of the registration exam had said that it wasn't that important because you would still be able to get a job. I guess since she was grandfathered in, since registration was something new to our field, I don't think it occurred to her that having the initials RD next to your name would come to mean what it does today. It means you have a certain authority, expertise, and statue in the field of nutrition science.

I was glad that I had been accepted at Case Western. I think I was in denial as to how much this hurt. I was not used to failure, didn't like failing anything I put my mind to do. However, I knew I'd had some obstacles, and I was furious about them. Eventually, I wanted to talk to my instructors at Southern about it. There were others from Southern who had to take the test as well; I don't know how many passed or how many failed. What I do know is that I was not properly prepared, nor was I told about the examination while I was in college, and I should have. The one course I took that would have been most helpful to passing the exam was a diet therapy course that was a two-credit hour class and was taught to me over the summer at Southern by a visiting professor. I didn't take the course that seriously and definitely did not keep the book. So when I failed the test, I tried to forget about it as I headed to graduate school at Case Western Reserve University, a private university in Cleveland, Ohio.

Case Western Reserve University— Master's Degree (1970–1971)

I didn't know what to expect at Case Western Reserve. I had never heard of the university and knew very little about private universities. I was not prepared for all the old buildings on the campuses. SU and UW had fairly modern campus and a mixture of the old and new buildings. In the taxi, I was surprised to see that most of the people on the streets were black. It seemed the campus was close to a poor black neighborhood. Later, I would see that on the other side was a rich mostly white neighborhood (Shaker Heights). I was impressed with Shaker Heights because to me the big buildings or mansions that were single-family homes and not apartment buildings looked like some of the buildings I had read about in my romance novels. In the novels, the families were always having parties, but instead of coming for a few hours, the guests would come to spend the weekend. It was like a hotel, so you needed a lot of rooms. The single-family homes in Shaker Heights were huge.

When my taxi pulled up, I thought, *This can't be my dorm. It is too old.* This time, I had flown to Cleveland instead of taking a bus, like I did when I went to Wisconsin the year earlier. I'd gotten a stipend of $200 a month during my internship and saved some of it. Of course, flying meant I couldn't buy any new clothes. So here I was in a new town and a new university with some of the clothes I had been wearing since my freshman year at Southern. It didn't matter at the University of Wisconsin because most of the time I wore uniforms. Even with that, for some reason, I got compliments on my clothes. Compliments I would just smile and say thank you to, but inside I was thinking, *This old shit.* Yes, by now I knew how to curse, even in my thoughts.

When I got to my room in the old dorm, both my roommates were there, and they were both from foreign countries. One was from the Philippine Islands (Judy), and the other one was from Greece (Marie). I couldn't believe I had gone from all black, to all white, and now all foreign roommates. I think I got along with my two foreign roommates the best, especially the one from the Philippine Islands. She and I were both naive about a lot of things. She was a virgin, and I was one except for one experience I'd had in Wisconsin. My Greek roommate was not a virgin. When I asked her when had she lost her virginity, she said she didn't know because she'd had been worked over so much she had probably broken her hymen before she actually had sex for the first time. Okay, doctors need to define virginity.

That first evening in the dorm, we went to dinner together and ate together for a few days. After a while, I noticed that most of the black students began to sit together. One day, someone invited me to join them, and so I did and ate with them from then on. Most of the black students were from Ohio, but some were from other states. They also had a variety of majors, but it seemed most of them were in law school at Case. So most of the conversations at the dinner table was about what happened in their law classes. I remember them laughing about how obnoxious one of the black students was in class. They said that he had kept interrupting the law instructor with his antics, and it was obvious he was making the instructor mad. Well, at the end of the semester, that student got an A and most of them got Cs or something lower. Well, it seemed his fearless antics impressed the instructors; no one wanted a lawyer that wouldn't speak up for them. Also, at the end of the year, most of them decided to not return except for the loudmouthed student who never sat at the black students' table. He chose to sit with his white law student counterparts. I really think some of the students had flunked out, but no one admitted to this defeat, and I understood. It was embarrassing.

Cleveland was another northern city, another year in the cold weather—what was I going to do? I really hadn't learned how to dress in the cold weather in Wisconsin. At first, I thought I would be walking from class to class in the snow most of the time. Another new thing was registering before I even got to the campus. Man, I thought Southern could use this technique. So I didn't have to stand in line because I was already registered. I did go to apply for a student loan so that I could have extra cash because by now my parents had too many kids in college and could barely help me out.

I walked over to Food and Nutrition building before my first day of class. I found out it was a large old house turned into a department. It was a far cry from Southern's School of Home Economics, which was an immaculate fairly modern large building. The Food and Nutrition Department at Case's kitchen had only a few stoves, whereas Southern's had many cooking units. The classrooms at Case looked like they had been large bedrooms in the day. Both undergraduate and graduate students attended classes in the building. I never met any undergraduate students, mostly graduate students. Most of my classes would be in the same building. My schedule seemed to have been developed with that in mind, so most of my classes were back to back. When I left the building, I was heading back to the dorm for lunch or dinner.

In most of my classes in the Food and Nutrition building, I was the only black student. There were a few other black students, but I never had more than one other black student in the class. In one of my classes, I met a black student named Debra. I was very impressed by the way she spoke. She evidently had a lot more confidence in herself than I did. She was from California and had an excellent speaking voice. She seemed to be too smart for our class. She eventually did attend medical school at Case after a short foray into the world of nutrition and became a doctor. She had married a dental student, but it didn't work out. It seemed he wanted a wife that was home most of the time, making him home-cooked meals from scratch. I think he came home one day, and Debra was gone. Debra and I kept in touch until I got married myself, and she started her medical practice. I think both of our lives got too busy, but I often wonder what happened to her. I don't think her husband ever finished dental school. I knew she would be successful in whatever she decided to do. She made smart look effortless. I am so glad our paths crossed.

Case Western University had once been two private universities, Case and Western Reserve. They had merged by the time I got there. The graduate students' dorm I lived in was coed. The boys lived on the first few floors, and the girls lived on the top floors. But you could go from floor to floor without hesitation or fear of getting into trouble, a far cry from Southern University, where men were not allowed beyond the first floor in the all-female dorms. My Greek roommate met a young man from Thailand whom she was enamored with, and soon she started spending more time in his room than ours. So Judy, my Filipino roommate, started to get close with a young student from Puerto Rico. Her name was Carmen. Both of them were public health nutrition majors as well. They were both very smart young ladies as well but were a long way from home.

In graduate school, we had a lot of papers to write. I was always able to find a typewriter to type my papers. I am so grateful that Ms. Gunn had demanded that we learn to type the right way and fast. Carmen didn't know how to type, so for her first paper, she hired someone to type it, and they charged her an exorbitant amount. After that, she started pecking out her own papers, and that took forever. I couldn't help her out because I had a lot of work myself.

None of the young black ladies—Landa (Ohio), Merline (Georgia), Sandra (Tennessee), and Audrey (Harrisburg, Pennsylvania—that I met in the dorm that I ate most of my meals with were majoring in public health nutrition. I had no one to study with. I really felt alone, but I was determined to do as well as I could. The teachers made it easy for us. Whenever, there was a paper due, they would put all the books we needed in the library in a special section. Not only that, they gave us a list of resources to use. I couldn't believe it; we had our papers handed to us by the teachers. What I surmised was that they wanted us to spend time learning and not chasing after books in the library, and I thought that was genius. I couldn't help but remember my days of coming up with my own outlines and chasing after books in SU's library only to get the reference books and find the pages torn out. It was so frustrating; this was before the personal computer and internet days. But the teachers at the white school made it easy on you, and that made sense to me.

I met a student that was twenty-four and getting his PhD in physics. I was so impressed. His name was James Smith, and I thought he was so quiet and cute and immediately developed a crush on him. I thought he was also very nice and naive, like moi. He had a brother that I would meet later who was getting his PhD in operations research in mathematics. They were from Jackson, Mississippi. I think they went to a private HBCU university in Jackson or somewhere. I do remember it was an HBCU.

The brother was married to a former queen of this university. She wore her hair in a natural style like me at the time, and I thought she was gorgeous. Then her husband, James's brother, was gorgeous as well, except he was taller. The wife asked me if I thought it was possible for her to go to Case and get a master's or medical degree. It seemed she had majored in biology. I looked at this beautiful girl with this beautiful husband who should have had all the confidence in the world, and here she was asking me, the queen of no confidence, but had goals and guts. I told her, of course, she could. Later, I found out from my friend Debra that she had indeed gotten into medical school at Case. Not only that, after the guys got their PhD degrees, they decided to enroll in medical school as well. Later, I read in *Jet* magazine that the wife was a neurosurgeon. Debra said that James was a neurologist, and his brother, I believe, became an orthopedic doctor. She also said that the husband and wife had divorced. By then, Debra had divorced her dental student husband as well. Needless to say, these would have been two power couples if they had stayed together.

Debra had said that in her marriage, she had to choose between medical school and a successful marriage. Even though her husband was in dental school and knew the rigors of studying in a professional program, he still wanted her to be a dutiful wife and cook everything from scratch like his mother (stay-at-home housewife) did when he was growing up—no shortcuts. I think she felt that his demands were hampering her studies, and he had to go. I am sure she was disappointed that he was not more understanding.

Most of the students at the table were obviously smart and had plans on being professionals in their field. I was so impressed by them and wished more so now that I'd had the gumption to major in business while at Southern. Now, in graduate school, I still found the nutrition classes boring as hell. Or like I said maybe it was the instructors, the material, or the methodology.

One of my classes was taught by the dean of the program. It was my very first class. Her name was Dr. Hunscher. We used a book she had written as the textbook for the class. I couldn't believe it; she'd actually written the textbook. Some of the other professors had written books as well. Plus, most of them had PhDs. I found the quality of the instruction excellent. On the first day of class, Dr. Hunscher told us that participation was important in her class and counted toward the grade in the class. I was the only black in her class and the only Southerner. I had to talk with my Southern accent. I was petrified of talking in front of people. Would I make any sense? Would people understand anything I said? But I was more scared of getting a poor grade, so I learned how to speak up. This was a turning point for me. I started speaking up and asking questions in all of my classes then. Afterward, I started making myself speak up in situations that were scary. My motto was, "If God wanted me to speak perfect English, I would have been born in England." This motto really worked for me. I would see people squiggle whenever I murdered a verb or pronounced a word wrong, but I figured I would never get better unless I tried.

I could never understand how some people grew up in my situation. They had poor and uneducated parents and Southern backgrounds, yet they accomplished the English language and became very articulate. I decided that I had either a learning disability or hearing issues. I knew I was tone-deaf, at least I thought so. Maybe it was a lack of confidence. It would be years before a co-worker would tell me that a lot of people from the south joined choirs to improve their articulation, even if they couldn't sing that well. I then remembered how my principal Mr. Hayes kept putting me in choir in high school. He didn't know that I was not following the protocol and was just mouthing the words as the others sang. I was happiest when she worked with groups other than the second sopranos because then I could sneak and study math or biology. Most of the students that were in the choir became very articulate. I noticed that the students in drama did as well. This was one time I was too smart for my britches and should have followed Mr. Hayes's lead. I wish he had told me why he was putting me in the choir, which evidently was to assist me with my articulation.

Even though I was quiet at school, with my family and friends, I talked a lot. As a matter of fact, I think I talked too much, so I didn't realize I had mispronounced so many words. It was in high school that I started to realize that many of the words that I heard over and over again at home were really being pronounced wrong. It took me a while to correct some of them in my head, but not before some people would laugh and make fun of me. Even though I had many more degrees than my husband, he would often correct my English. The one thing I remember him correcting was this: I used to say "raise the window down." He would correct me and say, "Laura, that doesn't make sense. You can't raise a window down. You raise a window up. You let the window down." I remembered that the first time he did that, I gave him a puzzled look. I remember saying, "What do you mean?" He said, "Think about it. When you raise something, you put it up, not down." Then I got it. I probably still said "raise the window down" sometimes, but not without thinking back to that conversation and, most importantly, correcting it in my head.

I said so many things wrong and eventually would tell my husband before he spoke up that I knew it was wrong, but he knew what I meant to say, so shut up and do whatever the command was. For instance, if the window was down already, it was obvious I wanted it up. I did this because now I knew I had a lot of correcting to do with my language skills. But it was not going to be done overnight, and I was so tired of him correcting me. The funny thing is, I don't remember any of my Southern teachers correcting me like my husband did. I don't know if it was because I spoke so little in class, so they didn't realize how poorly I spoke, or it could have been that they were used to the mispronunciations as well and didn't catch them. I should not have gotten all the way through high school without some of my bad habits not being caught.

I am so glad I had my motto though of always speaking up no matter how it comes out. Later, becoming a teacher myself, I knew how important it was to communicate well so that the average person could understand you. I also knew how important articulation was to getting promotions. I am sure my poor language skills hindered me more than I know. I believe Dr. King knew we were smart and didn't have the articulation skills, but with Affirmative Action programs, we could learn and get better and better. I see this all the time with minorities on television. Now, if you close your eyes, you would think everyone was white on television. But no. Often it is an articulate African American. Many think it is speaking like white folks, but no, it is just being more articulate. We grew up with articulate whites on television, but in our neighborhoods, we heard something different, so we thought being articulate is being white. I really appreciated my articulate African American instructors in college; otherwise, I would not have graduated. Most of my white instructors, I felt, thought they were automatically articulate; but no, they weren't. To me, often they spoke too fast, and therefore some of their words were not as articulated as they thought. To me, they sounded like foreigners, and I'd wish they would speak more like my African American instructors.

I found that most of my white instructors at Case spoke well. For some reason, I could understand them, and I was grateful. I think because they wrote the books, they wanted you to understand. Or was it because they had mixed classes, so they spoke as if they were teaching white students? I figured my white instructors at Southern, who had 100 percent black students, really didn't care if we learned or not. They had not been able to get jobs at white universities like they wanted to, so why try?

A turning point for me at Case came when Dr. Neville, one of the instructors, questioned me about why I was always getting Bs on my book reports, papers, etc. She said that she wanted my opinion, not just the author's. She said she wanted my papers to be more colorful and with more of me in them. When I wrote my papers, I really didn't write in my own voice; the voice was more sterile because I didn't think my voice was enough to get an A. I didn't think I'd had enough experience to be colorful in my writing. Most of the books I had read other than schoolbooks had been romance novels, especially after I left Minden, because I couldn't afford any of the other books.

Because I had no social life, these books would add to my daydreams of being more social and having a boyfriend.

In Minden, I used to go to our little small library on Crichton Hill. I'd literally read almost every book in the place and started on the encyclopedias. I thought this was silly until a *Britannica* salesperson told me years later that she had read them from cover to cover. I was so amazed that I bought her books. It was at Case that I started to realize that I needed to expand my reading and to know that when you read books, somehow many of the words become a part of your vocabulary without you knowing it.

After Dr. Neville had approached me about my writing, I decided to work on being colorful and being myself in my writing. I couldn't believe it when I got an A from Dr. Neville on my very next paper. It was weird. I thought when I was writing the paper that it was stupid. I had compared the author's ideas to a rainbow. Dr. Neville loved it and said I was on the right track. I knew then that both Webster and Southern had failed in teaching me how to write. I knew that white instructors had expected me to be me, even if my experiences had been of the low-income country variety. But white instructors should know that not all black students speak as I did and still do sometimes and indeed do speak like white people and deserve As on their papers.

What I didn't realize was that the way you spoke in class or with your professor in private was the way they expected you to do on your papers. I don't think they expected poor English. They expected you to put it in quotation marks or do and/or type of sentence. Plus, students should not anticipate that their lives don't matter to all of their teachers and to share their experiences; just use good English. Then again, test developers should consider that all students do not have the same experiences and to use some of the experiences of less-fortunate people in their tests items as well. What I mean is, instead of "when I drove my car to school," use "when I walked or took the bus to school"—and not poor English! I believe some poor students would make better grades if they could see themselves and their experiences in the test items every once in a while.

At Webster, by the time I was a senior, the instructor who taught senior English had become our first high school counselor. Students had praised her for her ability to teach English. So I was looking forward to learning English under her and was so disappointed to find out that Ms. Lillian Mitchell would be my senior English teacher. Ms. Mitchell was also my homeroom teacher. Mostly what I learned in her class was that there were different types of paragraphs, descriptive, narrative, etc. I did not learn how to put those paragraphs together in different types of compositions and nothing about consistency or transitioning. I remember thinking not having Mrs. June Turner as my English teacher for my senior year was going to haunt me for the rest of my life, and it has. She had made a reputation for herself as an English teacher, which was positive. But to me, she was probably the worst counselor because she always discouraged C students from going to college.

After a few nutrition classes at Case, I figured I was only going to make Bs on most my paper, no matter how hard I tried. It had nothing to do with my researching or writing ability but everything to do with my skin color. One of my white classmates explained it to me. She was married and lived off campus. She noticed how hard I tried to transcribe my sentences so I wouldn't be graded down for plagiarism. She said the teachers didn't expect me to write that way because of my speech pattern, whereas if she quoted the authors word for word, the instructors didn't catch it because they anticipated that she would write that way because she was white. So right before my eyes, she proceeded to copy her paper word for word from the resources and later showed me that she had gotten an A on the paper. I appreciated her telling me that because after that, I didn't work that hard and still got Bs. I needed to spend more time on my other subjects because I was not making good grades in those classes, and I knew I needed to have a B average to graduate. I made enough As and Bs in my nutrition classes to compensate for the Cs I made in the other classes.

My social life at Case improved even if most of the activities were in the dorm. Like I said earlier, the dorm was coed. We'd have social events catered by the cafeteria staff. We had several wine tastings that were interesting. I had never drank wine, and I kind of liked some of them. I tried not to drink too much, but I tasted quite a few of them and found myself with hangovers in the mornings afterward. We were able to also dance and eat hors d'oeuvres and canapés. I even danced with some of the white guys.

One event that is forever singed into my mine is Valentine's Day 1971. I was at the table eating with the same group of African American students per usual when Merline, one of the girls, sat down and began to fuss at the black guys at the table and to tell them that they could have at least bought us some flowers. I think she said roses. Harold, one of the guys, said that his father never bought his mother flowers for Valentine's Day. That made Merline even angrier because Harold had been trying to woo her. I think that statement brought an end to their relationship. But Harold was right. If you never see it in your own household, it's hard for you to imagine it in real life. As a girl, I couldn't help but think, Why would I want flowers from strangers? None of these guys were my boyfriend. I had never seen my father give my mother flowers or any other gift. My mother never seemed to mind, probably because she never saw her father give her mother flowers or any other gift. I am pretty sure Merline got the habit from television and not from her own family, but maybe I am wrong. She'd once told me that the first man she loved left her with a baby, and the rest would leave record players, clothes, etc. She said she was not going to be used again. I thought she had a warped sense of thinking.

Like I said, I decided to spend more time studying for my other classes (i.e., epidemiology, social science, biochemistry, etc.). I had a hard time understanding my professor in my social science graduate course. He invited us to his home one night for a study session. I went with some of the other nutrition majors. All of a sudden, our professor started smoking a cigarette, and the smell in the room was putrid. I finally figured out that he was smoking marijuana in our presence. I was beside myself; this was illegal. I had to get out of there. I couldn't believe it. How dare he put all of our lives in danger that way? I was glad when the session was over. I didn't remember anything that was discussed during the study session. I lost all respect for that professor. I think I got a C out of his course.

I was scared of the grade I was going to get in biochemistry. My experiences in biochemistry taught me a lot. I made a D on my first exam. The head professor invited those of us who had not passed the exam to his office for a retest. We went in small groups. He would go around the room and pose each of us questions. I was surprised at some of my white counterparts' answers. I thought, *Wow, they don't know any more than I do.* It was the first time I felt confident that my education was indeed not inferior. That if you knew how to read, you could learn; you just had to spend the time studying. Who knew?

I grew into adulthood at Case. I even enjoyed the food. For the most part, the food in Wisconsin and Cleveland was not as spicy as the food in Southern Louisiana, but it was spicier than my mom's cooking. In Wisconsin, I had been introduced to cauliflower that was breaded and fried. I loved it. In Cleveland, I learned to love liver with bacon and onions. I had already gotten over my disgust of liver in Southern Louisiana when my roommates cooked it with their twist in seasonings. Now add the bacon and onions, and my mouth just watered.

The black students sat at a table near the kitchen of the dorm, so we got close with some of the staff. I guess since we were in graduate school, we couldn't help but talk to the young men who helped out about what their goals were in life. One of the guys said that he wanted to be a gangster and join the mob. I can't remember exactly what I said to him, but I am pretty sure I said something like, "So you want to die or go to jail." I remember him looking kind of funny, but I am not sure if he was dismayed.

I even threw myself a birthday party while at Case in my dorm room. This would be my first adventure into planning any type of social event. I am not sure what gave me the gumption when everyone there would be a stranger to me. I had a gotten a $1,000 National Defense loan and used some of the money to buy some clothes and throw the party (a mistake, I know now, but this would not be the first). When I went shopping, I bought separates so I could mix and match. But most of my clothes were purple or black. I loved black, and purple became my new favorite color. I got a lot of compliments on my old clothes and now on my new clothes. I had been wearing those old clothes forever. I even bought me a hot-pants outfit. Hot pants were in vogue at the time, but I don't even remember ever wearing shorts before, maybe pedal pushers. I didn't know what my body looked like until I was eighteen years old when I locked myself in my parents room, got naked and used the mirror in their room to look at my entire body.

I had met a guy; I can't remember where, maybe on the streets. He had taken me to my first Muslim restaurant in Cleveland where I had pork roast with the best mashed potatoes. To this day, no one believes I had pork in a Muslim restaurant, but I did. The Muslim community was not too far from the university. The guy was my escort to my birthday party. I have a picture of us together, but I can't remember his name, and I don't think I saw him after that night. I don't think he could dance, and I loved dancing. I know it was stupid, but I used to judge guys by the way they danced. It was my shimmery period, so I wore a shimmery blouse and a shimmery pair of pants. I thought they fit me nicely, especially the pants. I was becoming aware of my body.

I wore the hot pants to another party. I have one picture of me in those pants. I had stockings on, and I don't know why, but I think I did look hot. At the time, I thought men were only attracted to pretty faces, not a girl's body. I never dressed to impressed men; I just tried to wear what was in style at the time.

The other black girls and I would often play cards in the basement with some of the other black guys. I had learned to play cards in the girls' dorms at Southern, and that was where I learned my first curse words. The only problem was that cursing at Southern was made in fun. But when I did it at the card table at Case with men, it wasn't. One day, one of the guys (Leonard, a dental student) pulled me aside and told me that my cursing made me look tramp-ish (or something like that), that good girls didn't do it. I really didn't understand what he meant, but I did stop cursing. I figured since cursing by men didn't appeal to me, since I had not heard any cursing growing up, this was a similar situation, and they were not used to women cursing.

One day, I did go to Paul's room (Paul was an older guy that had PTSD from the Vietnam or Korean War) and asked him just what did Leonard mean about how I looked. Paul was too kind to say, but his roommate (a guy that we all thought was gay) said that I was acting like a whore. I couldn't believe he had said that. Here I was with one night of sex under my belt, and the men at Case thought I was a whore. I cried like a baby, so the guy apologized to me. Later that night, I wore my hot pants, and Paul said, "I see you got over the incident that happened in my room." It didn't dawn on me that he might have been talking about the hot pants I was wearing. Man, was I naive. I didn't have sex that night or any other night while I was in Cleveland.

Before I graduated from Case, I had to complete an apprenticeship in Public Health Nutrition. I was assigned to do mine with the Chicago Board of Health. I couldn't help but remember my first foray into Chicago when I was on a field trip as an intern, and how it looked so dirty to me. I grew up in Minden, Louisiana, and we often got the award for being the cleanest city in Louisiana. So you can see my embarrassment when I first drove into Chicago with a bunch of white dietetic interns and see mostly black people and trash all over the place. I wanted to get out of the car and pick up the trash. After I returned, now to do my apprenticeship in Chicago, I did pick up a lot of trash until the AIDS epidemic, and then I stopped. Trash on the streets is still an ongoing problem in Chicago, even on my own block. But when I came back to Chicago, this time I flew in, and man was, it was a different sight: the city looked wonderful. The lights were beaming; they looked like stars. I wondered what was in store for me in this big city for a small-town girl.

Chicago (Public Health Nutrition Apprenticeship)

I was staying at the Y for young women because I had limited funds. Another Board of Health apprentice from Tuskegee Institute (Mozella) was also staying there. Her room was next to mine. We took the bus to the Board of Health main offices downtown together that first day. To take the bus in 1971 was not that expensive, but I thought it was because I had never ridden a city bus before. The trip to the Chicago Civic Center, where the Chicago Board of Health was housed, was quick. We got off the bus a few blocks from the Civic Center. Once we got into the building, we located the offices of the Nutrition Section of the Chicago Board of Health. I couldn't believe it; they were in the basement. One of the reasons I didn't want to be a dietitian in a hospital was because they seem to be located mostly in the basement of buildings. Basements of buildings made me feel like I was suffocating. The Civic Center was a huge building, more than ten stories. I never felt comfortable there, not one day.

We walked into the Nutrition Section, and the first person I saw was a black woman sitting behind the desk. Mozella and I introduced ourselves, and the woman (Helen Carroll) said, "Just a moment," and went to get the Director (Virgina Jauck) and the assistant director (Betty Tate). After speaking a few minutes, we were joined by Florence Smith. Florence was going to be our supervisor for the duration of our apprenticeship. One of the first things I noticed about Florence was her green teeth. She had this big smile with green teeth. She was a prolific smoker, and that's how her teeth became discolored. I felt sorry for her. She was nice, however; and I, for the most part, enjoyed the training. I got the chance to visit high-rise federal projects. Most of the inhabitants were black, so I was not scared. I did notice that people kept throwing things over the banisters, and the elevators were filled with graffiti. Plus, there were a lot of little kids. There didn't seem to be a lot of playground equipment, so I couldn't help but wonder what the kids did for fun. Even though I had not grown up with a lot of playground equipment either, we did have big plots of land to do whatever we wanted to do. These kids didn't have much land to play in at all.

Living on the near north section of Chicago was an eye-opening experience. I saw so many different people. I lived close to Michigan Avenue, so I saw a lot of rich people. I lived one block from Mister Kelly's, one of the most famous jazz clubs in Chicago. It was where Ramsey Lewis would play often. The Playboy Club was nearby as well. But you'd see little black boys roaming the streets at 10:00 p.m. I found out that there was a federal project called Cabrini Green that was nearby. There were evidently prostitutes on the streets, but I couldn't tell them apart from regular people. A lot of people worked in the area and would party there as well. There were a lot of restaurants and clubs in the area close by the Y.

I had noticed that whenever I went out on the streets on the weekend by myself especially, men would honk their horns or whistle. I would just ignore them. I had no idea they thought I was a prostitute working the streets. Man, was I in the wrong section of town.

Before I left for Chicago, Merline had schooled me on how to protect myself from men to keep myself from being raped. She told me that he couldn't hold my legs and my hands at the same time, so when he opened my legs to place my hands over my vagina so he couldn't penetrate, then when he moved my hands to close my legs again. I thought she was wasting her time because I didn't see myself getting into that type of situation.

The second weekend I was in Chicago, Mozella went to visit relatives in the city, and I was by myself and alone and felt a little lonely in a crowded city. I went out to get something to eat and passed by some pay phones in the lobby. This guy that was talking on the phone got my attention; he hung up the phone and started walking with me. He smiled at me and asked me where I was going, and I told him to get something to eat. He walked me to the restaurant and walked me back to the Y. He asked if he could take me out to dinner the next evening. I said okay, and we agreed on the time. When we went out to dinner not too far from the Y, I thought I was safe. We decided to just walk around a bit after dinner. He started pointing out girls he thought were prostitutes. Later I would find out that they were his prostitutes; he was a pimp. At least, he said he was a pimp, and I believed him after he had tried to rape me.

While we were walking, he said that he'd forgotten his watch in his apartment around the corner. I really didn't know where I was; we had walked several blocks from the Y by then. He said he wanted to run upstairs and get it before he took me home and that I could wait in the lobby. However, when we got to the lobby, he said, "Come on up to my floor. I don't trust leaving you in the lobby." I followed him and decided I was going to wait outside his door. He said to come on in because nothing was going to happen to me—famous last words. I followed him in, and there were no chairs, so I sat on the bed and waited for him to get his watch. He had turned on the television. He came back into the room and sat next to me. The next thing I knew, he had pushed me down on the bed and was on top of me. I remembered what Merline had told me and started closing my legs to protect my vagina; and when he opened my legs, I would put my hands over it. We played this game for about thirty minutes—all the while I was talking to him.

I cursed (not a norm for Christian me) him and told him that in a few weeks, I would be getting my master's degree and starting to work after being in college for six years, and he wanted to take that excitement from me, that I was a poor black girl that wanted something for herself and had worked hard for it and was still a virgin. I told him that when he finished to just kill me because even though I was small and looked timid, I definitely was not and that my father had five brothers and my mother had six, and they would find him and kill him. I also told him that his face would be front page on the *Sun Times* tomorrow because I was not one of those mealymouthed girls who wouldn't go to the police and not testify. I told him if he didn't want to go to jail, he had to kill me. By the time I gave up, his dick was limp, and he couldn't have penetrated a grape. When I told Merline about this later, she said I should have kicked him then. He got up and decided to walk me home.

As we walked home, he did educate me on why I should never go into a guy's room. He said that he could have called his friends over, and they could have gang-raped me. He also said that he was a pimp. I had been in town less than a month. Plus, here I was, broke and vulnerable. After that event, I knew dating in Chicago was going to be hazardous to my health, if I was not careful

I appreciated the education, and eventually I took it to heart, but I should have called the cops anyway. Why I didn't, I don't know. I think a lot of girls never call the police, and we should—then we could stop some of this molestation of young girls. Men are molesting girls younger and younger these days. The female body is not at a man's disposal. Our bodies are not to be used and tossed away like trash. No means no, but we send a different message when we don't press charges. We need to change this scenario now. I think black girls don't want to send black men to jail, so by not reporting the offense, we doom young babies to these heathens. I think some black girls don't want to send black boys or men to prison because so many are incarcerated. I remember thinking when I was in Wisconsin that there were not that many black men there, but when I went to Waupun State Prison with the other dietetic interns to tour their food-service operation, I noticed that there were so many "fine" young black men there, and it was then I realized where all the black men were, and it was a pity. I had even met one of Waupun's black prisoners. He had been a patient of mine, and I thought he was the finest man I had ever met. We even wrote to each other after he left the hospital. To this day, I don't know why I gave a prisoner my address.

While I was in Chicago, a friend (Henry Banks) from Webster High School who also had attended Southern invited me over to play cards. He said other Southernites and Gramblingnites would be there. I was excited to go, but he lived on the south side of Chicago, and I didn't know how to get there on the bus. He said for me to take a taxi, and he would pay for it. During the taxi ride there, the driver pulled into an alley and asked me if I wanted to make some money. I cursed him out and told him to get me out of that alley and to take me where I was supposed to go. I have no idea how often this happens to girls, but this should be sexual harassment as well and should be against the law—I was scared to death. I was lucky he did take me to my friend's house in the end, and I enjoyed the evening playing cards. Thankfully, someone gave me a ride back to the Y later. Again, I should have gotten his cab number or license plate and called the cops. The cab driver was white.

Another evening in Chicago, a friend of a friend from Case came to town and invited me to dinner. I had met the guy before; he was a friend of a guy (his name was James) I had met from Africa. I had gone on a double date with the both of them in Cleveland. I'd had a pleasant evening, and James was a nice guy. I remember he got tuberculosis and had to stop school. I couldn't figure out how he got TB. Maybe he had it before he left Africa because only few people still had it in the United States. I did go to visit him in the sanitarium, and I was surprised at how many people were there. I felt so sorry for James; he was so far from home.

After dinner in Chicago, the guy invited me up to his room. I can't remember what he said to me to get me to go to his room (this was after the pimp incident), but I never imagined it included sex until he closed the door. After he closed the door, he started looking funny and making innuendos leading toward sex. I told him I had to go home, and he strongly encouraged me to stay. I got a little scared, but he allowed me to go. I was so disappointed in him because by then I had a lot of respect for African men, maybe because James had been so nice.

After that fiasco, I decided not to date any more. So I just finished my apprenticeship, and to my surprise, I was invited back to be a part of the nutrition staff. I had met one black nutritionist, and she said that if I came back, I could stay with her and her two kids until I found a place to stay. Wow, I thought, I already had a job and a place to stay, and I had no family in Chicago. I even got another offer from Detroit Board of Health. My friend Debra from Case had done her apprenticeship in Detroit and made sure I'd gotten an offer there. I chose Chicago because I was used to their program by now and didn't need much training. So, Chicago, here I come.

(After almost twenty years after finishing at Case, I decided to get a doctoral degree. Now, I am working full time as a community college administrator, is married to James, and we have a son named James Jr.)

Northern Illinois University— Doctoral Degree (1990–1994)

I had been a community college administrator for several years when another administrator informed me that Northern Illinois University was starting a doctoral cohort for community college teachers and administrators. She said that we would have to take classes one weekend a month for two years and then complete a dissertation. I thought one weekend a month didn't sound too bad. I wouldn't be away from my family too much, and I could still work full-time. Later on, I would find out that it would cost me $200 a month; and by the end of the program, I should be finished paying tuition. I thought, *No loans? Count me in!* So I applied for the program and got accepted.

When I became an administrator, my professional circle changed, and I was in the company of people with doctorates or PhD degrees. I started to want the knowledge that they had so I could be more in the conversation. So when James Jr. was four, I applied for the doctoral cohort group with Northern Illinois University and got in. I figured that I could get the degree out of the way while James Jr. was still young and didn't need me as much. It was weird because I had never thought of getting a doctorate before. I knew that I loved learning, though.

In order to move from lane to lane on the career ladder as a college professor with the City Colleges of Chicago, you had to take courses. When I started at Kennedy-King, one of the City Colleges of Chicago, I was an instructor. I took some graduate courses and was able to move up to assistant professor. I think the next step was either associate professor or full professor. I never did get the chance to apply for those lanes before I became an administrator. With each advance in lane, you got more money. I enjoyed taking the classes; every time I would learn something new. So I was looking forward to starting the program at Northern.

Before we started our coursework at Northern, there was an orientation for our families. James, James Jr., and I went, and we were able to meet the other families. I hope I didn't imagine this; I am pretty sure it happened, but it was over twenty years ago now. It seemed that the class was about half and half, half black and half white, students. There were several Hispanic and, later I would learn, one American Indian. It was weird because I had been working with the American Indian about four years. She was the director of Academic Support Services at Truman College on the north side of Chicago. I met with her and other support service directors monthly at the City College's headquarters with the associate vice chancellor. I think her name was Deidra Jackson. We had been meeting for years, and I had no idea Dorene was American Indian. I had assumed she was either Hispanic or Filipino. I had no idea she was American Indian. I never asked, and I don't remember her or Deidra ever mentioning it directly. She must have talked about her culture at some point in time, but whatever she said must not have registered with me. I think I found out when she introduced herself in our class at Northern; or Phyllis, our instructor, may have mentioned it.

I think Phyllis loved the diversity of our group. We had Southern black Americans, Northern black Americans, white males, white women, Jewish men and women, Hispanic male, Hispanic woman, black males, black women, and one American Indian; single women, divorced men and women, married men and women, low-level college administrators like myself and Dorene, one vice president, college faculty, and administrators. Most of the doctoral students were from the City Colleges of Chicago. Quite a few were from Kennedy-King College, one of the city colleges of Chicago, and where I was employed at the time. We had a pretty big class; I think we started with about thirty-six people. It was quite an eclectic group. Someone could have done a dissertation on just our group.

The orientation was held in a room across from the hotel (the Holmes Student Center) where we would be staying in if we stayed on campus. My plan was to stay on campus. I knew it was going to be expensive every month. I also had to pay for parking. I don't remember if the Holmes Student Center provided room service, but I do know they had a restaurant and a vending area. Plus, there were a lot of food services near the campus. All of our classes would be together and in the classroom where the orientation was held. We were in the LEPS (Leadership and Educational Policy Studies) program. Primarily, our doctorate would be in adult and continuing education. We would be learning how to teach adults. Looking at the curriculum, there was only one course that dealt with higher-education administration. My aim was to become a dean or vice president of a college. I had not intended on going back to faculty, but here I was, learning how to teach adults. My whole teaching career, had been teaching adult students. These were going to be classes that I needed prior to teaching. Here I was again, going against my desires.

I had never ever figured on teaching as a career. Even though, whenever, my siblings and I played school, I always played the part of the teachers. I think it was because I was the oldest. Now, looking back, I probably bullied my way into being the teacher every time. I think sometimes I would let Bobbie be the teacher. But as a profession, I never saw myself in that role. But having never seen anything but teachers and principals as black students in the South, it was a logical career for most of us because they were our role models.

We were able to meet most of our instructors during the orientation as well. I wondered if we were going to have any black instructors. As it turned out, we had one black instructor. He was the chairman of the English Department. I am always amazed at an African American who chooses to major in English. English was always my worse subject. When my sister Bobbie chose English as a major, I couldn't believe it.

We were given our class schedule during the orientation. Our first class would start on July 1990, only a few weeks away. All of our classes would be held in the room where the orientation was being held. The instructors would come to us instead of us going to their classrooms. This was the advantage of being in a cohort. I thought it was so cool since we were all working full-time, and most of us had families. This was very helpful to us and cut down on the confusion of finding your way around campus.

I knew I was going to be one busy sister, with working full-time and being a wife and a mother. Plus, my mom and dad and James's mom were advancing in age and would probably need more care than usual. But I knew with God's help and if it was His plan, whatever I started, I generally finished; so I knew that in a few years, I would have a doctorate.

On the first day of class, I loved walking right across the street to the classroom. The first day was nerve-racking because I had been working all day, then drove about one and half hours to Northern's campus in DeKalb, Illinois with some of my Kennedy-King colleagues. I think it was Nellie, the person who had told me about the program in the first place and a colleague I will call James S. Nellie was the Assistant Dean of the GED program at Kennedy-King and James S. was one of the GED instructors. We had to sit through four hours of class. To my surprise, we had a homework assignment on that first evening. We were given something to read and to report on that next morning. It may have been a group assignment (I can't remember now); we had so many late-night group assignments we had to work on before our class the next day. By the end of that first weekend, I was insane; I was so tired. What kept me going was that I found the material that we discussed interesting. Let's face it, I just loved learning. We would be talking about lifelong learning, and here I was, a real lifelong learner.

To top it off, I couldn't sleep that first night in the Holmes Student Center. It was a high-rise, and after I developed a thyroid condition and had my car accident, I had a fear of heights. I am not sure when or how it started, but it did and I hated it. The Holmes Center was not that high, but it took some getting used to. Plus, I missed sleeping with James, and I missed my son. I was lonesome. For most of my life, I was always with people. Now here I was, alone for a whole weekend, and it felt weird. Here I was, so tired, and I couldn't sleep, and I had to be in class at 8:00 a.m. I had never been a coffee drinker, but I think I started drinking decaffeinated coffee just to wake up for class that first weekend and every one afterward.

I was nervous that second day of class because of the assignment. I am pretty sure we had to give some type of report. Who can remember? It was so long ago. Whatever, it was, I got through it and many assignments afterward for two years. Most of our assignments were research papers. For the most part, I got Bs on my papers. By the end of the first semester, I was driving to Northern with just James S. On his first paper, he got an A. I asked him how he did it, and he told me that he'd had help and that I could get help as well. It seemed someone had written the paper for him. I wanted no parts of that. How could you learn if someone else wrote the paper for you? I knew it was going to catch up with him.

After our first or second course, the instructors told us they were going to give us a written examination because it seemed some of us were probably not writing our own papers. My mind, of course, flew to James S. I had remembered how the instructors had made him lead us in discussion one day, and he proceeded to do what I call bullshit everybody. It was obvious he didn't know much about the subject, and here he was getting As on his papers, which indicated just the opposite. I figured he was the main reason we were taking the written examination.

Before we started the program, we had to do an essay; that was to provide them with a sample of our writing. And then of course, someone else could have done the essay. I was upset with Northern for not doing a better job of vetting the cohort group members, but grateful I'd taken that adult education English course from Governor's State University a year before I started the doctoral cohort because English compositions had always been a weakness of mine. As director of Academic Support Services, I had access to videotapes with instructions in math, English, etc. Since English is my weakness in written and oral expression, I decided to look at the English videotapes to see what I could learn to improve myself. I think you should always work on your weaknesses. In one of the videotapes on English composition, the instructor said that she taught freshman English and that she sometimes would take it from another instructor herself just to refresh herself, and that made sense to me. Why not just take English composition again! I don't know how I found this class, but I found an adult education English composition course from Governor's State University. It was not that expensive, and it was in the evening. This course changed my life. My poor writing and English usage skills had a damaging effect on my confidence level.

The first evening in the English composition course, the instructor (Dr. O'Connor, I believe) introduced herself and said that she was a linguist. I think she had her PhD in linguistics. I really didn't know what linguistics was, but I knew it had something to do with languages. In the class, she talked about how people speak differently and how you should write for the audience you intended to reach. She emphasized the importance of prewriting a composition first. As I understood it, it is where you write down what you knew about the topic prior to doing any research. She also asked us to write two pages in a journal every night. It's been a while now, but I think she said it was to exercise our fingers. Whether she said it or not, that is what I found happening with me. Writing those journal pages every night helped me to write more. It not only exercised my fingers, it exercised my brain. I had to really concentrate to come up with two full pages every night. She had us turn the journaling in, so we had to do them. It wasn't just an exercise in futility.

Until her class, I had never thought much about the flow of the paper. She taught me about consistency and transitioning between paragraphs and sentences, the importance of the beginning and ending paragraphs, details, etc. I finally began to get some confidence in my writing. I still lacked confidence in my verbal skills. I realized in high school that I was probably tone-deaf because I couldn't carry a note, and that was probably hindering my ability to hear myself talk. I could write using standard English; I just couldn't do it while spontaneously speaking. I was getting better; I realized that all those years of shyness and not talking had hindered me. Later on, I would realize how my parents, teachers, and friends spoke had an effect on the way I spoke as well. But one thing my mom and dad did probably had the most hindrance, and that was making sure babies were kept in a quiet room. I learned that even though you were little and not speaking yourself, the words that people were saying somehow found the way into your brains. There is no way for that to happen if you are in quiet room the first few years of your life. Plus, there was no television, radio, music, maybe a little singing by my mother. To top that, my parents were shy, both of them, so they seldom had company over. So loud discussions weren't heard so they could penetrate our brains and add to our word pool. After Dr. O'Connor's class, I was at least more confident in my writing ability.

Somewhere along the line, I learned about Black English or Ebonics, and I realized that was the style of English I was using. But according to my linguistics instructor, if I wanted to write so that the majority of people could understand what I was writing, I had to use standard English. She said that it was okay to speak or write using what is called poor English, if it would be understood by my audience. By saying that, she liberated me. I figured if God had wanted me to speak or write perfectly, I would have been born in England. If I was supposed to use the king's English, then I would have been born in England and not in Louisiana to poor, uneducated parents. I was doing the best I could do, but it would not hurt, to continue to work on my English skills so that I could be understood by the masses.

I made my first legitimate As on compositions I wrote in an English class taught by a linguist. My final grade was an A. I had never been that proud of a grade in my life. I loved the textbooks that she used in the class. I have them to this day. The books to me taught English composition like science. I had always made As or Bs in science, so these particular books hit home with me. Conquering English composition really added to my confidence level. It still wasn't where it should be and probably never would be because of my poor English usage. But when they said we were going to take a writing composition examination, I knew I had that in the bag.

On the day of the exam, I sat by James S. I noticed that he only wrote one or two paragraphs. I knew he was not going to pass the test, and he didn't. There was another young lady in the class that I had gotten to know who didn't pass the test either. She and James had both majored in criminology at the same university. They both had master's degrees in the subject from that university. I had taken courses at that university and had been very impressed with the quality of instruction, so I knew it had to be the program and not the university that gave those degrees that they did not earn. Neither of them could write a research paper. What else do you do in graduate school except write research papers? I remember going to the library with the young lady at this same university (I often used their library to do my research; it was familiar to me because I had been taking graduate courses there myself for years) to research a paper for one of our classes in the doctoral program, and she didn't know where the stacks were. How could you get a master's degree from the university and not know where the books were? She knew where the reference books were located, but sometimes you actually needed to go to the actual source (reference books only summarized), and she had no idea where the "books" were located. I knew James S. did not write his papers; I was wondering if she had gotten someone to write hers as well.

They were both put out of the doctoral program, but the young lady was able to get back in because she complained to higher authorities. I could understand where she was coming from; the entrance criteria should have weeded her out before she even took a class in the doctoral program. I knew even if she got back in the program, the instructors would make sure she never finished. They didn't have to do that though because I don't think she ever turned in a proposal for her dissertation. I think the program they were in had a reputation of being an easy A because one of my nieces went to the same university and majored in criminology and graduated with a master's in it and never worked a day in it in her life. After having a hard time finding a job, she went back to school to get a degree in what I told her she should major in before she even started to college. She didn't finish it either. Sometimes it's not the program; it is the student using every hook or crook to get through a program and skirting the actual learning process only to discover that they need that knowledge later on in a job or in life.

My niece eventually found a two-year program that she liked and graduated from and is now making a living in the field. Our paths crossed when in her new position as a ECG technician at a local hospital near us, when my husband had a ministroke and was taken by ambulance to this hospital, she was the one who found that he had a small hole in his heart that caused the stroke. Imagine how much money she could have made if she had started this job at twenty years of age (it was only a two-year degree) instead of, I think, thirty-six or so.

I was not that surprised when I passed the writing composition test. The instructors had said it would help them decide whether to keep us in the program or not. What I knew for sure was that when it came to me, that decision was mine, not theirs. The decision was totally mine and only mine. I had to decide if I wanted to kill myself studying and robbing my family of my time or not and whether it was worth it. For some reason, I decided it was worth it, and I do not regret it, but I have really never recouped the financial losses or brain matter from those four years. When I finished the program, I really questioned my sanity, and I've been questioning it ever since. I was definitely "at risk" of failing because I was not an education major. This "at risk" student needed to get a bachelor's and master's degree in education essentially while she was studying for her doctorate it seemed.

I am glad I finished the program because I learned things that I never would have otherwise. It was amazing reading all the studies and what the researchers had discerned. I also learned things about myself, and I think that was most surprising thing of all. One of our instructors asked us to critically journal every day. I started it in his class, and I continue to do it today. I had been journaling before; I'd started it in the adult education English composition class I took and continued it. But now exactly what is critically journaling? The way I understood it, it was not only writing down what you did that day but also why. I was amazed at what poured out of my brain. Even though it seemed like I was the type of person that whatever came up came out in conversation. My feelings really poured out in my journaling, and I discovered that I held back in conversation, that I still had trouble explaining myself in the moment. When I went into the doctoral program, I spoke in sentences. When I came out, I spoke in paragraphs; therefore, I was able to express myself more fully. I am still a work in progress, and I know it is because of my background and not a lack of smartness.

We were informed that we had to choose a dissertation chair. But first we had to decide what type of dissertation we wanted to do. One weekend, we had instructors whose expertise was in particular types of research come in to talk to us and explain the type of research. Dr. Rose's expertise was in historical research. I felt a warmth from her that I did not feel from the other instructors. For some reason, I felt I would be able to talk with her comfortably. She was the youngest of the instructors. The problem was, she was historical, and I wanted to do a quantitative dissertation. It was explained to us that all the instructors could help us with whatever type of dissertation we chose. I wanted to do a quantitative dissertation because I didn't trust my writing well enough to do a qualitative dissertation.

I had always loved working with numbers. I knew I was going to have to learn how to do statistics, and I had always wanted to learn more about statistics ever since my friend Pearlie took it in college, and she hated it. She hated it, but just listening to her, I wanted to learn more about the things she was talking about like standard deviation and analysis of variance.

I met with Dr. Rose and told her I wanted to do a quantitative dissertation, and she said that she could help me; but since that was not her expertise, she could recommend a professor to serve on my committee that would guide me in quantitative research. She suggested Dr. Abrams, I believe of the educational psychology department. Dr. Abrams proved to be invaluable. What I did not know was that each university had their way of doing things when it came to quantitative analysis. What I am trying to say is that each university had their own uniqueness, and Northern was no exception. Dr. Abrams understood what that was and guided me expertly. I had no idea how important this was until one of my cohort members was pulled from his defense when the information he presented was not in the form that Northern's research specialists wanted. He had used someone that was not familiar with Northern's way of doing things. I felt sorry for him because he had to do extra work, but he eventually completed his defense later. I did not have the same trouble, so my defense went as expected, and I was so grateful. Dr. Rose was invaluable as well; she guided me every step of the way.

Dr. Rose stuck with me even when I decided to change from my original proposal. It was explained to me that I was going to have to survey participants to get my data for my quantitative analysis. In order to test my hypothesis, I was going to have to survey a large number of people, and I may have to send out the survey more than once to get back the desired number of surveys. This was going to require that I develop the survey instrument, participant lists with addresses, buy stamps, send out the surveys, etc. This was not only going to be time-consuming, it was going to be expensive. It was also explained to us that whatever we did our dissertation on, we would be considered experts in that area. I began to put two and two together and realized that maybe I needed a change. First of all, I did not want to be an expert in the GED program or its students. Fortunate for me, we had lecturers in one of my classes that had done research on minority students. Most of my students were minorities. After their presentation, I asked if I could use their data since I was interested in data regarding minority students. They agreed to share their data, and I developed a proposal around the data they had already gathered. I was lucky; they had ten thousand surveys returned for data analysis. This took some time, but I was able to develop my own instrument using their original surveys and their data for my own research. I got my proposal approved.

Instead of taking a class in statistics, I decided to use statistical software. The committee member that was an expert in quantitative research helped me come up with the form that fit my research proposal. The company that developed the statistical software was located in Chicago, so I took several classes from them to learn how to do the analyses. I am still mystified as to how I did it to this day. I think I even surprised Dr. Rose and the other members of my committee.

Writing and defending my dissertation was the hardest things I've ever done. I had the best chairperson. She's an excellent writer, so she guided me all the way through even though I was doing a quantitative dissertation, and that was not her expertise. I owe a debt of gratitude to Dr. Rose and to Dr. Abrams. I was able to finish the program because of them.

I was also able to finish because I followed the directions of my chair and my committee members to the letter. I was a good student. I had noticed other students arguing their points of view with the instructors wanting to do things their way. I thought it was a useless way to spend their time; they had plenty of time to do things their way when they graduated. But for now, they needed to get through the program; plus, who knew if their way was right? We were all students. The students who had trouble being a student themselves still do not have their doctoral degrees to this day.

It took me four years to get my doctorate, and I learned so much during that time. One thing that I learned that will always haunt me was the fact that I was an at-risk student. At first, I fought that moniker, but I realized by the end of the class that introduced the term to me that I indeed was at risk. Even though I had a sound enough foundation to finish the program, I realized that my foundation was full of holes from birth, and at any time I could have fallen through one or more of those holes. I had achieved in spite of, but I suffered mentally and physically as a result, and that is why I support reparations for African Americans. We are still suffering astronomically because of illegal, ill-moral, un-Christian enforced slavery that impairs African Americans to this day. The disruption to the family lineage is unforgiveable and hampers our emotional intelligence to this day.

When I see how whites can trace their history back for generations and African American heritage often stops at slavery, I get angry all over again. Because we couldn't speak the language and were segregated, so chances to learn were minimal. Our inability to communicate effectively keeps us from succeeding even today, in life, relationships, and careers. Our ability to not fall through the holes laid out for us by whites is a challenge daily and a tribute to God and Him only. To have endured slavery says to me that I have a heritage of very strong men and women to whom I owe my life, and for that I will always be grateful and dedicated to proving to them that I was worth it.

Before that class, I thought others blacks, whites, anyone who had trouble learning were at-risk students. I thought they were at risk of learning. You can imagine how surprised I was when the teacher said that we were at risk if we were a minority, born in a rural area, poor, uneducated parents, etc. When he said those words, I sat up and listened then because I was a minority, born in a rural area, and raised in a small Southern town to poor and uneducated parents, I was, by definition, "at risk," or shall I say *super at risk*. How dare this white man say that I was at risk? I thought. When I calmed down, I realized how hard I had worked all those years and how hard I was still working. What if it had not been so hard? I would probably be so much further. Here I was in my forties and still living paycheck to paycheck, comfortably, but still...

I looked around me and realized that no one in the class met all those characteristics listed by the instructor but me. Even the blacks from the South came from educated parents. One black student in the class had a street in her hometown named after one of her relatives who was a lawyer or doctor (or some profession) in the early 1900 or maybe even the late 1800s. I doubt if anyone in the class had ever picked or chopped cotton but me. Tears came to my eyes, and I tried to hide them. I cried and cried for myself and for all of my people, but mainly for myself because I was sitting in a class that I was not supposed to be in. Why was I here? Why had God made it so that I thought I was supposed to be here and had no fear that I would be successful? I knew without a doubt that it was going to be harder for me because I was a nutrition major and not an education major, and I knew that going into the program, but I was ready for the hard work. But why should it always be so hard for me? Why couldn't something come easy for me? By the end of the program, I felt like I had gotten a bachelor's, master's, and a doctoral degree in education all in those four years.

Another thing I learned about was incidental learning. I was so excited about this term because I couldn't help but to remember how I learned what to do or especially not to do from my friends in high school and college. This type of learning to me was just as important as classroom learning. I also thought about how doing my research I would find interesting studies that had nothing to do with what I was researching, and I couldn't help but to read the studies and learn from them as well. At some point, I realized that I just loved learning, and I was a lifelong learner. I spent hours and hours in the library. Whenever I had time, I would spend the whole day in the library. I would take my lunch or go get lunch and come back. I loved the library at Chicago State University (CSU), and the Harold Washington Public Library downtown Chicago, had rooms you could sign up for where you could study alone or in a small group. I spent most of the time at CSU because it was close to my house. Normally, you couldn't eat in the library, but you could eat in the group-study rooms at CSU. After they built a new library, they got rid of these rooms, and I think that was a mistake. During final exam days, CSU's library would be open until midnight. I took advantage of that as well.

I am not sure what class I learned probably the most important lesson of all in, and that had to do with a philosopher named Paulo Freire. Freire indicated that after years of being controlled by the upper class and the underclass came into power, influence, and money, they started to treat the current underclass the same, if not worse, than the upper class had formerly done. In my years of working, I noticed this scenario being played out time and time again. I saw minorities being placed in top positions with no change to the circumstances of their contemporaries. To me, in the case of the War on Poverty pioneered by the Johnson administration, I believe, it seemed to me, that the middle class got richer and moved to the suburbs, leaving the underclass in the same financial position or worse as they were before and fending for themselves with fewer knowledgeable human resources in a world they were not accustomed to—therefore, leaving the humanity in many urban communities in shambles and worse off after the War on Poverty ended.

I think I am the epitome of the person Dr. King had in mind when he pushed for Affirmative Action. He wanted African Americans and other minorities to have a chance in programs that they may not qualify for due to their backgrounds but with hard work and dedication they possibly could master. I don't think he wanted people to just give minorities grades; he wanted us to earn them. However, I think some instructors, black and white, thought if you were a minority, due to Affirmative Action, they should just give you a grade. That would mean that people would graduate with degrees they didn't earn and disappoint employers that hired them and sour the field for other African Americans who did work hard for their degrees in spite of their "at risk" categories.

Personally, I can say I grew as a result of the graduate programs I participated in, but I cannot say that my immediate family as a whole benefitted, especially financially, and that had been one of my hopes, and I am pretty sure my husband's as well. I do know that as a result of my improved ability to analyze and reason; it is the reason my husband and I are still married. I recognized that my husband was a product of his environment, and if circumstances had been different, he would have handled challenges in our marriage, jobs, society better. He hated conflict, so he would walk out of the room whenever we had a disagreement. I had to learn how to not suffer in silence but to approach him and let him know that this type of behavior was unacceptable and that I valued his opinion. He had grown up in a household where his father ruled and only his opinion mattered; even his mother had no say-so. James and I both had to learn how to talk things through. We both had come from poverty with uneducated parents, so mentally we were limited in the rhetoric. But now with the doctorate, I had matured somewhat and could guide us through the maze hopefully with our marriage still intact. What I didn't realize until much later was the burden this would place on me. My health has suffered as a result, and to this day, I struggle with my own sanity.

Before college, I had no idea how dangerous it was for women in the world. Looking back, I know that night during my apprenticeship and being twenty-four and foolishly thinking I could take care of myself could have been the last time my parents and siblings saw me. I could have been put on a ship to foreign country, given drugs, and even I could have forgotten who I was. It is imperative that women learn how to protect themselves and avoid being with strangers alone unless you are in a public place. I know casual sex is common these days for both women and men, but all I can say is, you can't be too careful. Once you leave your parents' home, you still have a lot to learn. You can't put your guard down, even in the company of women, because sometimes they are the ones who lure you into being trapped by men. Go figure. Other than a few creeps, I can say that majority of the guys I met in college were nice, respectful guys.

Chapter 7

THE WORK WORLD I

The Chicago Board of Health (1971–1975)

When I finished the graduate program at Case in 1971, I applied to only two public health nutrition programs in the US, and I got both jobs, Detroit and Chicago. I was beyond happy but scared at the same time. These were both two big cities, and I was a small-town girl. I decided to take the one in Chicago because that was where I had done my training. One of our assignments as apprentices was to bring back to our fieldwork class at Case a list of available jobs. There were about ten of us or more in apprenticeships all across the country. I had been hoping to apply for a position in California, my favorite state. I can't remember if there was anyone assigned to California, or they just didn't have any positions available. I had no idea when I chose Chicago how out of my league I was going to be and that maybe I should have chosen a less-populated, less-progressive state. But here I was, twenty-four years old at the time and ready for the challenge—or at least I thought so.

I walked into the Nutrition Section that first morning with a smile on my face and ready to work. I was happy to finally, after being six years removed from high school, to be working in a full-time job and making more than a stipend. Remember I told my friend Calvin in Wisconsin that I'd planned on making a starting salary of $10,000. Well, that was exactly what I was making. Several new nutritionists were hired right along with me. I was assigned to number 12 clinic of the Chicago Board of Health and located in the Englewood Neighborhood, a black neighborhood. I would serve as the nutritionist for station 12 with mostly black patients. It was located just off Sixty-Third and Racine on the south side of Chicago. The clinic was not too far from where I lived. I only had to take two buses.

Esther Emery, the only black nutritionist in the Nutrition Section at the time, made good on her word and allowed me to live with her until I found an apartment. Esther knew a classmate of mine from Southern, Ruby Fredericks/Stadeker. Ruby had been a very good student; and Ms. Thrift, the dean of the School of Home Economics, seemed to like her a lot. Ruby had come to Chicago the summer between our junior and senior years. When she returned to campus, she announced that she was engaged and would not be doing an internship. Ms. Thrift's face told the story of how disappointed she was in Ruby. I think she had questioned us about Ruby's decision, and none of us knew what had happened—we didn't even know Ruby that well. We saw her in the classroom, and that was about it. We all figured she would be at the top of our class when we graduated, but that honor eventually went to Mamie Gray/Finney. We all knew Mamie, but had no idea her grades were that good.

I forgot to mention that during the summer I was doing my apprenticeship in Chicago, I did get in touch with my classmate Mamie. She was living in Chicago by now. After Southern, she had done her internship at Hines Veterans Hospital and decided to stay in Chicago. She invited me over one Sunday, I believe, while I was doing my apprenticeship. I met her husband. I believe they introduced me to a guy, and we went out on a double date. It was a nice evening, and I began to soften up to Chicago a little bit. I was beginning to see that the city would have a lot of strange twists and turns for this Louisianan.

Esther lived in a two-bedroom apartment on 50 W. Seventy-First Street. She had two kids, Melvin and Delphia. Melvin was the oldest. I slept in a room on a small cot with Melvin and Delphia.

Esther's ex-husband, Melvin Sr., lived in Chicago as well. Esther and I believe her ex-husband both had graduated from Tuskegee Institute.

I remember the first time I visited in her apartment that summer that Esther's kids went outside to play. There was a small playground outside of the apartment. It was close to the building's parking lot. There was no grass for the kids to play on. I felt sorry for the kids. Esther could keep an eye on them from her apartment.

By the time I got back to Chicago, which was only a few weeks later, Esther had quit the Board of Health and was now working for Miles Square Health Center. I was really surprised that she had quit. I assumed she left for more money.

Esther's birthday was the following week. She said that Miles Square's policy was that you could have your birthday off. So on that Friday morning, she left for work, and we didn't see her again until Sunday evening. She had Monday off because that was her birthday. She needed it because she had a terrific hangover. She never asked me to babysit the kids; I just assumed it because she hadn't asked for any rent money from me. But man, was I surprised when she stayed out the whole weekend.

The first time we played cards with her friends, I noticed that she placed alcohol in her milk. I thought that's just like a dietitian having a healthy drink. By the time we finished playing cards, she was inebriated. After a few weeks, I figured out that she was a functional alcoholic. That was someone who only drank on the weekend. We went out with her boyfriend one Saturday or Friday evening. I think one of her nieces babysat. I noticed that Esther did most of the drinking. Her boyfriend seemed to me to be a nice country gentlemen. He never said anything to her about her drinking. After we left the establishment, she asked him to stop by the liquor store. I got out with her; we were only a few blocks from her apartment building. I got black walnut ice cream, which was delicious. Ice cream was my favorite dessert. Esther got a pint of alcohol. We had been drinking all night, and here she was, getting something else to drink. It was then that I figured she was an alcoholic.

To my knowledge, this was my first experience with an alcoholic. I say "to my knowledge" because in my upbringing, people didn't drink around children and some women. My mother's brothers never drank around her, and it was obvious that they did drink. So I was not accustomed to people drinking around me. My mother's family also considered her very religious, so they didn't smoke, curse, or drink around her or us, her children. I caught my father drinking beer several times in the yard, but never in the house. I don't think he drank excessively, though, because he worked too hard. My parents didn't allow us to go to parties. Whenever I would visit my friend Pearlie's house, I noticed some alcohol bottles. Other than that, I didn't even know what the bottles looked like. I think I was afraid to touch the bottles even. I grew up in a dry town, so alcohol was never in the stores. You couldn't order alcohol in the restaurants. Eventually, I figured out that Esther was putting her alcohol in milk to save her stomach; she was a nutritionist, after all. I moved out after about five or six months because I figured out I was enabling her. Unfortunately, she passed away about four months later from what I believe was accidentally mixing alcohol and medicine.

Station 12 was in an old building, and all the desks were in one big room and the examining rooms on the sides made from curtains. I got to know most of the nurses. It got cold soon after I arrived in Chicago. I knew I was going to need boots and a coat for the winter. I still didn't have a decent coat for the Northern winters. I went downtown and bought some boots. The first day I wore the boots to work, one nurse approached me and asked me if I knew that I had on two left boots. I said I didn't know. I looked at the boots and realized she was right. Everybody had a laugh on the country girl from Louisiana that day. When I took the boots back, I tried to get the same salesperson; I couldn't believe he or she let me leave the store with two left boots. Not having worn boots that much before, if ever, I don't know how long it would have taken me to notice. Other than that little incident, I got along with most of the nurses and doctors at station 12.

At lunchtime, I would go to the stores nearby. One day I was in the nearby grocery store when two gentlemen approached me and asked me if I wanted to go to an orgy. I asked them what that was, and they told me. I told them "no, thank you" and hurried out the store. I knew I was in the big city then. I told some of the nurses about it. To my surprise, several of them told me they had been to some orgies. Looking at them, you wouldn't suspect that they had. I decided I really needed to get to know my coworkers before I went to parties at their homes.

I had been in the Nutrition Section for a week, I think, when I was asked to train two new nutritionists. I was happy to see that they were black. One was Thomasine, and the other was Diana. They had both worked at Michael Reese Hospital and were tired of the hospital routine. They complained about the hours they had to work. At the Board of Health, you worked 8:00 a.m. to 4:00 p.m. Monday through Friday, no paid overtime. They loved it, especially Tommie, because now she could get a few hours' sleep before she had to be at work, no matter what night she decided to go out. Tommie loved to party. I think Diana was already married and had a daughter, so she was not the partying type. Tommie was not married, so she and I started to party together and became very good friends for over forty years.

Before the end of my first year at the Board of Health, I was moved to the Woodlawn Neighborhood Health Center with, again, mostly black patients. The Board of Health was expanding its clinics to new buildings that housed more services for the community. I was happy to leave station 12, which was centered in an old building and had limited services and no office for the essential services, including nutrition (which was my job). I was delighted to find out that at the Woodlawn Neighborhood Health Center, the specialties would have offices. My office was in a corner, and I had no problem with it.

While I was at Woodlawn, I had trained two black dietetic intern students (Hilda and then Veronica). They both would come to work with the Board of Health after they finished their dietetic internship. I got to know both of them quite well. Both got married and had children while working at the Board of Health. Veronica retired from the Board of Health, and Hilda became a lawyer and ran for a judgeship later after serving as the head of the Nutrition Section. Tommie served as the head of the department after Hilda quit.

By the end of my first year in Chicago, my sister Juanita called. She was looking for summer employment and hadn't had any luck in Memphis. She said that she and our cousin Tressie wanted to come to Chicago to look for positions just for the summer. I had not been living by myself that long and really wanted more time to be alone to figure out my path in life, but I agreed, went out, and bought a sofa sleeper for them. They came and worked the summer, and both of them went back to college. That spring, I had met a young man that I fancied myself in having good chemistry with at the time. Helen, the department's secretary, had invited me to Sunday dinner at a friend's house (I'd met the friends previously at Helen's house). The husband's son was visiting as well. When I met the son, he gave me the biggest smile, and I loved it and felt an immediate attraction to him. I remember dancing, really dancing, into work that Monday and telling my intern (I think it was Hilda) that I had met someone, and I remember her saying that I must really like him to be dancing the way I was. I knew immediately this was one man I was going to have sex with. I was drawn to him. I don't even remember us going out on dates before we had sex. Our dates seemed to be in his apartment.

My parents came up that first summer (1972) with my sisters Bobbie and Vickie and my cousin Queen. My mom and dad stayed with me, and probably Bobbie and Vickie did as well. My cousin Queen stayed with her uncle Willie Shepherd, who didn't live too far from me. I had met him and his wife and daughter. I tried to be a good host and took them to see the city. My mom and dad loved touring the Johnson Publishing Company and meeting John Johnson. They didn't like the idea that I had walked them to death because we had missed our train stop. Ronnie's father and stepmom came over to my apartment to meet my parents. Helen came as well. I guess my mom and I cooked dinner for them, but I can't remember. Ronnie and I took Bobbie, Queen, and Vickie to the John Hancock Observatory. We got tickets for two adults, Ronnie and me, and our children, Bobbie, Queen, and Vickie. When we got on the elevator, they all started laughing because Vickie was the only child. We laugh about that today. After all my visitors left for the summer, I settled into a single life and dating Ronnie.

Around November, my college friend Jackie called me. She said that she was being put out of her apartment because she didn't have the money to pay the rent. Jackie had accepted a scholarship to Case Western Reserve the year after I left. Unfortunately, she had flunked two classes, and so she didn't finish in a year, and her scholarship had run out. She had been living with her sister, and at the end of the year, she went back to Kansas City instead of staying and helping with the rent with Jackie. I asked Jackie, Couldn't she stay with some of her other friends? And she said she didn't think so. I felt sorry for her. She kept calling me and saying she didn't know what to do. I think she asked if she could come stay with me while she finished her classes in December. I said okay (mistake) against my better judgement because I was just getting used to staying by myself, and I needed that time to think about my future.

I went to Cleveland, and she and I drove back to Chicago. She continued to study for her two classes but failed both of them. I don't think I ever saw her pick up a book, so I was not surprised when she didn't pass. She started looking for jobs in Chicago. Her sister came up to visit around Christmas. She evidently liked Chicago because, before I knew it, Jackie was asking me if I wanted to move into the two-bedroom apartment next door to us. She said her sister Carolyn wanted to come back and move into it with us. I looked at the apartment, and it was much bigger than my own. So we moved. Then that Summer, three of my sisters asked if they could come and stay with me so they could work for the summer; they were all in college. When they left, Juanita, who by this time had graduated, wanted to know if she could come to Chicago and look for a job. She came. Carrie had stayed because she said she wasn't going back to college because she had flunked out.

The second year I was at the Board of Health, I was moved to the new Englewood Health Center, which was the now home to station 12. It seemed I was the go-to girl whenever they opened up a health center on the south side of Chicago. I did have more seniority than any of the other nutritionist on the south side. Englewood was much larger than Woodlawn. I had a larger office. It was one where I could not only do individual nutrition counseling, but I could do group counseling as well. I decided I should put my public health nutrition training into action.

The first thing I did was figure out what I thought were the most pressing health problems in the community (black community) I worked in. Most of my patients that had been referred to me were overweight, diabetic, and hypertensive. So I decided to start a program that was diet- and exercise-oriented. I told my supervisors that I wanted to start a weight-loss program that incorporated dieting, exercising, and cooking. Englewood had a small stove in the basement, and I thought we could cook tasty low-calorie meals or cooking what my patients normally ate in a healthy way. I thought my program was a novel idea. I did not know about aerobic exercise programs or health clubs with exercise programs. I just knew that weight loss was more proficient with a diet-and-exercise regimen as I had learned throughout my coursework.

There was a large waiting area and hallways in the basement of Englewood Neighborhood Health Center. I thought this would be an excellent idea for us to have a fashion show after my patients lost the weight in the weight-loss program. I got my directors of the center to go along with it. So around Christmas, we had a fashion show. The directors even participated in the program. I was pretty proud of myself. The patients seemed to really have a ball. We had a potluck dinner after the program that the staff had contributed to. Someone made lasagna that I thought was great. It turned out it was one of the nurses. She gave me the recipe, and every time I cook it, I get rave reviews.

The white directors of the Nutrition Section (Virginia and Betty) did not seem to like the changes that I had made. Basically, most of the nutritionists just did one-on-one counseling. I did not think group counseling was far from what we were supposed to do as nutritionists. We had been asked to give group lectures from time to time. To me, it made nutrition more exciting. One-on-one counseling was boring. Plus, seeing a patient one time did little to help them change their ways. I understood why educational psychology had been a part of my undergraduate curriculum and also nutrition education. We had to develop goals and objectives for our nutrition lesson plans. This was for group learning and not just individual learning.

One day the directors asked me, What was the purpose of my weight-loss program? Every time I think about that discussion, I am perplexed. Two white nutritionists with master's degrees in nutrition and training in nutrition asking me what the purpose was of a weight-loss program. Had they not heard of Weight Watchers (and I think there was another program at the time, but I can't think of the name)? Somebody had figured out the need for a weight-loss program and was making a lot of money off it. Here we could give our low-income patients the same training for free. Maybe they were not ready for change. Then again, maybe if one of the white nutritionists had come up with the idea, they would have loved it. I had noticed that in meetings, when it was reported that a black nutritionist (mainly me) had had a large number of patients that week, they would question the quality of the instructions. Whereas if a white nutritionist had large numbers, they would get congratulated and told "great job."

I was having a difficult time in the department. It came to a head when a conference on nutrition education came around, and the directors chose a licensing nutritionist, who was white, to attend. Even though she had more seniority in the department, in her job, she never counseled patients. Her job was to license nursing homes and day-care centers. I thought I was the one who needed the training because of the educational programs I had instituted and approached the directors about it. I think I was a little too vocal, and maybe I accused them of being racist. I think Virginia felt threatened by me and wanted to write me up. I know that after that, I decided I had to leave; that the department, the way they ran it, was not for me. I hated to leave my patients, but I was going if I found a new job.

I loved the job I had created for myself, but I hated the oppressive leaders. The oppressive leaders were the director and codirector. They were both white. I felt like they were about making the salary and not about preventative health or preventive medicine. We clashed on so many levels. My impression of them was that they were wasting taxpayers' money and setting black people up for diabetes, heart disease, poor dental care, etc. in the future. This was 1971 to 1975. Fast-forward to now 2020, and the obesity, diabetes, poor dental care, heart disease, etc. are out of control in the black neighborhoods. If the nutritionists and health-care educators at the Chicago Board of Health had been doing their jobs early on, I don't think we would have such a poor health-care problem today among minorities, and they wouldn't be as vulnerable to the COVID-19 virus today as they are in Chicago.

The bosses didn't seem to have a problem if nutritionists saw one or two patients a day. I had a problem with it: I thought it was wasting my time. I could not be satisfied with just sitting all day long. I found that so boring. It never occurred to me to do something part-time, like sell Avon or Tupperware (even on the job as some people did), or making plans for my future when I was not busy. Instead I went about drumming up business, and I was very successful, but evidently my bosses were not happy. If one of the white nutritionists saw twenty patients in one day, they would be the topic of conversation at the departmental meeting. Whereas if one of the black nutritionists saw twenty patients in one day, the topic of conversation would be, How could you give each patient quality diet counseling? I eventually, along with the other black or minority nutritionists, felt that they were being racist. We had one Hispanic nutritionist, and she got upset when she was not assigned to a majority Hispanic clinic. It didn't make any sense. There were so many incidences that spiked of racism, too many to discuss here, and some I don't even remember now.

I had been involved in the "Civil Rights Movement" at Southern University and in Minden and believed in the causes. I thought when you improved yourself as a black person, you should work to pull other black people up. While working in the clinics, I didn't see this happening. Everyone, including the parents, seemed to work well with the babies, making sure they arrived healthy and got off to a good start. But when the babies started to school, if their parents didn't demand good health care—and they didn't because they didn't know what they needed sometimes—no one was going to stuff it down their throats. Everyone seemed okay with making money and doing as little work as possible. I was not because I knew it was hurting my people, black people.

I wanted to be an asset to my community, African American community, so I decided to quit my job at the Chicago Board of Health. By the time I quit, the nutritionists were just giving out WIC (Women Infant and Children) food stamps. I saw myself wasting my master's degree. I thought clerks could give out those stamps without any degrees. Some nutritionists settled into their roles without complaining. I just couldn't do that.

The nutritionists had also been asked to inspect and license the food service operations of nursing homes and day-care centers. I remember that there was one church day-care center that I had been asked to inspect. I kept denying their license because they were not serving balanced meals to the kids. I think I denied them twice, and the third time another nutritionist went out, and she licensed them. I asked her why, and she said they had promised to add certain foods to the menu. Well, I thought, this was horrendous, you are going to just take their word for it. It turned out that the black female minister of the church was well known in Chicago. I could have cared less about that. Regardless, she was supposed to give the kids balanced meals while they were under her care. I decided that the problems in the Nutrition Section and maybe the Board of Health itself ran deep. I started in earnest to look for another job.

Every day I passed Kennedy-King College. Since I had a master's degree, maybe I could teach home economics. I called the school to see if they offered home economics. I got a copy of the home economics curriculum and found out that they had a program called Food Management and most of the courses I'd had, and I would later find out that they used the same textbooks. So I decided to make an appointment to interview for a teaching position. I got the position, and that should have been the end of my relationship with the Board of Health, but it wasn't.

Soon after I resigned, several of the other black nutritionists approached me about filing a complaint with the EEOC, the Equal

Employment Opportunity Commission. I was definitely in favor because I felt I had been discriminated against because of my race. We did get an attorney, but it never went that far. The young lady that was leading the complaint and had put us in touch with a lawyer eventually became the director of the Nutrition Section. One of the other black nutritionists became the director after she resigned. I am not sure how the Nutrition Section changed after they became the directors. I started to work for Kennedy-King College in September 1975. They were paying me $3,000 less than I was making, and I accepted it. I would find out later that some of the gentlemen in my department without a master's degree were making more than I was with two degrees. The person interviewing and recommending me for hire at the time was a black female vice president at the time. I wish I understood her reasoning for giving the men more, or did they demand more and I had not due to my naivety?

Kennedy-King College (1975-1997)

In 1975, I decided to apply for a job in the Home Economics Department at Kennedy-King College. I was passing the school every day. I believe I called and found out that they had a Home Economics Program and Food Management Program. I was interviewed initially by Ms. Witherspoon. She was, at the time, the chairperson of the Home Economics Department. I met her in the parking lot of Kennedy-King College. I don't believe school had started, and she said that the faculty had planned on going on strike. So the college probably would not be opening on time. I noticed that she had on a polyester pantsuit that was wash and wear. The pants were too short; they were flooding, as my younger sisters had taught me. She also had on a wig. I thought the wig had been hastily thrown on her head. There was one other person in the Home Economics Department at the time, Ms. Parmer, the clothing instructor. Ms. Witherspoon taught both clothing and foods courses. She said that if I was hired, I would teach mostly food courses.

Later, I was interviewed by the dean of Applied Sciences and the vice president of the college. I was surprised that the dean was white and that the vice president was a black female. I even remember the color of the suit I had on the day they interviewed me. It was a solid rust color with a colorful blouse. I was hired and would start soon after the strike ended.

I was hired primarily to teach the foods classes; at least I took the job anticipating only teaching food classes. I loved the freedom you had in teaching your classes. Once you closed the door, it was you and your students, and you were allowed to interpret the departmental syllabus (the objects and outline of the course) any way you wanted to. However, I didn't know you had to get tenure before you had job security, and that would take three years. I never thought I would be there no more than three years. Unfortunately, I started to enjoy the job and felt like I was an asset to my students, so before I knew it, I had been at Kennedy-King twenty-two years. Remember, my plan when I came to Chicago was to stay here three years and to head for sunny California. I was already four years in by then, so why didn't I take off for the California instead of looking for another job in Chicago?

Ms. Witherspoon had given me copies of the books that I was going to use for my classes and the syllabus I was to use for the food-preparation courses. The food management classes were new, so I had to develop the syllabus for those courses. Okay, I had never taught before, had limited food-service experience. I had to draw upon the time I worked in the cafes with my mom when I was in high school. I'd had only limited experience in the kitchen while I was interning at the University of Wisconsin Hospital. I was a little over my head. No one else in the department had any experience either. I think they both had gone from college to teaching. To tell you the truth, I would not have hired me to do the job.

My classes initially were huge. I had between thirty-five and forty students in all of my classes. I kind of used my former instructors as my model for how I taught my class. I had never planned on becoming a teacher and probably should never have been a teacher. You get to a position where you need to support yourself, and you do what you have to do. When I walked into my first class and saw this eighty-six-year-old (I believe) woman and very few eighteen-year-old students, I knew I was in for trouble. After I gave my first test, I knew I was in for even more trouble. I was shocked not only at the scores on the test but the misspelled words, poor sentence structure, poor math skills, etc. At first I thought the Chicago public schools really didn't prepare these students. Then I found out some of the students had not only not graduated from high school; some didn't even get to high school. I was confounded. What was I going to do with this huge number of students who were ill prepared for the course I was going to teach and were seemingly ill prepared for college-level work?

For most of them, I was not only their teacher; I was also their advisor. Soon after midterm, I invited them one by one to my office to advise them on the classes they should register for in the spring and future courses they were going to need to graduate. It was then when I found out what grades they had made in English, mathematics, etc. while in high school. By now, I realized that most of them did not read, write, or do math at the college level and that they really needed remediation. Some had never taken a science class. Some were registered in the lowest level of science class at the same time they were taking my class.

What further perplexed me was that there were some students in my class who were not food management or home economics majors. They were close to graduating and just needed additional credit hours. They were having just as hard a time as the other students.

I started to study the college catalogue. I found out that the students didn't need mathematics to graduate. I couldn't believe it. I'd had to take Algebra I and Algebra II in my freshmen year at Southern. In my thinking, mathematics was necessary for life. Who had developed this curriculum, and what credentialing organization had approved it? I figured I had my job cut out for me in advising these students on what courses to take.

To the students who were not doing well in my class, I advised them to drop my class and take remedial English and mathematics courses. Some of them balked and others took my advice. Some of the students who went back eventually ended up in my classes again, and others just dropped out or decided on another major, I guess. I found out that most of the students couldn't add three place numbers and definitely had trouble with division and fractions. You needed to be familiar with basic mathematics at least for all the courses I was teaching.

I found remedial math and English books that I thought would help them in the field of food service management. I had the students purchase the books and gave them assignments in it that I graded. I believe it helped somewhat. I just couldn't help but feel that things were not right. I started to gain weight.

I was helpless to help students who couldn't help themselves. Now I know I was overempathizing with the students. I couldn't just teach and move on; I cared too much. I wanted to grow and develop, and I wanted my students to grow and develop, and neither one of us had the rudimentary material to do just that. I hustled to be the best teacher I could be and paid the price. No job is worth a person losing themselves in. If I had been thinking properly, I would have quit and looked for something more to my liking, but I didn't have a clue as to what that was at the time. I was lost. When I look back on it, there are a lot of people I could blame, but I am not going to do that; I am just going to blame myself. Settling into a job in a disadvantaged community to teach was a mistake from the beginning for an untrained teacher and inexperienced teacher in a college community that did not provide sufficient training or support for its teachers. I was drowning in a cesspool and did not know it.

At the end of my first year, I decided that my students and I would host a dinner for the home economics graduates. By this time, James and I had gotten closer, so he helped me. I know Ms. Witherspoon didn't help, but I believe Ms. Parmer, the other instructor, came in and helped wash the dishes at the end of the evening. She'd had on a beautiful fancy red outfit, but she put on an apron and helped out. I couldn't believe the amount of dishes we had. The dishwashers we used were those for the home, and some were not working.

The chairperson of the Applied Science Department was our main speaker for the evening. He brought his wife along with him. He had beautiful dark skin, and I loved dark-skinned men. I was very impressed with him, so I was hopeful about our department. Unfortunately, I think he left our department at the end of that first year, and I have no idea where he went. He was an automotive instructor, so I believe he took a job in that industry, but I am not sure if it was teaching.

Initially, I was very disappointed in the department chairperson, deans, other faculty, etc. I didn't understand the lack of professionalism. My job evaluations were a joke. I wanted to be evaluated critically because I wanted to know whether I was doing a good job or not. I didn't want to cheat the students, my black students. Instead, I got excellent evaluations. I was not a trained teacher, so in no way was I excellent. The evaluations that I received as a teacher were not going to help me grow as a teacher, and I knew it. So one time I asked a new assistant dean of Applied Sciences if he could evaluate me. I knew he had come from the Chicago Public Schools and that he had been a teacher before becoming a vice principal. I was pretty sure he had retired from the Chicago Public Schools because they kept promoting younger people to principal positions, overlooking him. He said he would evaluate me. He came to my room to observe me, but before we could sit down for the evaluation, he had a heart attack, I believe, and passed away. I was pretty sure he passed away from duress of having a new job and not achieving his goal to become a principal. That could have been my imagination working overtime; I hardly knew the man. After that, I decided to take any workshops, seminars, etc. that I thought would help me become a better teacher. I couldn't get reimbursed for workshops and seminars, only classes in my field or the field of education.

James and I had been going together about two years when I started working at Kennedy-King. James proposed to me around Christmas 1976 on the phone. I was home for Christmas in Louisiana, and we were talking on the phone. Before I left for Louisiana, we'd had a long conversation about our future together. I told him that I wanted to get married, and if he didn't, I thought we should go our separate ways.

We'd had a trial separation a month before. I can't remember exactly what happened, but I do know we stopped seeing each other.

Then my sister Bobbie came to town maybe for Thanksgiving, and we needed dates, so I called James and asked if he would escort me, and I arranged for a friend to escort Bobbie. After Bobbie left, James and I got back together. I had missed him terribly, but I wasn't sure it was love or separation anxiety. Juanita was working at night, so James had spent many nights in my apartment. I knew that he was a good guy and that I liked him a lot. I really enjoyed having sex with him. He had old-fashioned values and was more conservative than I was. He had the three major character traits that I wanted in a man, and those were trust, trust, and trust. I knew what he said he would do, he would, and that was very important to me. He also was not averse to trying something new.

One problem I had with him was that to many of my questions, he would often answer "maybe." At the time, I thought *maybe* would be good enough, so I settled. So when he proposed, I said yes and announced to my family that we were getting married. Now, I know *maybe* is not the answer you want from your husband prospect. What you want is *evidence* because even if he says yes, it is too easy to lie to get what you want from a woman. Lying is one skill men seem to have down pat. By evidence, I mean does he talk about doing this or that, or has he done, or is doing this or that—something that is important to you in your future. If not, then the answer is probably no. Now, I know that marrying someone with not the same vision as you have is hard because it is always like swimming upstream by yourself. If you are successful, then he benefits, but you got high blood pressure or some other disease because you were so busy (thinking for the both of you or how to convince him to go along with the program—forget about collaboration, who can even define that) and not taking the time for your own health.

Between December 1976 (I am not sure, but it may have been Christmas Day) and April 9, 1977, about three months, I put a wedding together. I decided to get married in my hometown, Minden, Louisiana, because that's where most of my family lived. I knew it was going to be a problem for James's family to travel to Louisiana, so I stupidly decided to plan a second reception so they and our Chicago friends and my students could attend. I got so busy until

I almost felt I was losing my mind. I should have saved that money because I don't think anybody really cared, not even James.

This was the year that Ms. Witherspoon had decided I should take Ms. Parmer's clothing construction courses so that maybe I could teach them if necessary. So not only was I teaching my classes, but I was also taking her classes and sewing my head off trying to learn. I even bought myself a sewing machine. I decided I would get the extra experience by making most of my Christmas gifts that year. So just after having one of my most difficult semesters of my new teaching career, I now only had a few months to plan a wedding (mistake, I should have held out for June or August). If James still balked, then we could have gone our separate ways.

I did, however, learn how to stand up for myself after that semester ended with Ms. Witherspoon. I had a talk with the union representative. I told her that I was being forced to teach clothing classes that I felt untrained for and did not enjoy and did not want to limit the students. She said that if I did not have a degree in clothing, they could not make me teach it and to file a grievance. However, I think before I filed the grievance, Ms. Witherspoon acquiesced and did not assign me to teach the clothing classes.

After, I returned to work after my wedding in Louisiana, about a week later. Ms. Witherspoon and Ms. Parmer had decided that the department would do the graduation banquet and not just my food classes. I thought this was a great idea; I just didn't realize that none of my ideas would fly. This time, it seemed they wanted the banquet to be on a grander scale. We were using the college's cafeteria, and we were including a fashion show. They decided on most of the details. I was asked to wear my wedding gown and James a suit and model in the fashion show's final scene. Everything turned out nice, except most of the food went in the garbage. Ms. Witherspoon had decided against my wishes and served Jimmy Carter's Peanut Butter Chicken. I also knew that the banquet was a lot of hard work and doubted that it would happen again, and it didn't.

The next year, the Applied Science Department had a banquet for all of our graduates and at an off-campus venue catered by that establishment. I think we did it for two years, and then it stopped as well. I had wanted something on a smaller scale that was planned by my students for them to get experience. I had experienced something similar at Southern, where the junior students would plan and prepare a dinner meal for the senior students. It was not that grand of an event, but the students got much-needed experience.

When I took the job with Kennedy-King College's Home Economics Department as an instructor, I didn't realize that you had to become tenured for job security. I was used to a probationary period of about six to nine months, but here the tenure or probationary process was three years. Every year my teaching performance was evaluated by the other teachers in my department. When I started at Kennedy-King, my department was Home Economics, and we had three female instructors, including myself. About a month into my job, it became the Applied Science Department and now included Automotive Technology, Electronics, Air-Conditioning, and Photo Offset Printing programs as well. These disciplines had all-male instructors. I tried to make the best of it, but I should have seen the handwriting on the wall, especially when I found out that because of their vocations, they didn't need to have a master's degree for their jobs. Supposedly, a master's degree in one of the areas of home economics was required for my job.

By my second year at Kennedy-King, we had a new dean as well. His name was Herman Bryant. He'd been an automotive instructor. He had never served as a dean before. I really liked him as a person, but I think he made a lot of mistakes as the dean. We also had a new president, Dr. Ewen Akins. Maceo T. Bowie had been the president when I started. He and Ms. Witherspoon had known each other at another college. I believe that was how she got the job as chairperson of the Home Economics Department. Another faculty member had applied for the position at the same time. She was now a professor in the Child Development Program. I could not understand why Child Development and Home Economics had not combined into one department. I knew at Southern they were combined. When I found out that this instructor had left Home Economics because she didn't get the chairperson position, then I knew why. It seemed

Dr. Bowie, the new president, had worked with Ms. Witherspoon at another college.

Dr. Maceo T. Bowie retired or quit after my first year at Kennedy-King. I was told that during the Civil Rights Movement, there had been demonstrations at Kennedy-King, and one day the white president left, and the students demanded a black president be installed. So Maceo T. Bowie was installed. It was his first job as president of a college. He seemed to be a popular president. I do know that we had a football team, a Ms. Kennedy-King contest, and a homecoming football game. We had graduation in the gymnasium, and my first year the speaker was the CEO of *Ebony* and *Jet* magazines, John Johnson. His speech was very motivational to me and I believe the students as well. Things seemed to be progressing well under Dr. Bowie.

After Dr. Bowie left, it seemed all the creativity at Kennedy-King left with him. He had been instrumental in helping to rename the school. It had formerly been Wilson Junior College. At first I thought Kennedy was named after John F. Kennedy, but it was Kennedy-King after Robert Kennedy and Martin Luther King. They had both died in 1968, hence *Kennedy-King*. I didn't particularly like the name because of the initials *KKC*. It was too similar to Ku Klux Klan.

Dr. Ewen Akins replaced Dr. Bowie. It was his first job as president of a college as well. I found out that the presidents were not the only new people in positions. It seemed the whole staff almost was new. What I was told that one day during a protest the black students ran all the white staff members off the campus. The students who had been work-study students working with them then became full-time staff members. I am not sure if some of them ever completed their associate degrees. To me. they were never trained in public service because of the way some behaved. After I heard this, everything seemed to fall into place and why the institution had stopped progressing.

I had noticed a lack of courtesy between staff and teachers. The staff members all knew the teachers' salaries, so I am sure there was some jealousy. The staff seemed to enjoy the power they had over the teachers, processing their grades, etc. The secretary of the Applied Science Department seemed to take offense that she now had to type for the home economics instructors. Any time we gave her papers to type, they always came back with a ton of errors. Eventually, I figured she could definitely type better than that and was doing it purposely to get us to do our own typing, which I started to do. Most of the time, my tests were not ready until the night before, so the morning of the tests, I would be copying them. I could not even depend on getting them copied and stapled correctly. Since this was my first time teaching college classes, I preferred to type my own exams anyway because I could correct errors as I typed, so I never complained about the lack of secretarial support. Now I realize if they had done their jobs, I would have had more time to perfect my teaching skills or more time for my personal life. I should have complained and hopefully gotten more support, but I doubt it since the administrators worked so closely with the secretarial staff; they seemed to favor them and not the faculty.

One of my teachers in my doctoral program had done her dissertation on the influence secretaries make on institutions—especially since most of the administrators were males, and women were more accustomed to serving males. I even remember attending an Alpha Kappa Alpha Sorority luncheon with someone I think was hoping I would decide to join the graduate chapter and the then president telling the women to use their womanly wiles to get ahead. She followed that up with, "And you know what I mean." What did she mean, that women should prostitute themselves? I knew I wasn't joining that sorority. This had to be before the women's liberation movement.

In order to get your tenure, you had to do more than teach your classes; you had to participate in other college events. So I became an advisor to the Home Economics Club. I was used to colleges and high schools having home coming parades. So when I discovered that when Kennedy-King was Wilson College and majority white and had homecoming parades and homecoming dances before the homecoming football game, I talked the current president, Dr. Akins, into having one for the black students. I worked along with the Student

Government Association to get this done. I never anticipated that I would have to organize and direct it myself, but I think the different clubs that decorated cars and rode in the parade enjoyed it. I had to get permits for us to circle through the Englewood Community. I was so tired by the end of the evening, but the parade was a success. I didn't want to take this on as a responsibility yearly. It was too much for one person, and no one stepped up to the plate, so there was never another homecoming parade.

The president or the director of Student Services should have developed a homecoming committee. There were not that many nontenured instructors at Kennedy-King that needed to make an impression like me, even though I didn't do it to make an impression. The tenured faculty didn't seem to want to do anything but teach their classes. Dr. Akins was only a few months removed from being in their position, and from what I understood, he never participated in extracurricular activities himself, so he was not going to demand or motivate the faculty to do so.

Later on, Kennedy-King would get rid of football altogether, and the director of Student Services left (he had been somewhat creative). I remember him bringing the Count Basie Band to Chicago for one of the events. I thought it was a little overboard because the concert was held at the Palmer House. Why not at Kennedy-King? It must have cost a fortune, but it was well attended and a lot of fun.

When I first started at Kennedy-King, there were big headlines in the student newspaper that we had about ten thousand students, and then the enrollment started to go down and down. Absolutely no one seemed to care. I think more to the point no one had any ideas as to how to stop the tide. To their solace, other city colleges' enrollments were also going down. What they didn't notice was that the popular colleges were not going down as much, if at all. Kennedy-King was a community college, but you would have had a hard time seeing the community in the college. We continued to have a large group of students taking food management classes and, initially, home economics classes.

I received my tenure after my third year at Kennedy-King. Ms. Parmer was still at Kennedy-King, and she and Ms. Witherspoon and the dean at the time, Mr. Herman Bryant, had approved it. I was happy to get the tenure but at the time didn't see that it came with shackles. I say *shackles* because with this tenure, you got complacent after you realized that no teacher had ever been fired before that had tenure in the city college system. Plus, you no longer had to do the extracurricular activities to impress the faculty. Only a few faculty members were hired after I got hired. I never experienced that sense of complacency, though. I was always busy.

After my third year at Kennedy-King, the clothing instructor Ms. Parmer announced that she was leaving to go get her PhD. She said she wouldn't leave until after we hired a new instructor to replace her. I should have questioned whether she should have been involved in the process of hiring a new instructor, but I didn't because I figured she would be helpful in hiring a clothing instructor. I was wrong. I foolishly believed that she would make sure we hired someone with a master's degree in clothing and textiles, or at least a master's degree in home economics. I was wrong.

We settled on interviewing two people for the clothing instructor position job. One had a master's in home economics or clothing and textiles, and the other one had a master's degree in special education. Ms. Witherspoon and Ms. Parmer voted on the person who had a master's in special education. I argued against her employment because of this variation. However, I was outvoted. I couldn't see how the outgoing faculty member had a vote, but there were no personnel rules and regulations for the individual departments. Plus, the instructor they wanted had come from the Chicago Public Schools and had never got tenure, and she had been there around ten or more years.

Unfortunately, now the dean of Applied Science (a former automotive technology instructor serving in his first term as dean) sided with the other two instructors. Everybody tried to get me to change my vote, but I knew it was a mistake to hire this person without an advanced degree in home economics or, better yet, a master's in clothing and construction since those were the courses she was going to teach. I had preferred the other candidate. She had the credentials, or at the very least continuing to search for a reputable candidate. I really think it came down to who was the cutest, and that is so sad.

I am pretty sure that after she was hired, she found out about my voting history on her employment because one day she asked me why I didn't like her. Unfortunately, she was my officemate, and we couldn't avoid each other. I don't remember the whole discussion, but I remember saying to her that our working together did not mean we had to like each other. I later voted against her tenure later on, and again I was outvoted, the dean and Ms. Witherspoon against me. Even though we had a large department now, when it came to hiring new instructors and voting on tenure, we kept our individual disciplines.

But she was correct: I didn't like her, but not for the reasons she thought. I didn't like her because shortly after she started to work at Kennedy-King, she started to go with one of the administrators, who had just gone back to his wife after a separation. They had met when she went to get her keys for the office and the classrooms from him (he was the building manager). He eventually left his wife, and she left her husband. I am not sure if they got married or not. I just hope they loved each other because they broke up two families to be together. I am very family-oriented, and I am deftly against single women or men dating married people. I think if married people are unhappy in their marriages, they should get divorced before dating other people because most of the time they stay with their spouse, and the on-the-side person is deeply hurt.

After she was hired, I felt like the odd man out. She and Ms. Witherspoon seemed to get along well, whereas Ms. Witherspoon's and my relationship was going downhill fast. We taught the same classes, but in different ways. Like I said earlier, at the end of my first year, I decided to have the students do a small banquet for the graduating home economics and food management students. I invited other administrators to the banquet, and the students could invite their relatives. We had a program and gave out certificates. My sister Juanita and my friend Tommie came. We served a variety of food, but most of our serving utensils were more like those you would use in the home. My sister Juanita really enjoyed herself and talks about the event to this day. The students really seemed to enjoy themselves. But I think Ms. Witherspoon thought I was overstepping my boundaries or being too aggressive.

Looking back, my first years at the Chicago Board of Health and Kennedy-King left scars of post-traumatic stress syndrome. I would like to say it was more due to my lack of experience, but I think it was more lack of a professional organizational structure in both instances. Before I left Case, we were told what a professional was and that we should exhibit those traits. I had a hard time seeing professionality at either of the institutions.

My job at Kennedy-King College was stressful from beginning to end. I developed high blood pressure while working there. I didn't recognize the stress because when I went inside my classroom, it was just me and my students, and I was in charge. But outside of the classroom, so much was happening that I didn't understand. I didn't understand what I know now was the organizational culture of the college.

The first five years or so, the college seemed organized, and then it changed central administration, and that seemed to go out the window. Kennedy-King was part of the City Colleges of Chicago. There were about six or seven colleges with a central administration headed by the chancellor and associate chancellors and various directors. So we just didn't set our own rules, curricula, etc. Every college had a president.

Dr. Akins was not a seasoned president when the central office changes occurred. He had kept Mrs. Barker (the vice president who hired me). She had to be one of few women in administrative positions at the time. They were both more like figureheads while the central office ran the show. Later, I would learn that both top central administrative positions were held by individuals who never were administrators before; they went from the classroom to those top positions. I was beginning to see how political the city college system was. It seemed the students were being sacrificed. I loved the idea of a community college system because of the vocational training and academic aspects. Not all students wanted or needed a four-year degree, and some needed more time to figure out just what they wanted.

Even though I said the first five or so years seemed organized, I was never really happy with my plight. I had been hired to teach, but had no teaching experience. I remember that at Southern that I had taken a class called (I believe) Nutrition Education. Primarily, it was to teach us about counseling patients on diets or leading small groups on nutrition-related topics. I remember I chose diabetes mellitus. But here I was teaching food preparation, food management, food service, etc. I had the basics of lesson planning.

But what I was not prepared for was assessing students' prior knowledge. So that first year, I was in for a rude awakening. I found out that some of my students couldn't read or write at the college level. Forget about high school level; some were illiterate. I couldn't help but wonder how they got into the college. I found out that no requirements were required; even adult students without a GED could take college-level courses. The college had some remedial courses, but I guess no means of deciding who should take them when I first started teaching. Later on, they instituted an entrance examination, but they had no standards. Needless to say, I flunked a lot of students those first few years. I even advised a few who were relentless in their pursuit of a degree to drop out of my class to take remedial reading and math courses. Some did and eventually came back to take my class. So the supposedly two-year college ended up being longer than a four-year college for most of the students. Many never graduated.

What I realized was that the federal government had instituted the PELL grant system, meaning that students could now get a grant to go to college, one that they didn't have to pay back. I don't think they had this system when I was in college, or it was never offered to me. Knowing Southern, it may have given it to some students with high GPAs like a scholarship of sorts; I wouldn't put it pass them. Some of the students were also veterans with the Vietnam War wounding down at this time (1975). So the students were eligible for grants and GI bills to go to college. Some of them went from being poor to almost middle class until the money ran out. After the money ran out, some still were missing a degree in any one thing and therefore no more qualified for jobs in the outside world than before. I thought this was an abomination. I tried my best to advise students to not only get the two-year degree but to go further and get a four-year degree. Some students took my advice, and one of them even took my place when I went from faculty to administration at Kennedy-King.

For the most part, I enjoyed teaching and being with the students. If I had to describe my students, I would say they were hopeful. Many of them were just hoping to pass my class and get a decent job. Some of them hoped they had what it took to pass the course. Many of them hoped I would pass them no matter what grades they made. Some of them didn't have a clue as to what it took to pass the class. I think some of them thought cooking was easy, so my class would be an easy A. What they didn't realize was that cooking is a science, and to most of them, science is never easy.

When I realized that so many of them were passing up this opportunity to get an education and to better themselves and their families, I started preaching to them to take advantage of this opportunity. It wasn't until I learned in my doctoral program that these were adult students and therefore responsible for themselves. They had to make the decision for themselves as to whether they wanted the education or not. It was my job to lead them to that decision, not preach to them. While I was preaching, I was wasting valuable lesson time. I was a frustrated teacher until then.

I started to work at Kennedy-King when I was twenty-eight years old and about 125 pounds. I was a size 7 dress and a size 7 shoe. James and I were still going together when I started to work at Kennedy-King. I'd bought a car in the spring of 1975 and had a car accident a few months afterward. I simply did not see the other car. I'd looked left, then right, and pulled out, and a car hit me on the left side. The force of the accident pushed my car through hedges and ended up a few inches from a house on the corner. I was heading to work at Englewood Neighborhood Health Center. I did go to the hospital, but I had nothing but a few scratches on me physically. But internally, I was shook up. I started to have panic attacks soon afterward and still do till this day periodically. Most of them occur when I am in a car. Later that year, 1975, I started to work at Kennedy-King.

Things started out okay with my teaching, but I soon started to have anxiety attacks. I would give my students group assignments so I could calm down. All of a sudden, I was spacy, and I would lose my train of thought. I started putting my lectures on overhead projectors. My lectures were many times too wordy, especially in classes I didn't feel comfortable in teaching. I was too thorough and too bookish. I started not to enjoy the experience of teaching as the attacks progressed into panic attacks. I seemed to have them mainly in three places: grocery stores, expressways, and in places with a large group of people, like concerts. I refused to let it cripple me, so I continued to go out to work through my issues.

I had gone to college at eighteen years of age and finished with a master's degree at twenty-four. Here, most of my students were older than twenty-four, most older than me when I first started to teach, twenty-eight years of age. They were, what I found out later, nontraditional students. In my first class, I had a student who was in her eighties. By the way, when she graduated, she had a job waiting on her. She was a delight to teach. She was the one who taught me that I shouldn't call my students *children* or *kids*, which I had the awful habit of doing. I was not prepared to teach adult students.

City Colleges did not offer training for new instructors. I don't think there was even an orientation. After I became tenured, I remember taking a class in "mastery learning" from some professor from the University of Chicago. My confidence level as a teacher would never be the same after that class. I started using the mastery-learning method of teaching, which was to spoon-feed the students even more than I was doing before. More students passed my classes then, and I was happy about that, and I think they learned more, but I suffered professionally.

With mastery learning, you were not to surprise the students. It was important for them to get everything they needed in the class. They were tested more, even given a nongraded pretest at the beginning of the class and a post-tests at the end (the final exam), which was comprehensive and included materials from the beginning of the class. Other tests included weekly quizzes, midterm, and final examination. You were not supposed to introduce new vocabulary to the students on the tests. Plus, you could make available old exams to the students. I placed copies of old exams in the library where students could browse through at their leisure. I was to keep the lectures at the student's level of understanding. As a result of trying to dumb down my course, I lost my own confidence in my abilities. I forgot the usual vocabulary for my nutrition class. I only used mastery-learning methodology in my nutrition course. It was the hardest course for the students to master.

I felt sorry for my students and felt as if they were being cheated, primarily because when I took the same nutrition course using the same book in college, I'd had four years of science in high school (two biology courses, one chemistry, and physics) and two courses of science in college (two biology and two chemistry). Now most of them were sitting in my class with none of those courses, and they were expected to master it. Here I was with black students that I wanted to succeed more than anything because I knew they were coming from a deficit incurred during slavery when their ancestors were stolen from their own land, brought to this country, and treated like animals or worse. As a matter of fact, it was against the law to teach slaves how to read or write. They were always to be less than their masters, less than the animals. One of the reasons we know as much about our heritage as we do is because masters kept logs on their animals and therefore their slaves.

After I started using mastery learning, the majority of them started to pass my nutrition course. Plus, I still felt that they would be ready for the next nutrition course if they chose to go on to a four-year college. I had worked very hard on the course. It took a lot out of me. Every night and every weekend, my head was stuck in books preparing for the lecture, dumbing down the material as best I could. Some of the students surprisingly still thought my class was too hard.

One semester, the president of the student body took my course. She got an A out of my class. She would later tell me that the only reason she took my course was because she'd heard that I was a hard teacher. She said that she found out that if you studied, you would definitely pass my course and that evidently some of the students didn't want to study. All I could do was smile at her findings.

I found that so many of the students didn't know how to study. I remember asking one of my students why he thought he'd flunked one of my exams, and he said, "I don't know. I studied for twenty minutes." I was too dumbfounded to respond. I noticed that after he finished his exam that he'd taken out a radio to listen too. I asked him what he was listening to, and he said the radio; he wanted to see what was happening to Jesse and Angie. Jesse and Angie were very popular black soap stars on the show called *All My Children*. Some people allowed soap operas to control their lives. Everything was scheduled around soap operas. Most of these shows were on during the day when you should be at work. Some people would rather watch soap operas, draw welfare checks, than work or go to college.

My siblings and I had watched soap operas during the summer. We would really get into them; then we'd go back to school and forget about them until holidays or until the next summer vacation. We always were able to catch up easily on what was happening. When I went to college, I didn't have a television, radio, or telephone in my room. Some of my roommates had radios. I was not accustomed to radios because we never had one before I graduated from high school. It kind of irritated me to listen to music on it for some reason. We didn't even get a television until I was in high school. School was our entertainment. When we finally did get a television, we could watch it for about an hour after we got home from school, and then we had to turn it off and do our homework. My mom was not at home, so I was in charge if my dad was not home. My dad worked full-time and would go to our farm after work to tend the animals (cows, hogs, horses) and plow or harvest the fields of peas, beans, tomatoes, watermelons, etc. Even though they weren't home, we did as we were told and turned the television off.

My mom had a sixth sense; she would call home at certain times in the evening to see what we were doing. It was eerie how she would know just where we were all sitting. Most of the time we would all be sitting quietly in the living room doing our homework; it didn't even cross our minds to not mind our parents. Since my siblings did not have as much homework as I did most evenings, I would go to the bedroom and finish while they watched television. I had to learn how to study in a home with a television playing and kids playing. This talent would come in handy when I had roommates and suite mates at colleges.

But here a student was listening to a soap opera during an exam (a male student at that). When he left to go outside of the classroom, some female students followed him and were listening as well. Every last one had flunked the exam. I wonder how many students had failed classes or dropped out of school due to their fixation with soap operas. I didn't know how to fight that, primarily because these were adult students, not teenagers. It seemed with the adults, it went in one ear and out the other. Whereas teenagers were somewhat impressionable and could be led down a productive path, these adults had somehow escaped teenagedom without anyone impressing upon them the fact that they had to make a living, and that meant getting some type of skill which required separation from television and the real world.

Now most of them who had children would guide their own children down the same path. I really think that is the problem now: adults who were poor students in high school did not know how to guide their own children to be productive individuals. Some of them recognized the mistakes they made in high school when they see students who were diligent students leapfrogging over them and doing well in life. I say "some of them" because the rest will latch onto the demise of good students who later become seduced by drugs etc. and fail to make something of themselves and say, "Look what happened to them, and they were good students. It really doesn't matter." Some of them will even use the fact that they are black to do poorly, saying, "It doesn't matter if you are black. The white man is never going to let you get ahead." To them I would say, "Look at Jesse and Angie. They made something of themselves. They are on a television soap opera for which they are being highly paid while you sit on the couch watching them, and they are black. One thing, for sure, if you don't put in the effort, you definitely won't succeed."

When I look back on my time at Kennedy-King College, I think of how naive I was. It was not that the city was too fast for me; it was that I didn't know anything about anything. I had been brought up in a very strict Christian orthodox household. For the most part, we didn't socialize with people outside of the church. For us, it was school, church, and family. However, outside of school and my immediate family and church family, we had very little contact. Both my mom and dad knew people on their jobs, but they did not socialize with them outside of their jobs. If my mom was trying to convert them to Christianity, then she would take them to church with her; but outside of that, she didn't see them. Sometimes the neighbors would talk in the yard, when my mom was either sweeping the yard or hanging clothes on the clothesline. But rarely did they visit each other in their own homes or even talk to each other on the phone.

When I first started teaching, I was shocked at the experience my students had in food service. Many of them had worked in kitchens before. After Ms. Witherspoon and Ms. Parmer took over planning the graduation banquets, I had to think of some other activities for my students to do. One of my students worked at a large local hotel and served as a waiter or server at large dinners at conventions etc. Another was a chef at a prominent hotel on Michigan Avenue in Chicago. He couldn't spell the names of the foods he cooked, but he sure could cook them. Most of the students were in all of my classes and the Home Economics Club, so I decided to have a major activity each year and include all of my classes and the club members. Unlike eighteen-year-old students, some of my students had experience in their field already. If you happen to be in the class and you were eighteen, you were blessed because you were going to learn from me and the adult students in the class.

The first activity we had was a mock wedding. This was right after I got married, so I considered myself an expert. We held the event outside in May. I had no idea that it would be so cold in Chicago in May, but it was. The sun was bright, so it helped. My students in my classes prepared the food and participated in the wedding. I had bought two bottles of real champagne for us to celebrate with after the wedding; however, someone stole the champagne. Go figure!

The second activity we had was a mock restaurant. The student who worked for the hotel as the waiter said he could get us some table linen from his job. He did just that, and we turned a classroom into a restaurant. I asked the building manager if he could get the room painted, and he did. The room went directly over a street, so at night the atmosphere was unique and a little romantic. Another student said she could get her friend to loan us some plants. She had them delivered, and I couldn't believe the transformation of the room. We sent out fliers with the phone number people could call for reservations to our mock restaurant. I got a calligrapher to do our menu. I asked the male students who were going to serve as waiters to put on black suits. To my amazement, most not only didn't have a black suit, they didn't have a suit. So I decided to rent tuxedoes for them, and they looked amazing. I saw their confidence grow just by putting on the tuxedoes. Even though I could hardly walk at the end of the evening, my students obviously had a ball. The student who was the chef at the large hotel served as the head chef and prepared most of the food. I had put students whom I had observed as very good cooks in my food-preparation classes as cooks. They all did an amazing job.

Later, we had a gourmet luncheon, and later a gourmet festival. I led all of these activities by myself. I thought they all turned out great, considering the work that went into them. For the most part, my students and I not only held the activities. we also had to do fund-raising so we could purchase things like shrimp, lobster, rabbit, etc.—all along doing all these activities by myself. I did all the planning and shopping for all the food while using my car (small compact Datsun) to deliver the food to the college. Ms. Witherspoon had said that I couldn't get it delivered by the store. I figured out later how to get it delivered. After getting the food to the campus, I had to find a way to get it to our labs on the third floor. I remember going to get supply carts from the janitors, putting the bags of food on the carts, and pushing the cart to the elevators (sometimes by myself) if classes were out and my students had gone for the day.

After these students graduated, I had to rent items so that we could pull off these activities. This expense was tremendous. Our events grew bigger and bigger. Some students were members of churches or had large families; they bought tickets to the events or raffle tickets. Those are the benefits of having adult students.

These creative activities inspired the students to work hard, but later I would realize that it took a toll on me raising money to put on the events and then hustling to make them a success. The students and I worked hard. However, some of them didn't see how hard I was working behind the scenes. It was not easy getting the college to allow us to host events on the weekend, being in the building from 6:00 a.m. to beyond midnight. I tried to take as many students home as possible when we worked late, especially the girls. Most of them rode public transportation, and I knew it was not safe at night. Plus, most of the students lived in the community (Englewood), and it was known as not being a safe community. It still has a reputation of being a high-crime area today.

Because my students and I had been planning so many events, I felt comfortable in suggesting to my family that we plan a surprise thirty-fifth wedding anniversary for our parents at the same hotel where my mom worked. It was a magical evening; my mom and dad were so surprised. They were both dressed up because they thought my brother and his wife were taking them out to dinner. I don't think I had ever seen both of them as happy as they were that night. I am so happy we took the time to plan the event for them because by the time of their fiftieth anniversary they were both sickly, and my mom and dad died soon after. The pictures from that night are precious; we have pictures of our parents, family, and neighbors enjoying themselves, many of whom have gone on to glory. I was glad I had started the event planning segment in my classes.

It would be later that I would realize that the time we spent hustling for our events should have been spent studying or spending time with family (especially on my part). One year, I read in the paper that Kennedy-King didn't spend all the money in its budget and had sent back money to central office. I was furious. I started hustling in their direction. I should have had some support from Ms.

Witherspoon, but I didn't. She kept telling me year after year that there was no money in the budget. Eventually, the administration helped us with events monetarily, but most of the time, it was paying me back. It was hard coming up with the money and then getting a refund later, but I did it for my students. Now we did not have to hustle bake sales, raffle tickets, donations, etc. for our events.

Most of the time, I would be the only faculty member present to supervise my students. Ms. Parmer helped before she left to get her advanced degree. Ms. Witherspoon and Mrs. Anderson (Ms. Parmer's replacement) would never help. Sometimes they didn't even come to the events. My husband was my life savior. He would take the tickets, sale the raffle tickets, etc. I didn't want students handling the money. As it was, they were stealing whatever food they could. I remember cooking gumbo for one of our events. When I left to go to a meeting, the gumbo had lobster, shrimp, crab, etc.; and when I came back, it only had crumbs of these items. Another time, I had made crayfish bisque, and I had promised our vice president and her husband, who were in attendance, some. But when I went to get it, it was gone; plus, one of my students had disappeared. I couldn't believe this student had taken off with a whole pot of crayfish bisque. I had worked hard on this bisque. The vice president had worked in Louisiana at one time and was familiar with crayfish, so I was looking forward to surprising her. I just couldn't keep an eye on everything and everyone. Sometimes I would have over a hundred students working with me. They were all working for a grade for the events, so most of the time I could depend on them. The events we held were very popular with the students, faculty, and the community.

As a young faculty member, I didn't realize that I was stepping too far out of the box with my department and making others jealous. The one thing they didn't talk about in my graduate program was being careful not to step on people's toes; it might come back to haunt you when you need their support. Plus, all of my money, my husband's money (he didn't know, of course), was going out the door. If I thought we needed something else to make our events successful, I would put in the cash at the bat of a hat. Now that I am retired and broke, I wish I had put that money in the stock market. That's not being mean; that's just reality. Because long after the students were gone, the faculty would still be there, and eventually I would need their support, and it would not be there. Even though I was getting along with faculty members in other departments, the relationship in my own department was cold and getting colder.

I simply did not like the direction my department was going and tried to voice it gently at first, but it was obvious I was not being heard, so eventually I blew up and told the chairperson, Ms. Witherspoon (she was chairperson of the Applied Science Department for years) that she was incompetent. I would come to hate that I said that to her because, evidently, she spread that around to other faculty and staff members. The vice president of the college started treating me coldly and saying things that reflected it. It was obvious Ms. Witherspoon had a lot of support on the faculty; besides, she had more tenure than I did. Ms. Witherspoon wanted things to stay the same all the time; she didn't want to venture out. I knew that if a department didn't spread its wings, updated its curriculum, motivate the students, etc., eventually its very existence would be threatened. I asked her if we could meet over the summer to make strategic plans. She said, "I play golf during the summer." I gave up then. I was tired of leading from the bottom up.

After Ms. Parmer left the college, Ms. Witherspoon had wanted me to teach some of the clothing classes. She even had me audit Ms. Parmer's clothing construction classes. I had to make a several outfits while preparing for my own classes. I realized during the classes that Ms. Parmer's expertise was extensive, and I didn't have the time or the inclination to become an expert in clothing construction, and I was not prepared to cheat the students by acting as if I knew what I was doing. Plus, I did not like sewing, even as a hobby. That year, I was sewing by the end of the semester. I had a crook in my neck that took a long time before it went away. I decided that I had enough to learn how to teach the food-management classes—forget the sewing. I went to the faculty union and asked for their support and got it. It seemed if your degree was not in something, you couldn't be made to teach it. Ms. Witherspoon's degree was in home economics, which means she could teach clothing and food, whereas mine was only in food and nutrition. My relationship with Ms. Witherspoon soured even further after I won that battle. She and Mrs. Anderson became a team after that. I was the odd man out.

In 1980, I paid my own way to New York City for a workshop on computers in food service. I wanted to keep up with anything new in my field. The college did not pay for faculty to attend conferences. I thought this was stupid because how do you keep up with what is happening in your field if you didn't attend workshops, conferences, or conventions in your field? I simply could not afford to attend these conferences on my dollar; I was putting too much already into my classes without James knowing about it. He never questioned how I spent my money and some of his; he expected me to pay our bills. But I had to go to this workshop on computers in food service because this was breaking new grounds. If we started to incorporate computers into our program, we would be ahead of other programs, and recruiting other students interested in going into the food-service industry would be a cake walk.

James and I went to the workshop and toured New York. I found out that New York is the city that never sleeps. There was something going on all the time. From our tour bus, we saw the World's Trade Center, the Twin Towers, Harlem, etc. I would never have guessed that years later I would be training to be a stock broker in one of those Twin Towers just a few years later terrorists would bomb them and they would come down, killing so many people, some I probably met during my training, but I would never know. I was so happy that James was willing to go with me to New York. He seemed delighted to go. I knew I had married the right man. I think he was a little hesitant to venture out into New York by himself, so he would wait until my workshop was over for the day, and then we'd tour the city. I would be so tired, but he was so nice, so I wanted him to enjoy New York as well. I learned so much from the workshop.

When I got back to Kennedy-King, I was so excited about what I had learned at the workshop. However, when I presented it to the department, it was met with cold skepticism. Ms. Witherspoon said she didn't see how computers could be used or how they would help our department. I thought I was speaking English when I explained how it could be used in inventory, development of recipes, storing information, word processing, etc. I was heartbroken. It was then that I decided to run for chairperson of the department myself. We were never going to make it anywhere under Ms. Witherspoon because she didn't want change. I was drowning in complacency.

At first, Ms. Witherspoon had said that she was not going to run for chairperson, but when she found out I was running, she changed her mind. Early on, out of desperation, I told her she was incompetent (mistake); she would turn against me after that. We all met at the house of one of the teachers and voted on a new chairperson. Ms. Witherspoon won; she would remain as chairperson. I was devastated. When we were walking out of the house, one of the teachers said to me that he didn't vote for me because he knew I would have them working. I felt so defeated after that, so when the opportunity came for me to go to administration, I jumped at it. I was tired of working with faculty members in my department who had no vision.

Afterward, I decided to run as the department's representative on the faculty council at Kennedy-King. I won, and when I went to my first meeting, I arrived a little late. I had not even taken my seat when I heard someone put my name up for president. I knew I was not going to win, so I did not object. But I did win, so I went from arriving late to taking over the presidency. I don't remember who ran against me, but I stupidly did not decline. I felt honored that they thought I could be the president. It didn't occur to me that no one wanted the unenviable position.

After I became president of the faculty council, I took an adult education class at Chicago State University in Robert's Rules of Order because I knew so little about them. I was so grateful for the class; it helped me a lot in my position as president. I wanted to be successful. As president, I was an ad hoc member of all the committees. Stupidly, I tried to go to all the committee meetings. I also had to go to the All City College Faculty Council meetings. Somehow I got on the personnel committee at this meeting and became the chair. Again I felt honored that they thought I could handle this. What I would later find out was that this was an unenviable position as well. I had to learn the hard way that if you are new to something, learn the lay of the land before you try to lead the group. I not only was the youngest person in the room. I was probably the dumbest because I didn't know what making decisions on this committee meant, especially if you went against the administration. I would later learn that the decisions I made on this committee would haunt me forever and probably cost me my job of twenty-two years later.

After I became president of the faculty council, I was determined to make a difference. One of my committees recommended that we host an alumni reunion. I thought it was a great idea. The only problem was the committee did not work efficiently, and as it turned out, I did most of the work; they just chipped in sometimes. Because of my untrained and inexperienced eye, I didn't realize that I was being manipulated again. Just like I had been manipulated on the personnel committee (I had been elected chair because the older and more experienced faculty knew it was a thankless job and could be detrimental to my future with the City Colleges), and I was clueless. Now the faculty, all of a sudden, couldn't do anything for the reunion, find the place, send out the invitations, design the invitations, etc. I wanted it to be a success, so I persevered on it, and it was mildly successful. I think we had seventy-five people attending. Majority of the faculty council members themselves did not attend. Forget the rest of the faculty. Believe it or not, some of them had even attended Kennedy-King when it was called Wilson Junior College, so they would still be called alumni.

Like I said, as the president of the faculty council, I was an ex officio member of all faculty council committees and stupidly thought this meant I should attend all committee meetings that I could. So when I was available, I went to every committee meetings. Looking back, I should have allowed the committee chairs to control their meetings. Not that I was controlling; it was the very presence of the chair made it seem like I was controlling, and I did not know that. I was surprised at the lack of attendance at the meetings and late start times. At first I would get to the meetings on time, and they would never start until almost fifteen or thirty minutes late. Once I decided to be purposefully late, and I was still the first to arrive. One time, I went to the committee chairperson's office to see if I had gotten the date and time wrong, and she said she had forgotten about the meeting. One committee that I thought was extremely important was the Curriculum and Standards Committee. I was taken aback by how it was run. There did not seem to be any wholehearted interest in updating the curriculum or the standards. There were two changes that I'd hope to incorporate: one was a requirement for mathematics in the general education course requirement needed for graduation and standards for remedial English and mathematics.

I thought it was inhumane for students to graduate without ever taking one mathematics course. Everybody needed mathematics in their lifetime. In some form or fashion, mathematics was required in every course I taught, from increasing and decreasing recipes, counting calories, food check balances, totaling or estimating market orders, etc. When I realized that most of the students couldn't add or subtract past three place numbers, I felt defeated. Plus, all the books we used were college-level reading books, and very few of the students read at the college level. To me, it was not realistic of us to expect the students to pass these courses.

Some of the students passed because they were good at memorizing or attaching themselves to other students' work. I realized I had to make a change when I passed a student, and she came back and told me she didn't do anything and that she hadn't read a chapter in the book. At the time, I would place students in groups, and everyone in the group would get the same grade. So my grading method accounted for the C that she got and did not deserve. After this discussion with the student, I did more research on group teaching and realized I had to give them a group and an individual grades. After, I took a course at Roosevelt University, and the teacher required that the students give each other a grade. I'd wished I had included this method as well, but I had retired by then. I was not able to get the curriculum updated, but I was able to get the remedial standards for entry-level mathematics and English courses upgraded. There really were no standards before that, and you could have an illiterate student taking your class, and your textbook was college level.

As the president of the faculty council, I was also a member of the All-City Faculty Council. Soon after being elected to the presidency of the faculty council, I went to my first meeting of the All-City Faculty Council. There was one other member from Kennedy-King, Joe Wormack, of the Automotive Department at Kennedy-King. I don't think he ever said a word at any of the meetings. I wondered how he got selected as the representative; he did not seem to have an agenda. I am not sure, but I think he urged me to get on a committee called Committee M. I believe that was the name at the time. It was the personnel committee. It was the faculty committee that screened candidates for higher administrative positions. I went to my first meeting of Committee M and was immediately selected as the chairperson of the committee. Again I was surprised and wondered how I had impressed people to be selected. And again I was too stupid to decline. I was the youngest person in the room. It didn't occur to me that no one wanted the position because it meant squabbling with central administration, and that could hurt you in getting positions, money, etc. in the future because they had the last word.

There was one central administration position open, so I called a meeting of Committee M to discuss how to proceed. We were to interview all the candidates and make our decision as to whom to suggest to the chancellor to hire. What I did not know was that there was a committee of administrators as well. In the end, we recommended different candidates. The chancellor suggested that we meet and decide on one candidate. I did my homework so I would be able to defend my candidate. I did an excellent job, and the combined committees chose my committee's candidate. Again, what I did not know was that the chancellor had already promised the job to the other candidate.

Dr. Wayne Watson had chaired the administration's committee. He was at the combined meeting and pushed heavily for the other candidate. Dr. Watson was black, so I was surprised that he was pushing so heavily against the black candidate. The other candidate that evidently had been promised the position unbeknownst to me was white. My committee's candidate had a PhD in chemistry, had served in administration before, was from Chicago, and graduated from a Chicago public school and had a GPA above 3.0. I can't remember if my committee was privy to the reference letters or not.

At the time of this selection process, Harold Washington had been elected the first black mayor of Chicago. My committee's candidate had graduated from the same high school as the current mayor. So when I wrote my recommendation to the chancellor for the candidate supported by the combined committee of faculty and administrators, I cc'd Mayor Harold Washington. For some reason during the Christmas holidays, I received a call from Hermene Hartman, one of the assistants to the chancellor. Hermene was black as well. She asked me why I sent the information to the mayor, that he didn't care about such things. I told her that I did it because I thought he was the ultimate boss of all of the City Colleges employees. What she did not know was I had not mailed the letter yet and only made up my mind to put it in the mail after she called me; otherwise, I never would have mailed the letter. What I really wanted to do was scare the white chancellor into hiring the black candidate. I still didn't know he had already promised the position to the white candidate. He chose the black candidate. I was elated that he was hired. Again what I did not know was that because of my pressure tactics—which I considered as going the extra mile for someone who I believed was qualified for the position against someone who was not qualified— my name became mud with the central administrators, especially Dr. Wayne Watson, the black person who chaired the administration's committee. I think he was looking to impress his white boss, the chancellor, by getting his nominee selected. He never expected an aggressive young black female from the South whose aim was to help her people whenever possible and when she was placed in the position to do so, and the black person was the best candidate, at least in her view.

When I came to Chicago, the "Civil Rights Movement" and its principles were embedded in my mind. One of those was fighting against discrimination against blacks and other minorities that had been perpetuated by white people for centuries. I thought it was the right of black people who got in positions of authority and could hire qualified black people that they should. I felt it was my duty to promote the most qualified candidate that my committee interviewed for the central office position; he just happened to be black. I would not have promoted him if he had not been more qualified than the other candidates in my opinion.

After the candidate my committee suggested was hired, he was under Dr. Watson's supervision. He called me one day and told me that he had an office in a corner with a desk, no phone, and no secretarial support. I thought he had to be kidding. We were in touch several times during his tenure at the central office. He was never given any real authority. He stayed in the position for several years, probably looking for another job all the time. He called me on his last day at City Colleges and told me to watch my back. I really didn't know what he meant then, but I would find out.

At the end of the year that I served on the faculty council, I did not run again because I knew I was pregnant and would be taking a year off. I knew we were going to need the extra money, so I taught summer school. I got big so fast. Everyone seemed really happy for me. Here I was, thirty-eight years old and pregnant. James and I had been trying to get pregnant for five years by then. We had been married for eight years. I didn't try to get pregnant the first three years because I wanted to make sure we were going to stay married. I think several of my girlfriends were watching to see if my marriage lasted as well because after I was married about two years, all of a sudden they started to get married, or get engaged at least. My friend Delores Evans got engaged, but never did get married and gave us, her friends, no explanation. She had a baby, but still didn't get married. She later died from ALS or Lou Gehrig's disease while the child was in high school, I believe. My friend Tommie, probably the most skittish of them all, got married, and the marriage lasted until her death from breast cancer in 2018. My friend Connie got married and is still married to her husband.

After James Jr. was born, I did take a year off without pay. This was difficult for James and me because he was sometimes laid off in the winter, and we hadn't saved up a lot of money as a result. But the year before, he'd gotten a job with the Chicago Park District and didn't get laid off anymore and even got paid for sick and vacation days. By now, we had been married eight years. When he depended on the union for jobs, he was constantly being laid off, especially when he was single. Now that he was married, he was working steadier, but he was still being laid off at times, and I would have to pay most of the bills. He always applied for unemployment, and that helped. I tried to pay off most of my bills so that I could take the year off. The one problem I am not sure I anticipated was that I would have to pay for my health insurance. James had insurance, but I wanted to go to my own doctor, so since I was not working, the money had to come out of my own pocket (a mistake, I should have used James's health insurance). I also wanted to James Jr. to use the same clinic. We would never recoup this year of salary.

While I was off work, Dr. Akins was terminated as the president and went back to faculty at another city college. I couldn't help but wonder if I was somewhat responsible for his demise because we had some type of run-in when I was on the faculty council. The previous president of the council had encouraged me to go against him on some issue that I can't remember now. Now I know she was using my naivety. I had no idea the man might lose his position.

So while I was off, a search was conducted for a new president. The vice president served as the interim president. Dr. Akins had terminated Ms. Barker, the vice president who hired me, and she was back in the classroom at Kennedy-King. I could tell she was miserable, but she made the best of the situation. Later that year, I heard that she was taking a leave of absence. She'd call me the day after I returned home with my new baby and invited me to her wedding anniversary celebration. I told her about the baby, and she said, "Now you have to go right back and have another one." I told her that it was too painful having a baby. She said that I would forget it, but I didn't. I never used birth control, but I never got pregnant again either. Mrs. Barker died about five months later. Mr. Bryant, the dean of Applied Science Department, died a few months after that. I couldn't believe they were gone. I went to both funerals.

Before I left Kennedy-King for my maternity leave, a few black faculty members and I had formed the Concerned Black Faculty of Kennedy-King College. We were a part of a larger group called the Black Faculty in Higher Education, which was a national group or Midwest group. This group supported certain individuals for union positions, normally black faculty. I would vote for these black candidates on their recommendation because I was so dissatisfied with the system. Later, much later—it might have even been after I retired—I found out that one of the candidate's husbands (that I had met) was a leader or even chairman of the Communist Party of Illinois and that she was a member as well. I remember how a fellow Kennedy-King employee and a member of Concerned Black Faculty and staff at Kennedy-King had told me this. She followed up this statement by saying that if I wanted to go to a meeting, she could help me. I looked at her and said, "No, thank you." I was adamantly against the Communist Party and had been since I learned about them in high school. If I had known that certain members of Concerned Black Faculty at Kennedy-King associated with members of the Communist Party, I would never have aligned myself with it.

I know that certain black groups had been represented in the press as to having ties with the Communist Party, but I thought it was a lie. Now I knew better. Now I know better than to align myself with a group just because it has "black" in its title. I needed to do research not only on its history but the members' history as well. I say *members* because later on I found out that certain members of Concerned Black Faculty had at one time been agnostic, wondering why God had abandoned black people during pre and post the Civil War. I have never doubted God and definitely didn't want to align myself with agnostics.

The Concerned Black Faculty at Kennedy-King decided to endorse a candidate for president at Kennedy-King. All the candidates accepted their invitation to interview. I decided to attend some of the interviews. My friend Dr. Rose Brown was chairing Concerned Black Faculty at the time. She seemed very impressed with Dr. Harold Pates. Dr. Pates had been transferred to Kennedy-King as a counselor. He had never served as a president of a college before. Two of the current Kennedy-King administrators were candidates as well. None of these candidates had previous experience as president as well. I had raised this concern, but most faculty members in Black Faculty, including my friend Rose, who was the chair, seemed to be more concerned with them having knowledge of the city college system. Rose went out of her way to get Dr. Pates the position. She got up early one morning and went to each home of the current city college board of trustees and left his résumé on the doorstep. By then, Rose and I had made friends with Florence Brown. I think all three of us went to the board meeting where they announced Dr. Pates as the new president of Kennedy-King.

I was still on maternity leave, but I went to the reception that was given for Dr. Pates. We thought one of the first things he would do would be to get rid of those two administrators who were also up for the position, but he didn't. I found out that Rose wanted the position of vice president of Arts and Sciences. She applied for the position, and maybe she interviewed, but she did not get the position. She was disappointed because she thought she had earned it and that Dr. Pates would reward her for it, but he didn't. I later found out that she was interested in him personally. I think she was just enamored with him because he was so tall. I couldn't help but wonder if he had gotten the position if he had not been so tall. It seems in America, if you have anything going for yourself and you are tall, you are employable.

After I came back from maternity leave, Rose suggested that I apply for the position of director of Academic Support. I was tired of teaching by then and felt that the department had stalled under Ms. Witherspoon. So I applied and got the position. This was the start of another new chapter in my life that I was not trained for. I did get the chance to speak with the outgoing director. Primarily, all she did was introduce me to the staff. Most of the staff was paid through the Disadvantage Student Grant. She gave me copies of the grant and her reports, which I appreciated.

Kennedy-King had a nice Academic Support Center. The center provided academic support for students in all of the programs in the college, even the GED or General Education Diploma program. I had no idea that the GED had a literacy component. Now I see how some of those students ended up in my college-level courses. I believe many of the GED students, after finding out they didn't need a GED to take the college-level classes and because they were in close proximity to the college, could enroll in the college and get a PELL grant. I think before they graduated from the college, they had to have a GED—though, one of my students who had her first baby in the eighth grade and dropped out of school went back and got as far as the eleventh grade, I believe told me. She studied hard and turned out to be one of my best students.

When I started at the center, I was surprised that the secretary for the department was not using a computer to do her typing. She was still using one of the old typewriters. I decided to offer a word-processing workshop for her, interested staff, and myself. She seemed to enjoy the workshop. I know I loved it. To be able to save your work, correct the misspelled words before printing it, to me was a lifesaver. So I bought her and myself personal computers. I think she had gotten into a rhythm of typing and filing over the years and didn't want to change. I think the fear was that she would now get more work because of the computer. She had figured out how to stay busy for eight hours a day, even though her job could be done in much less time. I think because of the constant turnover in her department, she had considered herself to be a pseudo-director.

I took on the job of being the director the same way I did teaching the food classes. I worked to increase the number of students we saw and was eventually rewarded with more funds and more tutors. I realized that no training program had been in place, so I initiated a training program. I noticed that most of the staff would arrive late and set up penalties for arriving late for work. When the tutorial supervisors left, I hired new tutors. I even established a position as Academic Support Center manager. I bought new computers for the center for student use. I purchased academic software programs for literacy, English, and mathematics. At the end of the year, we had an awards program. Tutors and counselor assistants could recommend students for an award. The awards program grew every year. We started off having the program in the center but had to move it to the cafeteria and made it a full-scaled banquet. I purchased videotaped learning material. Sometimes I would use the learning material myself, take some of the tests, etc. And I grew personally. I surprisingly enjoyed the job.

I had one problem: most of the administrators had PhDs and would engage in conversations that I didn't understand sometimes. I had not majored in education, so I was not familiar with some of the philosophers they would mention. So like I said earlier, when the opportunity came around for me to join a doctoral cohort at Northern Illinois University, I did. It was hard working full-time, raising my young son, and being a diligent wife to my husband, but I did it and got my doctorate in four years.

A year after I got my doctorate, my family and I went on vacation for a week. I had wanted to take longer; but President Pates, for some reason, told me to come back after a week. When I came back and went to my first administration meeting, he informed us that he was retiring and that Dr. Wayne Watson would be transferring from Harold Washington College to be the new president. When he said that, my heart just sunk, I knew that under Dr. Pates that I probably would have gotten a deanship at some point in time, and maybe even a vice presidency, but Dr. Watson meant red lights for me ever since we had gone head to head on the Personnel Committee while I was on the All-City Faculty Council. I remember the statement that was made to me to "watch my back."

Plus, while I was in administration, I had voted against the chairman of the faculty union for distinguished professorship. After I left faculty, quite a few changes had been made. Now the faculty received funds for conferences; they could take paid sabbaticals to take courses or get an advanced degree. They also could apply for distinguished professorship for which they would get $5,000. The year the union chair applied for distinguished professorship, Dr. Pates asked me to serve on the committee. He and I both knew that my friend and his ardent supporter for his job, Dr. Rose Brown, was going to apply for the distinguished professorship. The first time the committee met and voted, I noticed that Rose came out at the bottom of the list and that she had gotten scores like 40 or 50 out of 100. This was a lady who had gotten her PhD in mathematics, advisor to the mathematics club, chairperson of Concerned Black Faculty, and planned a black history program every year for the college. She also worked with me to supervise the cheerleaders when no one else stepped up to the plate.

My problem with the chair of the union was that he had not formed a recruitment committee among the faculty so that we could curtail the continuation of the drop in our enrollment, and this was a part of the contract. I knew faculty members were going to lose their jobs, and they eventually did. Programs would be closed, and they eventually were. To me, he was just as much at fault as the administration because if he had urged the faculty, I am sure more would have been done to market the programs in the Chicago Public Schools. The faculty and the administration needed to join hands, and nothing was ever done.

When I stupidly told Rose about the scores after she pounced on me after the first meeting, she was livid. She told me at the next meeting to give everybody else a 0 and her 100. I knew this was going against my principles, but I also figured that I'd have the backing of the president because I knew he wanted to reward Rose since he had denied her that vice president's position. So I did as she had instructed, and to my surprise, she won. Everybody else had voted the same way; plus, they probably didn't score the union chair 100 like I did Rose. None of the candidates deserved 100 points, but Rose definitely did not deserve their low scores either. They were all union members or officers mostly and had planned on the chair getting the distinguished professorship. They were all shocked that Rose came out on top of the voting. I could feel the heat in the room, and I couldn't wait to get back to tell Rose she had won. The votes were not supposed to be shared, but I believe they were because the next thing I knew, I was being called to the president's office, along with the other members of the committee, to discuss the voting. I had figured right: the president sided with me, and Rose became the distinguished professor for that year. Now here I was with the union against me and a brand-new boss against me

Dr. Watson's and my path seldom came across each other after the personnel committee where my candidate had gotten the job and his didn't. At the end of that year, I was pregnant and took a year off. Then a year after I returned to work, I became an administrator. Mrs.

Witherspoon passed away from a congenital heart condition. Now the department consisted of Mrs. Anderson and Mrs. Ross (one of our former students that I recommended for the job when I became an administrator; by then she had her master's in food and nutrition or was working on it). I was too busy getting my doctorate and being director of Academic Support to keep up with what was happening in the Home Economics Department, but I'd heard rumblings of low enrollment.

Eventually, Dr. Watson's and my path did cross again, in a way I had never imagined. I thought his path to leadership was to become the chancellor of the City Colleges of Chicago. Instead, here he was, going from vice chancellor to become president of Harold Washington College at first and then president of Kennedy-King College. The Harold Washington faculty did not like him and said so very loudly in their actions. I think the Harold Washington faculty were majority white. Kennedy-King's faculty didn't like him either as an administrator, but the faculty was majority black and evidently weak to the core. Evidently, everybody was out for themselves and their individual departments. It seems that the status of presidents had risen above that of vice chancellor, and now here he was, my boss. He treated me as if I was invisible the whole year I served as an administrator under him. I hated his administrator meetings because all he did was complain about the central administration and what a terrible job the chancellor was doing. It was obvious that he wanted the chancellor's job and was campaigning for it all the time. Forget the fact that he was a lousy college president himself, at least to me.

The only thing I remember him doing is hiring some chefs from New York to come and evaluate the food management program. It seemed that since City Colleges had taken over Washburn Trade School, they were looking for a college to align it with. The chefs even interviewed me since I had been an instructor in the Food Management Department at one time. I had thought that the two programs could merge since our program was training food service managers and Washburn was training chefs or cooks. Why couldn't both programs work together while merging the faculties?

So at the end of Dr. Watson's first year at Kennedy-King, he removed me from administration and sent me back to the classroom. I was just glad I still had a job (at least I thought I had a job). A few months into the semester, Dr. Watson brought the other food management instructors and myself into his office and told us if our enrollment did not improve, he was eliminating our department. The home economics discipline at Kennedy-king had already been eliminated due to low student enrollment. After the instructor I thought was not qualified replaced Ms. Parmer as the main clothing instructor, students started dropping out of the clothing classes because they knew she was incompetent. Even though many black students were looking for teachers to give them a grade sometimes, I felt the majority of them wanted to learn something from their teachers and that they recognized when the teacher didn't know the discipline that well. So then she started teaching the food-management classes. Then students started to disappear from those classes as well. Her background was not foods, and they recognized that. Plus, she was now the social secretary for the union, so she used her food classes to cater their meetings. I think the students felt used, and they were being used to hoister their instructor's reputation with the union.

Dr. Watson told us he would give us one semester to get our enrollment up. I couldn't believe it; it would take us at least a year. Here, I was just getting back use to teaching; I really didn't have time to go to the high schools to recruit students. I begged him to give us a year, but he refused. So we went about trying to campaign to save the program. I should say I went about trying to save the program to no avail. So in January, Dr. Watson called us into his office and told us since we were not able to get our enrollment up, he was closing the program when the students we had graduated. The former clothing, now food, management instructor was allowed to move to another department. Ms. Ross was allowed to move to Harold Washington College to teach Food Sanitation courses.

I found out that things had changed, and now all food sanitation instructors had to take an examination. I had thought maybe I could teach at Malcolm X college's program in dietetic assistants, but

I was not a registered dietitian, but neither was one of their instructors. I wasn't even given the opportunity to become registered. I was told that if I became certified in sanitation, maybe I could be hired. I went about working to pass this examination. The week of my examination, my mom passed away, and I had a breast-cancer scare. I was really a mess taking the exam, and I came up two points shy of passing. So I couldn't take the job at Malcolm X. I was told to get fifteen credit hours in English or mathematics (graduate courses). I knew that math was out of the question, and English was my worst subject, so I was fired as far as I was concerned.

My last day on the job was in May 1997. One or two people had taken me out to lunch, but otherwise no one said a word to me. One of my students told me that everybody was looking for me to break down and cry, but I held my head high for one reason. I knew that if I was losing my job, that was the way God wanted, and he had new experiences in store for me.

I had put twenty-two years of blood, sweat, and tears into my position, and I walked out alone and miserable. I was mad because I was sorry that I had stayed in a position where I was not appreciated. I felt I had been fighting upstream the whole time. I was a dedicated employee, and I should have been in a position that appreciated my efforts. Now here I was, almost fifty, and being employable was suspect. I had no idea what I was going to do. There were no other home economics programs in the city. Even the Chicago Board of Education had gotten rid of all of its home economics programs. For some reason, they thought the students could get what they needed at home; obviously, they didn't know that all homes weren't equal. Now we have a generation of moms and dads who do not cook or sew or manage their lives better.

I left Kennedy-King without a plan. Not only didn't I have a plan, all the stress had caused me to gain weight. I also felt like I had disappointed God because I had stayed at the college when I'd only planned on being there three years or until I found another job or started my own business. I was never supposed to be at Kennedy-King. I believe I had gone against the path God had laid out for my life. I thought I had been in charge, and I wasn't all the time. I left

Kennedy-King with hypertension, high cholesterol, hyperthyroidism and hypothyroidism, anxiety—devastated and depressed at fifty years of age and no plan.

After leaving, I decided to fight back by filing a lawsuit against the city colleges. I didn't know any lawyers, so I called the Chicago Bar Association to ask for references of lawyers that had filed discrimination lawsuits because I felt I had been discriminated against for my age. I made an appointment with the law firm they had recommended and was impressed with him. After I had made the initial payment and agreed to terms, I found out that the lawyer I had interviewed would not be my lawyer; his son was to be my lawyer instead. The son and I disagreed on what my fight should be. He thought it should be protected language since I had protested with my students against the termination of the Food Management Program from the curriculum, and I thought it should be age discrimination. When we met with the judge, she disagreed with my lawyer and said I had a case but chose the wrong path. I was so upset with my lawyer and myself. I could have used that money to look for another job. Under Dr. Watson, Kennedy-King was dropping the Food Management Program and instituting a chef-training program.

My students and I had decided to fight back. We went to one of the city college board meetings, and several of them spoke, and I did as well in an attempt to convince them that the program was needed, but to no avail. We decided then to stage a protest during a visit by the accrediting association, the North Central Accreditation body. I'd asked faculty members to join us. I even asked Rose, who had retired at the time. No one joined us, not even Rose; I thought she had nothing to lose. It was then I decided that I didn't know how to define friendship. That I thought I had friends among my colleagues, and what I really had were associates. I had shown up for someone whom I thought was my friend, and she had gotten $5,000 as a result. Now I was fighting for my job, my livelihood, and she couldn't show up for me. Here I was, fifty years of age, and still had so much to learn about friendship. I was more of a ride-or-die-type friend, but they weren't, and now I realize I shouldn't have been either, especially if it meant going against my principles. One of my boyfriends had told me that he didn't have friends, that all he had were associates. I thought he was being a cynic, but now after being brought to my knees time and time again by people I thought were my friends, I knew better.

Another friend at Kennedy-King, Florence, came to me when she realized that our program was being eliminated, and I was losing my job and suggested that they form a committee of faculty members to see if they could save our program. She said that one of the white faculty members would chair; she thought that would add more weight. I couldn't believe she wasn't chairing; it seemed to me that she was scared of losing her job as well and going against Dr. Watson. She figured Dr. Watson would not fire one of the white faculty members. I had no idea I was working with such chickens, or maybe they knew something that I didn't. Certain fights were not worth losing your job over. I didn't have that thought because I had never planned on staying in my job in the first place. I knew I would not make the money I wanted in the job at Kennedy-King—but now I was fifty years old—had I stayed too late. Nothing happened with Florence's committee. I think they suggested that I go and make a personal appeal to Dr. Watson, and I did.

I will forever remember the day I went to his office to meet with him. I was sitting in the outer office with his secretary. Around this time, I had decided to go ball headed. I had alopecia, and most of my hair was gone anyway. I was sitting in the outer office when a couple showed up in the doorway, and the young man got the attention of Dr. Watson. Dr. Watson came to his door and spoke to them; he evidently knew the young man. The young man introduced the young lady as his fiancée, I believe. Dr. Watson said, "You got a good one."

"A good one." The young lady had long hair, and she was light-skinned. Here I was, sitting with dark skin and no hair. I felt defeated before I went into his office. I went in anyway and made a vain attempt to save my job, but after the conversation I'd overheard and rumors I'd heard about Dr. Watson, I knew I was not his type, and he would not help me. I felt humiliated and ugly. I thought no matter what degree you had, your looks always followed you and possibly could prevent you from getting a job. Until this point, I had gotten every job I had interviewed for, so I was venturing into new territory at fifty years of age, unemployed and not attractive.

A few days later, the board of trustees voted to terminate my contract. Dr. Watson came to the area of the college where my office was located and saw me, turned, and signed the termination right in front of me. I thought, God, had I deserved that? Maybe I had for working in a job where I was not appreciated that long. I had been a naive country girl with no experience of working in a big city. I should have found a college or even a high school that was more of a training ground before I ventured into the vulture land of the City Colleges of Chicago.

Chapter 8

THE COURTSHIPS, WEDDING, AND SETTLING INTO MARRIED LIFE AND MOTHERHOOD

The Courtships

By the time I met my future husband, I had been living in Chicago for a couple of years. I had moved to a two-bedroom apartment with my friend Jackie and her sister Carolyn. I was still sleeping on bedframes and a mattress. We started having parties. We didn't know a lot of people, but those we knew came and brought or invited random people with them. Most of our parties were fairly successful. Most parties we went to just had snacks and alcohol. So we only had alcohol and a few snacks. Some people would come to the party with a bottle of some type of alcohol or wine. We started to accumulate quite a stash of alcohol. None of us drank, so we had plenty for our next party.

When I arrived in Chicago, I had very little experience with dating. I had dated one guy Esther had introduced me to who turned out to be a bed-wetter, and another guy who had erectile-dysfunction issues. By the time I moved in with Jackie and Carolyn, I had been dating Ronnie for almost a year. I felt so comfortable with him that I invited him to meet my family that summer. He drove me to Louisiana so that I could attend my sister Linda's wedding.

Linda had just graduated from high school. She walked across the stage pregnant, and nobody knew it. With seven girls, my parents were lucky that she was the only one that got pregnant in high school. At that time, you couldn't go to school pregnant. I think you had to stay out until you had your baby and come back the following school year. My parents knew that Linda was pregnant. I am not sure when I found out. My parents insisted that Linda go to college that summer. My mom, especially, had encouraged all of my siblings to go to summer school. She wanted everyone to graduate as soon as possible. She tried to get me to go every summer, but I told her that I needed a mental break, so I only think I went two summers. Going during the summer meant that I could get by with twelve credit hours of courses during fall and spring semesters and not work so hard. I found fifteen hours challenging, but I had several semesters with fifteen or more hours.

When Ronnie drove me home, my parents arranged for him to stay at my neighbor's house. I think he slept on the couch. I was so busy preparing for the wedding that I don't think I had the time to introduce him to my hometown or any of my friends. Linda got married on our front porch like most of my relatives and friends did at the time on their front porches. I think my mom had made her the dress she wore. She looked pregnant. Her husband was handsome. He'd been a young man in my sister Carrie's class when I met him in elementary school. I remembered him as a short, chubby little boy. He grew up to be a handsome guy. My sister Linda thought she had a catch.

I knew she didn't have a catch and probably shouldn't have married him. My parents told me that even though he had been working at the shell plant (ammunition plant) all summer, he didn't have $25 to put down as a deposit for their apartment. Of course, they didn't tell me this until after Linda got married. They were both so embarrassed that she was pregnant and had to get married that they weren't thinking clearly.

Linda was only married about three weeks when she miscarried the baby. She probably could have returned to Southern for the fall semester but decided to skip it. In the spring, after being married about five months and catching her husband with another woman in her bed, he told her that he thought they should divorce until after she graduated and then remarry if they wanted to then. They gave up their apartment, and Linda moved back in with our parents. Of course, that would be the last she would see of him.

After the wedding, my new friend Ronnie whom I was so smitten with drove me to Florida so I could meet his mother and some other relatives. I was surprised that in the midst of the wedding preparation, he started talking about "when we get married, we're going to…" I thought it was a little early to be talking about a wedding between us, but I played along. I was twenty-five at the time and was feeling like I was never going to get married for some reason. I'd always had doubts because of my feelings that I wasn't attractive enough to catch a man. I'd had a few dates at Southern that weakened those feelings somewhat, but they were still there.

When we got to Florida, we stayed with his mother. She seemed a little standoffish. I seemed to get along with his sister. I met his grandmother and was surprised that she looked white. Ronnie had told me the story about how his father and mother split because his brother came out of the womb looking so white, and the father felt that the mother had had an affair with a white or very light-skinned black man. I'd met the brother, and he was light-skinned. However, the father would have nothing to do with him. This situation was a thorn in the family. They didn't have DNA then. I am pretty sure this light-skinned kid was his; he just took after the grandmother's side of the family (and besides, the mother herself was light-skinned). It didn't make sense. Evidently, he knew very little about genetics. The boy was raised by his mother's sister in Chicago, and the mother went back home to Florida. The father married someone else. Ronnie's father and stepmother were both very nice to me.

When we got back to Chicago, however, he started treating me differently. He was distant for some reason. His family had a problem with my dark skin and had mentioned it to him. He only told me they had a problem with my skin color, but I am pretty sure they said I was ugly as well. Of course, my thoughts ran the gamut. I was very hurt because this was the first time that I felt I was "in love." I felt we connected and that the chemistry was right. I knew I had to get over it, though.

One night he had agreed to go to a party with me. We were to leave around 10:00 p.m., but he never showed. I called him, and he said he had forgotten and had been gambling with some guys and would be on. He never came. I never called him again because trust is something I value. He did call me and come by, but I knew it was over because I was distant this time. A relationship can't survive if both of you are distant. I am not sure now if we officially broke up, but I do remember him telling me that he wasn't ready to get married, and he knew I was, so he thought we should cool it. I was surprised with his thinking because we didn't know each other that well yet, but I agreed with him that neither of us needed to waste our time. I was really hurt.

Later on, my roommate Jackie told me that she saw him out partying with another girl. She had gone out and came home and headed straight to my room about 2:00 a.m. to tell me this. I was sound asleep at the time, but of course, I couldn't sleep anymore. I was having trouble getting over him, and this stirred the pot. I knew I had to move on. I made a promise to myself, though, never to wake someone else up and tell them I saw their boyfriend cheating on them or ever.

The funny thing was that Ronnie's next girlfriend looked a lot like me. I met her because his sister came to town and called me asking if she could stay with me. I think Ronnie's sister had spent one night with her and felt uncomfortable. I said of course. I had met his sister when I had gone to Florida that one time to visit his family. I think she was still in high school at the time. She was a really cute little girl then. I had to pick her up at his current girlfriend's house, or we went to pick her up, I am not sure now. I know that I did get the chance to meet the new girlfriend. She was my skin color and had a shape and size similar to mine. I don't know how long he had been going with her. By then, James and I were in a relationship. It still hurt somewhat that Ronnie had moved on, but not as bad now. My sister Vickie was staying with me as well. She and Ronnie's sister got along well. Vickie was still in high school. I know that they met some guys and went out. Ronnie's sister was not only cute, she was busty now as well. Vickie told me that she thought Ronnie's sister was a little too friendly with the guys. I had a talk with her, and it turned out that at home in Florida, she had a friend; and from her description, he seemed like a pimp. I am pretty sure he was grooming her to be one of his girls. I told Ronnie about it, and he looked hurt. But he said that there was nothing he or I could do about it. For the first time, I felt lucky that neither me nor any of my sisters were light-skinned or in the beautiful category.

When Jackie, Carolyn and I moved to our two-bedroom apartment, we had a huge (at least to me, it was huge) living room. So we had plenty of room for dancing and throwing parties. Plus, our view was somewhat spectacular from the seventeenth floor. We had a view of Lake Michigan and downtown Chicago. We had so many windows; it had been expensive finding curtains for the windows. Plus, the windows were from floor to ceiling and all the way around the living room and bedroom areas. I still had my sofa sleeper, which was the first piece of furniture I had in my life. I don't think we had anything else for the living room (maybe a chair).

I started to date. Jackie and I went on one double-date together. When the guys brought us home, it was very late, so they offered to take us to what was called "Jew Town" to get some polishes. They wanted to know if we had ever had a "Jew Town" polish, and we told them no. When we got to Jew Town, all I could smell were onions grilling. I thought the polish was okay, but nothing to write home about. I'd had polishes in Wisconsin, and I thought they were much better. I didn't think the food was worth the trip to Jew Town. I also dated a guy from Southern that was living a block from me. I think we had met getting off the train together from downtown. There would be a lot of people getting off the train in professional attire heading to high-rises on South Shore Drive where I lived. When the guy invited me on a date, I accepted. I think we went to dinner or to a movie, but when he was taking me home, I noticed that he passed my apartment, so I pointed it out to him. Then he said, "Your place or mine?" I realized he thought we were having sex. I told him to take me home, and he said, "What do you want, a pair of boots?" I am not sure what I said to him, but I know it amounted to something like, "My ass is worth more than a pair of boots!" I was furious with him and never ran into him again.

There was another guy from Southern that wasn't living too far from us. He invited Jackie and me over, and we went. I think he was interested in dating one of us, but he didn't ever make a move. His name was Sylvester Love, and his brother was Nathaniel Love. They were just two nice guys. My sister Juanita eventually dated Nathaniel, but nothing came of it. Sylvester was the first black guy that I met when I first got to the University of Wisconsin that I had already known from Southern. Then imagine my surprise when I saw him getting off the train on Seventy-First Street in Chicago about a week after I arrived. He had finished his master's degree at the University of Wisconsin and had taken a job in accounting in Chicago. I had been downtown to make my first purchase on my new credit card; it was panties. I had never had enough panties and was constantly washing what I had. Now here Sylvester and I were not living too far from each other. Knowing him and his brother made me feel a little safer in big Chicago. They would often come to our parties.

You are not supposed to date someone you just meet on the street, but that is exactly how I met James, my future husband. James lived at 7201 South Shore Drive, and I lived at 7251 South Shore Drive, just across the street from each other. To get to the grocery store (Nationals), I had to go by James's apartment building. I would often walk to the store or go with Jackie in her car. I had passed James on the street one time, and he spoke to me and said, "I like the way you walk." I said, "Thank you," and kept walking. However, the next time I passed him, which I believe was a few days later, he said it again. But this time, I stopped and invited him to a party I was throwing for some friends (Larry Houston and Pearlie Jean Winzer, friends from high school who were visiting me in Chicago). I wanted the party to be a success, so I was inviting everyone I knew and obviously didn't know. James said that he had a date. I immediately thought, *This guy has a girlfriend, and he's coming on to me.* But I appreciated his honesty, so I told him to bring his date to the party. Both times I saw him, he was covered in soot. I thought it was from working on his car, but it turned out that he was working as an ironworker in a steel mill. I noticed that he did not come to the party, but it was mildly successful anyway.

The next evening was a Sunday, and I decided to take Pearlie and Larry to a lounge that Jackie had been too on the near north side and said it was nice. I very seldom visited the near north side after spending my summer there when I was an apprentice with the Chicago Board of Health and had all those negative experiences. Plus, it was on a Sunday; and even though I was not going to a church yet, I still felt that I should keep it holy and not party or drink on a Sunday and definitely not go to a nightclub. But I wanted to impress Larry and Pearlie and show them Chicago, so I acquiesced and took them. While we were there, someone tapped me on the shoulder and said, "Laura, can I have this dance?" I asked him how he knew my name, and he said, "Dance with me, and I'll tell you."

While we were dancing, he told me his name was James and that he'd met me on the street beside his apartment, and I'd invited him to my party, but he couldn't make it. I remember inviting a guy to my party, but didn't recognize him. He said it was because he was covered in soot from his job at the steel mills where he worked as an ironworker. So when I met him, he looked dark-skinned, and now he looked lighter-skinned. I enjoyed dancing with him especially when we slow-danced. I fit real nice in his arms. He seemed just the right size for me. Whenever I danced with a guy, I would revert back to that experience I'd had at a dance at Southern when the guy was too tall for me and almost broke my back. But dancing with James felt just right. We danced quite a few dances before Larry and Pearlie reminded me that they had an early flight home to Washington, DC, the next day. I said good-night to James, but he followed me to the door and asked for my number. I gave it to him and told him I was leaving the next day to go to Louisiana and would be gone for three weeks.

When I returned to Chicago, James did call me. He had to remind me of how we met, but what I remembered was our dancing together at the club. He invited me to go out, and I enjoyed his company. He seemed like a nice guy. A few weeks later was his birthday, so I took him out to dinner at a nearby restaurant. I felt it was okay to do so since it was a cheap soul food restaurant. He seemed to appreciate the gesture. A few months later, I took him to Helen Carroll's, the African American secretary for the Nutrition Section and the one who had introduced me to Ronnie Miller. I asked her if Ronnie would be there; she said that she had invited him. I was not quite over him yet, and I'd told James about him and that I didn't want to get serious about anyone just yet. He told me that his wife of only six months had just died and that he didn't want to get serious yet either. We went to the party, and Ronnie did come, but without a date. I often wondered if we would have gotten back together if I'd gone to that party without a date.

After I'd known James about three or four months, we started to have sex. He had been trying to get me to have sex with him, but I was still holding out to get to know him better. I enjoyed having sex with him. I loved the fact that he had nice soft lips, so the kissing was great. I would often spend the night with him. He had a car, so he took me everywhere I asked him to take me, even to work when the weather was bad and he was laid off work. He seemed to be laid off too often. He was able to pay for our dates most of the time, but sometimes when he was laid off, if we wanted to go out, I would have to help out, and I didn't mind because it was seldom.

For James's next birthday, I decided to throw him a surprise birthday party. I am not sure why I did that because I hated surprise parties. One of my roommates in the Villa—I believe it was my senior year—had a boyfriend, and he enlisted my help in throwing her a surprise birthday party. He made a mistake and invited her to go to a frat party with him. She didn't like the frat parties because she wasn't a member of a sorority. Her boyfriend was a member of a fraternity, and she didn't like going to the frat parties because of the sorority sisters who would be all over the guys. He should have just said they were going out for her birthday. He had to take her to the party, let everybody surprise her, and then bring her back home to get dressed. Then my other roommates and I could get dressed and go to her party. She came back smiling, but I was mad because of all the trouble she put us through refusing to go to her own party. I decided then never to throw a surprise party for anyone. But I found out that James had never had a birthday party or even a birthday cake, and neither had I; and by then I'd met James's family and most of his friends, so it was easy to throw him a party.

I asked James's mother if I could throw it at her house, and she said yes. I told her that I would come over to help clean up and decorate. James had lost his father and his brother Clifton around the same time he lost his wife. I knew he had to be in some terrible pain because of these so recent losses, and I think that was another reason I wanted to throw him a party. When I arrived to help with the cleaning, it turned out to be just me cleaning. His mom and his sisters had disappeared on me. I noticed that the house was extremely cluttered and dusty (mistake, didn't take this hint about James's upbringing, maybe because I grew up in a cluttered house as well, but never this cluttered or dirty). By the time the party started, I was tired from cleaning. I bought balloons and a beautiful cake. It made for a festive atmosphere even if the house left something to be desired. There was a nice crowd of people there when I returned with James, and he was definitely surprised; he had a smile on his face all night. I think he was proud of his girlfriend and extremely happy because a smile never left his face.

I wasn't surprised that James had never had a birthday party because the only party I'd had was one that I'd thrown for myself in my dorm room at Case. My mom never made us cakes on our birthdays. Our birthdays would often pass by without any acknowledgements at all. Melvyn Thomas's family was the same way. When we got older, we started giving each other our favorite candy bars on our birthdays. Her birthday was March 5, and mine was March 6. We would sit on her back porch and eat our candy bars.

For my next birthday, James and Jackie surprised me by throwing me a surprise birthday party. Man, was I surprised. I don't think I ever was so happy. It was amazing, and I enjoyed myself tremendously; and this time, I never stopped smiling. I'd bought a long party dress and put it on after we got back from dinner. James had taken me out to dinner for my birthday and had to invent some reason to take me back to my apartment. After dinner, when we were headed back to I thought was his apartment, where I'd hope we would have birthday sex, he said that he had to take me home instead. It was only around 10:00 p.m. When we got on the elevator in my apartment building, we saw some people that I knew (they were going to the party); they stayed on the elevator when we got off. When we got to my apartment, I was a little put off, but went inside, and almost had a heart attack when everyone yelled "Surprise!" The picture that I took that night is the only one that I declare that I look beautiful. I had a short natural hairstyle that was perfect that day. My skin, my smile—everything was on point that night.

Jackie and I had trouble with the rent checks. My name was on the lease, so she would give me her rent check. Her check bounced on me several times. Therefore, my checks I had used to pay my bills would bounce, and all of these fees would devastate my checking account. Plus, there was a problem with food. Every time she and Carolyn bought food, it would only last until the middle of the week. They bought too many snacks and not enough solid food—surprising since Jackie was a nutritionist. I decided that we needed to go our separate ways.

Before we moved from our apartment, we threw James another surprise party in our apartment. This time, I think we had gone to the Playboy Club for dinner. While we were there, James saw his sister Pam and his cousin Mary. I tried all night to tell them I was throwing James a surprise party at my apartment, but I had a hard time getting them alone. James loved his cousin Mary, and I did too. She was a lot of fun, even though most of the time she had been drinking. It turned out that she was an alcoholic. I had a hard time getting James to take me back to my apartment because, I think this time, he wanted to have birthday sex or continue the evening at another lounge. I eventually told him that I had started my period and had to go get tampons or something. He took me home then.

When we got to my building, there were people getting on the elevator at the same time who were going to James's party. I had to give them a hint to stay on the elevator when we got off so James wouldn't get suspicious, and they did. I don't think I have ever seen a more surprised man than James when he entered the door of my apartment and everyone yelled "Surprise!" I thought he was going to faint. His family was there, even his mom. I think having his mom there was the icing on the cake. The evening went quite well.

I'd already decided to visit California that summer (1975). California was the state I had dreamed all of my life of living in. I had imagined great weather and palm trees. I planned my itinerary carefully. I was going to visit my uncle in San Francisco, my cousins in Sacramento, and some friends in Los Angeles, San Diego, and Tacoma, Washington. I ate myself silly all up and down the West Coast. It was such a fun trip, and I loved the hospitality. My uncle took me to a lot of places I wanted to go and some I didn't want to go. He took me to visit some relatives that had cocaine on their cocktail table. I didn't know what it was and asked Jimmy about it after we left, and he told me it was cocaine. He took me to a bar where he introduced me to a man that had on a trench coat when it was so hot outside. Jimmy told me he was probably a heroin user.

To this day, I cannot understand why he took me around those types of people. I hate people—and I know that is a strong word, and I don't normally use it—but I must be adamant about my dislike for people, no matter what the age, who bring drugs into the black community (or any community, for that matter) that has the potential of killing them, especially illegal drugs. When my youngest uncle and some of my cousins started selling drugs in my hometown and some going to jail, I couldn't help but wonder if my uncle Jimmy had not been at the bottom of it.

When I came back home from my trip to the West Coast, I found a condominium was available a few doors down from our current apartment. I really didn't know what *condominium* meant, but after touring the building and finding out that all they needed was a $200 deposit, I was sold. My sister Juanita and I moved in a few weeks later. Jackie and her sister moved into another apartment near Hyde Park that they liked. James did not like me buying a one-bedroom apartment; he thought it was too small. I thought it was perfect for me, a single woman, and it was affordable. I loved the fact that it was just off the lake and near Rainbow Beach.

My baby sister Vickie came up to visit that summer before starting her senior year in high school. It was a weird summer because Ronnie Miller had called me and said that his sister was visiting him, and she wanted to stay with me because she knew me and not his new girlfriend. I had met her when I visited his family in Pensacola, Florida. She came and I noticed that she had grown into a lovely young girl (or should I say young woman) who was well endowed bust-wise. She attracted a lot of guys. It seemed at home she was afraid some guy was trying to turn her into a prostitute. I called Ronnie and told him what she had told me, and he seemed puzzled about what to do. She was grown. After she and Vickie left that summer, I never heard from her or Ronnie again.

That summer also, my sister Dorothy and Frankie Brown (whom she had married unbeknownst to our family while they were both doing a summer internship in Minnesota with the Kellogg Cereal Company, I believe) moved to Chicago after they both graduated from Southern University. They had even come to Chicago-probably on their honeymoon and spent time with James and I while they were interning (but didn't say a word about already being married). The last I had heard, Dorothy was marrying this guy named Ronnie, whom she had met in her freshmen year. Dorothy had asked that my mom look for a Catholic church to hold the ceremony because Ronnie was Catholic. My mom did look, but before she finalized things, Dorothy had called and said she and Ronnie had broken up and he had left the college. Now who was this guy Frankie whom she had supposedly married? They slept on my sofa sleeper, and Juanita and I shared my bedroom. Dorothy and Frankie found an apartment soon and moved after about two weeks.

Before the summer was over, I took Vickie shopping, and she had a ball with all the new clothes. I decided to throw my first party in my new apartment. It was kind of like a going-away party for my friend Iris. She was a social worker that I'd met at the Englewood Neighborhood Health Center, where I had been working before I started to work at Kennedy-King. She was leaving to go get her PhD. The night of the party, about midway, the cops beamed a light into my windows, so I went down to see what they wanted. They said someone had called the police on me because of the noise. I told them we would turn the music down, and we did. The party broke up soon afterward. The next day, there was red punch and cigarette stains all over my beautiful brand-new carpet. I decided that my new condo was too little for a party and never threw that type again.

That fall, my sister Carrie, whom I had taken back to Minden because she wouldn't or couldn't find a job in Chicago, came back because she got a ninety-day job at the post office that Juanita had told her about. At first, she stayed with her boyfriend that she'd had before she left Chicago. Then, for some reason, either he put her out, or she just left. After her first ninety-day stint, she got another ninety days, but I told her she would have to leave after that.

By this time, a friend of my sister Linda called me and said she needed a place to live for a few weeks until her parents could send her money to come home. I allowed her to come. I then had Juanita, Carrie, and Julia (Linda's friend, not her real name) all living with me. Julia ended up staying more than a few weeks, more like a few months. Before she left, one of my payroll checks was cashed and money withdrawn from my account. I had been mailing my payroll checks to the bank. I remember Julia asking me if I wanted her to put the letters in the mail she had seen me writing, letters that included my payroll check, since she and Carrie were on their way downtown. Later, when my checks for my bills started to bounce and I went to the bank to check on what had happened because the money should have been in the account, I discovered that someone had deposited my check but had withdrawn more money than I had in the bank.

I questioned Julia and Carrie about it, but neither admitted to stealing my money. I even found a piece of paper around my house where it seemed someone was trying to copy my signature. The bank eventually returned my money to my account, so I gave up and dropped it. By then, both Carrie and Julia were back in Minden. My mom and Juanita were mad at me for sending Carrie back. They both figured she would eventually get on with the post office. Well, until then, I could not house Carrie. What I really was trying to do was to get her to go back and finish her college degree. This was probably the first time I had said no to my family, especially my mom. I stuck to my guns, and unfortunately, Carrie never did go back to finish college.

About a year or so after I met James, I started to work at Kennedy-King and bought a condominium and moved. Jackie and Carolyn got an apartment in Hyde Park. I'd had some trouble with bouncing rent checks, so I thought it was best we part ways. By then, my sister Juanita was living with me. She was trying to get herself settled in Chicago. She'd tried teaching in Webster Parish in Minden and said that was not for her. She'd had some trouble with her bosses, I think. She'd lived with Bobbie in Memphis but couldn't find anything, so she came back to Chicago. At first, she went to work at the McDonald's she'd worked in the summer between semesters of college. It didn't pay enough money, so eventually she got a full-time job with the post office. She worked the night shift and loved it. She also took the time to go to graduate school during the day to get her master's degree in library science from Chicago State University. I was scared for her to work at night, but she didn't seem to mind.

My sister Carrie was already living with us. She had come up over the summer to work (I thought before going back to college) along with Linda and Dorothy. They had all found jobs at a manufacturing plant in Niles, Illinois. To my surprise, Carrie decided to stay in Chicago because unbeknownst to me she had flunked out of Southern. The other girls went back to college, and Juanita returned to Chicago.

The Engagement

James and I had been going together for almost four years when I approached him about our future together. Even though when we started going out together, neither of us wanted to get serious at first. But before the year ended, I think we were seeing each other exclusively. I had dated several guys. As a matter of fact, my mom called me one night, and I told her I was going out on a date. She was surprised that I was not going out with James. She wanted to know how James would feel about my dating if he saw me because he lived across the street. I told her James might have been going out on a date as well. But my dates were few and far in between, so I started exclusively dating James. My dating policy then was not to put more than three years in a guy. I think a friend of mine had put about six years into a married guy and decided to quit him. I thought six years was too long to waste your time. I told James just before I left to go home for Christmas that we needed to move on if marriage wasn't in our near, very near, future. I was now almost thirty years old, and I was not getting any younger, and I wanted to have children. That Christmas, we got engaged over the phone.

After James and I announced our engagement, Juanita found an apartment and moved out. She had met a man on her flight to Chicago when she came to live with me, and they were still dating. He owned some apartment buildings, so Juanita took an apartment in his building. They broke up after she moved in, and she figured he was spying on her. Juanita finally came around and told me that she understood why I had sent Carrie back home and that she should have moved out much sooner because everybody needed their own space. She never invited Carrie to come and live with her. She really enjoyed having her peace and quiet.

James told me he wanted to get married before his lease was up, and his lease was up April 1. It was now December 25. So I had three months to plan a wedding. I told him he could move in with me after his lease was up, and we could get married in June. That would give me at least five months to plan the wedding. I told him that I wanted to get married in my hometown, Minden, Louisiana. He was adamant about not shacking up; he said he thought my mom would not like it. Looking back now, I should have stood my ground and taken more time to plan the wedding. If I had, maybe I would have called it off, because while shacking with James, I probably would have discovered some flaws that I didn't like. I should have given him an ultimatum—either June or later, or we go our separate ways. If he refused and we went our separate ways, then I would have known how immovable he was with his decision-making. Me giving in to his demand and having the wedding in April showed who was really in control.

The Wedding

My mother had to do most of the running round for me in Louisiana. Plus, my mother decided to fix up her house after I decided to get married. I thought she was going to hire reputable contractors, but she tried to save some money, so she hired some handymen for whom she had to get something to drink before they even started to work that day. When I found this out (my sister Carrie was going to Dixie Inn to buy them wine or beer every day), I was very upset.

Every time I would ask my mom how the repairs were going, she would complain about the workers. I got scared that the house I grew up in was not going to be ready for my wedding. I wanted to have dinner at the house for my family after the wedding. Why? I don't know. I think I decided to do it after the wedding because I knew the house was not going to be ready for a rehearsal dinner. The kitchen was ready, so we were able to cook all the food.

I was going to have twelve bridesmaids, so I needed twelve groomsmen. I had to find the groomsmen because James didn't know anyone in Minden; plus, he only had a few friends in Chicago that he was close too, and I don't think he even asked them if they would make the trip to Louisiana. I don't think he wanted to be bothered. I should have taken this as a hint that over the years, when I set the standard, I would be the one being bothered all the time. I also decided to have the bridesmaids' dresses made. I had to make my two in-laws' dresses and the flower girls' dresses.

My dress had cost me $800, if my memory is correct. My friend Jackie had gone with me to pick it out. We went to Marshall Field's in downtown Chicago. That dress was probably the first thing I had bought at Marshall Field's. I had always thought it was too expensive for me. Jackie and her sister Carolyn loved the store; they often shopped there. My colors were apricot (orange) and kelly green. They were selected because in the fabric store, they had enough fabric of those colors for my twelve bridesmaids. My maid of honor was going to buy her own dress in kelly green or close to it. I had really wanted rainbow colors for my bridesmaids but couldn't find enough fabric or decide who should wear what color. Even choosing two colors was difficult, but I was willing to risk it. I chose a pattern (I was into sewing at the time) that I thought was somewhat sexy but could be worn to church or to a party. I didn't like the idea of people spending a lot of money and only wearing the dress once. I bought the fabric and mailed it to my bridesmaids and sent the pattern number. I only had to make two of the dresses, the ones for my sisters-in-law. I think I also made the dresses for my two young junior bridesmaids, my six-year-old niece and James's six-year-old niece. We were having white pinafores to cover the kelly green and apricot dresses they were wearing.

I wanted my own reception dresses to look professional, so I had one of my students who was an excellent seamstress to make both of them. Yes, I decided to have three receptions beside the dinner I had at my house. We had a small reception at the church for those who could not go to the reception I had planned at a hotel in Shreveport, dinner at my house, reception in Shreveport, and the following week, a reception in Chicago for my husband's relatives and our friends who couldn't make it to the wedding in Chicago. Yes, I was stupid. Trying to please everybody was insane. It cost James and I over $3,000, a down payment on a home at the time. We should have just gone to city hall. But then I would not have gotten to see the smiles on my parents' and grandparents' faces when I walked down the aisle. They were so proud of the occasion. Most of my family and friends made it. It was a magical day. The sky was so blue. It was a beautiful day, April 9, 1977. The house was ready around 2:00

p.m.; the wedding was at 4:00 p.m. We had to clean the house, put all the clothes back in the closets, set out the food, etc. and get to the wedding in two hours. It was hectic. I was so tired when I walked down the aisle and at the end of the day that I don't even think James and I had sex on our wedding night. I am pretty sure I fell asleep on him, and maybe he passed out from the drinks. We made up for it the next morning, though.

Even with all the nerves unraveling, the wedding was beautiful. When I stood at the entrance to the Fourteenth District Building and looked at the altar, I couldn't believe it. I was stunned at how gorgeous everything looked. I had not been to a wedding in my hometown of that magnitude. The caterer had come through big time. The orange and green flowers with the greenery were stunning alongside the lit candelabras. The girls looked beautiful, and the guys looked dashing in their tuxedoes. James never looked more hand-some. He had spent the night with a friend of mine and would be meeting us at the church. I was so stunned how everything had fallen into place.

My mom had suggested a caterer in Minden for the wedding. She would do everything, including decorating the church. I was apprehensive about using someone I did not know, but my mom and my aunt Elnora were adamant that everything would be okay. She was my aunt Elnora's neighbor. When I got into town, I stopped by her house to finalize our plans. I think it was a week before the wedding. When I went to her house, she had cats all over the place. I got itchy (not realizing at the time I was allergic to cats). I could not believe the number of cats at her house. I did not know if I wanted to eat her food, but I had no choice; it was too late to make a switch.

At the wedding, I was so surprised at her decorations and her food. The night before the wedding, the church looked horrific for the rehearsal. It was like night and day when we got to the church around 3:00 p.m. the day of the wedding. Everything was so gor-geous. The cake looked beautiful and the hors d'oeuvres and canapés she'd prepared were too. I was pleasantly surprised. I would never doubt my small town again. I'd wanted to get married in my hometown because I knew that was where most of my family lived. Now I was happy that it did not disappoint.

Like I said, when I stood at the entrance to the church, I was taken aback by how beautiful everything was. Then I heard a young boy, the boy my friend Jacquelyn Bradford had when we were in college, who was now about twelve years old, say "You look beautiful." That was all that mattered. His statement was the icing on the cake. I had never been called beautiful in my life until that day, my wedding day. I thought my husband looked so handsome standing at the altar waiting for me. I'd helped him pick out his tuxedo, but he looked great in it. My friend Pearlie had gotten her friend and someone who had gone to junior high school with us to sing a song for us at the wedding. Her name was Rose Johnson. Other than that, we had no other entertainment. I think she may have played "Here Comes the Bride" on the piano as well. It's been forty-three years now, so my memory is a little fuzzy.

After the wedding, my wedding party and other family members went back to our house for dinner. I had prepared this huge lasagna. My cousins loved my lasagna and have me make it now at every opportunity possible. I had gotten the recipe from a nurse on my first job at the Board of Health. I can't remember what else we had that day, but everyone loved the food. My now husband and I took a limousine to the hotel. Someone had to drive his Buick 225 to the hotel because we would drive it back the next day. We were only spending one night in the hotel. The next day was Easter Sunday. The reception at the hotel was nice. I wore an orange dress that one of my students made for me. She made a white one for the reception in Chicago. I don't think I have any pictures of my wedding reception at the hotel in Bossier that night. I remember when we made our entrance, my husband grabbed me, and we did a walk dance. We had never done that before; we should have practiced. He thought the music was appropriate for a walk. It was like waltzing around the room. It was appropriate. I just tried to follow along the best I could.

After the reception, some of the people came to our hotel room for more champagne. We put them out so we could go to bed. Plus, most of the people had to go to church for Easter Sunday. I can't remember if we had sex or not; all I know is I was tired. If we did, it was not memorable. But the sex we had that morning or early afternoon the next day was great.

Settling into Married Life

My new husband and I headed back to Chicago on that Monday or Tuesday after the wedding with about three hundred wedding gifts. I was glad he had a big car. The back seat and trunk were filled. When we got back home to my small one-bedroom condominium, which was our home now, the gifts filled the living area. We still had a reception coming up the next weekend, where we were going to get more gifts. This was before wishing-well weddings. I wish I had known about them then, especially since my new husband refused to open any of the gifts. This was my first glimpse that being married was not going to be a cake walk. Once I opened the gifts, I had nowhere to put them. I gave as many of them away as I could. Some were surprising, like how my sister Juanita gave us decorative shot glasses. What were we going to do with decorative shot glasses? I still have those shot glasses, and they are still out of place in our home. It was so unusual because Juanita has not had a drink in her life. I think she thought they were cute. I should repay her the favor of regifting those shot glasses to her one day. I know she doesn't remember them.

We did get a Mr. Coffee pot. That coffeepot made my husband a coffee drinker for life. We have had many derivatives of this coffeepot since then. What I loved are the bath towels we got. I didn't have to buy any bath towels for years.

For our wedding reception in Chicago, we bought a cake that cost $300. It was big and beautiful. It was a fiasco because most of the guests had left before the caterer cut the cake. He packaged the cake and gave it to me and my husband. We had nowhere to put all this cake. After the reception, we went to my husband's brother's house; we took most of the cake there and gave it to people. We kept the top of the cake to be cut in a year on our anniversary, which we did. I was so upset with the caterer. The cake should have been cut earlier so it could have been boxed for people to take home.

When it was all over, I'd wished that I had not tried to please everybody by having all those receptions. It didn't make sense. I never thought of the tons of gifts we would get and what to do with them or the stress it would put on me. Like I said, all James had to do was show up, look good, and smile. I must say he never looked handsomer. I was and still am attracted to my husband, but I prefer him naked.

My wedding day was not the last time I would wear my wedding dress. By the time I got married, I was working for Kennedy-King College in the Home Economics Department. The clothing teacher asked me to wear my dress at the end-of-the-year banquet and fashion show. My husband obliged with his reception suit, and I wore my bridal gown for the wedding scene. It was nice to be able to show off the gown one more time before retiring it to our crawlspace where it mildewed, and I was only able to save the headpiece. So at the time, I thought if I have a daughter, she won't be able to wear my gown at her wedding. But then again, I doubt if it would have been sexy enough.

We got married on Saturday, April 9, and moved in together afterward. James had been against our moving in together before we got married. After we got married, I figured out why: he had a lot of bad habits that he knew would be red flags. Unless I asked, he didn't help with the housework. His favorite thing to do was to plop his body down in front of the television and watch it all day. The only time he seemed to notice me was when we went to bed, and he was all over me then. I think he enjoyed having a ready piece of meat. He didn't even help me open wedding gifts and send thank-you notes. I opened every gift and sent every thank-you note. I got really tired of opening the same gift every time. One thing we got that we didn't have was a coffeemaker. I didn't like coffee, so I never drank it in the morning. I am sorry to say that I was more likely to drink a Coke in the morning to get me going. Someone got us a Mr. Coffee, which was very popular then. James loved it and used it for years to make coffee every morning until the poor thing broke.

The only thing James could cook when we got married was chili. His deceased wife had taught him how to cook chili with beans.

I loved chili without beans, and he felt it wasn't chili unless it had beans. Most of the time, we had his chili with beans so that I could get him to cook for a change and to give me a break.

By the time we got married, I had moved into my condominium just off of Lake Michigan. It was down the street from my apartment at 7251 South Shore Drive. James did not like the building. He was in construction, so he had a lot of complaints. I told him that I had planned to buy other buildings and renting them out. He said that he didn't like dealing with renters. I thought he would eventually change his mind, but he never did. The *maybe*s he'd had before we got marry became definite *no*s after we were married. Now I know not to go by what a guy says when you are dating him but what he does. James was thirty-four years old and seemingly didn't have any goals. I had plenty that he stopped dead in their tracks. I was a dreamer and he was not. He'd never had very much in his life, and after he got his training to be an ironworker and made what he called "good money." That was it for him, but it wasn't for me. We had different definitions of "good money."

After James and I were married, I decided to wait three years before I would attempt to get pregnant, so I took precautions not to get pregnant. James and I had been having sex for a while now, and I had been using the "sponge," so I never got pregnant. After we got married, I knew we were going to be having sex on a regular basis, and my chances of getting pregnant were more likely, so I decided that maybe it was time to start on birth-control pills. It was when I decided to start taking birth-control pills that I found out I had a problem with my thyroid. I had gone to the University of Chicago Hospitals to see a gynecologist to get a prescription for the pills. She said I would need an annual checkup, and so I did.

When reviewing my laboratory results, she asked me if I knew that my thyroid gland was overactive. I said no, I didn't know that. She asked me if I had any unusual changes in my behavior lately. I told her that I was nervous all the time, that I couldn't hold my fingers straight, that I had an overactive sweet tooth, and that I couldn't climb one flight of stairs without breathing hard (I didn't mention that I had been losing my hair because I didn't equate that with hyperthyroidism at the time). All these things I had noticed for about a year, but I thought it was because I had been planning my wedding and was supertired. I had gotten married in April and through a hurried three months of planning. This was now September, and I was still feeling the fatigue of what I thought was my wedding. But the doctor told me that I had an overactive thyroid and needed to see an endocrinologist to get it under control. As I spoke to her nurse, she told me that no matter what happened, I needed to stay in control without taking a lot of medications. I did see the endocrinologist and was surprised to hear that I would have to take a pill for the rest of my life. Here I was, a girl who didn't even like taking aspirins. Now I was going to have to take a pill for the rest of my life.

I was only thirty years old when I got my diagnosis of hyperthyroidism. I had worked in a medical clinic and majored in public health nutrition. Why wasn't I getting annual checkups? I guess I was just young and stupid and thought I didn't need it. Plus, being raised in a black community, there was a scarcity of doctors seeing black patients. So unless you were very sick and home remedies didn't work, you didn't see a doctor. Also, I think there was distrust in white doctors. I am sure there was a feeling they didn't want to get their lily-white hands dirty while attending to your black body.

You can bet after that diagnosis I started getting annual checkups. I was able to get my thyroid under control. I even shared my experience with my coworkers and found that my friend Iris, a social worker, also had been diagnosed with hyperthyroidism. She had a goiter. I had not gotten to the stage that I had a goiter, and I was thankful for that. When I started teaching nutrition at Kennedy-King, whenever we got to the point in the class where we were discussing iodine, I would tell them about my hyperthyroidism and the symptoms I had been feeling before being diagnosed. One day a student walked up to me and lifted her head up, and her goiter jumped out at me. She wanted to know if she had a goiter, and I said I thought she did have one and that she needed to see a doctor. She said she was seeing a doctor, her gynecologist. I told her she needed to see a specialist, an endocrinologist. She did and was scheduled for surgery within weeks. I felt really good about helping, even possibly saving, this student's life. I wondered why her gynecologist hadn't referred her before it had gotten to the goiter stage. She might not have been testing her for that. Possibly the student may not have told the doctor what she had been experiencing, her symptoms. I am not sure if she recognized these symptoms as unusual. Sometimes you think the symptoms you are feeling are normal; you have had them for so long. Plus, growing up poor in Chicago as a minority was definitely not a cake walk. You had a lot to endure most of the time.

I think of all the classes that I taught, I enjoyed teaching nutrition the most. It seemed to relate to the students more or touch them more deeply. We often talked about common day diseases or conditions that were related to nutrition. I would often tell them about my experiences as a nutritionist with the Board of Health or the University of Wisconsin hospitals. I was so grateful that I'd had these worldly experiences in the field because I was able to make real-life connections to my lecture and keep the interest of the students.

When James I got married in 1977, I was in my second year of teaching. I was diagnosed with hyperthyroidism nine months or so after I got married. I had started to feel anxious before I got married, but now I had started to have panic attacks. It affected my confidence level and my anxiety about public speaking. Sometimes I would space out in class, and I would forget my lecture. I started to depend on my notes more. As a matter of fact, I started writing everything down on transparency film. Before that, I would write on the board because many of the students couldn't spell the words correctly from my lecture. Couple the panic attacks with the use of mastery-learning methodology, and I say my confidence was shattered. But I persevered, and eventually I learned how to control the panic attacks somewhat. Also, I figured out that my hyperthyroidism was caused by the lack of iodine in the salt James used at his apartment. At some point, I had noticed that his salt did not have iodine and had thrown it out, but it was evidently too late for me since I ate most of my meals with him at the time and it had already affected my health. Neither James nor I had noticed that his salt lacked iodine because the Morton's salt boxes were the same (in color)—the one with iodine and the one without iodine. You had to read the small print to notice the differences. Being a nutritionist, I had always paid attention to the notice when buying my own groceries, but James and I bet a lot of people do not. As a result, I have suffered from Graves' disease most of my adult life, and it has caused me to suffer tremendously as a professional due to my fear of having "brain fog" or "memory issues"—one of the symptoms of thyroid-related illnesses at inappropriate times. It was the reason for what I called at the time "my spacing out" while lecturing in class. It would be years after reading an article on the symptoms of thyroid disease that I would figure this out.

After James and I got married, I focused heavily on my job. James didn't seem to require much of my time; all he needed was a television. If he wasn't watching the television, he was reading the paper. These were his favorite pastimes. I thought I knew a lot about James before I got married, but little did I know there was a lot to come. I knew that he was smart and loved his job. I was very impressed by the way he approached his job. He seemed to be a perfectionist. I noticed that about whatever he did around the house. He replaced our tiles in the bathroom, and it was the first time he had done something like that and it looked like it had been done by a professional. He didn't like painting, however. We had a small condo, and I wanted to paint the bedroom. He said that he wasn't a painter; it wasn't his trade. I didn't understand his reluctance. I thought it didn't have to be perfect because we would be the only ones to see it. I ended up starting the job, and eventually he acquiesced and painted the ceiling because he didn't want me to hurt myself. I think our thinking was different because I was raised in a house we owned, and we did the upkeep, and James was raised in rental apartments where a landlord was responsible for the upkeep. Growing up in my family, we put up different wallpaper every summer in the living room and would move the four pieces of furniture we had there around to keep ourselves busy. Our walls always looked like crap, but we would be proud of ourselves as kids and our parents never complained. I think James's perfectionism sometimes gets in the way of him doing things around the house. He was a journeyman and he wanted a journeyman to do the work. Thankfully, he worked with a lot of journeymen, so they would do our painting, plumbing, etc. Most of the time, I didn't complain about the work that they did. I think they used the bartering system, and James would do any ironwork they needed on their properties. One of the things I insisted on was that he, along with myself, go over to visit his mother more often.

James sometimes wouldn't go over to his mom's house for a year. In my household, as I was growing up, my mom would go visit her mom and dad at least once a week, mostly after dinner on Sundays. Most of the time, I would go with her or some of my other siblings. I enjoyed going to visit my maternal grandparents. My paternal grandparents had passed away before I was born. Some of the time when some of my mother's siblings came by, I would sit and listen to them talk and laugh for hours. They would regale in old stories from their youth.

My mom was the quiet one, but she would say something every once in a while. It seemed all of her siblings loved to talk except one, and her name was Lillie. She was nicknamed Carolyn, and that is what I always called her. She would be off in a room somewhere by herself. My grandparents were pretty quiet as well, especially my grandfather. Often he would be in a room by himself, and I would go sit with him. He would tell me stories that he knew were not true, but we would laugh about it. He was good about making up stories. I felt like my grandfather was a genius. But I felt my grandmother was really the one who controlled her family. Whenever she was not around, my aunts and uncles would talk about how mean she had been when they were growing up. I know she didn't mind putting them out if they misbehaved because I had seen her do it to several of my uncles. James would eventually acquiesce, and we would go see his mom.

It seemed like every time we went over to his mom, I would see something that I couldn't believe. First of all, the house was never thoroughly or modestly cleaned. My mother-in-law seemed to be a hoarder. The bathroom was always the cleanest spot in the house, thankfully. James's mother and I seldom sat down and talked; most of the time, I would be playing cards with James's sisters. I had bonded with them through card playing; we all loved it. When I did sit down and talked with her, I asked her if she wanted to get married again. She had been in her forties, I believe, when her husband died. Dear (that was the nickname her kids and everyone called her) actually starting shaking because of my question, and she said, "Noooo, no way." James had told me how his father had controlled his mother and would sometimes beat her. I believe his mother was emotionally handicapped because of her upbringing and her husband. By the time I met her, I think she was suffering from PTHD, post-traumatic husband syndrome. She'd allowed him to control the whole family; she had very little say in anything according to James. He said every time he looked around she was pregnant, and he hated it. She'd never had a life of her own. She'd left her mother's home (I think her father had passed away by then) and entered married life like a child. She was evidently running from one ant's nest into another one. She soon found herself with twelve kids (one of her kids passed away soon after birth from pneumonia) that she had to raise with their own identities, and she didn't even know her own.

James's maternal grandmother eventually came to live with them, and she was his saving grace. James loved his grandmother. His mother told me that she left her parents' home where she was controlled only to marry a controlling man. I always wondered if she had a happy day in her life. I often wondered how she felt with both of her controlling forces in the same home. The grandmother had come up north to help her raise the twelve kids. James, for one, appreciated it. He often spent long hours just talking to his grandmother. By this time, he had very little respect for his parents—his father because of the way he treated his mother and couldn't afford twelve kids, and his mother because she kept having children and never questioned anything the father did. I am sure he thought she was a coward. Since James was the oldest, he was made to help with his siblings. He had to wash their dirty diapers often. His mother had some of her babies at home, and he'd have to help clean up the blood afterward. He did all this when all he wanted to do was play basketball with his friends. He grew very angry because of this. I believe the meanness in James that Juanita saw and that I eventually saw, especially after we had our son, was from the anger he felt toward his parents and growing up poor and not even having the essentials at times.

After James's father died (his grandmother, brother, and new wife passed away around the same time), Dear very seldom left her home without one of her children. She bought this huge house (six bedrooms) for about $10,000 that needed rehabbing, which she got when her husband passed away at the age of fifty-two. One by one, her children moved their boyfriends or girlfriends with them into one of the bedrooms. Nobody paid rent. James was furious. He never liked the idea of couples shacking up before marriage. As a matter of fact, one day James' mother asked him to cosign for a furnace for the house and he told her as long as she had adults in the house rent free he wasn't cosigning anything and that she should let those worthless adults pay for the furnace. One of her daughters eventually cosigned for the furnace. After the mother passed away the company tried to garnish her paycheck and she gave them James' phone number and employer. The funny thing was that they both worked for the same company, the Chicago Park District. When my husband got wind of what was happening, after they threatened to garnish his paycheck, he sent them straight to his sister (Precious) and she eventually paid for the furnace to get them off of her back. She was not even living in the house at the time, she moved out after her mother passed. The worthless adults continued to live in the house.

I never met James's grandmother, but he talks about her often. I think he had more respect for his grandmother because of her morals and values. James himself has very strong morals and values; that was one of the things that attracted me to him. Some of his values sometimes clashed with mine. Our first argument was over abortion rights. I believed in a woman's right to choose and still do, and he is totally and ardently against abortion. He knew that my mother was against abortion, being a staunch Christian, so he would ask me what would my mother think if she thought I was for abortion. I told him that I didn't agree with everything my mother believed in, but she had her right to her ideals, and so did I. You can still love your mom and your husband even though they disagreed with you on issues.

I was not going to change their minds, and they were not going to change mine.

I wish I'd had the chance to meet James's grandmother. He said that whenever they moved, she would move into the same building. She was there to help James's mother look after the thirteen kids. Being the oldest, James was generally her helper. She couldn't read or write, so he would help her cash her checks and pay her bills and go to the doctor. He said that she had arthritis really bad and a very bad back. She would move in an apartment upstairs from them; she wouldn't stay with them because she didn't like James's father because he beat his wife, James's mother.

I think it can be said that James hated his father, primarily for beating his mother but also because he was so controlling. Plus, he also beat his children. I believe James and all of his siblings, plus the mother, lived in fear of being beaten every day. This had to be a horrible way to live. James's father has been dead for years, but James still resents him. I remember whenever we socialized with people and they would get in conversations with James, James would monopolize the conversation with his father's negative antics. By the time everyone had moved on from the conversation, James would not know anything about them. That is why I finally realized that he probably needed to see a therapist about his father because James was probably suffering from PTSD (post-traumatic stress syndrome) from his childhood and maybe from the Army as well, he is a Vietnam Era veteran.

James had several brothers who left home and never came back because of his father's beatings. James especially hated that his brother Clifton left home. He said that after one of his father's beatings Clifton left the house wearing James's shoes, and he never came back, James never knew where he went that night. He was really worried about his brother being out in the streets by himself. Clifton seemed to be a well-liked person by his peers; plus, he had a girlfriend at the time. Clifton eventually joined the Black Panthers and was killed trying to set off a bomb along the rail track. Unfortunately or fortunately, he only killed himself. I say "fortunately" because some lives were probably saved as a result of his death.

At Clifton's funeral, there were several women claiming to be his girlfriend. One of them said she was his wife. I think she arranged the funeral and James's family just went along with everything since they didn't have to pay any money. It seemed she and Clifton had been married by the Black Panthers. The marriage was not recognized by the State of Illinois. She was also pregnant at the funeral. From what I understand, there were several women pregnant at the funeral. James didn't see any of those women after the funeral, so he never met his nieces that were born shortly after Clifton's funeral. What I understand, the wife did attempt to get his social security, but was turned down because she couldn't produce a valid marriage license. She came over to James's mother's house trying to get her to sign some papers saying she was Clifton's wife. The mother said that Clifton never said he was married and that she should use her marriage license, which of course she didn't have, to get the social security. By then, of course, the baby was born, and the mother had a baby to take care of. James didn't know any of this had happened. He probably would have signed the papers because he knew that his brother just didn't have a chance to tell the family about the baby or babies on the way. His brother was a rolling stone, and James knew it. He also said that he thought that Clifton had beaten his girlfriends, including his wife. He knew Clifton was following in his father's footsteps, and he felt bad about it. He was never told about the baby or babies.

One day on the job, he was talking with one of his coworkers and found out that he knew his brother Clifton. He said I knew him, and I know one of the women that he had a child by. He eventually gave James's phone number to the young woman (Erica). We all talked, and she told James about another daughter named Karma. She gave Karma our phone number, and she called, and we talked for a long time. She was happy to talk to some of her father's family. We arranged a dinner at our house so she could meet some of the other family members. We are still in touch with her even though she moved to Sweden soon after we met her. Her mother came down with cancer, so she would come home often. Her mother and grandmother had some bad feelings about James's family, so they never even attempted to bring her around the family. Karma tried to get them to meet James and me, but they wouldn't for a long time. They eventually agreed to meet us, so we all had dinner together in November 2016. Clifton died before I even met James in 1972. So it was a long time. Unfortunately, both the mother and grandmother died in 2017. James and I went to the funerals; none of his other siblings did.

James's brothers Ricky (short for Julius Morgan Jr.) and his Carl left home running from their father as well. They were either in elementary school or around seventh or eighth grades. I believe Ricky's girlfriend had a baby for him, so I believe he went to live with her family. Carl left home and went to live with his then girlfriend's parents. His girlfriend soon got pregnant as well. Ricky did not marry the girlfriend; he went into the service. When he came out, he got a job with the phone company and eventually married another woman by whom he had two kids. They separated, and afterward Ricky didn't seem to have anything to do with his former wife or his children. His former wife eventually was killed by her cousin while they were both doing drugs. From what I heard, he cut her up in pieces while they were out of control and high on drugs. Ricky lost his job with the phone company and went back to live with his eighth-grade girlfriend and his now-grown child and some of the girlfriend's other children by other men. Carl never did marry Sabrina. He eventually had about five other babies by different women (we only met a few of these children). Sabrina would die at a young age from cancer. Both Ricky and Carl were known to be cruel to their women. Later, the youngest brother Craig would do the same. What they had observed in their own home when they were little kids, they perpetuated in their own affairs with women. Plus, all of them overly indulged in alcohol (and some even drugs). I didn't see this coming when I first met the family (mistake).

Even though James grew up in the same household, he never even raised his hand on me. I think he knew I would leave him if he even did that. James was smart with his cruelty, though: he was mostly mentally cruel. When I wanted him to do something, he would initially say no, and later, mostly in bed, he would say he would do it. I found out much later that this was a way of him getting control. He didn't want to seem like he was doing everything his wife (a girl) wanted him to do. While I was being crushed by his first refusal and then exuberant when he eventually agreed, this type of behavior played out in my own family. I remember how my mom would ask my father to do something, and he would just ignore her. He wouldn't say yes or no; he would just ignore her. He wouldn't even look into what she had wanted until it was almost beyond control; then he would have to go get professional help with it, and it would cost him more money. My mother would nag and nag until he finally would do what she wanted. I refused to do it. I got tired of her nagging myself. It seemed my mother and my father had strict rules about the male and the female roles in a family. One thing, though: I never heard them argue about things; my mom would just incessantly nag.

James told me that once his father got so mad at his mom that he hit her so hard, and she came through their bedroom door and landed on their bed. He and his brother Clifton were asleep in the bed. When he relayed this story to me, I couldn't believe she didn't leave him then. I wondered if she or any of the kids had to go to the doctor after the beatings. I think some did, but there was always an excuse.

James's outbursts of anger perpetuated in short uncontrolled and unnecessary anger toward me and eventually toward our son. Whenever he questioned something, he wouldn't wait to hear the details before he would get angry. He would already be about to explode with nostrils flaring and eyes beaming. I would calmly tell him what had happened, and he would calm down. I, on the other hand, needed to know the details before I would get angry. He was often quietly watching television by himself. I often thought he was avoiding us so he wouldn't have any opportunities to hurt us by getting angry and exploding at us. As a matter of fact, whenever we argued, he would often say his piece and leave the room, whereas I would be sitting there ready to talk things through. When he cooled down, we did talk things through because I didn't like to go to sleep angry. Plus, James knew that if I was angry, I would say no to his sexual advances, so he was always ready to talk things out over pillow talk.

I had noticed that James was much like my students. I'd notice that they often spoke too loudly, and it seemed like they were angry when they weren't. On the other hand, with his friends, James was friendly and spoke civilly. He seemed to have two or even three personalities at a time. Even though James and I were both the oldest child in large families, I didn't fear leadership, and he seemed to. However, whenever I was in a leadership positions, especially in the community, he seemed to want to make sure people knew that he was not my puppet. I don't think he ever tried this around his family and friends, but I often saw this side of him in the community. However, he didn't want to lead himself. Once when he was promoted to foreman on his job, he gave the position up the first time somebody questioned him. I was happy for him and wanted to celebrate because it meant more money, but James was anxious about it, so I was not surprised (disappointed but not surprised) when he quit.

After James and I got married, we focused heavily on our jobs. I gave very little time to getting to know my neighbors or my neighborhood. After my son was born, I focused heavily on him. I wanted the best for him. I think I loved him too much. I think he was James's crowning glory of manhood. I don't think he nor I thought much about training him to be an independent and confident adult. I know we didn't know how to do it coming from our own childhoods. At least I'd had a loving home; James didn't even have that.

One thing that James feels really bad about is that one of his siblings died in infancy while she was in his care. His parents had told him to take the baby to the hospital. He was underage, so they would not see the baby without the parents' consent. He had to wait with her in the waiting area, so when his mother got there and the baby was finally seen, she was so sick that she died soon after. It turned out the baby had pneumonia. James has not gotten over that heartache. The baby was a twin; her twin (Priscilla) is still living.

Looking back on things, I believe social awkwardness was the norm not only for James and me but also for our families. I only got the opportunity to meet James's mom. His father had passed away when I met James. His mother, however, was extremely shy to me. She did not have a friend to speak of. She never threw a party that I knew of, and James said that she seldom went out socially when they were growing up. She didn't even go to church. James's grandmother, who always lived in a building where his family was living in order to help her daughter out (James's mother) with her twelve children, belonged to a church. James would escort her to church on Sunday. James was very close to his grandmother. She was elderly, so she would need an escort most places. James took her shopping, to the doctor, to cash her check, etc. He spent hours with her. It seems that she had the most to do with James's moral upbringing than anyone else. James's grandmother's one downfall was that she would not go to visit "Minnie," her granddaughter and James's second cousin, or her own sister who lived in Chicago as well at the time. James did not understand this but did not question his grandmother as to why. Minnie still lives in Chicago, and on some of our visits with her, she tells us often that their grandmother had treated her and her siblings extremely badly when they were growing up. James found this hard to believe of his beloved grandmother. Minnie told us that her own mother had deserted her and her siblings when they were young. She left them with their dad and didn't come back. Minnie is now ninety-five years old, lives alone, and cooks for herself. Funny thing, Minnie left her children down south when she came north following a man. She said she did keep in touch with them. This not speaking to each other seems to be normal in James' family. Several of his siblings do not speak to each other, and one of his sisters has not spoken to her son in almost twenty years (mistake).

James is so different from all the rest of his siblings except for the temperament. James says that his grandmother hated his father. She hated him because of the way he treated her daughter. To me, it seems that he treated his wife, at least the way James's and his other siblings describes it, was as if she was another child instead of a partner. He often beat her. James says he never understood why she didn't leave him. She had tried to leave him once but had so little money that she had to come back home with all of her kids. She couldn't make it on her own, so she came back and endured the beatings (both hers and her kids). I get the impression that there were very few peaceful and enjoyable moments in their household.

The members of James's family were always at each other's throats about one thing or the other. The only time I saw them enjoy each other was when we were playing cards or drinking alcohol. Like I said earlier, I bonded with them over playing cards. We had a lot of fun playing cards together. I should have worked harder to talk with them and to get to know them individually. I don't think we ever just sat down and talked to one another. Cards or some type of games always seemed to be in the mix.

When I met James, a few of his siblings were still in high school. One brother (Eric) had returned from Vietnam mentally disabled. Some of his siblings were in college or trade school of some sort or working. His brother Ricky (his real name was Julius; he was named after James's father—James always fretted over why his father didn't name him Julius because he was his first son). James was named after his father's father, who was James Morgan. James thought that was weird because Julius's father did not raise him, and he hated him (Julius's father never married his mother). Julius was raised by his grandparents, who evidently were very hard on him.

Most of the men in James's family liked to drink and do drugs. I think it is reasonable to say that they were alcoholics and drug addicts. James enjoyed drinking alcohol, so I was always afraid that he was an alcoholic. I don't ever remember seeing him sloppy drunk or even inebriated where he could not drive except for once. Once, we were at an event, and he left to go to a hotel room with some guys he didn't know; they just happened to be sitting at the same table we were at. When he came back to the table, he was smiling too much, and his eyes looked funny. When we got ready to go, he told me he'd smoked marijuana and that I should drive home. I tried to drive, but it was so icy, and I was afraid. The weather had changed while we were at the event. I told him I wasn't sure I could get us home safely. We probably should have gone back into the hotel to get him some coffee or something or even spend the night. He said that was okay, that he could drive. And he did. James was always a careful driver, so I was not surprised that he got us home safely. He never smoked marijuana again. I scolded him about smoking marijuana just because the other guys were doing it. He said that he'd had it before and thought he could handle it. Now he knew he couldn't, so he would never smoke it again; and to my knowledge, he didn't.

James and I had many discussions about alcoholism being in his family. I think as a result he was careful and controlled about his drinking. He would get upset when I talked about his drinking. He said that I thought everyone who had more than one beer was an alcoholic. I did not grow up around people who drank. I now know that my uncles and aunts drank but never around me when I was younger or my other siblings, to my knowledge. My mom never had alcohol in her house. I saw my father drink once or twice, but never in our house. I saw him drink straight liquor at one of his relative's houses when I was in college. For some reason, he took me with him when he and my uncle Nathaniel went to visit them. By then, I was in college and had drunk some straight liquor. I was at a friend's house who lived off campus, and there was a bottle of vodka with a little left in it. I took the bottle and turned it up. I couldn't believe how nasty it was. I couldn't help but wonder why people liked to drink it. That taste stays with me to this day—even though vodka is the only alcoholic beverage I can drink that does not make me sick to my stomach with a hangover the next morning. Even with that, I seldom drink more than two shots of it. When James and I would go out when we were courting, he would get upset with me for letting my drink turn to water. I could drink it when it turned to water. I just didn't like the taste of alcohol and still don't. I do not understand James's and other people's infatuation with alcohol. I do not like anything that dims my senses. I like to be in control at all times. The operative word is *control.* This word would come back to haunt me later in life.

James will admit that his father was an alcoholic, and several of his brothers are as well. I saw his brother Ricky beat his wife from the rear of their mother's house to the front. He beat her in the street in front of the house. By the time I saw them, his eyes were blaring. It was obvious he'd had too much to drink and was totally out of control. I don't remember why we were at James's mom's house.

James didn't like to go over there much because he didn't like the way she ran her house. She allowed several of her unwed children to live in her home with their boyfriends or girlfriends and James didn't like it. Things came to a head when his mother asked him to loan her some money to buy a furnace for her house. James told her he wasn't loaning her money to pay for furnace in a house with grown people who could work living in it rent-free. She got so upset with us that she didn't speak to either of us for some time. He said that would have never happened if his father was living because he was very strict. James has strong morals and values. When we were courting, he wouldn't shack with me. He would say, "What would your mother think?" James had a lot of respect for my mother, just as he had for his maternal grandmother, who was a full-blooded American Indian, but James does not remember which tribe now.

James didn't know his paternal grandmother. He'd only met her couple of times. According to James, his father hated his mother. He said that when he was very young, she took him to live with his grandparents, and they had raised him. From what it seems like, they were very strict with him and often beat him to make him behave. They were spare-the-rod-spoil-the-child disciplinarians, and he turned out to be just like them. He never forgave his mother for abandoning him and hardly spoke to her; therefore, James and his other siblings didn't really get to know their father's side of the family. James would later get to know Annie, his second cousin, who would fill in some of the details of his father's family. It seemed there was a mean gene in the family. She said that her own mother was mean and that some of her siblings seldom came home after they left because of her meanness. So she was not surprised when James told her of how mean his own father had been to them.

I remember when I met James, and we would go to parties. I would often overhear him talking to someone, and his conversation would always be about his father and how mean he was. I would later ask him what was the name of the person he was talking to. He wouldn't even know their name. He'd say, "I forgot to ask." He had shared so much about his father, but he knew nothing about the other person. At the time, this struck me as being socially awkward,

but I did not know it as a problem and an indication of socially ineptness and immaturity. I just thought it was a lack of experience—I
am still perplexed about it—but he still talks about himself in social
situations. I just think now I am the butt of conversations more than
his father because I often meet people, and they say, "Your husband
talks about you all the time," "Your husband must love you." I have
a doctoral degree, but in casual conversations, I don't bring it up. It
doesn't even cross my mind, but James does somehow evidently with
people he meets for the first time. I know this because when I walk
up to them, they will say, "Your husband said you have a doctorate." I
am not sure if this inappropriateness is due to James' social ineptness
or social awkwardness, or something deeper, like autism spectrum.
At various times during our marriage, I have felt that all of us were on
the autism spectrum. However, it didn't occur to me until I noticed
our son's own social awkwardness. Now I believe he got this awkwardness from both sides of our family.

When I look back on it, my family was very large on both sides.
In my mother's family, there were thirteen brothers and sisters; and in
my father's family, there were six. Most of the time we got together, it
was just family. We socialized with very few other people other than
at church. I don't remember my maternal grandparents ever having
friends over when I was around, and I never went with them to visit
friends. It was always family. Often when I visited them after the kids
were grown and gone, my grandfather would be in one room and my
grandmother in another. On my dad's side, other than family members and at church again, I never saw them interact with friends. My
father only had one friend that I saw him socialize with, and that was
Mr. Judge, and you can't really call that *regularly*. We never had parties at our house, not even birthday parties. My mom didn't allow us
to go to parties when we were younger. I don't ever remember going
to a birthday party or even being invited to one. I think I got invited
to one or two parties when I was a teenager, but she did not allow me
to go because she didn't know the parents.

James and I didn't have a child for the first eight years of our
marriage. It seemed as if we were coasting along until James Jr. was
born. I think it was then that I realized that I became extremely frus-

trated with our not being in sync when it came to the finances especially. We were not in sync with other things, but we came to terms with that. But when it came to our financial future, we could not agree. I wanted to get into real estate for profit. I wanted us to buy rental property and land. I wanted to buy land or property in an area in Chicago now called Bronzeville. The properties are now worth millions. In the '70s, we could have bought them for thousands. James's problems involved a lack of vision and fear of success. I think growing up with his father always filing for bankruptcy and never having enough money to feed or even house his family, James feared that for himself. He never wanted to file bankruptcy, and he always wanted to have a place to stay that was his. So when we bought our first home, he was happy. I just didn't know that it would be forever. I thought our first home was a starter home. It was a townhouse, and I wanted a house. I thought James and I agreed on that. I just didn't figure that this was his first real home, and he didn't care if he lived anywhere else. I found the townhouse, but without a basement especially, I didn't want to move into it.

There were houses going up west of the Dan Ryan expressway that I wanted to take a look at. I knew they were over $100,000, but I thought we could afford the monthly mortgage. We just didn't have the down payment just yet. I wanted to wait a year, and then we would have the down payment. James said he was ready to move then, that the condo we lived in was too small since we'd had James Jr. The townhouses were new and had three bedrooms, an attached garage, and a bath and a half. We had looked at some houses in the area by the same developer, but James didn't like them because they had too many windows that burglars could come through. So against my wishes, we moved into one of the townhouses (mistake). I put my condominium up for rent initially and eventually, and with much pushing from James, I eventually sold it. We had renovated the condominium before James Jr. was born, so it rented pretty easily to a single person. We rented it for several years, but had trouble with renters, except one. I hated when she moved out because she had been an excellent tenant. The rent was never late, and she kept the place immaculate.

After she left, I allowed my friend Jackie to move in because she was leaving her husband. However, after she moved in, I am pretty sure he moved in with her as well. One night about nine months into the lease, she called and said that she had to leave town because she feared for her life. She still had several months left on her least, and she asked if her sister-in-law could move in with her boyfriend and his child. I reluctantly agreed to this arrangement, even though Jackie said that the boyfriend was an alcoholic. I had an inkling that the sister-in-law was too, but Jackie said that she didn't think so. They were late with the rent, so when I called them to inquire, the sister-in-law said that I could pick it up. When I got there, she gave me $300. Well, the rent was $400 a month. She said that she had been told $300. I think my friend thought that I would accept $300 since that was about the mortgage and assessment, but that was not our agreement or the amount on the lease she signed.

The sister-in-law told me to come back Sunday, and she would have the additional $100. When I got to the condo, I noticed that the laundry room had been sabotaged. One of my former neighbors said that it had happened overnight and that the people had been after the money. Now it was going to take months before they would be able to wash their clothes again. I went on upstairs and found my tenants had disappeared; they had moved out overnight evidently. I put two and two together and figured that they had been trying unsuccessfully to get the $100 out of the washers and dryers, and when they couldn't, they left. There was no way for me to reach Jackie because I didn't know where she was at the time. Jackie stayed away from Chicago for twelve years; I had heard from her off and on. I never saw the sister-in-law again. I tried renting my condo one more time, and it didn't work out either, and one day they just disappeared without any notification. I had tried a management agency this time, and they hadn't told me that the tenant was late with the rent. I gave up after that and decided to sell the unit as James had been insisting for years.

A major drawback in James and my relationship early on seemed to be his relationship with his family. He never seemed to want to visit his family or, more specifically, his mother. James's family lived on the south side of Chicago, not too far from where we lived. He very seldom went over there for a visit. I would have to encourage him to go visit his mother. Initially, I thought it was because he was much older than his siblings, who were still at home. But later, I found out that it was partially due to his upbringing. His father had been a tyrant and his mother docile and submissive. James had regretted that his mother never left his father. But later, he realized that having twelve kids, it was hard for her to make do without him, even though most of his money went to boozing and womanizing, according to James. He said that fighting was constant in their home.

The only saving grace in his family life was his grandmother. She moved to Chicago to help his mother take care of her twelve kids. James resented the fact that his mother always seemed to be pregnant. Some of the babies were born at home, and he would have to help clean up the blood. He was so young and hated his circumstances. This resentment boiled over into an angry mean demeanor sometimes. What he hated most was how his family life interrupted his playtime (which at the time was playing basketball with his friends). Even to this day, he will give you a mean look if his playtime (which today is watching sports or wildlife shows on television) is interrupted. As he was growing up, most of his resentment centered on babysitting his younger siblings. Being the oldest, he was often called on to wash diapers, clean bedpans, etc. He hated it all and resented the imposition. His father would either beat him or threaten to beat him if he disobeyed. James, to keep from being beaten, would acquiesce. Much later, I surmised that was how he developed his passive-aggressive behavior, which I abhor. He learned this behavior at home to keep from being beaten or getting any negative feedback.

When I met James, his father (Julius Morgan) had passed. Not only had his father passed, but James had been married before for six months and his new wife had had a heart attack and died. She'd had some congenital condition that neither of them knew about (at least James did not know about it). He was devastated by her death and still to some extent to this day. I overheard him explaining to a friend that had just lost his wife that you learn to live with it, but it always hurts. James's wife died at home after going to bed with what she thought was gas. He said that when he went to bed later, she was breathing unusually hard. And when he tried to wake her, he couldn't, and then she started foaming at the mouth. When I met him, I think she had been dead about two years. She was twenty-six, and he was twenty-eight when she passed. James also lost the brother he had been closest to around the same time.

James's brother Clifton (Babatunde Omowali) had been a Black Panther, a radical black power group that was headquartered in Oakland, California. Clifton was a member of a Chicago chapter of the Black Panthers. This affiliation caused a rift between him and James. James thought they were too radical. Clifton was killed trying to blow up a train with explosives that he evidently did not know how to use. At least that was what James was told, his niece (Erica) says that he was only practicing. I feel I should include this note because after meeting her in 2019 long after her father's death, you can tell she is very proud of him and feels very strongly that he impregnated so many women because he wanted to populate the world with his own advocates. He died and left three babies, three babies who were estranged from James's family until recently (over forty years). His brother never told his family about the babies.

Clifton should have kept his family more in the loop about his relationships, but he didn't, and therefore none of his children grew up close to his family. Even when he died, he was estranged from the family. He had left the family home one night after a brutal fight with his father, only to never return.

James said to this day he doesn't know where his younger brother went that night and he hated he didn't intervene in the fight. He knew that the fight would have only gotten worse if he had intervened and maybe the cops would have been called. Much later, however, after James' father had beaten their mother again, he did intervene himself and ended up leaving home. He says that his father was much bigger than him, over six feet, and James is only 5'8" or 5'9" but that he had been in the service and was working out and strong as an ox, so he ended up picking his father up and tossing him into their dining room table that shattered to pieces. I think not only did he have anger in him, he had a lot of pent up emotions from years of his father's tyrannical behavior that helped him pick his father up that night. I think all of the kids felt some vindication that night.

James's father died of a stroke later on. He had been told that his blood pressure was too high, but he ignored the warnings. He was fifty-two when he died. The year James turned fifty-two, he seemed very anxious until it was over. As I write this, he is seventy-eight years old. He suffers from high blood pressure, but it is under control. He has had several minor strokes due to having a hole in his heart that he had since birth, but he is doing okay now. He still has a lot of resentment in his heart for his father and how he caused turmoil in the family. He specifically hated how he treated his mother. There did not seem to be a lot of indications of love in the family. James says they never got anything special for Christmas. They never had turkey for dinner either. Christmas was just another day for them.

James also hated being drafted by the army at twenty-five. He was always scared he was going to Vietnam and developed headaches that probably led to his high blood pressure later on in life. Plus, we learned later that his father probably suffered from PTSD from his tour of duty during World War II, but never sought care for it— probably didn't know he had it or could get care for it. James's cousin Annie told him that his father's personality had changed drastically when he came out of the service.

Like I said, the one saving grace for James was his maternal grandmother (Edith Brown). James loved his grandmother. She had come to Chicago to help with the kids. She cooked most of their meals, and she was a great cook according to James, whereas his mother couldn't cook a lick. I don't ever remember eating a thing his mother had cooked. I think she probably gave up because she knew she couldn't compete with her mother. James said that he and his grandmother often talked, and he had great respect for her. To me, James is the only one of his siblings that seems to be able to love and show love to another individual. Most of his siblings seemed to have a mean demeanor most of the time. James's admiration for his grandmother gave him an understanding of the meaning of love. She also died before I met him. By then, she had moved to California to live with another one of her children, and James's was not able to go to the funeral, which is one of his deepest regrets. I think I owe the sustainability of our marriage to her, and for that, I am grateful. Plus, I am a pretty good cook.

Most of James's siblings are not married right now. He only has one sibling that is married, and that is his sister Priscilla. Priscilla is sweet but also has some rough edges. Her marriage has endured some rough edges. She did not have any children by her husband, but they both had children before they married. Her husband and his previous wife and their children lived across the street from James's family after they moved into the house. He got James's young siblings into selling drugs for him at their high schools. They loved having some money in their pockets. I don't think they knew how dangerous drugs were or what a dangerous business they were in. They all got into smoking marijuana and the boys into harder drugs.

Four of James's brothers (Clifton, Ricky, Carl, and Craig) all grew up to be wife abusers. Most of them have problems with alcohol and probably are alcoholics. All were pretty smart and held good jobs at one time or the other. They were the products of a very dysfunctional home. As I said earlier, I observed one of James's brothers (Ricky or Julius Morgan Jr.) beat his wife from the back of his mother's house to the front. They were in the street when some of the family members were able to break them up. I was in the house and heard the racket and went outside and saw the aftermath. She was a beautiful small-framed dark-skinned girl, and Ricky was standing over her, hollering at her. They had two kids by then (Ricky had another child by a girl he had gotten pregnant when they were in the seventh or eighth grades). They would later divorce. I only saw her once after the divorce that I can remember. I do know that she was killed (chopped up into pieces, I heard) by a cousin whom she was doing drugs with. I don't believe we went to her funeral.

I do remember going to her mother's funeral. James and I went to her mother's funeral and then to the repast in Robert Taylor homes. The same Robert Taylor homes that I had visited when I was working for the Board of Health some ten years prior and had not been afraid. Now there were bars on the outside stairways, and it looked like more of a prison than an apartment building, and now

I was definitely afraid. James said they had put the bars up because people were tossing things off the balconies trying to hurt people. Plus, the elevators had so much graffiti that it scared you. Before we got to the apartment where the repast was being held, I could hear the music. James's brother Ricky was the deejay. Everybody was having a grand old time, it seemed—drinking alcohol, laughing, etc. This was unusual for me; I was familiar with repasses being solemn occasions and definitely no drinking.

James's brother Carl met and married a young woman (Tonya) who was about eighteen at the time. She was already in college and was tutoring others. At first, whenever I met her, she'd have the biggest smile on her face. After she got pregnant and they got married, the smile was soon wiped clean off her face. I think Carl's behavior wiped her smile permanently off her face. She seemed like a happy-go-lucky kid at the time. Carl was handsome and, on the surface, a fun guy. To be honest, I've never seen him mad, but according to his sibling, when he started drinking and drugging, he was a tyrant. I understand he started beating her. When he met her, he was living in his mother's basement, and I am pretty sure that was where one of her children was conceived. The second child was born after they separated, and Carl denies the child to his family, but I do not think he is sure. They eventually divorced, and I doubt if Tonya got much support financially; I know she got none emotionally. Carl still lives in his mother's basement. It is rumored that he has six or more children.

Craig is James's youngest brother. According to his siblings, before he moved out of his mother's house, he had beaten several of his girlfriends as well. He did get married, and his wife (now ex-wife) told me that he beat her as well. He didn't get much of an opportunity to beat her though before she left him. Craig's and her wedding had to be postponed because she had to bury her older sister who had been killed by her husband, so she was deathly afraid and rightfully so of wife abusers. After a chance meeting on the Lake Shore Drive jogging trail, she told me that she called the cops on Craig one time, and one of them held him down with his shoe on his neck and asked him how it feels. He begged his wife for help, but she did nothing.

Evidently, she had told the cops that was what he had done to her. But Craig said he didn't do it. I asked a friend of mine who worked with substance abusers if he forgot, and she said that most alcoholics don't remember what they did the next day. Craig has not gotten married again.

James said that he was pretty sure that Clifton beat Shirley. Clifton's daughter (Karma) confirmed that he was abusive to her mother. Like I said, James has never laid a hand on me. His actions toward me at time with his passive-aggressive nature could be mental abuse, but it never got too excessive, or otherwise I would have left him. We had sought counseling several times (three times) with little success. The first time, however, opened my eyes to what I know now as passive-aggressive behavior. I thought I had made most of the decisions, but the counselor showed me how he was really making them because I always considered him when making a decision. For instance, at the time we were looking for a house in the suburbs of Chicago. I would go and look at the houses and decide which ones I liked, and I would take him later. He didn't like any of the homes, so I would have to start all over. It was tiring to me. He was really controlling the situation, so we should have gone to look at the homes together. I thought I was controlling 90/10, but it was nowhere near that. My mom had been somewhat of a nagging wife, to the point that I got tired of her nagging. My dad would ignore her until he was ready. Now I know it was his passive-aggressive nature. I guess I got accustomed to that behavior and perpetuated it in my own marriage. It almost destroyed my marriage and nearly killed me. I also noticed whether it was a man or woman counselor, they seemed to side with James most of the time. James would sit and smile, talking easily now with them and the female counselors especially seemed to be moved. Most of the time, I left feeling like the majority of what was wrong with our marriage lay in my footsteps.

After his father's death, James's mother was able to buy the family's first house. His mother was living not too far from where we lived. Like I said earlier, I thought he should visit his mother at least once a month, if not once a week. My mom had visited her mom almost weekly, and she would take us with her often. On Sundays, the Hampton family would often gather at Monmon and Pawpaw's.

Most Sundays after dinner, my mom would herd us into the car, and we'd go over to visit her parents. Some of those evenings her siblings (my aunts and uncles) would join us. It was during these times that I understood the purpose of family. I loved sitting and listening to them talk and laugh about the good old times. I was surprised to learn that my mom had loved playing basketball when she was a kid, and that was how she met my father, I believe. Not only did she love playing basketball, she was good at it. My mom was short like me, so I was surprised that she was good at it. They also talked about how she had some pretty legs. We had similar legs, and people over the years have told me that I had pretty legs. I guess I take them after my mom. She had varicose veins that disfigured one of her legs somewhat. I have similar varicose veins, but not the extent that she had them. Our dark skin camouflaged the veins, so most people don't know it. In my mom's case, one leg was somewhat bigger than the other.

My grandparents had moved to Minden after we did. My aunt Elnora had lived in Minden first. I am not sure how she came to set-tle in Minden, but she moved there, and my aunt Annie Laura had lived with her in Minden so she could finish high school and go to college. She was the first in the family; I think, to finish high school and the first to finish college. The whole family pulled together and sent her to college. Even my family helped. I don't remember, but I understand my father had driven her to college some of the times. However, it seemed that there was a rift between her and my parents over something they failed to do for her I presumed at a critical time because she always seemed cold to our family. I don't remember her ever being kind to us.

With this big a difference in James and my upbringing, I should have given more time to make the decision of whether to marry him. I had a pretty strong nature, so I thought I was in control of things and could handle it. I didn't understand or even had heard of such a thing as passive aggression. If I had, I would have known how it eats away at your soul. My decision-making was already limited by my upbringing and lack of socialization due to being raised in a large orthodox Christian family in a small Southern town. I didn't figure that he would always be trying to undermine my control. I didn't have a manipulative nature; I was straightforward. So he always knew what I was thinking. I thought I understood him, but I didn't. Working together to make the best decision for our family was my "motto." His "motto" was making sure his needs were met.

I remember asking him once how, with a family of twelve, did his mother raise twelve selfish children. They all seemed to be selfish, with no understanding or caring about others' needs. James was a little more sensitive than the rest of the bunch. For the rest, it was always about them; others only fit in as long as they met their needs. They seemed to tolerate people; they didn't need them.

So I waited three years to try to get pregnant. I had plenty of time to decide not to continue with the marriage and probably should have bailed, but I didn't. James and I had settled into somewhat of a decent life together. I was fixated on my professional life, and he was more fixated on going to work and coming home and looking at television. We had a decent social life, at least I thought. We'd go to some parties, mostly given by people that I knew. We'd gone drinking at bars with some of his friends and maybe a picnic or two. However, I was surprised that even though he had grown up in Chicago, after moving here from the age of four, he really didn't have a wide circle of friends. His social skills seemed to be limited just like mine. I was surprised at that, but not suspicious, and didn't realize that would have an impact on any children we brought into the world.

One of the things that I had admired about James was that he had seemed to fit in nicely with my professional group of friends. I guess you would say he was blue collar, and I was white collar when it came to our work worlds. For the most part, at least I thought, he moved between both worlds well. I tried to move into his world, but even that circle was small. Most of the people he worked with were white when I started going with him. And from what James has said, most of them were racist. He said that he had even been called the *n* word by some of his white counterparts. James and I went to some social events together after he had been in his mostly-all-white union (Ironworkers Local 63) for twenty-five years. We went several times after that, and I noticed that James knew quite a few of the white guys and seemed to get along with most of them. Beyond work, however, he never pursued a relationship with them. He did meet one black ironworker that he got along well. They had been partners on the job. His name is Richard Hill. I met Richard and his wife, Mary. We would go to the union events together whenever James and Richard were being honored. But other than that, we never socialized together.

In his spare time, Richard liked to fish; and James, to his dismay, had never fished. That was one of the things he hated his father for, never ever having taking him fishing or doing anything else with him. This knowledge would mean a lot to me later, but I overlooked it because I thought this trait of not bonding with your children would not be perpetuated in my own marriage and with our children. James decided to learn how to fish after he retired and he and Richard went fishing a few times. I didn't have that much interest in fishing, but I would have done it just to please him. The one or two times we went fishing, I enjoyed it, maybe a little too much. When I caught a fish, no matter what the size, I would be so happy. I think my display of joy would upset James. I believe he liked to fish in solitude, and I was anything but quiet. I didn't mind being put in the background of his fishing trips because I thought spouses should have different interest. But I couldn't help but feel a little ignored, and I wondered why.

A couple of months after James and I got married, we received a flyer under our door inviting us to a tennis camp for grown-ups. We decided we would go. We didn't have to bring tennis rackets or balls. We went and had a great time. We even decided to ask one of the instructors if he did private lessons, and he said he did. We started taking lessons from him. We played until it got too cold. Soon afterward, they opened an indoor tennis club, and James and I joined. We started to take some group classes at the club. Eventually, we started to take private couples lessons and even private individual lessons. In the summer, we would play tennis at our local outdoor tennis courts.

James took it a little more serious than I did, so he started playing with some of the other tennis players. I would learn that my husband was competitive in whatever he did and hated losing. Our son is the same way. If they don't win, they will stop participating. My husband's favorite sport is basketball, but by the time I met him, he had stopped playing. He says it's because of his knees, but I am pretty sure it was because the younger guys could whip him. I just loved playing tennis and having fun. James started seeing himself playing professionally or at least teaching tennis. I knew he was dreaming, and that was okay, just not realistic. He was thirty-four when he started playing tennis.

One thing I was happy about was that James would at least try things he had never done. He tried tennis and liked it. He went to plays with me, and he liked them. He eventually, after much condoling, went on a cruise with me, and he loved it. I never had to beg him to go again. Some wives could not get their husband's to do anything with them other than sleep with them. You would always see the wives out by themselves. The men would continue to do things with their buddies. I had told James early on that I didn't get married to do things by myself. I could have stayed single if that was what I was interested in. I included James in my social life always, sometimes to my detriment because he would share a little too much information with my colleagues. He once told one of my friends that I didn't like our boss, and the next thing I knew, I was losing my job. The person James had talked to told my boss (Dr. Wayne Watson) that I didn't like him. There was nothing I could do to get this guy to like me. We'd had a history when he wasn't my boss, and he couldn't forget that either. He wanted employees who were yes men and women, and I always told the truth. I was not an ass-kisser. It was later that I figured out that ass-kissers always got the plumb jobs. I needed to be my own boss.

Over the years, I had accused my husband of drinking too much, and he heard me refer to people as alcoholic if I saw them drinking too much. He thought I was overly fixated on the word. Maybe he was correct, but when it came to his family, I was right. Several of his brothers are functional alcoholics. Some of his sisters also overly imbibe at times. They seem to have more control than his brothers. Like I said earlier, I saw one of his brothers get drunk one time and beat his wife from his mother's backyard to her front yard. I couldn't believe anyone could be that mean. His actions scared me to death. I was not married to James at the time, and I had never got the feeling that he would beat me or even hit me. He and his siblings had grown up with his father using their mother as a punching bag, drunk or sober. Looking back, I should have used that as enough evidence to break off my relationship with James because if I had any children, he would be around his family, or more specifically, at the time, I thought this particular brother.

As it turned out, my husband had not one brother who could serve as a role model for our son. His brother Eric had come home from the service mentally ill, but his family never took him for treatment. So to this day, he walks around like a zombie; he has no life. I never understood why the Veterans Administration did not insist he receive regular treatment with his veteran's disability benefits. He gets a certain amount of money monthly for his care. At first, his mother handled the benefits, and later one of his sisters handled the benefits. Getting him back and forth for treatment or counseling was too much for the mother by herself, so she never took him. After the mother died and the sister took over his care, she still did not make sure he received treatment. I think the VA did start to ask questions after they started to receive complaints about how they were taking care of the veterans, but he still walks around like a zombie. His brother David, who passed away recently from complications from diabetes, was an alcoholic also, I believe, or a drug addict. His brother Carl is a drug addict. His youngest brother, Craig, is a functional alcoholic—meaning he is able to maintain a job and support himself, but still subject to drinking too much and getting rowdy.

I realized much later that this was not a family I should have married into. I based my decision to marry James on the fact that he was not an alcoholic and we shared similar morals and values and he was very trustworthy. Trust is a deal-breaker for me. Initially, I thought James drank too much sometimes, but never to the point of being drunk. Most of the time, he drinks while watching television at home, and I have never seen him get rowdy with his drinking. I have seen him high, but not drunk.

If you want to hear me go on a tirade, all you have to do is mention drugs. I despise any type of drugs. Over the years, I have softened somewhat on the legalization of marijuana, but not on its use—period. I believe the use of marijuana leads to the use of more lethal drugs. Drugs destroy lives. Some people seem to be able to control their drug habits and not let it control them, but others lose all forms of control. When mothers start selling their babies for drugs, then you know they are not worth it. When I heard that mothers and/or fathers were selling their children as sex slaves to men for money so they could get drugs and using their children to push drugs for them to make money, it made me sick to my stomach, and I knew then the depth of immorality the community had sunk to. Our purpose in life is to protect our children. When something is so evil that it makes you abandon your children, abandon your parental responsibilities, lose your self-respect, it has no place in the community.

I knew marrying James that I believed in family and strong family ties. When I met him, he was not accustomed to visiting his family weekly. I would often ask him, "Aren't you going to see your mother?" and he seemed uncaring to me. Like I said several times before, in my own family, as I was growing up, my mom would try to visit her parents once a week, if not more. She would often take us with her. I liked visiting them because I had aunts and an uncle who were not that much older than me. Plus, often one or the other of my mother's adult siblings would be visiting, and I enjoyed sitting and listening to them tell stories of them growing up. I loved hearing the laughter rippling through the house. I am sure the neighbors could hear it as well. We would generally visit on a Saturday or Sunday evening. Whenever we visited on a Sunday evening, we had to drag my mother out of their house because we had homework or schooling the next day. She really enjoyed visiting with her siblings, even though she was as different as night and day from them.

Most of them, including my grandparents, smoked, dipped snuff, or chewed tobacco, and they all drank and visited juke joints. My mother did none of those things. They did none of these things in my mother's presence or in the presence of us children. Even if they went outside to smoke or drink, they would hide behind a tree or something. Even though my relatives evidently smoked and drank, they seldom did it in front of the children in the family. I never saw any of my uncles drink or get drunk, even after I grew up. Most of the time, I was with my mother, and she garnered a lot of respect in her family because of her religious beliefs. Plus, I never saw any of my relatives ever fight, even verbally. There was just a lot of laughter in my family. This was just the opposite from my husband's family, except when we played cards.

To this day, I think playing cards together was what bonded me to his family. I loved playing bid whist and spades. All of his siblings could play cards, but my husband cannot and does not even have an interest in learning. He hates board games, period. We used to go to parties, and they would play games. He would be the only one sitting in the corner by himself because he didn't want to play games. We've been married forty-three years now, and I still do not know his apprehension to playing what you call parlor games or board games. I think he doesn't want to be laughed at for having the wrong answer or not keeping up. I do not know if he was humiliated playing games when he was younger or what. He remains a mystery to me. He is known for keeping secrets. I had a lot of fun playing cards for years with his family. We would stay at his mother's house until the wee hours of the night until I became afraid of the neighborhood she stayed in, and then I would cut the card playing short. James would watch television or talk to some of the relatives not in the card game. We would play rise and fly. This is where whenever you lost, someone would take your place.

To this day, I remember the first time I played cards with James's family. One of his sisters was sitting in the corner with a head rag (wrap or scarf) on her head. She had a very deep voice, so I thought she was a man or a boy. I didn't realize until I was leaving that night that she was a girl. The next time I saw her, she was wearing dark lipstick and blonde permed hair at her graduation, and she definitely had changed her look. As a matter of fact, I didn't recognize her; she recognized me. I am not sure how we found out that she was graduating, but I am sure I was the one that convinced my husband or boyfriend—I am not sure which one he was at the time—to go to his sister's high school graduation. He could care less about graduation, but they had been very important to me and my family.

Graduations in my hometown at the time were a community event. You went even if you didn't have a kid graduating. Whereas, in Chicago, you needed an invitation or ticket to get in because graduations were so huge, so most of the time, they were only attended by family and a few friends. You just didn't go to the graduation because you knew the family. This was so different from what I was accustomed to. Throughout my marriage, I kept trying to make my husband's family fit into the box I had grown up into, and this was not possible. It took me awhile to figure this out. Some woman would have taken her husband's lackadaisical attitude and distanced him from his family; I kept trying to make him understand the importance of family and being close to his mother, especially. I had family dinners when no one else in the family did for over thirty or more years. Finally, one of his sisters started having everyone over around Memorial Day and Labor Day. This was after their mother had passed away, long afterward. After she passed, our visits to her home became few and far in between. Our son never really bonded with my husband's family. I had only allowed my mother-in-law to babysit him once or twice when he was little and I think once when he was four or five.

I remember she had fed him spinach that she had cooked, and my son said he liked it. I asked her how she cooked, and I tried to cook it with ham the same way, but he said he didn't like it. I think this was the first time anyone told her that they liked her food. My husband was adamant about the fact that she couldn't cook. I seldom went to her house when she was cooking something. She never cooked a meal for me. She would buy chicken or pizza sometimes from fast foods whenever we visited, but she never cooked herself. I think the harsh criticism she got caused her to give up trying.

Our son was in the stage where he did not like most vegetables, so I was glad to hear he liked her spinach. I did not like spinach particularly myself. I had developed a hatred for it when the cooks in my elementary school would put boiled eggs for garnish on it. The eggs would be green, and that was a turn-off for me for some reason. So spinach was not a regular vegetable in our household. However, now I can eat spinach any kind of way. I finally figured out that adult taste buds are not as vibrant as kids, so the bitter taste of some vegetables is not the same.

Looking back, we probably should have waited to get married and saved our money and started off just living together. We would have learned that saving money was not going to be easy for us due to our habits and his construction job. He was constantly getting laid off, and we would have to live off his savings and unemployment for the duration. He never knew how long the layoffs were going to be. We would be dependent on my salary then. By then, I probably would have changed my mind about marrying him. But then, I was not thinking sanely and James was adamant about not living together before marriage.

What I did not know at the time I was changing teaching methodology was that I had a thyroid deficiency and had developed Graves' disease. I found this out after I got married in 1977, about three years after I started teaching, when I was up for tenure. I figured out that I got Graves' disease because my boyfriend, *James*, whom I was eating most of my meals with at the time, had noniodized salt in his kitchen. Therefore, most of the meals I ate were cooked with noniodized salt. He had bought this salt because the boxes looked the same. Really, I am not sure who bought the salt. We were both shopping. We didn't live together, so he bought most of the food for his apartment. I was still buying food for my apartment with my roommates. Even though I was eating at James's house, I still took my turn as the cook in our apartment, which I think was once every other week. However, when it was my roommates' turn to cook, the food would run out around the middle of the week. Then I would just eat at James's and leave them to fend for themselves. I could not understand why they spent most of their money on junk food—one was a nutritionist, and one was a nurse. Who would have thought?

I noticed around November of 1976 that I was getting more nervous than normal. My hands would not stop shaking. I couldn't figure it out. In December of 1976, I got engaged to James and discovered my thyroid problem in September, 1977, almost a year later. He and I had been going together for four years, and I had given him an ultimatum. I told him that I wanted to get married, and if he did not after four years, we needed to part ways. We decided to go our separate ways, and then my sister came to visit, and I needed someone to take us out on the town. So I called James and asked him if he would take us, and he did. After that evening, we got back together. Sometimes I wonder how my life would have been if I had not made that call and just gone out with Bobbie myself. She wanted a date, so I got her a date with an English teacher at Kennedy-King, so I needed a date. I don't think James and I had been separated that long. We went out, and I thought we had a reasonably good time. I knew I had missed James, and I think he had missed me too.

After James and I got engaged, he insisted that we get married around April 1977. He said that his lease was expiring, and he wanted to be married by then. I couldn't help but wonder if he was marrying me out of necessity or love. I think with the trial separation, we both decided that we loved each other. I know I did. I loved the way James could make me laugh with his stupid sayings. To make my heart melt, all he had to do was smile. I knew hugging a lot made him uncomfortable as it did me because we were not used to it. To make up for it though, he was a great kisser. I knew I could live with this man for the rest of my life. So I went about planning a wedding in three months and nine days. So I thought my mood swings, sweats, nervousness, etc. was due to working full-time and planning a wedding in such a short time that was being held in another city. I was living in Chicago, but I wanted to get married in Louisiana. That was stupid and hard to do also. I had also noticed that my temperament had changed. I found myself short-tempered with people more than usual. I remember an embarrassing situation at the wedding when I tried to throw the bouquet to my friend Pearlie Jean and my sister-in-law Precious jumped in front of her and caught it. I think I said something to her that was negative, but I can't remember what it was now. I may have also been short-tempered with others doing the week leading up to the wedding. I had just thought it was a case of nerves. It's hard to start your marriage with your feelings being all over the place.

James and I settled into married life. He still tried to go out with his friends on Friday nights. One night he came home very late, and I complained; he didn't seem to understand. I told him I couldn't go to sleep if he was not in the bed with me; plus, I worried that something had happened to him if he wasn't home when he said he would be. Later, I got the chance to pay him back. I came home late after playing cards with my sisters at Dorothy's house, and he was still up when I got home around 5:00 a.m. He was upset and said he couldn't go to sleep because I was not in the bed. Now he knew, and he never came home later than was said again. As a matter of fact, he stopped going out with his friends altogether.

It was around the age of thirty that I went to a hairdresser, and she told me that the top of my head was hard, and it should have been soft and that my hair was thinning at the top. Later, I went to a dermatologist, and she confirmed that I had alopecia. I had no idea what that was. She said I would lose my hair at the top and maybe all over. She indicated that there was nothing I could do about it and that a lot of people wore wigs. After my son started school, he said that some kids were teasing him about my ball head, so he and my husband wanted me to wear wigs in public. I decided I would wear wigs in public, but if you came to my house, you would see me in the natural.

After thinking about things, I remembered that my mom's hair had thinned after menopause, but she still had a nice length to her hair. I remembered that my maternal grandmother and maternal great grandmother both wore head scarfs most of the time. Later I would see my Aunt Elnora do the same and noticed that my Aunt Annie Laura always wore wigs. I would later discover that they both had patches of very bad bald spots all over their heads. Evidently, alopecia was a genetic trait on my maternal side, something that I was never made aware of as I was growing up. If I had, I think I would have taken better care of my hair. After I left Southern, I started to wear my hair in a natural (short afro) all the time and sometimes washed my hair daily which was not good for my hair. Taking care of black hair is something that is not often talked about. Other than electric shock treatment, no black beautician gave me an idea of what to do. Now, I know one thing I should not have done was wear wigs without a wig cap, which I did all my life and still do, because I find wearing them too hot, especially in menopause and now in peri-menopause. I don't know if my relatives knew the name of their hair condition.

I didn't know also, that my thyroid condition could also con-tribute to my lack of hair growth and also stress. Who knew! Now wearing wigs is second nature to whites and blacks, but when I first started wearing them in my forties, they weren't. I am more of a nat-ural girl. This, coming from a girl who thought of herself as ugly all her life, didn't realize that hair and makeup could make a difference.

I remember complaining one day that I didn't know why young girls liked wearing fake hair down to their butts when my husband responded, "Laura, you don't see men complaining, do you?" I gar-nered from this conversation that my husband may like women with long hair. So yours truly surprised him on one of our weekend get-aways with long reddish hair, and he loved it. Too bad, I couldn't get used to long hair because our sex life that weekend was off the chart (we were celebrating my seventieth birthday). I understand now that taking care of your hair is a healthy thing to do and could affect your ability to get a job one day. People indeed consider it your crowning glory. No matter what you look like, having beautiful healthy hair (short or long) can be your ace in the hole.

Growing up, I don't remember ever focusing on when I would have children or if I would have children. I think I just thought as a girl that one day I would get married and have children; it was a given. I did make one decision, though, and that was if I ever had children, I would have at least two, so they would have someone to play with. I don't remember many people having only one child when I was growing up. Most people had at least two kids, if not many more. My siblings always had a lot of fun together, mostly spurred on by me. I would plan games and activities for us. I had noticed the kids enjoyed doing even the simplest of things, like rac-ing around the house; this kept them busy and avoided boredom.

Being the oldest of eight children, you take care of a lot of babies. I especially remember taking care of my youngest three siblings. When they were born, they were so small, but soon they grew to be pretty big babies, and I had a hard time carrying them. Because they were so big and I was so small, whenever I carried them, which was mostly on my right side, I would throw my hip. I had no idea that this was distorting my walk. I am sure I was happy when they started walking. I had to focus on my mom's babies every day, and it was tiresome and tied you down. I had little time to play. Plus, after my mom stopped having kids, it was now ten people in a two-bedroom house. There was absolutely no privacy, and I hated that immensely. I was a senior in high school before I managed to seclude myself in our parents' bedroom and got the chance to look at my whole body in the mirror on their dresser.

The house was unbelievably noisy and busy most of the time. I was always trying to hush my siblings so they wouldn't disturb the neighbors. For some reason, we were especially loud on the weekend. I was thankful that someone played loud music in our neighborhood on the weekend in the mornings, so no one could hear the kids fussing. Helping to get my little siblings ready for church every Sunday was a headache. As the oldest, I got first dibs on almost everything. I was the first to take a bath, first to choose where I wanted to sit in the car. Taking a bath first was wonderful because we had to share water, so everyone would have hot water; my water would be clean, thank heavens. The only problem was, you couldn't sit and enjoy your bath because seven kids had to follow you. The few minutes alone in the tub were priceless. The water in my home town is soft water; at least that's what I was told (it did not have a lot of chemicals). Plus, there was a window right over the tub, and a cool breeze would come in while you were in a hot tub. It made you want to stay there forever.

Riding in a car with all ten of us in a two-door car was my top pet peeve. Being the oldest, I could choose where I wanted to sit, so I always chose to sit in the front seat. When it was just my mom driving us to church, it was great. I got the chance to sit by the window, and my baby sister or sometimes sisters would sit in the middle. Whenever my dad was in the car with us, which was seldom,

I would have to sit in the middle with one of my baby sisters on my lap. I felt squeezed in all the time. The only time I sat in the back seat was when another adult went to church with us, and I had to sit in the back seat with the rest of my siblings. I felt like I was in prison whenever that happened. It didn't happen that often, but my mom was always trying to get someone to go to church with us. She got a few to go with us, but they didn't have their own transportation and probably didn't like traveling in a car full of kids or going that far to church, so they stopped going with us very soon.

Growing up in a house full of kids and being the oldest of the lot made putting having kids of your own off as long as possible. I think that was one of the reasons I didn't want to have sex early, I was afraid of getting pregnant and having to take care of another baby.

When James and I first got married, I decided that I would wait awhile before getting pregnant because I was not sure if we were going to stay married; we were so different. We both grew up as the eldest in large families, but our experiences were different. James had been forced to take care of his siblings. I had to take care of mine, but my mom knew that I needed time for myself, so she would allow me to go places when she got home from work and could take of the kids herself. I had a lot of fun growing up, so having a baby too early was not on the agenda.

When James and I got married, he said that it wouldn't matter of him if we had children or not. He'd had it rough as the oldest growing up. He was forced to take care of his siblings when all he wanted to do was play basketball. This was his constant mantra during our marriage and even to this day. Basketball was big among blacks in Chicago. He resented any time he had to take care of his siblings. He resented the fact that his mom had so many babies. She even had most of her babies at home, and he would have to take care of the bloody sheets. He said they had a scrub board, and he would have to wash the dirty diapers and other clothes in the bathtub, and he hated it. Growing up with this hatred left its mark, so he didn't necessarily need to have a child to prove his manhood; at least that's what I thought when we first got married.

So when we got married, I decided to give our marriage a trial run before we had a child. I was not sure we were going to make it. I knew that James had a lot of hatred inside of him from his childhood. It was all that he talked about—how much he hated his life growing up. The only good part to his life was his grandmother. This was a hint to me that raising a child with James was not going to be easy. We had such different backgrounds. We'd both grown up poor but had totally different experiences. My family farmed, so we never starved. James grew up in the city, and they often went hungry, it seemed. My parents put all of their money in the household, whereas James's father seemed to use his to chase women or gamble. I only saw my parents fight one time; this seemed to be a regular occurrence in James's family's household. James got his first job when he was eleven as a paperboy, and his father would take most of his money. He made James put the money in a drawer, and James did that until he got smart enough and started keeping some of the money for himself. He would make James give him some of his money from every job James had until James left home when he was drafted into the Army. James felt his father was unfair, whereas my mom and dad would let us keep whatever money we made and use it any way we wanted to. James had a passive-aggressive behavior, whereas mine was more aggressive. Even with all these differences, I decided after three years that James was responsible and an all-around good guy and extremely supportive, just as I had surmised before we got married. Maybe we would stay together and make plans to have children.

I was teaching when James and I got married and decided that whenever I got pregnant, I would do it so I could have the baby around the summertime, when I had time off anyway, and go back to work in September. At least that was my plan. James and I started trying to have a baby after we had been married for three years. By then, I still was not positive that James and I would make it—primarily because he had a temperament that I didn't understand. He would flare up any time I didn't agree with him. I had to explain to him that because we were married, that we didn't have to agree on everything. He would agree to almost anything in bed. I also loved the way he supported me in my school activities where often, without the support of the other instructors, I would need his help. He seemed to enjoy assisting me. So I decided, *This is a nice guy*, and that he would make a nice dad.

I stopped using anything for birth control around June of 1979. I expected to be pregnant the next month or at least by September 1979. I was shocked that I didn't get pregnant. For three long years, every month I looked to not have a period. Several times it was a few days late, but other than that, my period came every month. After three years of trying to get pregnant with no luck (1979–1983), I decided to see a doctor.

After the first year of trying to get pregnant, I persuaded James to have a fertility tests done to make sure it was not him. The doctor said that his sperms were moving slow but that we should still be able to get pregnant. After the second year, my doctor gave me some hormone pills to take, and I still didn't get pregnant. The third year, my doctor recommended a fertility doctor at Rush Presbyterian St. Luke. He was a white doctor. He told me that I needed to have a laparoscopy done of my uterus. I had never heard of a laparoscopy. He explained that laparoscopy was less-invasive surgery than normal. A small incision would be made near my navel; then a laparoscope would inserted into my uterus to take pictures of my uterus. I said yes to the surgery because I was desperate to find out why I was not getting pregnant. If there was something that could be done, I wanted it done right away because I was not getting any younger.

I was scared because I had never been under the knife before. I had never been in a hospital. The night before the laparoscopy, I was eating dinner in my room in the hospital, and a worm came out of my fresh cauliflower and scared me to death. I started to cry. I was wondering why God was putting me through all these tests to have a baby. Why were young girls getting pregnant so fast, and I couldn't get pregnant. I was thinking so negatively: Maybe God didn't want me to have a baby. Maybe I was too old. I know I was beside myself and at my wits' end.

After the laparoscopy was done, the fertility doctor told me that I had endometriosis and recommended some pills. He had drawn a picture of my uterus and where the endometriosis was located. He said that could be the reason why I was not getting pregnant but that I could still get pregnant. I wasn't happy with the endometriosis results but happy that I could still possibly get pregnant. The fertility doctor gave me prescriptions for some hormone pills that he said should help. I dutifully took the pills, not knowing what they would do to my body.

I went back to the fertility doctor about a year later for a follow up because I was still not pregnant, and he said that my surgical report didn't mention anything about endometriosis. I told him he had written me prescriptions for it, but still he said I did not have endometriosis. I was angry. He had said everything so matter-of-fact, so much so that I was beside myself. I wanted to scream, *You crazy motherfucker! This is my body you are talking about, and I want a baby.* Leaving his office that day probably was one of the saddest days of my life. I was so perturbed, but probably thinking saner than I had before. I decided I was through with fertility doctors and that it would be up to me and God. I decided that maybe I should stop exercising as much as I was doing (I had become an avid aerobic student; plus, James and I were taking tennis lessons and playing as much as we could) at the time.

James and I had been in baby mode for five years. I don't think we were enjoying sex anymore; it was just baby-making time for us now. Sex was scheduled around my fertile days. I had been taking my vagina temperature on a regular basis to see if I was fertile. I was counting the days that I would be fertile, and we would have sex during those times. I decided after my confrontation with the doctor—no more temperature taking. We were just going back to enjoying sex and having it when we wanted to and not on demand to make a baby and that we would do this for one year. After the year was up, if no baby, then we would just live our lives without baby.

My uncle Clyde Lawhorne died in February 1985. James and I had just been home for Christmas, so we didn't have enough money for both of us to fly back for his funeral. I decided to fly or take the train to Memphis so I could drive down with Bobbie to save some money. It was the scariest trip for us, two women alone, because ice was on both sides of the roads almost all the way to Louisiana.

We both stayed in Minden with our parents. My uncle's funeral was going to be in Homer, Louisiana.

It was while I was at his funeral that I started to feel sick. So sick that I asked the funeral director if she had cold medicine, and I took it. I never take medicine that I receive from strangers, so I had to be sick. When I got back to my mom's house, I spent the rest of the day and evening sleeping on the couch. My mom got up at some point and took my temperature and said I was too hot, so she and my sister Bobbie took me to the hospital in Minden. The doctor said I had an infected tonsil and to bring me back in the morning if I was still sick. I had gotten worse, so my mom and Bobbie took me back, and I was admitted into the hospital. They both spent the night with me. I was so sick I could hardly lift my head. I remember being so grateful they were there in the room with me because it took too much energy to talk. I could whisper to them that I needed water, and they would ring the nurses for me. I spent several days in the hospital. Bobbie had to get back to her job in Memphis. I hated she had to drive through that horrible weather by herself, but she made it back to Memphis okay.

When I got out of the hospital, my mom and dad put me on an airplane back to Chicago. I couldn't walk, so I had to be wheeled in a wheelchair. I know I must have been a sight for my husband when he saw me at the airport. I was okay, though, in a few days. I had to take antibiotics for a while.

Around my birthday and after the year was up, we went to a resort to celebrate my thirty-eighth birthday, our eighth anniversary, our getting out the baby-making mode, and my getting over a serious illness. While we were there, it rained the whole weekend. James and I bought a couple of bottles of wine and stayed in bed almost the whole time and, of course, had sex often. I assume we left that resort pregnant because my period didn't come in April or May. After it was late in April, I started to hope, but I had been late before and not pregnant, so I was not going to take a chance. I took several home pregnancy tests after a while, and the tests were positive. I told James about them, and I think he began to hope also. I had never been this late with my periods before, and I had never had a positive pregnancy test before.

We're Pregnant

In early May, I went to a super aerobics class that lasted for about four hours. I thought it would definitely bring my period down. When I didn't see even a drop of blood, I made a doctor's appointment. My gynecologist confirmed that I was pregnant. I had been keeping James abreast of what was going on with my period, so when I told him that the doctor had confirmed I was pregnant, he seemed as happy as I was. So success occurred when I left everything up to God and us, fertility doctors do not know everything. Some of my family said that the antibiotics cleaned me out so I could get pregnant. Another family member who'd had infertility issues got pregnant also after a serious illness and a bout with antibiotics. I'll never know, but I am forever thankful that I did get pregnant.

Later, I went to the doctor for an ultrasound. She told me that there were three sacs and that I could possibly have three babies. I drove home in total shock. I'd hoped that I would have twins because I would have the two babies I had always wished for, but three would be great. All I could think about was if I do have two or three, I didn't have to get pregnant and walk wobbly again. I prayed all the way home for the three babies. I was on cloud nine, so I floated home. I drove carefully, though, because I didn't want to harm my babies. I told James about the babies, and he couldn't believe it. I didn't tell a lot of people, just a few, and they were happy for me. Unfortunately, when I went back in about a month for another ultrasound, the doctor confirmed that I was only having one baby. I am not sure, but I think I cried for the other two babies that didn't survive. At the time, I didn't know what the Lord had in store for me. I was happy that one of the babies had survived.

After I found out I was pregnant, I kept a smile on my face all the time. After, I started showing, I told people I was pregnant. I waited at least three months just in case I had a miscarriage. I had signed up to teach summer school at Kennedy-King, and I started to get big right away, so I had to tell my students also because they had noticed that I was gaining so much weight. Everybody seemed to be happy for me. I was one of the youngest teachers at Kennedy-King even at thirty-eight years of age. My pregnancy went well; I didn't even have morning sickness. My taste buds did change somewhat, but I still had a healthy appetite. The one problem I had was people telling me bad things that happened to them or their friends while they were pregnant. I would think about what they said for weeks. I was in super praying mode that my baby be born alive and healthy.

My maternal grandmother passed away a few weeks after I found out I was pregnant. I was so happy that she knew I was pregnant before she passed because now she could tell my maternal grandfather (J. D. Hampton Sr.) that I had finally gotten pregnant. He had died about nine months before. But before he died, he had asked me on our last visit together when was James and I going to get pregnant. I had told him that we were trying. I had the deepest respect for my maternal grandfather. I thought he was one of the smartest men alive. He was so mild-mannered and hardly ever raised his voice and had such a rich laughter. I am not sure if he smoked cigarettes, but he did dip snuff, and I believe chewed tobacco—all of which I hated and could not understand the purpose. I knew he would be ecstatic that I was finally pregnant.

James and I (mostly me because I was still handling the finances) started to save as much money as possible for my year of nonpaid leave. I started listening to music more because the books suggested it. Now I know it was good for his vocabulary development even in utero. It was a wonderful time. I didn't want to buy too many pregnancy clothes because what was I going to do with them afterward? But I gained so much weight. I had to buy more than I wanted to because I couldn't wear any of my old clothes. Plus, my sister Juanita got married during my fifth month of pregnancy, and I had to have something for the wedding.

My friends, coworkers, and students gave me baby showers. It was toward the end of my pregnancy, and I was busy and tired. I enjoyed all the attention and definitely needed the gifts. James and I had the condo painted and bought a baby bed and linen. I got a year's diaper service as a gift. We were very ready for our little bundle of joy.

A friend of mine from high school told me to take a picture of me pregnant around the ninth month. There was a professional photography studio near us called Bonner and Bonner. A few weeks before I was due, James and I went to have some pictures taken, and to this day, I am so happy that I did that because I did not get pregnant again. I thought I looked pretty good for a pregnant lady. My hair had changed because it was thinning in the top because I was developing alopecia. So I did the best I could with my hair and wore my cutest outfits. James put on a blue jeans outfit, and I thought he looked slim and debonair.

About three weeks before my baby was due, my doctor had me come in every day to check my baby's heartbeat. I am not sure if it was because of my blood pressure or maternal diabetes now. It was hectic going every day, but anything to protect my baby. James and I also went to Lamaze classes and toured the operating rooms at Michael Reese Hospital (since torn down) where the baby was going to be delivered. We were probably the oldest couple there—I was thirty-eight, and James was forty-two—but it did not matter. I wanted to be ready when the baby was born. I was now walking wobbly down the hallways of Kennedy-King. I started to have Braxton Hicks pains. I thought I was going into labor several times, but it was only Braxton Hicks pains instead. I had never heard of Braxton Hicks. I knew that time was getting shorter, so I had to get everything ready for the baby. We went and got the baby bed, bedlinen, and car seat. I think someone gave us a baby carriage.

I was able to give my students their final exams before the semester ended just before the holidays, and all I needed to do was hand my grades in; I had already completed them. My baby's due date was December 29, so I thought I had plenty of time to hand them in. The grades were due to be handed in by December 20, I believe. Thursday, December 19, around 4:00 p.m., my water broke. When James came in from work, I told him we had to go to the hospital. I was in no shape to go to turn the grades in. I probably could have dropped them off on my way to the hospital, but that was the last thing on my mind at the time.

We got to the hospital around 6:00 p.m., and I was in labor. Young girls were coming and going, dropping their babies in minutes, and I was still in labor around 10:00 p.m. when the doctor came. The doctor told me to walk around the floor to see if that would hurry things on, and it did not. The doctor I had been seeing the whole time was pregnant herself (I think her name was Dr. Kramer) and said that she wouldn't be able to deliver my baby and that a Dr. Byrd probably would be the one to deliver my baby. I was so emotional at the time that I am sure I cried because I was used to her, and I didn't want a stranger. But she assured me everything would be all right, that Dr. Byrd had delivered plenty of babies.

After I got to the hospital, I assume Dr. Byrd was called. Around 10:00 p.m., he gave me medicine to speed up the labor pains; and later, around 1:00 or 2:00 p.m., he came and gave me an episiotomy so I wouldn't feel so much pain on delivery. I was afraid of the needle they used, but I acted like a big girl and did it. I went to sleep and slept until the morning. I was grateful for the rest, but now the pains were coming every minute, it seemed. They eventually took me to the birthing room; I was almost the last person in, I guess, was the predelivery area. I felt like a whale lying on the table with my legs up in the air. All I could see was the doctor's head. My right leg started to hurt; it seemed the baby was trying to come through my leg. I could feel him pushing.

Then all of a sudden, the doctor said, "It's a boy. Do you have a name?" All I could hear was my husband yelling, "James Morgan Jr., of course." Forget the fact that I had asked him all nine months if he wanted the baby named after him if it was a boy; he said he didn't care. That was James's patterned answer for most things, but he really does care. I think he was so used to not getting his way when he was growing up that he thought his opinions didn't matter. I was happy to hear him speak up, but why the drama for nine months? I had already decided I was going to name the baby after him because James had often complained about his father not naming him after him, even though he was glad he hadn't because he hated his father.

James's father had given his third son his name. He named James after his father (James's grandfather) and his second son, Clifton, I think after either his grandfather or James's mother's father. I didn't want to hear my husband say for the rest of my life, "I should have named him after me."

It seemed like an eternity, but finally I was pushed back to my room after the delivery. We had decided we were going to have James Jr. circumcised because my husband never was, and he wanted it for his son. James was adamant about it. He even decided to get himself circumcised because he had demanded that his son be circumcised. To me, this took a lot of guts and pain.

James Jr. was born around 2:00 p.m. on a Friday afternoon. I was in labor for quite some time; it was the most painful time of my life. I couldn't believe it was over. So many young girls had come into the labor room while I was there, and they were in and out in a couple of hours. Here I was, there all night and most of the day. I was so happy when he was born. Forget the pain—I have a son. I have a brand-new baby of my own.

The evening of our son's birth, a girlfriend of mine, Tommie, was having a birthday party. James and I had planned on going. James decided to go to the party alone, so he could tell everybody we had our baby, and it was a boy. We knew most of the people that would be at the party. I knew they would all be happy for us. So here we were, James going to party and me sleeping and attempting to breast-feed our baby for the first time.

Tommie told me how James had handed out a few cigars at the party, even though he doesn't smoke himself. I can just imagine how big his smile was. So having a baby or not didn't matter to him, huh? It seemed that he indeed wanted a baby to justify his manhood as well.

I had asked James to call my friend Rose and asked her if she would turn my grades in for me, and I was shocked to hear that she had said no. James said I should call her myself, so I did, and again she said no. I asked her why, and she said she just didn't want to do it. She never gave me any reasons. I had met Rose after I started working at Kennedy-King, and I thought we were pretty good friends (here

I go again using that word loosely). I really didn't have the energy to call anyone else, so I decided I would hand them in after the New Year. I knew all of my students would be getting incompletes, and that I would have a hell of a time filling out the paperwork to change the grades, but there was nothing I could do. My husband couldn't turn the grades in; he didn't have a clue as to what to do, so I was up a creek with a brand-new baby, and my students would just have to wait.

Raising James Jr.

Breast-feeding was something that I decided I would do for my son's sake. I knew as a nutritionist that breast milk was good for the baby. I also knew that colostrum, the first milk released for the breast, would be the most nourishing. James Jr. and I eventually got used to breast-feeding. I don't believe my mom breast-fed any of her babies. When I asked her about it after I started breast-feeding James Jr., she said that it just wasn't done. But I think black mothers at the time were just taking cues from white women. I assume I was too, in a way, because white women were now breast-feeding their babies again. I knew that the breast milk after the birth of your baby was extremely healthy for him, so I was determined to breast-feed at least four to six months.

When it was time for James Jr. and me to go home, the doctors told us that he had yellow jaundice and to bring him back to the clinic on Monday, if he wasn't better. We were being discharged on a Saturday, two days after arriving for the delivery and a few. I was devastated by the diagnosis and wondered what it meant. After we got home, James told me he had a tennis match to play, so he left right away. I couldn't believe it. Here I was, with a brand-new baby, nervous and anxious by myself. I'd thought two things: James would want to spend time with his baby and have some flowers waiting for me, and he did neither. I was really disappointed in him. I couldn't worry about it, though, because I had a newborn to take care of. I was so afraid I would harm the baby in some way. I don't think I'd ever been as nervous.

We made it through the evening with me trying to breast-feed. It seemed to be working okay while I was in the hospital. James eventually came back home, and I told him that he should not have left so soon after I brought the baby home. He might have been nervous too, but if so, he was hiding his feelings very well. I was so nervous I went into panic-attack mode. Here I was, alone with my baby for the first time, and I was scared of harming him. I had read a little bit about postnatal syndrome that was fraught with anxiety attacks and mothers either harming themselves or killing themselves. I needed James to be home with me at that time; I had never imagined that he would leave me alone on our first night home alone with our baby. To me, this was the most uncaring thing he had ever done. I had been married to this man for eight years, and I still didn't know him. He would do things that made me think he was the most considerate man in the world; then he would do something that went totally against the grain like leaving me alone with our brand-new baby almost the second we walked into the house. I don't think I'd had the opportunity to even put our baby down in his crib before James announced that he was leaving to go play tennis.

After I couldn't play tennis during my pregnancy, James had met a lady in one of his tennis classes that he hooked up with to play doubles. I had met her and thought she was very nice, and I was not jealous. But after he left to go play tennis with her that night, I couldn't help but wonder if something was not going on. James always returned home within a reasonable time after his tennis lessons or matches, so I was pretty sure nothing ever happened. It was hard for me to understand why my husband would leave me and our brand-new son alone on our first night home. It was only for a few hours, but it seemed like an eternity.

Plus, where were the flowers? I had just been through hell delivering our baby, and I deserved an award, or so I thought. I was hoping he would think to pick some up after his tennis match, but he didn't. I let him have it about the flowers when he got home. He offered to go out and get some, but I told him that was all right. Besides, it was the thought that counted. Wasn't he proud of me for taking care of myself and delivering a healthy baby with all of his fingers and toes? I guess not. James never missed a critical opportunity to give me flowers after that snafu.

I thought back to my days at Case when Merline had sounded off about the guys not buying the black girls at the table some flowers, even though we weren't their girlfriends—we were just their friends (here I go again using the term *friend* wrong)—and one of the guys, Harold, responding that he was not used to his father giving his mother flowers. I figured James never saw his father give his mother flowers. Eventually, I told James that on special occasions, I expected flowers. He started giving me flowers all the time after that until I told him that he could stop because I was tired of the same old flowers (from the local grocery store after his favorite florist retired and closed their store), and I thought we could save the money. I was about seventy at the time, and he had been giving me flowers for over forty years by then.

We brought James Jr. back to see the doctor on Monday afternoon, and he said to take him directly to the hospital. We didn't even get a chance to come home to get a change of clothing. I was still bleeding from the delivery. I think they had given me extra-large Kotex when I left the hospital, so I asked James to go home and get a change of underwear and the Kotex. I was not going to leave my baby. They kept our son in an incubator overnight. All I did was cry and pray for him. I loved James Jr. from the minute I knew I was pregnant and even more so after he was born, if that was possible. Seeing him lying in the incubator all alone was heart-wrenching.

We spent Christmas Eve with our son in the hospital. The hospital provided a meal for us and other families under the same circumstances on that Christmas morning, and my son was discharged that afternoon. I was just happy that James Jr. was now healthy and going home.

My sister Bobbie came up to spend a week with us after the baby was born. I was happy to have the company because James had to go to work after the holidays, so I needed help during the day. I was so happy when she told me she was coming up after I had the baby. She worked in a school as well as being the school librarian, so she had holidays off as well. Bobbie was a big help, and I was ever so grateful. I was still sore and developed a urinary tract infection, which was awful and lasted about three weeks. I was in so much pain every time I urinated. I started drinking cranberry juice. I couldn't take any pills because I was breast-feeding James Jr.

One day while I was washing clothes, I saw a sign that said "I am available for babysitting." I'd been wondering who I was going to get to babysit. I wanted to get back into exercising again, so I would need someone to babysit James for that and for a variety of reasons. I didn't want to take James Jr. out in the cold because he was born in December, so I would need a babysitter who would come to my house. It turned out the sign had been put in my laundry room by Mrs. Taylor, an older lady who lived in the twin building next door. We talked on the phone, and either I went over to meet her, or she came to meet me. She did babysitting for extra cash. She was fine with coming over to baby sit at my condo, if she didn't have any other babies. She was a total stranger to me. This was the first time I missed having my immediate family around. I missed my mom especially. I only had one sister in Chicago, and she was hardly ever home and was going through some things with her husband at the time.

Most of my friends' babies were much older by now, so they didn't have any babysitting suggestions. My husband's family was in Chicago, but other than his mother, I couldn't think of one I would trust with my baby who lived close by. His mother lived in a house full of people who were coming and going. I really didn't want my baby in that environment. Plus, there were a lot of kids in the house that might mistreat my son. I was in supermom mode when it came to my son.

After having James Jr., I felt a little vulnerable. Here I was, the girl who never thought men found her attractive, and I was still overweight, with a pretty big stomach, and felt very unattractive. My skin coloration was weird. I couldn't wait to get back to exercising. I'd thought I'd get off the birthing table weighing my pre-pregnancy weight. Instead, James Jr. weighed 7 pounds, 8 ounces, and it seemed that was all I lost. Before he was born, I was weighing 204 pounds. I couldn't believe I had gained 60 pounds. This was particularly heart-wrenching because I had worked so hard to lose the weight after

I had topped my weight at 160 pounds. Just before I got pregnant, I was weighing 138 pounds. When I went to the doctor, I weighed 142 pounds on my first prenatal visit. This had to be a shock to my body, considering I was 93 pounds when I went to college.

After I had James Jr. and took my yearlong maternity leave and went back to teaching, I think I only taught for one semester before accepting the position as director of Academic Support. My friend Rose had suggested that I apply for the position. I had really wanted to be chairperson of my department, but I applied and got the job. The job was not that hard, and now I didn't have to worry about lecturing with my anxiety issues. I had a small staff and only had a few meetings, so I didn't have the public-speaking issue. I did have to travel downtown for departmental meetings once a month. This meant heavy traffic, so again I had to be in control.

When James Jr. was almost a year old, we took him to one of my former students' renewal-of-the-vows ceremony. Her daughter had insisted that I bring James Jr. because she had babysat him, so we did against our wishes. We got there late and were trying to be quiet while we took off James Jr.'s snowsuit. I should have put him in my lap, but I put him in the chair, and somehow he slipped to the floor on his head and started screaming. We had to leave before we had even sat down good. This would be one of the events that would haunt me for the rest of my life. We took him to the doctor to see if he had any brain injury, but the doctor said he was fine. But I couldn't help but wonder if he didn't have a brain leak. The floor was concrete, and he was so small. Whenever James Jr. acted weird—and there were many times—I would blame it on the fall.

I took the first year of James Jr.'s life off from work. We really couldn't afford it, and thinking back, I probably should have worked. But I bonded with James Jr., and we still have that bond today. He and I are very close, sometimes I think too close because he is such a mommy's boy. I would even say Peter Pan–like. I remember when someone asked him what he wanted to do when he grew up, and he said that he never wanted to grow up. I should have taken heed to that statement and pulled back a little with the smothering-mother-hood bit, but I didn't. I couldn't help but want the best for my son.

I couldn't believe that I had gained sixty pounds with my pregnancy. I didn't watch what I was eating at all. I just ate. After James Jr. was born, I did try to exercise, especially during the summer, but I didn't seem to be able to get the weight off. I would still have some of the cravings I'd had during my pregnancy.

Soon after James was born, I found a note in the laundry room in my building offering to babysit. It was Mrs. Taylor. I called her and arranged to meet her. She came over to visit, and eventually I felt comfortable enough to let her babysit James alone. She had other kids she was babysitting as well. I got to know some of the other mothers. Mrs. Taylor lived in the building next door to mine; they were twin condominium buildings. She had seen me going back and forth with my big belly and thought I was due soon. She had even seen my sister in the parking lot and asked her if I'd had the baby because she hadn't seen my car move. My sister told her that indeed I'd had the baby.

Mrs. Taylor was a big help when I wanted to do something during the day. It got to be a little tiring and boring sitting around watching James Jr. all day. I developed a routine, but I was not the best stay-at-home mom. I missed work and felt that I was losing my professional edge. I tried to keep in touch with what was happening on the job. The president was demoted, and there was a search for a new president. I got involved in the interviewing process a little bit. I was a member of a group called black faculty. There were other black faculty groups on other city college campuses. I had always been a civil rights advocate. I credit the Civil Rights Movement and James Brown's song "Say It Loud, I Am Black & Proud" for helping me understand who I was. I knew I was somebody because I believed in God, but being proud of being black, I'd had problems with as a black girl. As a dark-skinned black girl, you were given the impression that you were ugly at every corner. I guess you could say I didn't believe the "blacker the berry the sweeter the juice" saying until the Civil Rights Movement came about. Not that I was better than anybody, but that I was not to be stepped on just because of the color of my skin. "I was somebody," as Jesse Jackson would later say. The person the black faculty supported won the presidency.

When I returned to work, it seemed impossible to lose the weight. I had so much to do. I had to get James Jr. to the day care and myself to work, pick him up, cook dinner, clean the house, put him to bed—it was a cycle. I didn't seem to find time for myself in the mix. I think I was trying to be supermom. Well, supermom kept the weight on, and as I write this, I am only 8 pounds lighter than I was when James Jr. was born. I was 204 pounds when he was born and went up to 216 pounds before I retired. I never got below 180 after he was born. Whenever, I would lose a pound, I would get so excited that I would eat that pound back on.

We put James Jr. in a day-care center after he was one year of age. It cost about $500 a month. It was so expensive, and it was tempting to let Mrs. Taylor keep him all day; and I think Mrs. Taylor, our babysitter, wanted to keep him, but I wanted him to be around other kids. Mrs. Taylor seemed to get angry with me; and when I would call her to babysit after that, she would turn me down sometimes, and I think it was out of spite.

After I went back to work, James Jr. still had not started to walk. I thought I was going to miss it. I had some classes at night, and then James would babysit. It seemed I would be gone all day. I tried to make sure I didn't have classes at night on the same day I'd had day classes, but sometimes it was inevitable. However, it just so happened that the night James Jr. took his first steps, James and I were both home. He turned a loose from the furniture and walked. He was about a year and three weeks old. I wish I had been able to capture that moment with a video camera, but they had not become popular just yet.

When James Jr. turned two years old, I decided to put him in another day care, one with fewer children. I don't think it was any less expensive. It cost us $500 a month for day care also. I will never forget the first day. He crouched in a corner and cried; I looked through the window on my way out and saw him. I started to go back in there to get him, but I knew he would get used to the place. He finally got used to the new day care.

Soon after I went back to work, the new president had taken office, and my friend Rose suggested that I apply for the director of

Academic Support position. I applied and got the position. I was a little bored with teaching by now anyway. It seemed the new president wanted someone new in that position. Rose had applied for a vice president's position and didn't get it. She was very disappointed because without her help, we didn't think the new president would have gotten his position.

When I became an administrator, my professional circle changed, and I was in the company of people with doctorates or PhD degrees. I started to want the knowledge that they had so I could be more in the conversation. So when James Jr. was four, I applied for a doctoral cohort group with Northern Illinois University and got in. I figured that I could get it out of the way while James Jr. was still young. I figured wrongly, I would later learn. These were developmental years, and there were things I needed to be on top of as his mother. It was much later that I realized that my husband didn't have the background or willingness to pick up the slack. I would have two years of coursework that would take me to Northern's campus once a month for a whole weekend beginning on Friday night and ending around 5:00 p.m. on Sunday. That would mean for two weeks in the month, I would not have a day off. I would essentially be working twelve straight days, sometimes twelve or more hours a day when you consider time for studying and doing homework. It was the most tiring two years of my life. I should say the four years were the most tiring because after I finished the two years of coursework, I still had to do a dissertation. The dissertation took me two years to complete because I switched subjects after I had already completed my first proposal. I switched because someone said that after you completed the dissertation, you would be an expert in that work. I was doing a proposal on GED students' transition into college. I didn't want to work with GED students for the rest of my life, so why become an expert in that field? So I changed to doing something with minority students and their perceptions of racism in college. I knew I would continue to work with minority students.

By the time I graduated from Northern, James Jr. was at the Harvard Elementary School. When he started there in kindergarten, I was already in the doctoral program and super-stressed out, but I tried to do what was necessary as a parent. However, when you are stressed, you are going to miss a lot of things. One of James's teachers had told me that he was too quiet in class and not participating the way he should. One of his teachers at the day-care center had asked me something similar. But I expressed to them both how vocal he was at home and would tell me about his day explicitly, so I was not alarmed that he was not participating in class as much as I should have been because he was so talkative at home. If he had been in a public school, I think they would have noticed his lack of social growth and worked with him; plus, he would have been around more kids. I noticed whenever we entertained the kids from his school at his birthday parties that James did seem to be a little socially awkward and would stick with me often.

He eventually made a friend with a young man called William, but even that friendship was awkward because William was social, and James was not. When other young people were around, he would drop James in a minute. They remained friends until William's family moved to the suburbs, and William left the school. James made no friends in high school. That I understood because most of the kids were white, and the few blacks didn't live in his neighborhood. He made a few friends in college, but nothing substantial. I have friends to this day that I met in kindergarten. Even though we don't see each other daily because we live in different cities, I still consider them friends. Whereas, my son would have a hard time calling anyone a friend. I think this social awkwardness started early on and if we (I) had caught it. We could have done something about it (maybe) with the help of professionals or knowledgeable teachers. It was obvious to me later on that most of the teachers at the private schools were not certified teachers because after the first teacher told me in kindergarten about James's social awkwardness, none of his other teachers mentioned it.

After I became a college administrator, I would take James Jr. to school every day, and his dad would pick him up. I hated this because I knew he would come right home instead of sticking around talking and getting to know the parents and the other kids. There was a playground across the street, so many of the moms and me would take our kids over there after we picked them up. I knew James would not carry on with this activity after a hard day at work, but I had no choice. Now, looking back, I should have made another choice and picked James Jr. up myself.

When James Jr. started to school at the Harvard School, he would often ask to stay late. I thought it was to play with the kids; but later, much later, James said that he noticed that James Jr. would be playing basketball by himself and that he wouldn't play with the other kids. James Jr. said that he wasn't fast enough to play with the other kids. He was the biggest and tallest kid at the time, but he refused to play on their elementary basketball team. The other kids wanted him to play, but he continuously refused. He said that he was uncoordinated, but I think it was because he was afraid of how he looked to the other kids and would be made fun of. My husband could have taken him out to practice basketball on the weekends or in the evenings, but he never did, even after I noticed the problem and begged him to. James Jr. started to pick up weight, and this made things worst. Eventually, I found out that he was gaining weight because my husband was stopping at McDonald's before they came home after school and before dinner, which was often late by this time. My husband refused to stop and continued this cycle behind my back. To this day, James Jr. is overweight, and my husband wonders why!

James Jr. made pretty good grades at Harvard, and I thought he was progressing well. My problem with private schools now is that the grades do not always reflect the child's learning because they do not want to make the parents mad enough to take their kids out of the school. So the grades were more to please the parents and not true tests of the child's academic abilities. If I had to do it all over again, I would never have placed James Jr. in a private school. James Jr. loved Harvard, and I thought he loved the kids as well. He always wanted to stay after school. I think it was more because he was lonely at home and not that he just wanted to be with the kids—because after he graduated from Harvard, he never wanted to see those kids anymore. Some of the kids continued to invite him to parties etc., but he would not go. I would go to be with the parents, and I would have to give excuses for him. My husband and I entertained all kind of reasons as to why our son was a loner. To this day, our son is now in his thirties. At his age, you would expect him to be going out with friends or at least with his girlfriend. But unless you count his internet friends, friends are nonexistent. We decided to stop worrying about it. I do believe he would have developed more social skills if he had went to a public school. Plus, if he did have a problem academically or socially, I think he would have been tested, and my husband and I would have been given some advice as to how to help him.

We really didn't discover how deep the problem was until James Jr. was in high school, when the school psychologist started seeing him. We had to stop this because every time he took him out of class, James would miss an assignment or material, so it was affecting his grades. We took him to see a counselor outside of the school. I think James Jr.'s problems escalated in high school because we sent him to a majority-white parochial school that was all boys and didn't provide any vocational classes or music programs. I think James Jr. needed a more diverse curriculum. When I asked James Jr. if he wanted to change schools, he said no, that he was already used to that school. I should have made the change anyway, just like I should have changed elementary schools.

I should have moved to the suburbs or close to a magnate school. James could not move to the suburbs because his job required that he live in the city. Mine did too, but I was grandfathered in, so I could live anywhere I wanted to. I should have moved, and James should have found another job. Now, looking back, I think it would have been worth it even if it required that I separate from James. With the social problems James Jr. was having, he needed to be in a more congenial neighborhood. In the neighborhood we raised him, people didn't trust one another, so they didn't socialize. Some of the people were transplanted Southerners like myself, and they didn't seem to trust any Northerner. It would be long after James Jr. graduated from high school that I would make more of an attempt to get to know my neighbors. It was after I noticed that the kids were being influenced negatively by gangs. There were gangs of kids always on the streets. Some of them from other neighborhoods, and they started to harass senior citizens on the surrounding blocks. Now I was a senior citizens, and this concerned me desperately. When James Jr. was younger, I never feared for our lives, but now I did.

I should have gotten to know my neighbors earlier; I would have figured out that getting out of the neighborhood was my best option earlier. Most of my neighbors didn't seem to care about working with other people's kids. They figured that they had raised their kids, and other people had to raise their own. When they were raising their kids, Chicago was a different city. Most of them were senior citizens like James and me. I had very little in common with most of them. They didn't want to get involved in the schools, and I most definitely did. I figured so goes the neighborhood, so goes the school. I knew that having a credible school could make a great difference in a child's life. I should have been able to send James to his neighborhood school, so he could get to know the kids in the neighborhood, form friends with kids he could play with on a daily basis. Instead I sent him to school with kids he only saw at school. He never saw them during the summers, not even on the streets. I never had no idea how this would impact James Jr. after he grew up.

I had grown up in a neighborhood with kids I not only went to kindergarten with, I also went to college with. I always had somebody to lean on. James only had James Sr. and me. When we first moved to the neighborhood, we had a neighbor next door that had two kids, but they were older than James and eventually moved away while James was still very young. They tried to keep in touch, but James Jr. was even shy around them after they grew up. It's important to have those connections after you grow up.

Instead of trying to get James Jr. more involved in programs outside of school, when I finished my doctoral program, I tried to get more involved in his school. I became the PTA president, and as a result, I was a nonvoting member of the board. I planned a dance class for the school when James Jr. was in the seventh grade. The kids loved the dance class. James Jr. showed me that he could dance in that class. I think he enjoyed it also. I went to all the programs the school held. I invited the kids to James's birthday parties. James went to sleep overs at one of the kid's home. I tried taking one or two kids to the movies with us. By then, James was vocal about not joining stuff. What I really regret is not joining a church. I tried putting him in Vacation Bible School at the church we visited most often. It didn't work out. It was only for a week. I was at my wits' end with trying to get James involved with other kids.

What I didn't realize was neither my husband nor myself were joiners. We didn't belong to any organized group. We both socialized with people from our jobs and a few people from our past, but most of them were from schools are previous jobs. Most of my friends and James's friend's kids were older than our son. I will say it again: I was at my wits' end. To top it off, my husband came alive when other kids were around. He went out of his way to entertain them, but with his own son he was stiff as a board. I literally begged him to do some things with James, just the two of them; he never, ever did it. When I asked him why he didn't, he would say James Jr. didn't want to go. I think our lack of social skills and social involvement had a double impact on James Jr. and would have an impact on him later on when he tried to find a job. What confused me was James Jr. was so smart; the only area of weakness was, he had no friends. He was a loner, and it disturbed me, and I think it disturbed him as well, though he never said so.

When James Jr. was about six, there was a girl that was several years older than James who would come over sometimes. One day, she and James were riding their bikes around the townhouse complexes, and some guys knocked James off his bike and stole it. It was a brand-new bike, beautiful lime-green bike. I think that was what attracted the guys to the bike. We had just bought the bike, and it cost over $200. It was probably the first time James had ridden it. My husband was sitting on the front steps of our townhouse watching out for James. He saw the group of boys go by, and James was out of sight. James Jr. should never have been out of his sight. He and the neighbor had driven their bikes in the back of our houses, and James Sr. was on the front. James Jr. and the young neighbor came running, with James Jr. crying, to tell us that the boys had stolen his bike. My husband went running after the boys, but by then they had scattered, and the bike was nowhere in sight.

We called the cops, and they came over, and we told them what happened. But the bike was gone for good. James Jr. told me that his dad would drive around the neighborhood when he brought him home from school trying to spot the bike for weeks afterward. It was an expensive bike, really cute; it looked like a motorcycle, so it was rare in those days. I don't really think I have seen another bike like it. James Jr. was never really comfortable living in the neighborhood after that. He started to seclude himself in the house more and more.

James Jr. loved our neighbor Pam's two kids, but they were older than him. Jamal was two years older than James, and Tanisha was, I think, six years older than James. Tanisha would babysit James for us sometimes. They loved James, but they moved before Jamal started high school, and that definitely left a social void in James Jr. life. The people who moved in after him never had any children.

There was one young boy who was younger than James Jr. that I tried to connect him with, but that didn't work out. James Jr. and I went to see *The Nutcracker* ballet with the young boy and his mother. The boy talked and fidgeted throughout the whole ballet. James Jr. complained about his talking, so much so that I had to change seats with him so he could sit by his mother. James Jr. sat there like a little man while the boy couldn't be still. While I was proud of how my son was behaving, so grown up, I was embarrassed at the way this mom's son was behaving. What I didn't know was that both behaviors were inappropriate for six- and five-year-old children. James Jr. was too grown up for his age, and the other child was too hyperactive. That was the end of that attempted connection. I was always concerned about James Jr. because he had older parents. I wanted him to be a kid and do the things that kids did and have fun doing it. The only time he really seemed to have fun was when he was in Louisiana with my nieces and nephews. He would act like a kid then. Then later on, he started acting weird around them too. He stopped having fun with them for some reason.

Around his dad and me, James acted normal. He talked and doted on our attention. I should say *my* attention because most of the time his dad eyes were glued to the television, looking at one nature story after another. At the time, this was my normal. It seemed as if when I was home, I had to be the mom and dad to James Jr. Whenever, I would request James Sr.'s attention with James, it seemed as if he didn't like being interrupted and would be short-tempered with James Jr. instead of compassionate. What I didn't know was that he was acting his normal for him, that he thought it was the mom's responsibility to raise the child(ren) because this was his norm.

I think it may have been the norm in the black family because in my own family, my own mom had been the most vocal in our upbringing. Daddy only got involved when she asked him to or when he observed us fighting or being disrespectful to adults himself. But most of the time he was home, he would be resting in the bed. He was seldom home because if he was most of the time working a full-time job and working on our family farm and serving as a Jitney cab to people in the surrounding areas near the farm. Even though he did not live in Athens now, where our farm was located, he was still one of few people who had a car in the areas, so more than my aunt and uncle (who lived on the farm) depended on him. Whenever, he came home, mostly he crashed. He never asked us how our day went or if we needed anything. I think James Sr. got this same let-me-ignore-them behavior from his father. Unless they did something wrong, then it was beating time. In James's family, they got beatings; and in my family, we got swoopings or spankings. There is a difference. A kid never deserves a beating. I think beatings causes a child to grow up and hate a parent(s) and others. With spankings, kids realize that a parent loves them and wants to teach them right from wrong, and they do not grow up hating their parent(s), unless the spankings are much too often and uncalled for.

Beatings also seemed to make a kid grow up with a lot of mean-ness in their heart and lack of trust and self-aggrandizement. I see that in my husband; it is all about him. If his peace is disturbed in any way, he first goes to meanness; then when he realizes he may be inappropriate, he will calm down. Whereas I go to calm first; and then much, much later, when I realize there is a reason for me being upset, I go into my anger mode. But even when I am angry, I am in control. Whereas if my husband never gets to the calm mode, he is angry without control, and the good thing is most of the time he doesn't lash out. With me, he leaves the room when he is angry. However, after our son grew up, he started lashing out when he was angry with him. I had to threaten to call the police in order to get him to stop. After our son grew up, I knew he was going to pick up some of James's bad behavior. I am thankful that he never lashes out though. I wonder, though, if he will lash out at his own children. There are two holes in the walls of our house: one from my husband and the other from my son. I am grateful neither ever lashed out at me. If they had, it would have been time for me to go or them.

My husband was also accustomed to fighting with his father. He and his brothers often got into fights with their father. In my family, we knew not to hit one of our parents. We just stood there and took our spankings because we knew if would have gone on much longer if we moved. I don't want to think about what might have happened if we had hit one of our parents. The worst part about getting a spanking in my family was listening to our parents' mouths for hours afterward. We got into fights as kids, but either another kid or our parents would break it up. But we never thought of lashing out at our parents.

I don't remember James Jr. getting into any fights with other kids ever. After Tanisha and Jamal moved away, James Jr. very seldom ventured outside. I remember when he was a teenager we had a block party, and I asked him to come to it. He came for a few minutes and seemed uncomfortable, and as soon as possible, he went back home.

James Jr. did get invited to one party when he was in high school. He left the house going to the party and had a flat tire outside of the house and called for his dad to come help him with the flat. He never did go inside of the house. The invitation came from a black kid at his school, and I am sure he didn't know him well. James Jr. seemed to be scared to death to go to the party. He did not like being in the company of people he did not know. I think his dad felt uncomfortable as well because whenever we'd go to parties and there were people we didn't know that well, if he could corner one of them, he would talk incessantly about himself. Later on, I would ask him who was the person, and he wouldn't even know their name or anything else about them. I think this was nervous behavior that he exhibited all the time. Every conversation always started and ended with him talking about how mean his father was, even with total strangers. We didn't have that many parties ourselves, so our invitations to parties got scarce as we got older.

James had nieces and nephews that were all older than James. I would get his niece that was closest in age to James and bring her over to play with James sometimes. It was obvious they had very little in common. The last time she came over, she broke a toy riding truck that we had bought James for Christmas. James Jr. probably only had driven the toy truck that was battery-operated one time prior to that. It was too expensive to get the truck fixed, so it went in the garbage. James Jr. always objected to my inviting her over after that.

James Jr. really had a hard time in high school. He had a hard time bonding with the black and white guys. He didn't talk to anyone that didn't talk to him. I am sure he seemed standoffish, so very few boys approached him. When it came to the prom, he didn't know any young lady to invite, so a friend said he knew of a young lady and would ask her parents. We went out to meet her and her parents. Both the parents were there, but we found out later that they were either getting a divorce or were divorced already. James Jr. didn't say a word while we visited. He sat still like a stone. I was so embarrassed, but the parents still allowed their daughter to go the prom.

James Jr. was friendly with one other guys at school. I think the guy felt sorry for James Jr. I am not sure how it came about, but he and James Jr. shared a limousine to the prom with their dates. The guy later reported to me that James Jr. hardly said a word in the limousine or at the prom. The guy felt sorry for James Jr.'s date, so he invited her to dance one time. The young lady was very pretty, and I'd hoped against hope that James would talk and dance with her. By then, he had participated in a beautillion, so he knew how to dance.

When James Jr. was a senior, the beautillion was my last effort to help him to become more sociable. A suburban chapter of the Alpha Phi Alpha fraternity held a beautillion every year. One of my coworkers' sons had been in it. I had been lamenting to her about my son's lack of social skills. Against his wishes, I placed James Jr. in the beautillion. The first day we went to practice in the suburbs, James

Jr. left the gymnasium headed back to Chicago, walking. One of the Alphas went after him and talked him into coming back. I think he and we should have let him walk back home; I think that would have been the best lesson.

What really surprised me about James Jr. participating in the beautillion was that he seemed to catch on to all of the dances. He was really good at it. He didn't look awkward or weird. We didn't have a young lady for James Jr. to partner with, so the Alphas assigned one to him. They had a list of young ladies who had shown an interest in participating in the beautillion as dance partners for the young men. The beautillion was for young men primarily, and cotillions were for the girls. James Jr. seemed to like the dancing, but even after practicing for about sixteen weeks, he didn't feel comfortable with any of the boys or girls. He would go off into a corner by himself when it was break time or snack time. He wouldn't eat at all, just to avoid the other kids and their parents. The parents took turns in volunteering to bring the snacks. When we were responsible for the food, James Jr. still didn't eat. I began to wonder if there were deeper problems with James Jr. than lack of social skills.

The beautillion was a beautiful event. All of us got a chance to participate in the program. I got the chance to dance with my son and my husband. My husband got a chance to participate in a manhood ceremony with our son. We invited relatives and friends. They were all proud of how James Jr. participated. I was afraid that he would run off the stage or not go on the stage with all the people in the audience, but he seemed to like being the center of attention.

After the beautillion was over, James Jr. complained about me putting him in it, but internally I think he was happy that he did participate. It's been over many years ago now, and he still mentions it every once in a while. When I was a teenager, I was so disappointed when I didn't get chosen to participate in a cotillion when most of my friends did. Of course, I thought it was because I was not pretty. But then I didn't think my friends were that pretty either. I think it had more to do with skin color; none of them were as dark as me. I wonder if that is why I pushed so hard for James Jr. to be in the cotillion—to live my own dreams. But whether or not it was, it was a good experience for all of us.

I've noticed that I keep saying my son, my friends, etc. Even though James Sr. was raised in Chicago and had relatives here, he really knew very few people. He really didn't trust his family members to babysit more than me. I knew more people than he did. Most of the people I knew I met through work. As a construction worker, James's jobs had very few black people. James only had a few friends when we got married, and soon after that, he stopped socializing with them or them with him because he became more of a homebody. His best friend was an alcoholic and a construction worker. He was married when we got married, and we had socialized several times with him and his wife. I kind of based our potential as a married couple on them because she was a teacher (public school) and he was a construction worker. I was a teacher (college) and James was a construction worker.

Unfortunately, they divorced soon after James and I got married. We didn't have them as role models any more. I started to realize after having my baby that James's social circle was very small. Plus, in raising James Jr., my husband referred to me often. Later in years, James would often say, "With all that you do for James Jr., why does he treat you like that?" I guess I came to think of our son as *my* son with James's absence in decision-making, discipline, etc. when it came to James Jr. I think it was because he didn't like his own role models, his own parents. It was obvious he hated, absolutely hated, his father; and even though he loved his mother, he didn't respect her job as the mother of the family. He thought she did a poor job most of the time; she always acquiesced to the father. It was obvious she was afraid of him. That on top of getting beaten constantly left her with post-traumatic stress syndrome (PTSD).

James had no idea how to discipline James Jr., I discovered. I remember one afternoon I decided to show James what I thought was one of the proper ways to discipline a child. I had James Jr. sit down on the bed because by now he was taller than either James or me. I had him extend his hand, and I proceeded to spank his hand with a ruler. He kept jumping as if the ruler was killing him. James

Sr. noticed how disturbed James had gotten just by spanking him on his hand. I don't remember us ever having to discipline James Jr. again after that demonstration. I don't think my husband liked the idea anyway since he was not used to it. I think he thought it was sissified. Well, his way may not have been sissified, but it could cause someone to get killed or mentally ruined for life (like a.k.a. James Sr. and his siblings) and end up hating your father for life.

Before this demonstration of spanking, the two times I saw him drag my son down the stairs and the two of them wrestling on the floor still disturbs me. Our son was giving as good as he got; he was not allowing himself to be beaten. When I asked my husband why he was fighting James Jr. like that, he said he had to get his bluff in. "I didn't want James Jr. to think he could beat me." I told him this was not a competition; parents should always be in charge, or the kids should find another place to live. James Jr. was not going anywhere, so there was no need to fight.

When James Jr. started his senior year, I decided to stop working and retire from my job because it was too far from home, and I was getting home later and later. Plus, I was so scared James Jr. would not graduate. It didn't dawn on me that not graduating might have been what he needed to jump-start himself. I have a niece who didn't get the chance to graduate with her class in high school, and she now has two master's degrees. I took off so that I could work with James. Even with all of that sacrifice, he still only barely made the grade so he could graduate.

We decided to have a graduation party for James Jr. We served the food outside and all of the neighbors came over. All the young people could talk about was the limousine that James Jr. had for his prom. They wanted one just like it for their prom. I think seeing what we did for James for his graduation, made quite a few young men in our neighborhood, who were probably being courted by gangs to stay in school and graduate.

James Jr. had applied to several colleges. We selected Hampton University for him to go to primarily because it was the farthest distance from home. James and I thought with him going away from home and being on his own that he would get a chance to grow up.

He didn't. I want go into it, but it seemed like James was on his cell phone calling me every hour of the day. He complained about everything. Eventually, he flunked out (purposely) and came home. He started to go to school online and eventually got his associate's degree. He took one baccalaureate course online and decided that was too hard, and he'd rather go face-to-face. So he enrolled in Chicago State University.

When he first went to college, he'd wanted to major in computer science. He had issues with calculus and programming and changed his mind. He decided to major in radio and TV production when he enrolled in Chicago State. Later he told me he did it because he thought it would be easy. After he graduated with his BS, he never found a job in his field. He did work part-time for the college for a while. He started looking for a full-time job after we gave him an ultimatum.

At the present time, he is still at home, still uncertain about his future. I have decided his main problem was his parents and their lack of knowledge of child rearing. Whatever we lack though, we did our best. I am certain of one thing: some people should not wait too late in life to have children. Wanting to have a child is not a good enough reason to have a child. You need to be dedicated to that child early on. I also think one parent should be home with that child until they no longer see the need to do so. Building confidence in that child with good social and emotional skills is crucial to his or her development. If I had it to do all over again, I would never have gone back to work after James Jr. was born until he was in high school or even college. Being a parent is not a part-time job if your child-rearing skills are limited, and ours were. I definitely would have moved to a more child-friendly neighborhood with quality schools. Plus, if James Sr. still refused to grow and learn to develop his skills as a parent and I didn't divorce him, we should have put our son either in a boarding school or found male-mentoring groups to put him in for his own maturity as a male. After James Jr. graduated from college, I had the feeling that James was jealous of him and didn't want him to make more money than he did; and that, I believe, was the reason he never gave James advice. I'd often hear him giving other young people advice but seldom his own son. I know James was proud of James Jr., but he just didn't know how to show his support anyway other than being the provider.

James and I both needed parenting-skills training classes. We both grew up in dysfunctional homes. Our saving grace was that we were good people and wanted the best for our son, but we had faults and a lack of knowledge about raising a child. Even with all our faults as parents, we seemed to have raised a respectful son with high self-esteem, and for that we are grateful. I recently asked James Jr. on a scale of one to ten, with ten being the highest, how he would rank us as parents. I was surprised and thankful when he said, "Ten." We must have done something right.

Chapter 9

WORLD OF
WORK PART II

Dean Witter/Morgan Stanley
Dean Witter (1997–1999)

The summer after losing my job at Kennedy-King College, I felt horrible and gained so much weight. Initially, I guess I went through a grieving phase. My sister Bobbie and my cousin Elsie came to town. I enjoyed entertaining them for a few weeks. They helped to keep my mine distracted from my problems. After I lost my job at Kennedy-King, I was so devastated and gained a lot of weight over the summer of 1997.

When I was essentially fired from Kennedy-King College, I went to work for Dean Witter as a stock broker trainee and eventually became a stock broker or financial adviser. I had always wanted to know more about stocks and bonds because I believed unless you owned a business that was successful, you were not going to get rich or achieve financial serenity unless you made some wise decisions in the market.

I saw an ad in the newspaper where Dean Witter was looking for applicants. I applied and was hired. I was hired because I was a former college professor and a member of a union, and they thought

I could entice my former colleagues to invest with the company. I was not able to get one of them to invest. I really didn't try too hard to get them to invest because I was still feeling bad about my termination. Also, I must have been one of the first tenured professors fired, and I was embarrassed. My goal at Dean Witter was to learn as much about investing as I could so I could have an influence on my son. My parents never said anything about investing in stocks in our home. They didn't have a clue or money to invest. However, my mom paid her tithes to the church every month, and this was 10 percent of her monthly income. My mom made $25 a week or $100 a month, so her tithes would have been $10 every month. Now, if she had saved another 10 percent for a year to invest, by the end of the year, she would have had $120. By the end of ten years, she would have had $1,200. She could have purchased stocks with that money at any time. If she had invested in Walmart just with only $1,200, I dare say we would have been out of poverty at some time. That would have meant she would have had $20 a week or $80 a month to spend. That would have been extremely hard for a family of ten. My dad's income was $100 a week or $400 a month. We would have had a total of $480 a month to live off of.

Dean Witter was located downtown Chicago in the finance district. I had to work in the Dean Witter offices on the twenty-fourth floor, and by now I was afraid of heights. Sometimes I would get so anxious I would have to go in the bathroom to calm down. They didn't have that many female brokers, so the bathroom was quiet. I struggled every day while I was on that floor. Once I got on the floor, I would very seldom go out for lunch because being in the area with all those high-rises caused me so much anxiety. One time, I tried to go do some shopping and got so anxious that I had to run back to the building.

Working at Dean Witter was a new world to me. I had come from working most of my life and going to school most of my life with blacks, and now I was with mostly whites, young white men at that.

At the end of the summer, I was hired as a financial advisor by Dean Witter. Dean Witter soon merged with Morgan Stanley and became Morgan Stanley Dean Witter. This was a far cry from being a college teacher or a college administrator. I figured I would never pass the Series 7 exam they required to become a licensed stock broker, so I would just stick around as long as I could and learn as much as I could. I think I received a small stipend, which probably didn't pay for my parking every day. But I wanted to learn more about stocks and bonds, and this was a way to do. I knew working for the man, you would never get rich. You needed to invest in the market.

For the first three or four months with Dean Witter, all I did was study for the Series 7 exam and get to know all the workings of all the departments. Plus, I got to work with some of their prolific brokers. But most of my days and nights (at home) were spent studying for the exam. I was intrigued by this new way of studying; after all, I had a doctorate in adult education. We had a book that had chapters of lecture material, tests, and answer sheets. So primarily, you were to read the lecture information, then take the tests and score them. If you didn't make 90 percent or above, you did it all over again until you scored at least 90 percent on the test at the end of each chapter.

At the end of the book, there was a test that was supposed to resemble the Series 7 examination. You were supposed to take it until you scored at least 90 percent or better. It also had an answer sheet. I think I scored my first 90 percent a few days before I was scheduled to take the Series 7 exam. I felt confident that I would pass the test then. There were three other people studying for the exam with me. They were three white men. They were surprisingly mature men. They all were familiar with the market and had invested before. I was the only black and the only neophyte. There were other black stock brokers at the company that were on my floor. Most of them were new to the business as well, and by the time I took the exam, some of them were gone.

Before we took the exam, one of the white men decided it wasn't worth it. So on the day I took the exam, the other two men I had been studying with and another broker with a degree in finance but yet to pass the Series 7 exam took the exam with me. The funny thing about this exam: you found out immediately whether you passed it or not. I think you had to make 70 percent or better to pass. I think

I made 75% percent and passed. I was ecstatic. I couldn't believe I had passed. But then I had used the test taking skills they suggested together with the one's I had learned from the material I had bought for students when I was director of Academic Support Services at Kennedy-King and those I had used all of my life. Only one of the other Dean Witter candidates passed the exam that day. You could tell they didn't pass because they didn't come back to the office. I knew they were devastated, especially the one with the degree in finance. It was not just your knowledge of finance that you needed to pass the Series 7 or any of the subsequent exams that I took; it was your test-taking abilities. I passed all the required tests the first time around.

After I passed the Series 7, the next step was to go to New York for three weeks. James would stay home and take care of James Jr. On the morning I was supposed to leave for New York, the white guy who also passed the exam called me to let me know he was not going to New York. He had been talking like he didn't think becoming a broker was worth it. He already had a seat on the Chicago Board of Trade (I believe). He said it was going to take too long to make any real money, and he had a family. He seemed afraid that his wife was going to leave him if he didn't start to make money soon. I told him that his wife loved him, and she wouldn't leave him. He said he lived in Northbrook, Illinois, and he had seen a lot of men lose their money or get fired from their lucrative jobs, and then their wives left them. The wives wanted to be kept in a certain way, love or not. It seemed love went out the window with the money. He was afraid his wife would do the same thing. He had just taken his whole family to Hawaii on vacation, and that was the type of lifestyle he thought she wanted, not what they now call staycation, where you vacation in your own home. She wanted to be able to go on trips with her girlfriends whenever she felt like it.

I couldn't help but wonder if all white women were like that. If so, they were totally different from black women in my circle. When my husband was laid off from his job, I picked up the slack and thought nothing of it. I never even entertained the idea of leaving him because of his on-and-off job status. So here I was headed to New York by myself. I had been once before with my husband, James, for a workshop on computers in food service. A trip that I paid for with my own money to get ahead of the game in my field (food service management) because City College didn't pay for faculty members to attend conferences at the time. I thought this was stupid because you should want faculty to keep up with the trends in their field so they could pass the information on to their students so they would be prepared for the job market.

Now, my trip was being sponsored by Dean Witter. I could have flown, but by then I was afraid of flying, so I took the train. I took the train from Chicago to Washington, DC, and then another train to New York. The train from Chicago to Washington, DC, was the nicest I had ever ridden on. I surmised it was because some US senators and representatives took that same train on a regular basis. The food was great. I couldn't help but remember my trips on the train when I traveled between Minden and Baton Rouge all those years for college. The one or two times I had money to spend on food on the train; the food had been fresh and tasted great. Years later when I took the train, the food was not that great. I was so disappointed. But on the trip between Chicago and Washington, DC, it was great again.

My train arrived in the train station in New York, and I was immediately thrust into the hustle and bustle of New York. I took a taxi to the hotel, which was only a few blocks away from where I was to go to classes every day at the Two World Trade Center. On the first day of class, I looked around, and I was one of only a few blacks in the room. We were on the ninety-sixth floor (I think) of the World Trade Center; I am not sure which tower. I was seated near a window. I could see the airplanes flying by. I kept thinking one of those planes could fly into the building. Years later (September 11, 2001), two planes would fly into each of the towers, killing all the people on the planes and many people in the buildings and on the ground. I couldn't help but wonder if some of the brokers I had met during my three weeks in New York had been among the dead. I had not kept in touch with any of them because by then I had changed professions.

I don't think I had ever been as scared as I was sitting in that classroom every day trying to listen to what the presenters were saying on investing in the market. I made it through those three weeks. I got to know several of the blacks and some of the whites that were there. I met one young lady from Cleveland, and we kept in touch until I left the Morgan Stanley Dean Witter. One thing that I noticed while I was in New York was that the traders dressed better than the brokers. I figured I had chosen the wrong field. I calmed myself down because I knew the job was only temporary because at fifty years of age, I was a neophyte in a market flooded with young people who had time to invest with few commitments. I had a family who counted on me. A family still in shock that my monthly income was missing and the bills (mostly credit card bills I had incurred) were not being paid in a timely fashion as before. I knew from the start that my days were numbered. I just wanted to learn as much as I could about investing.

While I was in New York, I was too scared to venture out by myself at night, so most nights were spent studying in my hotel room. My friend Cynthia Pittman (a mom I had met at the Harvard School and a mom of James Jr.'s friend, Williams) came to New York one weekend to shop. She and I went to a play and out to dinner. She took me to Harlem, and we had dinner at a soul food restaurant packed with white people called Sylvia's. I had liver and onions, greens, corn bread, candied yams, and it was all very good. I knew while the place was packed, the food was some of the best I'd had— and Chicago had a lot of soul food restaurants on the south side that I frequented. Cynthia and I had taken the train to Harlem. I got the chance to see the Apollo Theater—at the time, it was empty and looked a little run down. I'd heard a lot about Harlem, all negative, but I was impressed with the buildings. It didn't give me the impression of being a ghetto like it had been portrayed on television.

Cynthia had been to New York with her mother when she was much younger. She said her mother would take her and her siblings to New York on shopping trips. Cynthia's parents owned Carter's Funeral Home in Chicago; it was not too far from where I lived. Later, I would go there for one of James nephew's funeral. Cynthia and the rest of her family worked at the funeral home. I got the chance to go to B. Smith's restaurant as well in New York. B. Smith had been a supermodel and then a restauranteur. She was very popular. I often saw her on television. I eventually bought one of her cookbooks.

Over the course of the three weeks, I learned how to invest and how to market the investment vehicles (stocks, bonds, insurance, etc.). I wished I had been younger learning all of this stuff. But at an earlier age, I had never even entertained the idea of being a stock broker or financial advisor. Growing up, you never know what life is going to throw at you. I never dreamed of being a college professor or administrator either. When I think of it, I never dreamed of a career period. Maybe that is why I had so many twists and turns. Growing up, I really didn't know what I wanted to be so I grabbed the first straw that was handed to me, something familiar like teaching. But what I believe God was guiding me toward was business all along. I used to sell anything that wasn't tied down to make some money when I was growing up. I just thought it was due to necessity, not a vocation.

Now that I had learned how to invest, I didn't have the money to invest. I kept the job about eighteen months, passed the tests I needed to keep the job, but didn't get enough investors or money. I needed a millionaire relative whose money I could bring to the company and monitor his/her money while making money myself off the portfolio. Eventually, if I stayed long enough, I would inherit some accounts that would eventually bring in money as well. But alas, all of my relatives were poor, at least didn't have the kind of money or trust in me that I needed. I was fired after eighteen months. It was a whirlwind of eighteen months, however. I got the chance to experience life as a Fortune 500 company employee. It was totally different from working with a public agency where your promotions were based on who you knew or who you could impress. In the private world, your promotion was centered on *money*. If you brought investors into the company and increased the bottom line of the company, you got promoted. Your looks or who you knew had very little to do with it in the long run. I had always felt at Kennedy-King that I had been judged on my looks and not on how hard I worked or my education.

What I didn't like about the financial-advisor job at Morgan Stanley was the cold calling. You were really expected to call people and get total strangers to invest money with you. Some people called the company because they wanted to invest. You were lucky if you got some of those calls because you could convince them to invest with you (these were called warm calls because they already wanted to invest). Also, sometimes when brokers left the firm, you were given their clients. Several clients showed up in my account without my knowledge. They were always small clients, never big clients.

I was able to stay at the company for eighteen months because I met a black guy in the hallway who told me he was applying for a job there as well. He said his father-in-law had money to invest, and he wanted someone to hold it for him until he became a broker. I said I would do it, and just like that, I had $225,000 put into my account. I was told what to invest it in, and it was all mutual funds. Because of that, I had the largest mutual fund sales for the year for my branch. I got to go on a special trip for winners to Colorado Springs, Colorado. I had a ball at the resort they took us to. The food was great. We went on tours during the day. I had never been to Colorado before. I wish I had splurged and brought James with me. I slept in that big Queen Ann bed by myself. I had to jump up to get into the bed. The resort had a theater, golf courses, shopping stores, etc. It was amazing. I got just a glimpse of the life of people who worked for Fortune 500 companies. I could see how one could get used to this life and would be encouraged to work hard. Working hard at jobs I'd had before didn't entitle you to anything. I needed to be at a company where hard work paid off.

Triton College (2000–2003)

After I left Morgan Stanley Dean Witter—these two companies merged while I was working there—my sister Dorothy Brown had finished law school and decided she wanted to be a politician. I was so shocked when she chose this profession, especially having a political career in Chicago with its history of dirty politics and her being a devout Christian. But she was intent, so I had to help her because now she was divorced; and her daughter, I believe, was in college in another state at the time. I was her only relative in Chicago. I got a friend of mine, Barbara Parker, to volunteer as well. Barbara was attracted to volunteer because she was an accountant, and my sister Dorothy was a CPA (certified public accountant), MBA (master's in business administration), and a lawyer. Barbara was so impressed with my sister because she was an accountant herself.

Dorothy was running for treasurer at this time, but she didn't win. She made a good showing even though the Democratic Party and PUSH (People United to Save Humanity) didn't support her. So later someone would talk her into running for the clerk of the Circuit Court of Cook County. I helped her again as much as I could but I had a full-time job by the time. She won this election, even though the Democratic Party did not support her again. Everyone was impressed with her ability to win without the party's support because I don't think any Democratic candidate had ever won without their support.

I applied to work at Triton College. It was about twenty-five miles from my home and was also a community college. However, it was an independent community college and not a part of a system. I had to go through so many interviews, including a group interview. I accepted the position at Triton for half the amount of money I had made at Kennedy-King when I left. Hindsight, I should have continued to look for something that paid more money even if it was not in education or even if I had to leave the state. I let my husband's career trump mine, so mine just went into the toilet. I liked higher education, so I should have pursued a better-paying job in that arena, even if it was in another state. Now, looking back, I could have even trained to be a public school principal. That is something that I really think I would have been good at. I just didn't know.

I started to work at Triton, initially as the assistant dean of Health Careers and then later as the associate dean of Health Careers. Shortly after I took the position of assistant dean, the president had a heart attack, and the dean of Health Careers was moved up the vice president of the college, and one of the vice presidents was moved up to president. I was hoping I would move up to dean of Health Careers. I knew I had not been at Triton that long, but I was hoping; the job didn't seem that hard. Instead, they decided to combine two departments and make the current dean of the other department dean of Health Careers as well. I was moved up to associate dean. Later on, that dean told me I didn't get the deanship because the former dean, now vice president, said that I didn't have executive functioning skills and that I couldn't juggle two things at one time. He told me he couldn't understand that because he had witnessed me handling several jobs at one time. I really didn't know what she meant either but later found out that it had to do something with organization. Her office was neat, very neat, always neat, whereas my desk would start out neat in the morning and would look disheveled by the end of the day. I made an effort to be more organized, but it was hard for me. No one complained about that I was slacking on the job, though. I always got my work done and on time.

Another administrator that I had befriended did get promoted to vice president, but they did not allow her to move to the administrative wing. I think it had something to do with her lack of organization. Her office looked like a train wreck, but like me, she knew where everything was. She too got more than her share of work done and brought in a lot of money to the college through grants. She was allowed to stay in her office and not move. She didn't seem to have a problem with not moving to the administrative wing.

Having a neat desk seem to be a requirement for becoming an upper-level college administrator, probably not only at Triton but other colleges as well, remembering how neat the administrators' desk were at Kennedy-King. It seemed that counted more than getting work done. It didn't make sense to me, but I wished somebody had told me how important it was; then I may have made it a priority to become more organized and not just hide my junk when people came to my office. Evidently, I was not born as a good organizer. I even had a hard time keeping my house organized. If I had not worked hard at it, it would have been extremely junky. I just didn't like a junky house. My husband was no help; he seemed to like his stuff junky. Two junky people should not get married. James kept his clothes neat, but paperwork was another story.

Triton College was frustrating because I felt I was deliberately being overlooked for promotions, but then again, I hadn't been at the institution that long. I quit Triton after three years because I was tired of the commute and getting home so late at night. Plus, I was not sure my son was going to graduate from high school. His grades his junior year were not the best. I would get home late at night and tired; often James Jr. would need help with his homework. His dad had been too busy cooking dinner for us to help James Jr., or he didn't know how. It seemed James Jr. would sleep or play video games until I got home and then start in on his homework, needing help from supertired me. His grades were mostly Cs. He didn't flunk anything, but that was probably purposeful because the parochial school wanted the parents' money. I decided my first job was to be a good parent; plus, I didn't see any future for me at Triton with its current administration. So I was fifty-six years old with twenty-five years of pension, and decided to retire and take a year off to monitor James Jr.'s grades. I was desperate for him to graduate on time, as if I would have been a failure as a parent if he had failed.

I took the whole year off and started to participate in school activities that the Mt. Carmel High School mothers' club held. I had always gone to meetings in the evening, but did not have the time to help out during the day at school when the mothers planned activities such as bake sales, teachers luncheons, etc., but now I did. James's grades improved some, but not at the B or A level as I'd hoped. I decided he was just an average student, which surprised me because early on, he seemed like he was very studious while in elementary school. He may have had a learning disability that was not diagnosed. Sometimes he seemed like he liked his school, and then other times he didn't. He definitely had trouble making friends. James Sr. and I thought that had to do with the fact he was in a majority-white high school, and none of the kids, black or white, lived in our community.

The counselor had been trying to get James Jr. to apply to colleges. He finally did and was accepted at Hampton University in Virginia conditionally. He had to go to summer school and maintain a B average. We were happy that he had been accepted at Hampton. We were still scared that he wasn't going to graduate, though. We didn't find out until the Friday before graduation that he was graduating and marching on Sunday. He came home with his graduation cap and gown. I figured taking the year off to help him was the thing to do.

After James Jr. started at Hampton University, the fall of 2004, I went to Roosevelt University to take a course in event planning. I had decided to try my hand at event planning since I'd planned events with my students at Kennedy-King College—maybe I could do it for a living. My plan was to start my own business. After taking the class, I decided to start my own reunion-planning business. I worked very hard to make a success of my company, but it went under because of my lack of experience and not having more hands. James and James Jr. couldn't help me, and I had no money to hire anyone to help me; so the business, along with much of my retirement money, went by the wayside.

I applied for several jobs, but now I was about sixty years of age, and I guess over the hill. I started to get involved in activities in community after my neighbor's son was killed and found more turmoil than I had planned, so I decided to take a step back and figure out my next move.

In 2006, my sister Dorothy decided to run for mayor of Chicago. I couldn't believe it. Our uncle J. D. Hampton, my mother's brother, had run for mayor of our small segregated and racist hometown, Minden, LA. He was the first—and I believe to this date—black person to do so. I was home from college that summer and participated in the Civil Rights Movement in our small town. My uncle J. D. had been one of the leaders of the movement. He was very vocal, and I believe that was the reason the CORE volunteers had talked him into running. The main goal was voter registration. It seemed very few black people in our town voted, mostly because they didn't think their vote would count and a racist white person would win anyway. They may have been scared to do so as well. I don't know if they had to answer awkward questions or not. My parents had always voted and they never complained about it.

Uncle J. D.'s candidacy accomplished what it was supposed to, there had never been that many black people voting before. However, after the election, Uncle J. D. had a hard time finding a job whenever he was laid off. He eventually opened his own business, and I was surprised that black people didn't frequent it, so he eventually had to close it. Black people seemed to avoid him, and I believe he lost some friends. I believe blacks were scared to be associated with him after he ran for mayor, afraid the white people would be angry or losing their jobs as well. Uncle J. D. had to be strong to run; his life was threatened and his family's as well. My father and other black men with guns would hide in the bushes across the street from Uncle J. D.'s house to protect him and his family. The NAACP chapter in Minden finally honored Uncle J. D.; unfortunately, it was only a few weeks before he died. He had been in his thirties when he ran for mayor and now he was eighty-plus years old I believe.

I could see where my sister Dorothy (BS, MBA, JD) got her strength because she had to run against Mayor Daley and the Democratic Party in Chicago. Plus, she wasn't a native Chicagoan. The girl had guts and wasn't born with a silver spoon. She didn't win, but she kept her position as clerk of the circuit court of Cook County (an elective position) even when she was not supported by the Democratic Party for twenty years. She is an excellent role model, and hopefully, we all are for Rabb descendants and others.

Chapter 10

THE END

Enlightenment

It's been a long time since Bobbie and I walked obediently in that moonlit night with our mom to the outhouse together. I had no idea at the time how lucky we were to have married parents living on a farm that their family owned, especially a praying mother, and who were both what you would call servant-leaders. Servant-leaders to me are persons who see a need and answer the call. Both my parents did just that time and time again. My mother stepping up to the plate when she realized that her church did not offer what her children needed and what they were used to because she didn't want them to be bored. She stepped up to the plate and became Sunday school superintendent and started to offer programs she knew her children loved and needed to grow into healthy human beings.

My dad, because his own brothers left for war and left just him and two handicapped siblings on the farm, stepped up to the plate and provided the physical labor that was needed to feed not only their families but his own. After his brothers left the farm and went off to war or just left the state of Louisiana, my father was determined to make a living with the farm. In the end, though, he was only able to feed his family and the families of his two siblings that still lived on the farm. One thing for sure: we never went hungry too long with two inventive parents—our dad with his desire to feed us from the land, and our mom with her knack for coming up with meals when the shelves in the kitchen were bare. Our dad also provided much-needed transportation to town for the local citizenry. They both quietly led their varied communities (church, job, neighborhood, family, etc.) without asking for anything in return. Our dad became his union's grievance chair and a deacon in St. John Baptist Church and my mom supervisor of most kitchens she worked in and Sunday school superintendent at Spring Lake Church of God in Christ. I doubt they even got a thank-you at times, but didn't expect it either.

I remember in their later years when my mom and dad both were ill, and these two hardworking people were home all day, each in a different bed and a different room; and no one called, not even the Christian neighbors, whom my mom had lured to Christ, would stop by to visit them. My mom had given her all to the church for years; I was amazed that the sisters didn't call her just to see if she was okay. The church didn't have a benevolent committee like larger churches. I think the minister was expected to do the calling on the sick. When she could muster up the energy, my mom would call them. The only calls she got on a regular basis besides those from her children were from her oldest sister Elnora. I've never been more grateful for a human being than my Aunt Elnora. This woman was a Stallworth in our family. If you were sick, she would offer to help. When she got off work, often she would have her white boss drop her off at our house so she could clean our house (after cleaning her boss's house) because she knew my mom was sick and needed the help. She not only did this for my mom but for any of her siblings who needed help. Without Elnora's visits and calls, my mom's last days, I am, sure would have been extremely lonely.

My dad never got any calls or visitors. He would often complain that I didn't ask to speak to him when I called home. I started to make sure that I spoke with him, even though it would be more of a one-way conversation. Neither of our parents was healthy in their last days, but I think they knew they were loved by so many people, especially their eight children. Children they had raised to have high morals and values, unbelievable courage, and above all, a strong belief in God as their savior and protector.

Like I said, growing up, I had no idea of our background as descendants of slaves until high school, who may have been royalty in their African country, who were either stolen or sold by other Africans into slavery against their wishes (I found out after moving to Chicago). Later, much later, I found out that not all African Americans living in the US had a history of slavery in their backgrounds, that some were always free after their ancestors landed in America. But we are all black and subject to the same prejudices and discriminatory practices. Our parents never talked much about their upbringing initially. Most of what we learned came from their relatives. Another thing I know for sure: my siblings and I, even after our grandparents and parents passed away, still felt secure after having been reared by them. It's hard to tell anyone just how that feels, but it is something most children relish. Having a sound foundation gives children confidence when the ground is really shaky so they can have the fortitude to persevere even when things seem hopeless and to know innately that there is always hope and someone praying for them even in heaven.

James and I are both, I'd say, introverted, and that kept us from joining small and large organizations that we could have learned from and grew as individuals. Because we concentrated on work, that did not encourage our growth as individuals. We have labored often and felt oppressed in our jobs. I urge young African Americans to join organizations (church, fraternities, sororities, clubs, community organizations, professional, etc.), run for leadership positions, be observant, and not leave the organizations when you get defeated in some form or fashion. Learn how to overcome issues and move forward. I also urge you to seek a mentor early on in your career. Seek a mentor that you feel will guide you in your professional endeavors. Set goals in life, personal and professional, for yourself and your family. Seek a partner that shares in these goals. Above all, know yourself and your ideals and don't sway too far from them.

What I am most proud of is that my parents raised us in the church. Something, unfortunately, I failed to do for my own son, not for the lack of trying. Eventually, I came to the realization that I couldn't find Spring Lake Church of God in Christ in Chicago, a small-town church. I should have been more dedicated to leaving Chicago or paving my own road in Chicago. Listening to our son talk and the behavior he exhibits, my husband and I are grateful that we have been able to pass down to him strong morals and values that we both learned, me from my parents, church, and school, and him from his grandmother and school. We both knew that we were black, and for that purpose alone, we would face discrimination. But we also knew that with hard work, we could persevere, James as an journeyman ironworker (where he was called the n-word often in his training) and me as a public health nutritionist, college professor/administrator, financial advisor, sole proprietor, community activist, and servant-leader. What neither of us knew is that because of our race, America, or at least academia America, had labeled us as being "at risk." I wish I had come to understand what that meant earlier; then I would have believed that hard work on our parts would probably lead to high blood pressure, diabetes, etc., which could be detrimental to us not living a long life. That's not to say that James and I did not enjoy our lives somewhat, but our later years has been fraught with financial problems, which could have been prevented if we'd been born with silver spoons in our mouths—silver spoons that, in virtue of our births in this country, we were doomed not to have.

I was in one of my classes while I was getting my doctoral degree when I realized that James and I were both labeled "at risk" in general because we were both born poor and black—and me furthermore because my parents were uneducated, and I grew up in a rural Southern community. I remember the day I found this out. Ironically, I had just given a report on "at risk" students with some other doctoral students, most of whom were probably black students. The instructor had surmised that we didn't know what an "at risk" student was, even though we had given the report, so he defined it for us according to the research. When his definition fit me perfectly, I cried quietly to myself in the class. But later in my room, I openly cried because I realized when I looked around the room, nobody fit the definition like I did.

Most of the black students' parents were educators with even advanced degrees and all the students were my age or older. I had noticed that most of them were much more eloquent than I was in the way they talked and the way they dressed. Whereas I had been reared by ebonics-speaking parents and in a neighborhood where ebonics was the primary dialect even for the teachers, how was I to compete? I was not supposed to be in that classroom or in that program. I was supposed to have dropped out of high school and had babies and raise them as a single parent, but here I was, married with one child and in a program that I knew I could handle and would break my back to complete. I knew God had made a way, and my mom was praying for me every day that I would be okay. To be honest, if I had not been raised by dedicated Christian parents, I doubt if I would have made it. They had showed me what honest hard work, even if it was for meager wages, could get you or your offspring if you believed in God.

Even with that, though, I wish I had not been raised so sheltered, that I had been allowed to socialize with other people more than just at school and church so I could learn how to navigate the terrain as a Christian earlier. As it was, I always took people at face value. I expected them to be honest and do what they said, especially people that you called your friends, like I had experienced in my church. I definitely expected them to respect my hard work and not make fun of it. As it turned out, Northern blacks would make fun of Southern blacks for working hard on their jobs when they were making the same money and doing much less. They seem to relish in getting jobs that required extremely little of you but provided you with a so-called healthy living.

I remember someone calling Kennedy-King one day, and for some reason, I got the call. I was working as an administrator at the time, I believe. He wanted to know if there were any vacancies; he said he'd heard you didn't have to work that hard. I was working my butt off, so I was perplexed, but I knew that some people on the job didn't work that hard. There were two white female faculty members in our physical education department who were finished every day by 10:00 a.m., and they were gone. If you had a schedule like that, you could work another job, and many of the faculty were working another full-time job, I found out later, because our union contract only required that we work twelve hours a week. I knew the rest of the time we were supposed to be counseling and advising students and preparing classwork for disadvantaged students that needed our undivided attention. But I think I was the only one who thought like that. Very seldom did students come to your office seeking help; you would have to prompt them or motivate them.

One of the other faculty members told me that we should not have to motivate adult students. I think that argument is still going on. I told him that under normal circumstances with traditionally educated adult students coming from supportive households, maybe not, but these were disadvantaged adult students who were raised poor, probably with uneducated (definitely not college-educated) parents, who were working full-time and raising their own children more than likely as single parents. When the administration realized that most of the faculty was indeed only spending about twelve hours on campus, they negotiated a new contract and required that we spend fifteen hours on campus. I believe most faculty did just that, whereas I spent many more hours weekly on campus and off campus preparing for my classes and my type of student. I was dedicated to my students being ready when they either went to work or continued on to get their bachelor's degree.

I wish that someone had shared the serenity prayer early on with me.

God grant me the serenity to accept the things I cannot change; courage to change the things I can; and the wisdom to know the difference.

Living one day at a time; enjoying one moment at a time; accepting hardships as the pathway to peace; taking, as He did, this sinful world as it is, not as I would have it; trusting that He will make all things right if I surrender to His Will;

that I may be reasonably happy in this life and supremely happy with Him forever in the next. Amen.

(Reinhold Niebuhr 1892–1971)

Then I would have known not to go against the grain as often as I did. As a result of trying to change things and not knowing that it was impossible sometimes, I developed high blood pressure that threatens my own serenity as I age.

After I got from under my parents' umbrella, I became a social butterfly. I wanted to go to every party or club because I loved dancing and still do. But after my strict upbringing, I knew even to limit myself. I went to dances on campus. I did not go to a bar until I was of legal age to drink. When I started drinking alcohol. I took it slow; I wanted to always be of sound mind. As it was the first time, I drank a little too much. I got real sick because I had tasted alcoholic beverages that my friends had as well, not knowing that mixing alcohols or alcohol with anything (got sick once when I took a twelve-hour allergy pill and went to a bar and took one swallow of a slow gin fizz and got drunk; it hadn't been quite twelve hours, and the pill was still in my system) was bad news. Now I know to stick to one or two of the same alcoholic beverages all night and always ask my doctor about consuming alcohol with a particular medicine. I knew also to take it slow with men as well—get to know them first and make sure they respected you. I never understood why a man would want to have sex with a woman he didn't know. Because my job as a college instructor or college administrator was time-consuming, I did not get involved in my immediate community or my professional community and never found a home church in Chicago.

One thing I was slow to learn was how to keep my mouth shut and listen. I was quick to share my beliefs about marriage, infidelity, drugs, smoking, etc. While I was at Kennedy-King, I didn't realize that there were so many of the married faculty, administrators, security staff, etc. who were dating the students or staff members. If I'd had more experience, I would have known to keep my mouth shut because when people learn your beliefs, they were not going to trust you or be helpful to you when you needed it. Plus, I was really late to learn that secretaries run most organizations, so spilling your guts to them is definitely not a good thing, especially if your values clash; and in my case, most often they did.

One thing I definitely had to learn was just because people said they went to church and were Christian did not mean they had your same values or defined Christianity the way you did. One of my colleagues at Kennedy-King attended the same church I did most of the time. She was a member. I never joined, but loved the minister and the services. One morning she saw me before services started and told me she had just gotten off the plane from Las Vegas. Now here she was, conducting baptisms. I thought, *Isn't gambling a sin?* Evidently, she didn't think so.

It took a dramatic event—like my neighbor's twenty-three-year-old son getting shot and killed one block from our homes—to open my eyes to the fact that I had not been contributing to my community the way I should have. I thought I was being a good neighbor by tending to my property, going to work, and not being a bother to anyone. But if I had really been a good neighbor, I would have known my neighbor's first and last name when she knocked on my door that fateful morning to ask me if I would watch her house while she and her family attended her son's funeral—and I didn't. I heard her knocking on my door. She was saying, "Mrs. Morgan, Mrs. Morgan...they killed my son. They shot him five times right under the police camera one block from our homes." I knew some of her sons, so I asked which one, and she told me his name and that he was twenty-three years old. It turned out I did not know him because he had just gotten out of prison. He had been to visit his grandmother in the hospital, I believe, along with his twelve-year-old brother (I knew the twelve-year-old), and they had both gotten shot when they got off the bus one block from our homes.

I was in total shock, but I told my neighbor I would watch her home, and I did—all the time thinking, *How horrible, and what if this had been my son?* My son at the time was sound asleep upstairs, and he was also twenty-three years old at the time. I thought, What if I'd been my neighbor? When her twelve-year-old son ran down the street with blood dripping from his leg where he had been shot to tell his mother that his older brother had been shot, and she, in turn, ran down the street to find her son, riddled with bullets and blood everywhere. What if it had been my son? I would later find out that it had indeed been other sons and daughters (rumors had it was over fifty people killed) murdered on the very corner her son was killed. I know after I started paying more attention, I myself noted six murders on that corner and had met some of them at our block party.

The one and only block party I helped to plan as president of our block club I started after my neighbor's son was killed (turned out to be the last one to this day on our block). My neighbors had been upset when some of the street women came to help out at our party. We had put signs up on the street. The day of the party, the street women were the first to come out to help me and my husband with the setup, while my neighbors slept late. It seemed later they helped themselves to the leftover food. I guess for payment for their help. I had no problem with that because I knew the food would probably go to waste otherwise, but my neighbors were upset. Plus, kids came from other blocks to participate in the fun—I had no problem with that and was used to this type of community gatherings in my church and my neighborhood in the south. One of the street women and her boyfriend (I believe) were later killed on the same block my neighbor's son was killed. I served my tenure as our block club president, but the next president did not have the same zeal for helping kids as I did. I had started the club to set an example of caring for the kids on our block and to give them positive alternatives to gang activity. The next president's motto was, "I raised mine, now you raise yours," and not the "It takes a village" that I had expounded. It seemed most of our neighbors shared this sentiment, so my husband and I stopped our participation with the club, and I turned my attention to helping other community organizations.

Soon after my neighbor's son was killed, Barack Obama, an African American, was elected president of the United States. I was in shock and still is, that Americans had allowed an African American to become president. An African American born of an African doctoral student and American white female, it was like coming full circle. He is first-generation African American. It was like all the Africans who were stolen from their motherland and died either on the way to America or in the fields of America were cheering loudly. You could almost hear the cheering.

I had volunteered for President Obama when he ran for Illinois State Senate and won. He was a breath of fresh air. He was Mayor Harold Washington's heir apparent. I thought Harold had died without one, and I was wrong. At the time, I had no idea how far this young man would go. I could not dare imagine that the White House would be his home one day. I followed his every step to his new home, the White House.

President Barack Obama asked for a day of giving on January 19, 2009, the day before his inauguration. I went online to see what charitable organization I could volunteer with in my own community. I could not find any. I started to cry; it was if I was grieving for the children in my community. They deserved support as well—why didn't anyone care about my children? I went to work. I realized that I had never volunteered in my community. I didn't even belong to a church in my community. I had dedicated myself to my job(s). I did not find time to offer my assistance in my own community. I know now that it is so important that you select the right community to raise your child. It has as much to do with your child's upbringing as your own home.

I thought back on my own upbringing and how involved we were in the community and how I grew to love my neighbors even as a child. They added to the security that I felt every time I stepped outside of my home even when I traveled far, far from home.

After President Obama's plea, the first thing I did was to call the local park district near me to see if I could volunteer. They told me they had an advisory board that was open to members of the community. I joined the board and eventually became its president. The board grew because I invited my neighbors to join as well.

The next thing I did was call the alderman's office in my ward to see how I could start a block club on my block. I was given very good information and left the office with a new position, that of being the precinct captain. I had no idea what a precinct captain did, but I was going to learn. I had been given a booklet with steps on how to form a block club. I followed those steps and called the CAPS department of the police department (the Chicago Alternative Policing Strategy) and found the person who represented my ward. It turned out to be a Hispanic gentleman. He told me to invite two or three of my neighbors to my home, and he would meet with us to discuss next steps in starting a block club. I did just that. I invited the neighbor whose son was killed and one other person. The Hispanic gentleman kept his word and met with us. He told each of us to invite two people to the next meeting, and we did. All of us met in my small kitchen about a week later. We decided on the date and secured a place for our first full block club meeting of our neighbors. I made a flyer, and we walked the block and distributed the fliers. We took down names, addresses, email addresses, and phone numbers of as many of our neighbors possible. We were off to a good start.

We had over twenty-five of our neighbors to attend that first meeting. We met in a nearby church. We continued to meet in the church. I became the first president of the block club. We developed bylaws and values that we wanted to maintain in our block. We held our first real block club party. We found out that a block club was not just for planning a party; it was to maintain the values and standards in your backyard on your block that you want for your family so your children could grow up to be productive citizens and good human beings in general.

My foray into organizing this block club and joining the park district advisory board of my local park district were my first attempts at being a productive citizen. Other than voting in elections and teaching my students, I had done nothing in my community for my community and for my own son's healthy living style outside of my home, and this should have been of primary importance to me. I think my naivety stemmed from my southern heritage and my ancestors being born and reared enslaved. I realized and justly that like Dr. Joy Degruy Leary, PhD, said, as the descendants of former slaves, we were suffering from post-traumatic slave syndrome (PTSS). How can we not with all that we have endured as black people? Dr. Degruy Leary, in her book *Post Traumatic Slave Syndrome: America's legacy of Enduring Injury and Healing*, and at one of her lectures that I attended at the University of Chicago, introduced me to how during slavery blacks often downplayed the intelligence of their own children "to dissuade the slave master from molesting or selling them." The children probably didn't understand this reasoning and developed low self-esteem and eventually passed these habits on to future generations. In the Rabb household, our parents didn't belittle us; but they didn't praise us as well, which probably contributed negatively to our self-esteem somewhat. The word *love* was seldom used. I think I overused the word *love* with our son, but then to me you can't tell a person you love them ever enough. I will always be grateful for Dr. Deguy Leary's book because it helped me to understand myself and somewhat why blacks are the way they are in life. The universal question that has never been answered for me is this: Why Christians, throughout the years, have treated other human beings so cruelly and yet called themselves Christians.

I had started taking the lead in our Rabb-Herron family biennial family reunions because I saw the need to re-connect to our ancestors in order to build the confidence of the children in our family. My generation had the Civil Rights Movement to build our egos and to help us recognize that we were somebody, but the current generations seem to be floundering and wishing they were born white, as if that is more right. They needed to realize that being born black is indeed an advantage. Who else but us could have endured slavery and later become president of the United States? We were not only standing on the shoulders of the poor; we were standing on the shoulders of the poor, proud, and strong men and women who sacrificed much so that we could live. How dare the current generation disrespect these humble yet noble people, their own flesh and blood? Many young black people today think that white people will never let black people get ahead. To them, I say, "People, Barack Obama, first-generation African American became president, so you can too." But if you give up on yourself, everyone else will too. Happily I grew up not knowing that I was at risk of failure because I had God-fearing parents looking out for me. We need today's at-risk students to grow up with that same value.

I decided (2010) that it was important that I also start a scholarship fund in my parents' names to honor them. They were not educated but leaders in their own right. This organizing effort proved to be stressful as well. Some of the members of my family had strayed from the family for one reason or the other and never attended a meeting. Some members missed deadlines for making their contributions. It was and still is a challenge to continue with the scholarship commitment, but I am determined to do just that for as long as possible. The scholarship fund is still in operation.

I discovered years ago that I was an introvert and worked hard over the years to offset it. Being raised in a family that overprotected you did not help. So putting myself out there and starting a block club and joining organizations and taking leadership of these organizations goes against my grain. But I have determined that I am a servant-leader just like my parents. I see a need, and I rush in and try to right the ship. Now I know that serenity prayer, so I need to be fully armed.

After the block club and the advisory board, I continued to join other organizations, and I found none of them were really serving the community effectively, not even those in elected positions. One thing, in particular, I noticed in all the organizations was whenever bylaws were developed, the organizations would start to fall apart. No one wanted to follow the bylaws. I couldn't help but wonder why when they were all involved in the developing the bylaws. I decided I needed to know more about not only bylaws but parliamentary procedure in general. That is where I am now in my life. I am currently a registered parliamentarian (RP) and a professional registered parliamentarian (PRP), primarily to see how I can personally help groups navigate through the manure to get to the crust of the problems in the community in order to "Save Our Children" and our neighborhoods from crumbling. I think I can say I am truly enlightened. This time, I am not putting myself last or my family. We are doing this together, and we are growing together.

Currently (2020), America and the rest of the world are enduring a pandemic due to COVID-19, a deadly virus. People are dying, and there does not seem to be an end to it. Black Americans are dying of COVID-19 at higher rates than other Americans. Besides the pandemic, young black people are dying on the streets more and more at the hands of other blacks or the police. As a result, people all over the world have started to realize that America has done little to erase systemic racism and social injustices that threaten minority communities every day. It seems the rich get richer and the poor get poorer. Even when the poor get in high positions, even they often overlook the communities where they came from.

Because of the times, there is a lot of money being donated to organizations that supposedly serve the poor communities. I am afraid that what happened in the '70s will continue, where the middle class will move up to upper class, move out of their original communities, and the poor will not have been impacted at all, and their plight will remain the same: poor quality schools, no jobs, drug dealers standing on corners, and violence. I think there needs to be a clearing house or overseer of these funds that demand and ensure that the donated funds assist the poor directly.

I plan on offering my services as a professional registered parliamentarian (www.thehopetrainllc.org) to train leaders and members of community organizations in my own community so they can accomplish their goals efficiently and effectively and hopefully eliminate or reduce the violence that makes it impossible to feel safe every time you leave your home and sometimes even in your home. In my community, people have been shot while sleeping in their own bed or watching television in their homes. Babies have been shot while their moms or dads carried them in their arms. Girls and women have become preys of sex traffickers. Many of the churches and community organizations have been fighting to improve the community, but so far to no avail. I may be naive to think as a professional registered parliamentarian that I will be able to help them, but armed with the serenity prayer, I am going to work hard to make a difference and prove that God didn't make a mistake—I was supposed to be here. I can only hope that my son's children will be able to live their lives and not just survive.

About the Author

Laura Rabb Morgan, EdD, describes herself unabashedly as a shy country girl, even after living in the big city of Chicago, Illinois, for almost fifty years. One thing that Laura learned from her upbringing was that she was no better than anyone, and nobody was better than her. As a result, she never feared to venture into any situation no matter the status of the individuals in the room.

Laura always knew from early on that she would go to college. Even though she can't remember when the brainwashing started, she knows exactly where she was when she decided that she was going to college—in her father's cotton field.

After working hard to get her doctorate, she found herself a few years later without a job. To her, life got interesting after that because she was where God had intended her to be. In 1998, she even found herself on the ninety-sixth floor in the Twin Towers in New York City, a few years before 9/11, thinking, *What if one of those planes ran into this building?*

When Laura recognized that because of her race she was labeled as "at risk" of failing in life and not achieving much, she cried because she realized that her life did not have to be as hard as it had been for her or her parents. That being a descendant of slaves, having poor uneducated parents, growing up in rural America in the Jim Crow

South, and being black placed a heavy burden on her. She was and is definitely on a train—*A Hope Train* filled with prayers and the love of God because she was not supposed to be here.

She wrote *The Hope Train* memoir to make sure that at least one-tenth of her family's story was published because most of black history is oral and experts consider anything that is not in writing suspect. She also wrote it for her son and descendants in the family so they would know this chapter of their history. She tried, for years, to get other members of the other five branches of the Rabb family to contribute to a book on the Rabb family history to no avail. Not one word was ever submitted. It is up to African Americans to make sure their story is told not only orally but also in writing if only for historians to avoid distortions.